THE SECOND WORLD WAR, 1939-1945
A SHORT MILITARY HISTORY SERIES

GREECE AND CRETE 1941

CHRISTOPHER BUCKLEY

EFSTATHIADIS GROUP

EFSTATHIADIS GROUP S.A.
14, Valtetsiou Str.
106 80 Athens
Tel: (01) 5154650, 6450113
Fax: (01) 5154657
GREECE

ISBN 960 226 041 6

© **Efstathiadis Group S.A. 2000**

Printed and bound in Greece

Prefatory Note

TOWARDS the end of the Second World War the Committee for the Control of Official Histories recommended to the War Cabinet that the Government should commission and publish a series of popular military histories. These were to present a broad view of the military events of 1939-45, and each volume was to deal with a particular campaign. They were to be forerunners of, and not in any sense substitutes for, the more detailed Official Histories of the Second World War then planned and since published.

Soon after the war, distinguished authors were commissioned to write the texts for six books, and they were given full access to official documents and sources of information. The authors were, however, to be individually responsible for the presentation of their material, the statements they made and the opinions they expressed.

The first book was *Arms and the Men*. Written by Ian Hay, it was the story of the evolution of the British Army and how it acquitted itself throughout the war. The second was Eric Linklater's *The Campaign in Italy,* an account of the Eighth and Fifth Armies' fighting between May 1943 and May 1945. Christopher Buckley, the well-known war correspondent who was tragically killed in Korea in 1950, wrote the next three: *Greece and Crete, 1941,* a tale of heroic failure; *Norway, the Commandos, Dieppe* and *Five Ventures: Iraq, Syria, Persia, Madagascar, the Dodecanese,* which deal with smaller expeditions and campaigns, chiefly in country side that presented problems of unusual character. The last book, *North West Europe, 1944-5,* by John North, was the story of the achievement of the British 21st Army Group in the Allied invasion of North West Europe.

When these books were first published they were well received, and second impressions were produced of two of them. In recent years, the rapid expansion of interest in military history of all kinds—and in the Second World War in particular—has stimulated a demand from a wide spectrum of the public for copies of these volumes from libraries, museums and other sources. The demand appears to be growing and the reprinting of all six books in this new format is in response to it.

These new impressions are straight reprints. Except for minor changes to one or two of the preliminary pages, there are no alterations. The volumes are essentially just as they were a quarter of a century ago.

1977

Foreword

THE CAMPAIGN IN GREECE and the Battle for Crete, 1941, form a further contribution to this series by the late Christopher Buckley. The author and the publisher are very greatly indebted to the official historians of Australia and New Zealand who devoted much time and trouble to a critical reading of the narrative and supplying additional information; also to Lord Freyberg for his valuable notes and suggestions.

Contents

THE CAMPAIGN IN GREECE

THE BATTLE FOR CRETE

MAPS

All heights shown are in metres

PAGE

ILLUSTRATIONS

British Troops Arriving at Piraeus
Greek Welcome
A British Gun Passing Through Lamia
New Zealand in Greece
Transport Old and New on a Greek Mountain Road
Mount Olympus
The Pass at Thermopylae
On the Way to the Beaches: Australian Interlude

Suda Bay under Attack
Cretan Countryside
The King of the Hellenes and 2nd-Lieut. Ryan
A German Troop-Carrier
General Freyberg
Parachutes at Heraklion
Cretan Air-Raid Refuge near the Beach
Trophies from Crete

THE CAMPAIGN
IN GREECE

CHAPTER I
The War Spreads Eastward

1

Aims of the Axis Powers

THE fall of France and the declaration of war by Italy in June 1940 marked the beginning of a new phase of the struggle. With the British armies seriously weakened by the loss of the campaign in North-West Europe, the British Commonwealth and Empire faced the might of Germany and Italy, and continued to do so for a whole year, alone without ally.

There were, at first, two major theatres of operations. One was the sky over south-eastern England where the Battle of Britain was fought and won during the late summer and autumn; the other was the eastern Mediterranean and the Balkan peninsula. Throughout the autumn and winter Germany was in the process of conquering the Balkans by infiltration. German troops passed through Hungary. They took over control in Rumania in October, having previously retroceded half the province of Transylvania to Hungary. And during the winter signs were not wanting that they were preparing to descend upon Bulgaria and that Bulgaria was not in the least likely to offer them any opposition.

That had been the direction of the German land drive after the fall of France; and to many observers—the present writer included—it seemed that Hitler was about to pursue the traditional *Drang nach Osten,* that drive to the East which seemed to offer such rich prizes—the control of the Bosphorus and the Dardanelles; Mosul and the Persian oil-fields; the Suez Canal; ultimately perhaps even India.

Italian participation in the war seemed to point the way towards this strategy still more strongly. If Germany were to drive through Turkey to the Persian Gulf or the Suez Canal or both, the natural corollary was for Italy to thrust from Libya, the whole forming one gigantic pincer movement to eliminate the British forces in the Middle East, which, failing a direct attack upon the British Isles or their reduction by slow strangulation, furnished the best chances of dealing an early decisive blow against the one Power still in the field against them.

This was logical enough; and we know now that Germany's venture through the Balkans to the eastern Mediterranean caused the postponement of the invasion of Russia for a full four weeks. The decision was taken by the Führer at a conference held in Berlin on March 27th, 1941, when it was announced that Yugoslavia must be liquidated. The attack on Greece was to be carried out simultaneously. Later, the objective of these operations was described as 'that of driving the British from the Balkans and laying the foundation for German air operations in the eastern part of the Mediterranean'.

Nevertheless, the moves into the Balkans, which were initiated by Germany in the autumn, winter and spring of 1940-1 may be. regarded as a buttressing of her southern flank for the forthcoming campaign into Russia as well as preliminary operations against our forces in the Middle East. Germany needed Rumania as a base and jumping-off ground for the attack upon Russia in the following year, and she needed control of Rumanian oil. It was realized that Bulgaria and Yugoslavia must be absorbed into the German system. Thus the swoop of the German forces upon ill-equipped, unready Yugoslavia; the relentless drive down through the Greek passes; the bold and hazardous airborne invasion of Crete—these might be viewed as part of a strategically defensive operation to neutralize Turkey, and to prevent the possibility of a British diversion northwards from bases in Greece, whence British bombers might operate against the oil wells of Ploësti in Rumania.

Probably Hitler, and a *fortiori* the General Staff, who had still less liking for divergent operations, hoped that such action would involve the minimum dispersal of force and would take the minimum time to accomplish. When Mussolini's ineptitude did involve a considerable German commitment both against Greece and Yugoslavia, Hitler and the General Staff were certainly anxious to finish as soon as possible the spring campaign in south-eastern

Europe prior to the great offensive against Russia. Moreover, a swift and easy success in the Balkan countries would hasten the day for the opening of the aforesaid German air operations in the eastern Mediterranean.

Actually, as will be seen later, the course of events was to lead to German intervention in Africa.

But in any study of the Balkan campaign of 1941, and especially of the motives that conditioned the despatch of a British force to Greece, it is as well to see it as it must have appeared to us at the time. Though evidence was building up through the months to suggest the German intention of attacking Russia, it was not sufficiently sure-founded to act as a basis for British strategy. The direction of the forthcoming Axis advance was assumed to be towards the south-east, with Hitler and Mussolini pursuing a closely co-ordinated plan for the dismemberment of the British Empire and the destruction of Britain.

Under these circumstances, and following the decison to abandon the proposed 'Operation Sea Lion' (the code name for the invasion of Britain) which seems to have been taken as early as September 19th,[1] the centre of gravity of the war began to shift eastward from the English Channel to the vast area between the Danube and the Nile.

Germany enjoyed the prestige of continuous victory, the advantage of very much shorter lines of communication and the possibility of deploying her numerous magnificently equipped and battle-trained divisions against us; Italy was in a position to strike directly across the desert into Egypt or, from her advanced base in Albania, into Greece or Yugoslavia. Between them the two Powers appeared to have all the cards in their hands. The tide of the Axis advance across the Balkan peninsula was sweeping on, by means of conquest (Albania), military infiltration and disintegration (Rumania) and economic penetration and encirclement (Hungary and—as it seemed—Yugoslavia).

For months Britain could not hope to do more than play a waiting game, holding off the converging attack upon Suez—if it should come—until such time as sufficient reinforcements of men and material should have arrived in the Middle East to enable her first to safeguard the immediate Canal zone and then to take the offensive.

---

[1] See Peter de Mendelssohn, *The Nuremberg Documents*

Therefore the best that could be hoped for fully twelve months would be a series of 'delaying actions' on our part. Wherever there seemed some chance of temporarily staying the onset, the meagre British resources must be disposed—to parry here, to snatch advantage from an unguarded move there, to retard, even though it could not prevent, a *débâcle* elsewhere. That was the strategy planned by the Chiefs of Staff and executed by Wavell during those twelve months when we stood alone in face of the Axis Powers.

2

Italy Attacks

FOR Mussolini the Greek campaign represented aggression along the line of least resistance. By declaring war in June like one who buys on a rising market, he had hoped to secure easy profit, despite the fact that Italy was actually unready for war. Intervention in Spain had been a costly and exhausting undertaking. The armed services needed re-equipment with modern material, yet she could not hope to do this from her own resources. Her vulnerable position in the Mediterranean, so long as the British fleet remained in being in that sea, predisposed her to neutrality. But the opportunity seemed too good to miss. France was beaten to her knees, and good Fascists could not forget that it was only a matter of months since they had been clamouring for Tunis, Corsica, Savoy, Nice and Jibuti. Now it seemed that they might be secured with little effort. Most of Europe at that date would have endorsed Weygand's view that within three weeks England would have her neck wrung like a chicken. And when the three weeks came to an end and England still stood erect, most of Europe still thought that there might be peace by September; so Mussolini was able to reflect that there might be time after all for a victory campaign.

On the Alpine frontier the Italians had contributed little to the defeat of France. Malta, which many had believed would rapidly become untenable for the British, had been repeatedly raided from the air—at great cost to the attackers and very little to the defence. The Italian forces had hitherto had all the worst of the skirmishing on the frontier between Libya and Egypt. Their navy shunned a trial of strength in the eastern Mediterranean. Small penetrations across the Kenya and Sudan borders and the occupation of a number of frontier posts were a poor gesture on the part of the East African army which could at any one of these points have commanded a tenfold or twentyfold superiority in manpower. Mussolini might speak in florid terms at the opening of August of the forthcoming development of an all-out offensive against the British Empire in Africa to synchronize with the German air attack upon England, but the labour of the Fascist mountain produced only the *ridiculus mus* of the over-running of British Somaililand.

It is not surprising that in seeking easy triumphs and bloodless victories Mussolini's eye should have turned upon Greece. Of all the neighbours to whom he had issued his guarantee in June, Greece appeared the weakest, seemed to represent the easiest prey. Fascismo had long conducted a vendetta against its small neighbour on the further side of the Ionian Sea, and after Albania was annexed in the spring of 1939, Italian forces could be launched in a direct invasion of Greek territory.

On August 4th, General Metaxas, the Greek Dictator, had celebrated the fourth anniversary of his assumption of power—and the occasion had been signalized by congratulatory messages from the German and Italian Governments, but not, be it observed, from the British or American. The régime in Greece was dictatorial. It had copied many of the characteristics of the Fascist and Nazi models. It commanded some respect but not affection from the nation. Not only was it unpopular with the Venizelist (Liberal and Anglophile) party, but also with the Royalists. For these reasons Mussolini, with a misjudgement of the Greek character and Greek patriotism that was to prove disastrous to Italian arms, probably assumed that there would be little support for the régime in the event of an Italian attack.

On August 15th the Greek light cruiser **Helle** was sunk by torpedo at her anchorage off the island of Tenos. When fragments of the torpedo were recovered they were found to be of Italian origin. The Greek Government studiously refrained from publishing the facts, the torpedo being described as coming from a submarine of 'unknown origin', though the truth was well known throughout the country. The attack upon the *Helle* had been made by Italy to test Greek reactions, and quite the wrong deduction was drawn from the official silence. It was assumed that the Greek Government was silent through fear and therefore was unlikely to offer more than token resistance in the face of invasion. Actually the outrage provided the occasion for a closing of the ranks within the country.

The Campaign in Greece

The torpedoing of the *Helle* was not the only, nor indeed the first provocation which Greece had to endure from Italy during the period August-October 1940. Frontier 'incidents', so familiar a cause or result of friction between Balkan states, grew in number; the Albanian Press, inspired and encouraged by Italy, voiced many a grievance against the Greek Government and people.

Metaxas stood his ground against Italian provocation. He notified the Italian Ambassador that force would be met with force in the event of any military action being taken against Greece. The boldness of this decision, made in the very nadir of the fortunes of anti-Axis resistance, should never be forgotten. Greece at that moment was quite unready to face attack. Her armed forces were unmobilized, inadequate and hopelessly under-equipped even by Italian standards. France had collapsed. Russia was still in close alliance with Germany. Britain was fighting for sheer existence against the great air attacks which were to have been the preliminary to invasion, and it appeared unlikely that she could provide even token support to implement her guarantee of help against aggression given in April 1939.

Hitler gave no encouragement to his junior partner; which may explain why Mussolini held his hand for a time, continuing to reinforce his garrisons in Albania and trusting to a war of nerves to do nine-tenths of his work for him.

With October tension grew greater in Greece. Early in the month an Italian aircraft flying over Greek territory dropped three bombs between Thebes and Levadia, but the incident was hushed-up by the Greek censorship, as the Government was, very sensibly, striving to avoid any action that might be interpreted as 'provocation' of the Fascist Power. The Greeks, however, who had been quite unprepared in August, were now disposing their scanty resources to the best of their ability. The army, partially mobilized, was awaiting attack on the Albanian frontier. Metaxas told his Cabinet that the troops would be kept under arms until the threat to Greek independence was definitely past, though the cost of this continued state of semi-mobilization was appalling, and he could not begin to consider how it was to be met.

With winter approaching, the prospects of immediate aggression seemed to decline. Italy, indeed, might have been well advised to have delayed her offensive until the spring of 1941; but Mussolini does not seem to have regarded the Greek campaign as a serious military undertaking. If he envisaged a triumphant military parade of probably not more than a week's duration, it was immaterial to him at what time of year it might start. Italian forces had occupied British Somaliland; they had penetrated into Kenya and the Sudan; Graziani had gone forward nearly a hundred miles into Egypt; nowhere had the Italian troops as yet withdrawn. And so it was unthinkable that Greece should provide any serious opposition.

On Monday, October 29th at 3 a.m., General Metaxas was handed an ultimatum by Count Grazzi, Italian Minister in Athens. This ultimatum accused the Greek Government of having weighted its neutrality heavily in favour of England, of having allowed the British fleet to make use of its territorial waters, of having facilitated the refuelling of British aircraft and of having allowed a British Intelligence Service to establish itself in the Greek islands: the Greek Government was further accused of allowing Greek territory to be 'transformed into a base for warlike operations against Italy'; Italy therefore demanded the right of immediate occupation of certain unspecified strategic points in Greece for the duration of the war against England. It asserted that this was a measure of purely defensive character and that it would not be in any way prejudicial to Greek sovereignty over these territories. Greek troops were required not to impede the movements of the Italian forces.

General Metaxas promptly refused these demands. War was inevitable. With speed and unanimity the Greek nation responded to the mobilization summons.

It seems fairly clear that the Italian ultimatum was not meant to be accepted. Even before the close of the brief period allowed for acceptance or rejection Italian troops were moving forward in the frontier districts. Documents later discovered showed that every detail of the attack had been prepared. If the ultimatum had been accepted Italian troops would, of course, have moved forward to assume occupation of the unspecified districts of Greece in the interests of Italian security; but one can be safe in supposing that Mussolini preferred that the Greeks should put up at least some show of resistance. His prestige needed some indisputable victories to balance the sweep of Napoleonic triumphs of Nazi Germany.

The world was prepared to see Greece fall an easy victim of aggression. How could the courage and resolution of the Greek dictator and the spirit of the Greek people prevail over the Italian preponderance of force? Despite her commitments in Africa, Italy had massed upon the Albanian frontier troops which outnumbered the Greek defenders by nearly four to one. Possessing no tanks themselves and very few aircraft, the Greeks were ill-equipped to resist Italian armour or Italian attacks from the air. And yet the unexpected happened. Heroic Greek endeavour brought a triumph of Greek arms.

The principal Italian thrust was delivered in the Pindus towards Yanina and made some progress at first; but the Greeks proved themselves superior in the tactics of mountain warfare so that the invaders were soon driven back and pursued beyond the frontier. Further north the Greeks checked Italian attempts to advance, and then passed to the offensive, crossing the Albanian frontier on October 31st. Soon they were threatening Koritsa. In Epirus, where the open ground favoured the employment of mechanized forces, the Italians reached and crossed the river Kalamas, but the failures further north had their repercussions and a general retreat set in. By November 25th Greek soil was clear of the invader and a Greek counter-offensive was in progress.

This effort was crowned with remarkable success, a change of Italian commanders and the arrival of considerable Italian reinforcements having little effect. After the capture of Koritsa, the largest town in Albania, Pogradec on Lake Ohridsko fell to the Greeks, and only the onset of winter stayed further advance in the mountains. Near the coast Argyrokastron was captured on December 8th, Himare on the 24th, and Kelcyre on January 10th, 1941; but the port of Valona remained in Italian hands.

After weeks of inconclusive winter warfare the Italians, under another new commander, struck again with considerable forces. This offensive was pressed with something like desperation but only resulted in heavy losses: the Greek defensive victory near Tepelene in March 1941 meant that Italy's last attempt to prevail by force of arms had collapsed. For she did not try again.

Yet, although the prowess of the Greek Army was fitly rewarded by success, the efforts of the troops had left them overstrained and their numbers sadly thinned as a result of the hardships of the winter campaign. Re-equipment was a vital need, for all resources, military and civilian, had been used without stint to repel the invader. The whole Greek people sorely needed a period of recuperation, instead of which they were soon to be subjected to a much greater ordeal which ended in disaster.

It is now time to turn to the diplomatic developments of the winter of 1940-1, months which saw the small beginnings of Britain's assistance to her Greek ally and brought Germany to the point when she would intervene.

CHAPTER II

Swastika over the Balkans

1

British Aid to Greece?

THE Italian attack on Greece called for the British assistance against aggression guaranteed in April 1939; but the occasion was hardly propitious. Britain's exiguous land and air forces were urgently required for defence of the mother country against the most formidable threat of invasion that we had ever known. What could be spared for service elsewhere was required with scarcely less urgency for the defence of our position in the Middle East, based on the Nile and the Suez Canal and now much weakened by the defection of France, whose co-operation had of course been assumed at the time that the guarantee was given. The Middle East was regarded as the lynch-pin of the whole Empire; if that went, the war could be lost almost as surely as if Britain herself were to be invaded.

With France out of the war it became clear that, in view of our vital defence commitments elsewhere and our extremely limited resources, there could be no question of taking the initiative in extending our protection to Greece, though the guarantee remained valid and Greece, unlike Rumania, took no steps to repudiate it or to seek protection elsewhere. It was to be hoped—and it was little more than a pious hope—that with increasing strength we should be able progressively to extend our help to Turkey, Greece and Yugoslavia, all of whom were still nominally linked together by the Balkan Entente and by a common interest in opposing the further expansion of the Axis Empires.

The Campaign in Greece

The first definite plan for coming to the help of Greece in case of need appears to date from May 1940, before Italy came into the War and before France was defeated. The Middle East Command had then been ordered to prepare an expedition which, with the consent of the Greek Government already secured, would occupy the islands of Crete and Milos, in the event of Italy attacking Greek territory. Originally this was intended to be a Franco-British expedition, but the orders were confirmed in June, the Royal Navy being of opinion that Suda Bay, on the north coast of Crete, would form a valuable re-fuelling base for light craft. For the time being, however, it was our policy to keep out of Crete rather than provide Italy with an excuse for aggressive action. And when, early in August, the first clear signs of Mussolini's hostile intentions towards Greece became apparent General Wavell, then in London, reported to a meeting of the Chiefs of Staff that there was not so much as a single brigade available for the garrisoning of Crete in the event of an Italian attack on the mainland of Greece. Nor did it seem possible at that stage that we could provide even the most modest air assistance or anti-craft defence for the island.

By October, things were a little better. Graziani had stopped short at Sidi Barrani in his advance towards the Delta, and the Duke of Aosta was still trifling on the frontiers of Kenya and the Sudan. It was decided that it would now be possible to contemplate the occupation of Crete in the event of Italian aggression. With the consent of the Greek Government, at the end of the month a small British force was landed in Crete and became responsible for the defence of the island. Even so, we were still incapable of any considerable contribution to the Greek resistance, although Mr. Churchill's speech in the House of Commons, announced that General Metaxas had requested from Sir Michael Palairet, British Minister in Athens, such aid as we could give in accordance with our guarantee. It must be remembered that what resources were available in the relative proximity of Egypt were being carefully husbanded for a counterstroke against Graziani with the object of driving the Italian force from Egypt before it could resume its advance from Sidi Barrani.

Fortunately the requests of General Metaxas were not excessive. He was a realist, and he was perfectly well aware how little we ourselves possessed. Moreover, he knew that the appearance of any significant force in Greece might be the signal for Germany to come to the assistance of her Fascist partner.

Accordingly, Metaxas limited his requirements to an appeal for the naval protection of Corfu, air protection for Athens and general assistance in terms of finance and supply. The British fleet was already, to all intents and purposes, in control of the eastern Mediterranean; it was therefore improbable that any immediate danger was to be feared from the Italians at sea. The most urgent need was, consequently, for air support on the most immediate and the fullest scale possible. The Italians were in a position to employ over five hundred operational bombers and fighters; the Greeks had available a first-line strength of some 26 bombers and 28 fighters, and perhaps half as much again in terms of obsolete aircraft of quite negligible value under modern conditions.

Air Chief Marshal Sir Arthur Longmore, A.O.C.-in-C. Middle East, here acted on his own responsibility. To provide Greece with air assistance he disregarded our commitments in the Western Desert and ordered squadrons from Africa to Greece, relying upon reinforcements from the United Kingdom to fill their places. This course gained the entire approval of the Prime Minister who cabled 'You have taken a very bold and wise decision' and promised reinforcement as soon as possible.

Accordingly, No. 30 Squadron of Blenheims began to arrive as early as November 3rd, six days after the beginning of the Italian campaign. It was followed by No. 211 Squadron of Blenheims, No. 84 Squadron of Blenheims, No. 80 Squadron of Gladiators and No. 70 Squadron of Wellingtons; and on November 6th Air-Commodore J. H. D'Albiac arrived in Athens to assume command.

Two points of major importance arose in the first conference which D'Albiac held that same evening with the Greek Prime Minister and Greek Commander-in-Chief. The first referred to the general air strategy to be employed by the British forces; the second related to the selection of airfields from which they were to operate, and the preparation of new ones. On the first issue the British commander had his way; on the second the Greeks were able to impose their views—with far-reaching consequences to the development of the campaign.

Briefly, D'Albiac found the utmost pressure brought to bear upon him to employ his air force in direct and close support of the land forces. The Greek air force, which was under the control of the General Staff, was employed in this manner; the German air force, which had achieved such striking victories in Poland, Norway and the Low Countries had operated with great success during those campaigns in the closest co-ordination with the army. Such methods appeared to provide the pattern for air victory, and, which was a matter of importance to the Greek leaders, they would be of very great value in maintaining the morale of the Greek troops, since soldiers are always heartened by the spectacle of friendly aircraft immediately overhead.

D'Albiac pointed out that his small force of bombers could be best employed in striking at the enemy's disembarkation ports in Albania and at certain important centres of communication, and that the Italian advance could be more easily retarded by these means than by head-on attacks under unfavourable conditions upon advancing troops. In the end he was successful in carrying his point, and during the weeks that followed the maximum air effort was employed against the ports of Valona and Durazzo by which reinforcements and supplies were fed into Albania. Nevertheless, the British policy of long-term strategic bombing, still far from the peak of its efficiency, was not one that commended itself to the Greek military mind.

On the matter of airfields D'Albiac was less successful, for the question involved issues of diplomacy right outside the range of air strategy. Apart from the two at Elevsis and Tatoi (Menidi), both in the Athens area, the best airfields lie in the Macedonian plain around Salonika; and though much of the ground is liable to be water-logged in winter, the Larissa region would naturally be convenient for the concentration of our bombers engaged in operations over the Albanian and Italian ports.

But at this point the shadow of Germany—as yet a cloud no larger than a diplomat's hand—looms over the scene. Hitherto Germany had acted with the utmost correctness towards Greece. The Italian attack had been undertaken on Mussolini's own initiative. Hitler was definitely opposed to such action in October 1940; eventually he would incorporate Greece in the 'New Order', but the time was not yet. The German Government pointedly refrained from withdrawing its Minister from Athens or counselling German subjects to leave Greece. Everything was done to create the impression that in the German view the quarrel was one which concerned only Italy and Greece. General Metaxas had even been told privately by the German Minister in Athens that Germany would not be disposed to regard the presence of a small British air increment as a a *causus belli* provided that it was not permitted the use of airfields in northern Greece. We may assume that Hitler was genuinely nervous about the possibility of bombing attacks on the. Ploësti oil installations, perhaps also of the political repercussions that might result.

Consequently, D'Albiac found himself met with a firm refusal when he applied for the use of air bases in the neighbourhood of Salonika. Such a concession would provoke Germany, and to prevent Germany from intervening in the Greek war Metaxas was quite prepared to ban the Royal Air Force from bases in northern Greece.

It is difficult not to sympathize with the point of view of the Greek ruler. Greece seemed to have the measure of her Italian adversary, but a clash with Germany promised almost certain destruction. The fallacy lay in supposing that Germany could afford her ally to be beaten in the field. She must, inevitably, come to the rescue. General Wavell had drawn attention to this as early as November 16th when commenting upon an appreciation of the situation submitted by his Deputy Director of Military Intelligence. He wrote: 'I am sure Germany cannot afford to see Italy defeated or even held, and must intervene.'

In fact, Hitler had just begun to plan for this purpose. Only four days earlier he had issued an order to the General Staff to prepare for the invasion of Greek Thrace on the basis of a twelve-divisional operation. At the same time he was toying with the idea of sending a mountain division to help Mussolini out of his difficulties in Albania. Badoglio came up to meet Field-Marshal Keitel at Innsbruck a day or two later, and between them the first blueprint for German intervention was prepared.

Nevertheless, Hitler saw that no intervention would be practicable before the spring. His troops had entered Rumania during the month of October, though not in great strength, and were in no position yet to move down through the Bulgarian mountains to attack Greece. Besides, it was necessary to put pressure upon Yugoslavia to ensure her co-operation, since any advance across Bulgaria to Thrace would be exposed to a possible hostile reaction from the side of Yugoslavia which would threaten its communications with the north.

So it came about that our first attempts to bring aid to Greece were not carried out in the happiest circumstances. D'Albiac had to be content with the limited accommodation afforded him by two airfields in the Athens neighbourhood for his bombers, while his fighters had to operate from the most primitive stations behind the front line under conditions of extreme hardship and discomfort. He was not allowed even to reconnoitre, much less use, airfields in the Salonika area, and when a British aircraft crashed near the town members of the R.A.F. were forbidden to visit the spot to salvage which was left of it.

There remained the plain of Thessaly around Larissa, the only other area in Greece where the country is sufficiently open to provide a large number of suitable sites for airfields. But the rains had already begun, and the one squadron which was stationed here was soon flooded out. It was clear that the construction of further accommodation would have to be put in hand speedily. Having reconnoitred all available sites D'Albiac recommended to the Greek Premier the immediate construction of all-weather airfields at Agrinion (near the west coast, north of the Gulf of Corinth) and at Araxos (in the north-west corner of the Peloponnesus). The advantage of these sites was that they allowed a considerable margin for Greek withdrawals and could still be operated even though the whole of northern Greece were lost. D'Albiac was given assurances that they would be ready by the end of January 1941. Unfortunately, through shortage of labour, material and transport, and, it must be added, through a failure fully to realize the importance of giving a high priority to the work, this estimate proved sadly over-optimistic. Neither of these airfields was ready for use when the British troops evacuated Greece at the end of April. Araxos was almost immediately put into commission by the Germans after their occupation of the Peloponnesus. It was a melancholy comment upon the situation. We spent the winter getting the runways ready for use in the spring. Then, when the fine weather arrived, the Germans swept in and occupied them, completed what remained to be done with conscripted local labour and promptly turned them to their own use.

Meanwhile Major-General M.D. Gambier-Parry [1] had arrived as chief military representative of a British Inter-Services Mission to Greece, specifically charged to avoid giving promises or making commitments. Apart from the air squadrons, the first of which opened its operations on November 6th with a highly successful bombing attack upon Valona airfield, British help at the start had been limited to the despatch of nineteen anti-tank rifles, which had been flown over from Egypt to Patras and thence up to Yanina. These anti-tank rifles were hurried straight to the front line in the southern sector, where they are said to have done good service.

[1] He was succeeded later in November by Major-General T.G.G. Heywood.

· Still more opportune was the attack of the Fleet Air Arm upon the Italian fleet in harbour. On the moonlit night of November 10th/11th two waves, one of twelve and one of nine Swordfish flown from the carrier *Illustrious,* swooped down upon Taranto. Their brief and brilliant low-level attack with torpedoes sank two battleships, partially sunk a third, and damaged a cruiser and two destroyers. The price of their success was two naval aircraft.

On November 16th a British convoy arrived at Piraeus from Alexandria. It contained the base personnel for a British Expeditionary Force and totalled something over 4,000 men (284 officers and 3,913 other ranks) divided between R.A.F. and the Army with a slight preponderance of the former. Though a senior officer was privately informed that he should select a base which would permit expansion to accommodate two divisions for 'possible developments', the formal instructions forbade discussing with the Greeks an increase which must raise hopes which could not be realized. The force, apart from the crews of the operational aircraft, was mostly non-combatant, being composed of signals, supply and intelligence units, bomb disposal detachments and oil sabotage specialists together with a certain number of officers with specialized knowledge of modern weapons and mountain warfare. It could scarcely be regarded by the Germans as providing a *casus belli* and beyond noting its presence they paid it little attention.

Now began an elaborate diplomatic game in the Balkan peninsula, a game which extended throughout the winter months until with the coming of spring weather German armies were in position to attack.

German threats and blandishments were directed towards the three Balkan States, Greece, Yugoslavia and Turkey, but especially towards Greece. Bulgaria, true as ever to her tradition of siding with the bully, needed no persuasion. Germany knew that Greek resistance must be crushed, and if the Italians could not achieve this it remained for German arms to do so. Assured of the peaceful co-operation of Bulgaria, Germany wanted that of Yugoslavia; for the present she was content that Turkey should remain outside the conflict, though there was some justification for the current British assumption that the subsequent line of German expansion would be in the direction of Asia Minor and the Middle East.

For Britain, with her slowly expanding and still very meagre resources, the chief object was to avoid enticing Germany further into the Balkans and to be in a position to offer some sort of obstacle to her penetration to the eastern Mediterranean. The amount of aid that could be afforded to Greece required to be very carefully judged. The Greeks wanted enough to enable them to overcome the Italians but not enough to provoke Germany to intervene. As we have seen these two aims were incompatible; but the Greek Government affected not to recognize this.

At the beginning of December 1940 Mr. Churchill was already of the opinion that British intervention on an increased scale would probably become necessary against Italy and possibly against Germany with the coming of spring, and the Chiefs of Staff were requested to prepare plans on this assumption. By the end of the year, however, nothing had been done to increase the operational capacity of the existing airfields and no significant progress had been made with the new ones at Araxos and Agrinion despite promises to the contrary.

Since the commitment estimated at this stage amounted to no more than two divisions (and we should be hard put to it to find even these) and since the minimum force necessary to defend the Salonika and Larissa areas was estimated at four divisions, it was decided in principle that further airfields should be only constructed south of a line from Mount Olympus to the Gulf of Arta.

Then on January 8th the Chiefs of Staff came to the conclusion that no effective resistance could be undertaken if Germany intervened in Greece and that any formations sent by us could do no more than delay the outcome and would, judged in terms of the Balkan campaign alone, prove to have been wasted. Nor could our air strength be increased in the course of the next two months to more than five bomber and three fighter squadrons. Under the circumstances, therefore, there seemed little case for pushing the project further unless we wished to invite a second and more disastrous Dunkirk. Seen as a purely military problem divorced from any consideration of political expediency, the case against our intervention in Greece with land forces appeared to be complete and unanswerable.

On the German side Hitler's personal decison to attack Russia in 1941 had been made in the autumn of 1940. It was determined in part by the Russian occupation of Bessarabia at the end of June 1940, in part by the realization that 'Operation Sea Lion', the attack upon Britain, could not be launched under the cover of a beaten *Luftwaffe* with any reasonable prospect of success unless the potential threat from Russia were eliminated. The Russian pact had never been regarded by Hitler as anything more than an ingenious military expedient to free him from the danger of war upon two fronts, the nightmare of the General Staff. Ultimately, Soviet Russia was always the enemy *par excellence*.

Hence the entry of German troops into Rumania at the beginning of October 1940, while governed in part by a desire to safeguard the oil-fields for Germany's future use, served the further important purpose of lengthening the base for future operations against Russia. At the same time Rumania served as a strategic turn-table. Troops established there could be used for the invasion of southern Russia; equally, they could be employed for the subjugation of the rest of the Balkan peninsula by way of a complaisant, and probably actively co-operative, Bulgaria.

A secret directive had fixed May 15th, 1941 as the date of the completion of the German deployment for the Russian campaign. But Greece remained in arms against the Fascist ally, forming a potential British bridgehead for operations driving deeper into Europe and therefore a threat to the southern flank of the grand offensive against Russia. Accordingly War Directive No. 20 for 'Operation Marita' (the move against Greece) was issued on December 13th, 1940. Its purpose was to 'foil British attempts to create air bases under the protection of a Balkan front... for this would be dangerous above all to Italy as well as to the Rumanian oil-fields.' At the same time the Italian defeats in the Western Desert were opening up the possibility of the British over-running the whole of Libya and fundamentally altering the Mediterranean balance in their favour. Accordingly, a further War Directive, issued after the loss of Bardia, on January 11th arranged for the despatch of German forces to Tripolitania (the beginning of the famous *Afrika Korps*) and the establishment of a German air force in Sicily.

Thus, with the beginning of the new year, two German thrusts were developing southwards to the Mediterranean. One was destined to operate from Rumania through Bulgaria into Greece and the Aegean, the other into Africa by Sicily. Both were the subject of much speculation in the British Press at the time. It seemed reasonable to suppose that they represented the horns of Germany's 1941 summer offensive and that they aimed at converging by the conquest of Turkey and Egypt and driving through to the Persian Gulf. This, it must be repeated, was not the primary objective. Hitler, having considered and rejected the possibility of an advance through Spain to seize Gibraltar, was concentrating upon the campaign against Russia.[1] The two operations in the south were, therefore, both in the nature of divergences imposed upon Germany by the weakness of her Italian ally. Italy had embroiled herself in Albania and got the worst of it. Therefore, Germany must make herself responsible for the subjugation of Greece. Italy was on the run in Libya, and if this *débâcle* continued, there was a grave danger of an entire transformation of the situation in the Mediterranean. Therefore the *Afrika Korps* had to go to Libya and the bombers had to go to Sicily. Both represented a dissipation of force from the main objective.

So far as this narrative is concerned December 13th is the important date, when Hitler issued the directive for operations against Greece. A month elapsed before any corresponding—defensive—step was taken from our side. Then in mid-January General Wavell, at that time engaged in operations for the reduction of Tobruk, was instructed by the War Cabinet to proceed to Greece and make an offer to the Greek Government of armoured troops, field artillery, anti-tank and anti-aircraft guns to assist their forces in the defence of Salonika and Macedonia against possible German aggression.

With Air Chief Marshal Sir Arthur Longmore, Wavell journeyed to Athens, arriving there on January 13th and remaining until January 17th. During these days conferences were held with General Metaxas, the Prime Minister, and General Papagos, the Commander-in-Chief, in which future operations in Greece were discussed. Metaxas declared categorically that Greece would resist a German or combined German and Bulgarian attack with all the means at her disposal even though there appeared little possibility of either Yugoslavia or Turkey departing from her attitude of neutrality; and he called upon General Papagos to state the military needs of the Greek Government.

Papagos stated that in view of the German concentrations in Rumania (they had already twelve divisions in the country and were receiving constant reinforcements) and the preparations developing in Bulgaria for the passage of German forces, a thrust against Greek Thrace and eastern Macedonia must be anticipated. In this area Greece would have only three divisions. Accordingly the Greek Commander-in-Chief requested, in order to establish a defensive

---

[1] De Mendelssohn, *The Nuremberg Documents,* pp. 257-81.

position in adequate strength along the Greco-Bulgarian frontier, the despatch of nine British divisions with corresponding air support. He further advocated a rapid pressing on with the reconditioning of airfields in Greece, and the building up of magazines for the supply of the British troops in Greece; also the development of a 'cover plan' to create the impression that these forces were destined for large-scale operations in Tripolitania. The British divisions could be shipped to the ports of Salonika, Amphipolis and Kavalla and take up their positions on the right flank of the Greek forces, thereby extending the front as far as the Turkish frontier, an operation which might be expected to produce favourable repercussions in Turkey and Yugoslavia.

General Wavell may well have felt embarrassed by the scale of this request. He was obliged to point out that he could offer only two or three divisions and a relatively small number of aircraft, and that the troops were not likely to be available, owing to problems of shipping and reconcentration, for over two months. Thus they could scarcely begin to arrive before the end of March, whereas there was much evidence to suggest that a German attack might be expected at any time after the beginning of March.[1] The only immediate assistance he could promise was one artillery regiment and a unit of 60-65 armoured cars.

Metaxas naturally replied that such a force would be quite inadequate and could only serve the purpose of providing the Germans with a pretext for launching their attack upon Greece. He therefore could not accept the British offer, and requested us not to proceed with the despatch of the first contingent. The conference broke up on this note, and the question of military aid for Greece remained in abeyance for nearly three weeks.[1]

On January 29th, General Metaxas died after a fortnight's illness following a throat operation. In the critical situation in which

---

[1] When the occasion arose for the despatch of the force Wavell proved a good deal better than his word. The first flight of British troops landed at Piraeus on March 7th. By the end of the month over 30,000 had arrived.

[1] According to Papagos, *The German Attack on Greece,* this refusal to accept British assistance was communicated by Metaxas, in confidence, to the Yugoslav Government who passed it on to the Germans.

Greece found herself, the death of the Dictator robbed the country of the one man who, whatever may be thought of the nature of his régime, possessed greater prestige and authority than any other figure in the country. His successor, Alexander Koryzis, while lacking nothing in patriotism, was a man of less force of character and less dominating personality. The new Greek Government approached Great Britain on February 8th to ask what help could be expected in the case of a German invasion; it was requested, however, that no British troops should move until German forces had crossed the Danube into Bulgaria, the old fear of precipitating a clash with Germany being again in evidence.

The War Cabinet now formulated a new policy for the Middle East. General Wavell received a telegram from the Chiefs of Staff directing that no operations be undertaken beyond the frontier of Cyrenaica—Benghazi had fallen on February 7th—where a strict defensive would be maintained; all troops and aircraft which could be spared would go to help the Greeks against the expected German invasion.

2

Defence Problems

THE two Allies, with their slender resources, had now to evolve a defence scheme with the least possible delay; and, considering their divergent points of view, it was perhaps inevitable that difficulties and misunderstandings should arise. To give up large tracts of Greek territory—including the port of Salonika—or to relinquish the well-won gains in Albania was likely to affect gravely the morale of the Greek armies and the Greek people. Thus it was not surprising that General Papagos favoured the holding of a forward line, the more so as the Greek divisions lacked modern or suitable transport—there was a shortage of the pack transport essential on the mountain routes, and ox-wagons were largely in use for the heavier loads—and therefore moved so slowly that withdrawal and re-grouping would be difficult and tedious tasks. But a forward policy involved the active co-operation of Yugoslavia which could not be counted upon, though the Greeks seem to have hoped for it almost to the last. General Wavell was more immediately concerned with the military needs of the situation, and could not count upon the favourable turn of political events to simplify his problems.

If Yugoslavia did throw in her lot with Greece and Britain it would be essential to hold Salonika, the only port through which Yugoslavia could be supplied with war material. In that case it might be practicable to hold the so-called 'Metaxas Line' which consisted of a chain of forts from Mount Beles, close to the junction of the Yugoslav, Greek and Bulgarian frontiers, across the Struma by Fort Rupel to the Mesta river. The fortifications of the Metaxas Line lacked depth, and their length—over one hundred miles—was excessive in relation to the troops available to occupy them, for the garrison had been depleted in order to reinforce the Albanian front. These considerations apart, it would be absolutely necessary for Yugoslavia to concentrate sufficient forces in southern Serbia to prevent a turning movement by the Germans down the Vardar valley or through Monastir which would take the Metaxas Line in rear.

As there was really no justification for counting upon effective aid from the Yugoslavs, it is difficult to establish a case for holding the Metaxas Line, or even for occupying a position from Mount Beles to Rupel and thence down the Struma to the sea. This line, some seventy miles in extent, had been held by British forces in the First World War for two years (1916-18) but had never been subjected to serious attack; and in 1941 it was as much exposed to a turning movement as was the Metaxas Line.

If Yugoslavia could be considered as a neutral willing and able to deny passage to the German and Bulgarian armies a strong position—and a shorter one, for its length was little more than sixty miles—might be established from the mouth of the Aliakmon river across to Verria and Edessa and thence to the Yugoslav frontier at Kaymakchalan.[1] This line follows the edge of the table-land of western Macedonia, the mountains rising abruptly, from the flat Vardar plain. The roads that pierce this mountain line at Verria and Edessa do so by steep gradients which offer every opportunity to the defence. Towards the coast the country is flatter, but here, too, the defender would have the advantage since the steep mountain slopes south of the Aliakmon give excellent observation over the bare and open country. It was intended to harry the German advance by the action of covering detachments in selected forward areas, but this position, Aliakmon—Verria—Edessa—Kaymakchalan, which became known as the 'Aliakmon Line' was eventually accepted in principle as the main line of defence, to be held by British and Greek forces. Even on this position special measures would have to be taken to safeguard the vulnerable left flank. If Yugoslavia should display neither the will nor the ability to resist a German invasion, enemy forces might reach Monastir without much trouble or delay, and thence advance southward to Florina and Kozani penetrating to the rear of the Aliakmon Line.

A defensive position further in rear, sited to join at a point in the Pindus mountains with the main Greek armies on the Albanian front would be considerably longer; and it would involve the withdrawal of the Greek forces from Konitsa and all their conquests at the northern end of the line in Albania. Whether such a withdrawal could be carried out in the face of the enemy with the very limited means of transport which the Greeks possessed and without the morale of the army going to pieces was extremely doubtful. It was even doubtful whether some of the local commanders would obey orders calling upon them to surrender territory to the despised Italians in accordance with an over-all strategic plan which they could scarcely be expected to appreciate.

Thus, whatever dispositions they made, the attitude of Yugoslavia was of vital importance to the Allies; and time was running short.

For the purpose of co-ordinating defence measures in the eastern Mediterranean theatre, which meant gauging the possibility of support from any Balkan country not yet under the German heel, Mr. Anthony Eden, Foreign Secretary, and General Sir John Dill, Chief of the Imperial General Staff, left London for Cairo on February 12th. Unfortunately they were delayed *en route* by unfavourable flying weather and did not reach Cairo until very late on the 19th, 'five valuable days being thus lost at a critical time'. The words are General Wavell's. Delay was indeed serious, for the German forces in Rumania were steadily increasing and might be expected to enter a complaisant Bulgaria at almost any moment. And on February 17th Turkey had signed a non-aggressive treaty with Bulgaria. As the Germans were preparing for bridging operations on the Danube and German troops were awaiting the signal to cross the river, the treaty could have but one meaning: Turkey would not regard as a *casus belli* the entry of German troops into Bulgaria for the purpose of invading Greece. This triumph of German diplomacy was made possible by the presence of powerful German forces on the Danube. Von Papen, German Ambassador at Istanbul, displayed the iron hand within the velvet glove: Mr. Eden had nothing but the glove.

On February 22nd our Foreign Secretary and the Chief of the Imperial General Staff, accompanied by General Wavell and Air Chief Marshal Longmore, journeyed to Athens, and conversations were held in the greatest secrecy at the Royal Palace at Tatoi. No word of these conversations leaked out either then or for some time subsequently. Eden began by stating that there was little probability, according to his information, that either Yugoslavia or Turkey would intervene on the Allied side and that therefore defence measures should be taken with this fact in view.

On behalf of the British Government he offered a force of 100,000 men, 240 field guns, 202 anti-tank guns, 32 medium guns, 192 A.A. guns and 142 tanks. These figures included all categories of base details and what Major [1]De Guingand, who was responsible for preparing the list, has described as 'doubtful values'. In any case they considerably exceeded the total that actually arrived, although more would have been sent had the campaign lasted longer. Asked for a survey of the military situation General Papagos stated that the abandonment of eastern Macedonia-that is to say the Metaxas Line and Salonika—and also of certain forward positions in Albania would cover a period of twenty days; and at the end of this period he would be able to dispose thirty-five battalions along the Aliakmon Line. Before taking the irrevocable step of abandoning so large a strip of national territory, Papagos urged that the Yugoslav Government be informed of the decisions taken and requested to clarify their attitude.

Quoting the account published by General Papagos, this suggestion was adopted and 'it was resolved to send an urgent code message to the British Minister in Belgrade. According to the reply received, the order for evacuation and withdrawal would be issued or not, as the case might be. This was agreed upon by all...'

This was not the impression left upon the British representatives when the meeting broke up in the early hours of the morning. Both Mr. Eden and the two soldiers believed that while a reply from Belgrade was awaited the three Greek divisions would be on their way back from eastern Macedonia to take up their positions in the Aliakmon Line. To them it was obvious that this movement must be carried out at once or not at all. The lack of unanimity towards the close of the conference was noted by an eye-witness who described

---

[1] Afterwards Major-General, and Chief of Staff to Field-Marshal Montgomery.

Papagos as looking 'none too happy', whilst, when the party dispersed, 'Eden came in looking buoyant'. [2]

The British would certainly have cause for satisfaction if they thought that all available forces would be concentrated in the Aliakmon Line without delay; and General Papagos might well be a prey to anxiety, if in his view, the fate of eastern Macedonia and Salonika hung in the balance.

Mr. Eden and General Dill now journeyed to Ankara, but the visit produced little that could be regarded as encouraging. The Turks did not deny all intention of entering the War as an ally, but stated that they were in no condition to do so at this juncture: they certainly could not declare war upon the Axis powers if Greece should be invaded.

On returning to Athens, where they arrived on the evening of Sunday, March 2nd, the British party were greeted with two items of news, both unwelcome, one expected and one unexpected. The entry of strong German forces into Bulgaria on the previous day occasioned no surprise, but it came as a shock to learn that General Papagos had not begun the withdrawal of his divisions from eastern Macedonia. Nor had any preparations been undertaken along the Aliakmon Line.

Papagos pointed out that no reply had been received from Belgrade regarding the attitude of the Yugoslav Government and that therefore he had felt unable to take responsibility for giving the order to withdraw, and that it was now impossible to do so in view of the presence of German and Bulgarian troops deployed in strength just across the frontier: the slow-moving Greek divisions might be attacked in the process of withdrawal and destroyed in detail. Politically, too, any hope of Yugoslav co-operation would disappear with the abandonment of Salonika. He now recommended what was, in effect, a council of despair: the maintenance of a purely static front along the Metaxas Line with British divisions coming up to reinforce piecemeal. Mr. Eden and General Dill found themselves quite unable to agree to this.

Nothing, therefore, was decided at the meeting on March 2nd, and the crowds who next day acclaimed the British Foreign Secretary outside the Grande Bretagne Hotel, Headquarters of the Greek General Staff, in the brilliant spring sunshine little knew what an *impasse* had been reached. General Wavell was summoned from

[2] De Guingand, *Operation Victory.*

Cairo and discussions were resumed until they resulted in the following signed agreement:

(1) The Greek Army would leave in Macedonia three divisions to defend the prepared positions in the Mesta-Rupel Line (*i.e.* the Metaxas Line).

(2) The Greek Army would concentrate with all speed on the Aliakmon Line the following forces:

12th Division from western Thrace, already moving westwards by train.

20th Division from Florina.

19th Motorized Division from Larissa.

Seven battalions from western Thrace, provided that the Turkish Government agreed on the principle of their release from the neighbourhood of their frontier (where they constituted a potential check against Bulgar aggression), at the request of the Greek and British Governments.

(3) A separate Greek commander would be appointed forthwith for these forces.

(4) British forces would be despatched as rapidly as shipping would permit to Piraeus and Volos.

(5) The British forces would concentrate on the Aliakmon position, where it was intended that the Greco-British forces should give battle.

(6) The command of all forces on the Aliakmon position would be entrusted to Lieut.-General Sir Henry Maitland Wilson, but under the high command of General Papagos. The date on which General Wilson assumed his command would be settled by General Papagos in consultation with him and would depend upon the arrival of General Wilson's headquarters and the establishment of his communications.

This decision represented a not very satisfactory attempt to reconcile this British desire to base the defence of Greece on the Aliakmon Line and the Greek reluctance to abandone Salonika and a large portion of national territory so long as there remained any reasonable prospect that Yugoslavia might adhere to our ranks. But compromises, though the essence of successful diplomacy, are rarely justified in the realm of war. On whatever position the Allies decided to make their stand, it was clear that they would require the concentration of all their resources. It is doubtful if any of those who signed the agreement felt really happy about it. Certainly there were no illusions on the British side.

General Wilson, who had handed over his command in Cyrenaica to Lieut.- General P. Neame arrived in Athens on March 4th. At the urgent request of the Greek Government, fearful as always of doing anything which might be construed by the Germans as an act of provocation, the General appeared in plain clothes under the name of 'Mr. Watt'. His personal staff were likewise incognito, also our military attaché by whom he was greeted at Tatoi airfield. There is no reason to suppose that the Germans were deceived; but General Wilson, who required to make extensive reconnaissances and to supervise the arrival and disposition of his forces, was hampered by these restrictions for a whole month.

The first flight of our combat troops had left Alexandria and was due to arrive while the always threatening situation was still obscure. As ever, in war, time was the important factor. How soon the Germans would be ready to strike we could not know. Actually, the deployment of List's Twelfth Army along the Greco-Bulgarian frontier was barely completed by March 20th, and on the 24th Army Headquarters suggested an April date for the attack. Meanwhile the Germans were putting the squeeze on the Yugoslav Government and the Italians indulged in their futile and costly offensive in Albania.

Divided counsels were the ruin of Yugoslavia. The Regent, the Oxford-educated Prince Paul, was emotionally Anglophile, but weak and easily terrorized; Tsvetkovitch, his Prime Minister, was a mediocrity; Cincar-Marcovitch, the Foreign Secretary, inclined towards the Axis, and so the Government pulled all ways at once, now seeming to lean towards the Allies and now towards the Aggressors. They had no definite policy and were at the mercy of circumstance. It is true that the Belgrade Government despatched to Athens on March 8th a Lieut.-Colonel Perescitch, of the Yugoslav General Staff, under the not inappropriate pseudonym of 'Mr. Hope'. Mr. Hope had no power to commit his Government and did not seem to be aware of any plan for the defence of his country. The sole purpose of his visit appeared to be to ascertain the extent of British aid in the event of Yugoslavia joining Greece and Britain and to stress the importance of Salonika as a means of securing Yugoslav communications. It was impossible to co-ordinate any defence plan as the result of this visit.

Throughout March, German diplomatic pressure upon Yugoslavia was steadily intensified. Hitler spent precious weeks endeavouring to get a diplomatic agreement signed. Russian influence was effective in delaying this for some little time, but on March 25th the Prime Minister and the Foreign Secretary of Yugoslavia signed in Vienna a pact of adhesion to the Axis.

The signing of this treaty appears to have persuaded the Greeks that Yugoslavia was lost as an ally: they now asked if General Wislon could supply transport for the withdrawal of their divisions from the Metaxas Line. No more, however, was heard of this, for two days later came fresh and more hopeful news.

The pact did not commit Yugoslavia to intervention on the side of Germany and Italy, or even to allowing the passage of troops through their country. But it implied a benevolent neutrality towards Germany and it allowed 'sealed trains' to pass, bringing, in theory, medical supplies and stores. Its implications were obvious and they were fully recognized by the Yugoslav people. On March 27th, less than forty-eight hours after the signature of the pact, as a result of widespread and simultaneous revolution, the Government was overthrown, King Peter assumed power in place of the Regent Prince Paul, and the new Government of General Simovitch, was established by *coup d'état.*

It was an heroic gesture, by which the people redeemed the pusillanimity of their Government, but it came too late to make very much difference to the pattern of the campaign in the Balkans. And it gave Hitler the excuse for drastic and immediate action. He was determined to destroy Yugoslavia militarily and as a national unit. No diplomatic enquiries would be made nor ultimata presented. And so he issued his 'Operation Number 25' for the immediate destruction of Yugoslavia. No great redistribution of forces was necessary, and the campaign was to open concurrently with the attack upon Greece in the first days of April.

CHAPTER III

British Troops in Greece

WHILE the Germans were coercing Yugoslavia and completing their concentrations on the Bulgar-Greece frontier, while Mussolini was making his last effort to do his own work in Albania, troops of the British Commonwealth were crossing over from Egypt to Greece and taking up their position on the Aliakmon Line.

Throughout those vital months when the Italian entry into the war and the defection of France threatened disaster to our whole position from Gibraltar to the Persian Gulf the defence of the Middle East had been maintained by a mixture of bluff and daring on the part of our commanders and troops and almost incredible ineptitude on the part of the Italians. Increased reinforcements had supplemented the results of the victories in the Western Desert, but at the beginning of February 1941 Wavell still disposed of only four divisions and a Polish brigade in Egypt and the Western Desert; two Australian divisions in Palestine; two Indian divisions in Eritrea; and a South African division and two native African divisions in East Africa.

Not all these formations can be described as battle-worthy. The tanks of the 7th Armoured Division, which had carried out the advance to Benghazi, required a complete overhaul; the 7th and 9th Australian Divisions in Palestine were both short of training and equipment; the native African divisions were not suitable for operations in North Africa or Europe. The 2nd Armoured Division was newly arrived, and the engines and tracks of its two regiments of cruiser tanks were already giving trouble.

Wavell had to perform some intricate jugglery to produce even the modest contingent to which we had pledged ourselves for Greece. The expeditionary force, under Sir Henry Maitland Wilson's command, was to consist of the New Zealand Division (Major-General B.C. Freyberg, V.C.); the 6th Australian Division (Major-General Sir Iven Mackay); and the 1st Armoured Brigade Group (Brigadier H.V.S. Charrington). The Australians and New Zealanders were to form the I Australian Corps under Lieut.-General Sir Thomas Blamey. In General Wavell's words, 'the despatch of this force involved removing from the Middle East practically the whole of the troops which were fully equipped and fit for operations'.

Subsequently the 7th Australian Division and the Polish Brigade were to be added as soon as they could be got ready. As it happened, the German counter-offensive in the Desert, which began on the 31st March and made rapid progress, kept both these formations in Africa. In any case, considering the rate of the German advance through Greece, they could not have arrived in time to affect the situation.

While still posing as a civilian, General Wilson was able to make a fairly extensive reconnaissance of the Aliakmon Line where his troops were to take up their positions. Extending from the mouth of the river to the Kaymakchalan *massif* of the Yugoslav frontier, its great advantages lay in the excellent observation over the open Macedonian plain and in the restricted lines of approach; yet to hold it securely would require more troops than were likely to be available.

There were four possible routes of attack. [1] The first was directly down the coast following the line of the Salonika—Athens railway between Mount Olympus and the sea; the second by the pass that runs on the inland side of Olympus from Katerini to Elasson, a steep and narrow road, with wooded and precipitous slopes on either side; the third by the steep and exceedingly difficult Verria pass; and the fourth by the somewhat easier Edessa pass to the north. In addition a successful turning movement was possible by a penetration from Monastir in southern Yugoslavia through to Florina, and thence by the road that runs south-east to Kozani and Servia, parallel to and at an average distance of twenty miles from the Allied position.

A further weakness lay in the indifferent rearward communications. Piraeus, the port of Athens, was the only major port of supply available, but communications with the front three hundred miles to the north depended upon one railway and a road so narrow in many

[1] See Maps 1 and 2.

places that it had to be regarded as a single-line route. There existed a secondary port at Volos, much nearer the front, but possessed of quite inadequate means for unloading shipping. It was connected with the advanced base area at Larissa only by a single-track railway line and by a road which proved quite impassable for three-ton lorries. In addition, lateral communications were wholly inadequate, consisting of minor roads and mountain tracks, the latter at all times, and the former after rain, being quite impracticable for wheeled transport. There was the further disadvantage that the civilian telephone and telegraph could not be regarded as secure [1] and the mountainous country interfered greatly with wireless communication.

The Aliakmon Line had never won general acceptance from our Ally. General Papagos could not but regret the surrender of so much national territory without a fight. As we have seen, he would have held, in the greatest possible strength, the Metaas Line on which so much labour and treasure had been expended: and he had always felt that a forward policy designed to retain the port of Salonika was the best, the only, hope of securing the help of Yugoslavia.

At his request, on March 6th, General Wilson had promised that when the British armour arrived it should move forward without delay to manoeuvre in front of the Aliakmon Line.

Our own build-up developed well during the early part of March, and the first and second flights (the 1st Armoured Brigade and the New Zealand Division) had arrived in Greece on time. Both formations reached the forward area during the latter part of the month. In the towns and villages the troops were loudly acclaimed by the people who threw flowers and brought them gifts of food and wine. Spring had come to Athens, but travelling northwards the men had to endure the rigours of winter. The cold was bitter.

The third flight was delayed by exceptionally unfavourable weather, and the fourth by the naval battle off Cape Metapan. The Italian Fleet had been urged out by its German Ally, partly in the hope that it might catch one of the British convoys at sea, partly to distract the attention of Admiral Cunningham's Fleet from the convoys crossing with German troops to North Africa. Failing

---

[1] 'until the Germans attacked it was possible to telephone from Athens to Berlin...' Wilson, *Eight Years Overseas.*

completely in its first objective, it paid the penalty by being brought to action in the open seas by Cunningham on March 28th.[2]

The *coup d'état* of March 27th brought no closer liaison with the Yugoslavs. News of this development reached our Foreign Secretary and the Chief of the Imperial Staff after they had started for home and caused them to return to Athens; but although Sir John Dill flew to Belgrade on April 1st he could obtain no agreement to a plan of concerted action. We did not give up trying. General Wilson—no longer in civilian guise—and General Papagos met General Yankovitch, the new Yugoslav Deputy Chief of Staff, at the little frontier station of Kenali, south of Monastir, two days later.[1] It then transpired that the Yugoslavs had made no preparations to meet a German invasion and had a very exaggerated idea of the strength of the British forces. Nothing could be decided and so, when the Germans attacked on April 6th, the Allies were in no respect depending upon Yugoslav resistance.

It is easy to criticize the new Yugoslav Government which, at the eleventh hour, found themselves unable to control and direct the national will to resist German aggression. Yugoslavia was not ready for such a war and there was no time to prepare for it. The bulk of her forces were concentrated in the north, for Croatia was ever an uneasy part of the union, and a re-deployment to safeguard old Serbia would have been too long and too clumsy a process. It was useless for the Yugoslav Government to declare Belgrade, Zagreb, Ljubljana open cities; useless for it to obtain on April 5th, the very eve of the invasion, a treaty of friendship and non-aggression with Soviet Russia. Nothing at this stage could have saved her. The Yugoslav campaign was bound to repeat most of the characteristics of the war in Poland, and no one supposes that a better grouping of the Polish armies could have altered the issue of that campaign. This Balkan campaign was a combat between mechanical armies moving perhaps, at fifteen miles an hour and troops moving in bullock wagons at no more than three miles an hour. Tanks against ox-carts!

The Italians lost three heavy cruisers and two destroyers sunk, and a battleship and a destroyer seriously damaged. This our Fleet achieved without the loss of or damage to a single ship.

Mr. Eden and General Dill were also present but took no part in the discussion. Before they left the country they paid informal visits to some of our troops who had arrived in the Aliakmon region.

When the equipment and means of battle are so disparate, strategy scarcely enters into the matter at all.

The British commanders could not but regard the Greek troops sent to assist in holding the Aliakmon Line as a poor substitute for the well-trained divisions which they had hoped to welcome from eastern Macedonia. The Greek 19th (Motorized) Division consisted of 'just over 2,000 quite untrained and recently enlisted garage hands', with 'no possible prospect of fighting usefully as a mobile force, having only a few Bren carriers, motor cycles and small cars'. They had also a number of captured Italian lorries and some Italian and Dutch tanks.[2] The 12th Division had only six battalions, two machine-gun companies and three mountain batteries; the 20th Division could muster only six battalions, having no artillery. As originally planned the 19th Division was to occupy the coastal sector with the New Zealand Division on its left and the 6th Australian Division on the left again. The other Greek divisions, 12th and 20th, were allotted to the defence of the Edessa Pass and to the left flank. Our 1st Armoured Brigade was to operate in the Axios (Vardar) plain, well forward of the main position.

On March 20th, it was decided to move out the Greek 19th Division into the plain in an anti-parachutist rôle, which meant that the New Zealanders were called upon to extend their right to the coast, giving them a total frontage of 23,000 yards. Both the divisional commander, General Freyberg, and the corps commander, General Blamey, recognized that this was an impossible task for one division. They favoured a modification of the whole line, making Mount Olympus itself the principal bastion of the defence on the right flank: the New Zealand Division could defend the Platamon tunnel between Olympus and the sea, and the line would run from the mountain westward to the Aliakmon, southwest of Servia, along the river to Grevena, and in that region join up with the Greeks to present a co-ordinated defence against attack through the Monastir Gap. General Wilson recognized the advantages of occupying such a position, but knew that it would first be necessary to persuade the Greeks to pull back from Koritsa. And they were not yet ready to give up any of the conquered ground in Albania, even if they were capable of a successful withdrawal.

[2]The armament of the division was given officially as: 24 light tanks; 123 machine guns; 78 light machine guns; 30 mortars; 22 A/Tk guns; with one field and one mountain battery.

By April 4th, the day before he openly assumed command of what was given the name of 'W Force', General Wilson felt justified in reassuring the Greek Commander-in-Chief as to the state of preparations in the Aliakmon Line; but he was well aware that we could not compete with the German concentration. The enemy was estimated to have from nineteen to twenty-one divisions in Bulgaria, of which it appeared that not less than eleven were grouped opposite the three Greek divisions holding the Metaxas fortifications. Six or seven might be expected to deliver the initial attack upon the Aliakmon Line, which would be held by two improvised Greek divisions and the equivalent of less than two British divisions.

On the eve of the German attack our forces in Greece were still coming into position on the Aliakmon Line. The 1st Armoured Brigade Group, first to be landed, had been in the forward area since March 21st and was disposed in several detachments each with a different task. The 4th Hussars, with a company of the Rangers,[1] one battery of the 2nd Regiment R.H.A. and one battery of the 102nd Anti-Tank Regiment (Northumberland Hussars), had its head-quarters at Yannitsa and had pushed well forward into the Vardar plain, its mission being to cover the carrying out of demolitions and, by every means in its power, to delay the advance of the enemy towards our main position. The Rangers, wih the other battery of the 102nd Anti-Tank Regiment were near Skydra, east of the Edessa Pass which they covered with support of the second battery of the 2nd R.H.A. The 155th Light A.A. Battery held a series of positions stretching across the plain from Edessa. Further west the 64th Medium Regiment R.A., north of Lake Petersko, supported the 20th Greek division. Finally the 3rd Royal Tank Regiment was located near Amyntaion south of the Monastir Gap, and with it was the 27th New Zealand Machine-Gun Battalion, less two companies. This detachment, soon to be augmented, was under the command of Brigadier J.E. Lee who had been lent, originally, to General Blamey to command the corps medium artillery.

The 4th Hussars had 52 light tanks; the 3rd R. Tank Regiment the same number of cruisers. The latter, as has been said, were not in satisfactory condition. When the 2nd Armoured Division arrived in

[1] A London Territorial rifle battalion, the 1st Rangers (9th King's Rifle Corps) had been converted into a motorized unit in 1940: hence its presence in an armoured formation.

the Middle East, its commander had drawn attention to the poor state of the tracks of his cruisers, already nearly worn out, and to the engines which were in sore need of overhauling. There had been no opportunity to remedy these faults, so the 1st Armoured Brigade, supplied by the division for service in Greece, took the field in a condition which could not be described as battle-worthy. It may also be remarked that the 2nd R.H.A. and the 102nd Anti-Tank Regiment consisted of two batteries each, although the third battery of the anti-tank unit arrived later.

The new Zealand Division which completed its arrival during the last week of March had just taken over the coastal sector, its 4th Brigade and 6th Brigade, from right to left occupying the high ground overlooking the Aliakmon river from the south. Most of the divisional cavalry regiment (armoured cars and Bren carriers) was stationed in an advanced position on the river bank, with a view to carrying out a delaying action. The 5th Brigade occupied a reserve position on the Olympus Pass, the twelve miles south-west of Katerini.

Coming by later convoys, the 6th Australian Division was still in the process of arriving. Its 16th Brigade was actually taking over the Verria Pass locality from the Greeks, its 19th Brigade was in Greece and moving up towards the front; and the 17th Brigade was still on the sea.

The three Greek formations, ill-equipped and weak in numbers, already mentioned as co-operating in the defence of the Aliakmon Line had been formed into the 'Central Macedonian Army' under General Kotulas, with its headquarters at Kozani. The 19th Division was now well forward, echeloned between the Vardar and the Struma, the 12th Division was being relieved by the Australians at the Verria Pass, and the 20th was near Edessa with detachments further west towards the Monastir Gap.

As far as was possible General Wilson was contriving that our troops should hold the defiles and the Greeks defend the mountain positions so that each nation should fight on ground best suited to its own type of training and transport.

The Force was notably weak in anti-aircraft artillery. In addition to the 155th Light A.A. Battery with the forward troops there were one heavy battery and one light regiment on the lines of communication and one heavy and two light batteries for airfield protection under the R.A.F.

Whatever fortune we might expect in the military operations in

Greece, it was clear that we should be heavily and probably decisively outnumbered in the air. The five squadrons which had been operating in Greece during the closing weeks of the previous year had now been increased to eight by the arrival of No. 11 Squadron (Blenheims) in January, No. 112 Squadron (Gladiators) on February 10th and No. 33 Squadron (Hurricanes) on February 19th. Striking successes had been achieved in a series of air combats against the Italians. In one encounter a formation of Hurricanes and Gladiators destroyed many Italian aircraft—the number was reported as 27 at the time—without loss to themselves. But during March the demands upon our air strength had expanded considerably. D'Albiac, as the result of constant pressure by his Greek colleagues, had had to modify his strategy of concentrating against the Italian supply ports and lines of communication, being constrained to detach a part of his force to give immediate air support to the troops in Albania. This method proved successful from the point of view of maintaining or raising the morale of the front-line soldiers but the achievements of the British aircraft proved more spectacular than useful.

With the forthcoming German attack in view, D'Albiac organized his scanty resources into two Wings:

A Western Wing (one bomber and one fighter (Gladiator Squadron) to support the Greeks in Albania.

An eastern Wing (two bomber squadrons and one Hurricane) fighter squadron to support the Anglo-Greek forces operating against the Germans. The squadrons of this wing were under the necessity of occupying improvised landing-grounds on the Larissa plain which, though now drying, were still soft after the rains of a delayed spring.

In the Athens area one bomber and one fighter squadron were stationed. There was also an army co-operation squadron available, but since most of its aircraft consisted of obsolete Lysanders (there was rarely more than one Hurricane available at a time) it was able to do very little effective work in face of the enemy. Airfield accommodation was still limited, but had the German attack been delayed by even as little as a week we should in the opinion of D'Albiac, have enjoyed the benefit of several more satellite landing-grounds, whereby at least one subsequent holocaust might have been avoided.

Expressed in terms of numbers, the R.A.F. could muster some eighty serviceable aircraft to do battle with approximately 800

German, supported by 160 Italian aircraft based on Albania and another 125-150 based in Italy but operating over Albania.

The odds were heavy. They were the odds of Thermopylae, and the Royal Air Force in Greece could hope for little than to win for itself the fame of Leonidas.

CHAPTER IV

Germany Strikes

I

The Fate of Yugoslavia

At 5.45 on the morning of Sunday, April 6th, the German armies thrust across the Yugoslav and Greek frontiers, while the German Ministers in Athens and Belgrade were handing declarations of war to the Governments of these two small nations which had refused to be coerced by Germany. In the case of Greece the Germans justified themselves by claiming that they entered the country merely to drive out the British troops, whose presence was evidence that Britian was seeking to build up a front in the Balkans against Germany. This argument ignored the fact that the British force had only been despatched after the German troops, which had been massing in Rumania for months past, had actually crossed the frontier into Bulgaria and had penetrated to positions overlooking Greek territory. In the case of Yugoslavia no such excuse was proffered. That she had repudiated the pact of alliance and/or subjection was regarded as sufficient proof of her warlike intentions towards Germany.

The Germans had concentrated thrity-two divisions for the Balkan campaign, of which only twenty-one were actually committed to action. These were grouped in two Armies, the Second Army of von Weichs being directed to invade Yugoslavia from the north and north-west while the Twelfth Army under von List advanced into the country from the east and also attacked Greece. Von Weichs appears to have had two panzer, one motorized, one mountain and six infantry divisions; von List, who had the more important and the heavier task, was allotted five panzer divisions, two motorized, three mountain and eight infantry divisions, three independent regiments and the SS Adolf Hitler Division. Besides these forces, more than adequate to the task in hand in view of their vastly superior armament, the Italian Second Army could be relied upon, at least in a defensive capacity in the Julian Alps, while the presence of the two Italian Armies in Albania would prevent the Greeks from withdrawing troops from that front to reinforce central Macedonia.

The story of the campaign in Yugoslavia can be briefly told. Against overwhelming German mechanized strength and a plan well devised and executed with the utmost resolution and speed, the Yugoslavs could set only the unquestioned courage of their troops. It was the Polish disaster over again, in more difficult but by no means impassable country. The Yugoslav High Command quickly lost control of the situation: contact was severed between the Government and the General Staff on the one hand and the various army commanders on the other. As a result of the savage bombardment of the capital on the opening day of the war, Belgrade radio closed down for forty-eight hours. The first official war communiqué, broadcast by wireless on the morning of Tuesday, April 8th, opened with the remarkable statement 'On all fronts the situation is in our favour'. In fact, the Government , shifting constantly across Serbia and Bosnia, from Belgrade southward to Uzice, from Uzice westward to Sarajevo, and thence to the coast, constantly bombed from the air, can never have had much idea of what was happening in other parts of the country.

The main German drive came from von List's Army into southern Serbia, and it met with instantaneous and spectacular success. It took the form of a three-pronged drive in great strength upon Nis, Skoplje and Monastir. At the same time a further detachment attacked the Strumitsa Pass in the extreme south of Yugoslavia and by a swift turning movement by way of Doiran advanced into the Vardar Plain and thence towards Salonika.

Von Stumme, who commanded the advance on Skoplje met with some tough opposition at the frontier pass but his forward troops reached Skoplje by 5p.m. on April 7th, less than thirty-six hours after the opening of hostilities. In 1915 the Bulgarians had made their most powerful and their most swiftly successful thrust into Serbia in exactly the same direction, and Skoplje had been the first town of importance to fall to them. Now, twenty-five years later, the Germans had repeated the achievement, the defenders showing themselves much less prepared to resist.

The southern column of von Stumme's corps, after an engagement on the frontier, crossed the Vardar at Veles and reached Prilep on April 8th. The subsequent operàtions of this column and also those of the Strumitsa force belong to the story of the Greek campaign.

Further north von Kleist's corps did not occupy Nis until the morning of April 9th. Then, wheeling north, von Kleist advanced on Belgrade which he entered, after some fighting, on April 13th. While he had been hurrying up from the south, however, the German advance from the north had been equally rapid, and on the evening prior to von Kleist's arrival a very small party had reached the Danube from the opposite direction. The fact that these few men were able to cross the river and obtain the effective surrender of the capital shows what a state of demoralization existed, following the air bombardments and the disappearance of the Central Government.

The hardest fighting, and that in which the Serbs showed to the best advantage, occurred when the Germans, thrusting north-west from Skoplje, were held up some days in the Kacanik Pass and lost a number of tanks. This stand enabled many Yugoslav units to break contact and disband, thus avoiding capture as prisoners of war. But apart from the Kacanik action the Germans were at no point seriously checked. Zagreb, capital of Croatia, was occupied by the Second Army on April 11th, without having put up any defence, and on the same day German and Italian troops joined hands on the Yugoslav-Albanian frontier north of Lake Ohridsko. After a week's fighting, organized resistance was practically at an end. Sarajevo, one of the last of the inland centres to yield, fell to the Germans on April 15th and Split, on the Adriatic coast, on the same day. The formal capitulation of the Yugoslav armies took place on April 17th. As in the Battle of France, the losses of either side in the field were relatively light. Even the prisoners of war captured by the Germans were fewer than might have been expected, for many of the Yugoslav soldiers were able to break away and hide in mountain retreats whence many reappeared as guerrilla fighters under the command of General Mihailovitch or Marshal Tito.

2

Greece Invaded

THE German invasion developed along the whole of the Greco-Bulgarian frontier. In Thrace, at the eastern extremity the enemy met with little opposition, for this region lay beyond the protection of the Metaxas Line and it had never been the intention of the Greek Command to hold it—unless with the co-operation of Turkey. Attacking the fortifications, however, the Germans encountered the most determined and courageous resistance: heavy assaults against the Metaxas Line were hurled back with the courage of despair. The Greeks had been ordered to hold these positions to the last and delay the Germans' occupation as long as possible. This order was obeyed. The defenders were attacked by wave after wave of infantry, bombed by Stukas, shelled without respite by light and heavy artillery. Two forts were taken on the first day, but only after they had been destroyed by artillery fire and bombing from the air. Elsewhere the Germans forced their way into the underground galleries only to be driven out by counter-attack. In the Struma gorge parachutists to the number of about 200 were dropped behind the Greek lines: within a few hours two-thirds of these men were killed and the remainder captured. Assault teams with flame-throwers, hand-grenades and explosive charges were engaged and worsted in close-quarters fighting.

The tragedy lay in the fact tht the heroic resistance of the Greek divisions was of little or no avail. While they continued to give of their best and to hold the enemy at bay other German forces were penetrating the Strumitsa Pass, where Yugoslav opposition was of the slightest, to reach Doiran and begin an advance down the Vardar valley with nothing but open country between them and Salonika. The Metaxas Line was turned. We have seen how in February the prompt withdrawal from this position had been discussed, and then rejected by the Greek Command: useless now to stress the fact that the successful defence of the Metaxas Line depended upon Yugoslav active co-operation in which the Greeks had never had much cause to trust.

In the early hours of Monday, April 7th, Piraeus received a terrible reminder of the realities of war. At 3 a.m. an immense explosion, followed at intervals of about half an hour by two others, shook every house in the port. Even seven miles away in Athens doors were blown in and windows broken. A 12,000 ton ship, s.s. *Clan Fraser,* heavily laden with T.N.T., had been blown up by a delayed action bomb. Six merchant ships, sixty lighters and twenty-five caiques were sunk or burnt out. The docks office and two quays were wrecked. An ammunition barge and an ammunition train were blown up. The work of unloading the ammunition ship had apparently been suspended for the whole of Sunday, which in itself is hard to understand in view of the declaration of war by Germany early that morning. And the ship was left in port partly unloaded instead of being moved to an outer anchorage for the night, a normal precaution to take. We could ill afford to lose the cargoes, and another unfortunate consequence was that a Royal Engineer company destined for Amyntaion was kept in Piraeus to clear the debris while a light A.A. battery which should have gone to Larissa, was detained for the protection of the port.

Perhaps the moral effect was greater than the material loss. Having heard the great explosions and seen the resultant havoc, the populations of Athens and Piraeus were in no way deceived by the official communiqué of the Ministry of the Interior which announced that 'a steamer and some buildings had been damaged'. The incident was, indeed, nicely calculated to give a foretaste of the thunderbolt quality of the German offensive which had just been launched in Thrace and Macedonia. Coupled with the news of the air bombardment of Belgrade, it convinced many of the inhabitants of the Greek capital and its port that the hour of destruction of their own cities was at hand. As a matter of fact, apart from a little machine-gunning of roads in the outskirts of Athens during the last days of the campaign, the German raiders confined themselves strictly to military targets in Greece. Athens remained unbombed, but the port was raided with considerable thoroughness and efficiency night after night, and was very nearly put out of action, though there was nothing so spectacularly disastrous as the explosion of the munition ship on that Sunday night.

On April 7th the Germans pushed down through Thrace to the Aegean Seas, occupying Alexandroupolis and Komotini by the evening. This had been foreseen and caused no particular concern: what spelled disaster was the German break-through on the other flank of the Metaxas Line where a German armoured division, followed by a mountain division, reached the Vardar and swung south to cross the Greek frontier at Doiran and Gevgeli.

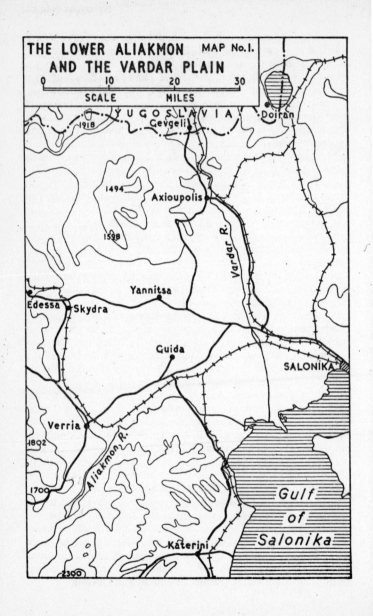

THE LOWER ALIAKMON MAP No. 1.
AND THE VARDAR PLAIN

SCALE 0 10 20 30 MILES

YUGOSLAVIA
1918
Gevgeli
Doiran
1494
Axioupolis
1598
Vardar R.
Yannitsa
Edessa
Skydra
Guida
SALONIKA
Verria
1892
Aliakmon R.
1700
Gulf
of
Salonika
Katerini
2300

By April 8th the magnitude of the Yugoslav disaster had already become apparent, and a Greek Government communiqué issued at noon was not calculated to hearten the people of Athens. It referred boldly, and somewhat vaguely, to the plight of the heroic defenders of the Metaxas Line. Further depression was caused in the capital by the pricking of another bubble. When, during the morning, it was rumoured that Turkey had declared war on the side of the Allies the people thronged the streets to salute the event. Turkish flags were carried alongside the British and the Greek, and there was a procession to the Turkish Legation, where the Minister very prudently refused to show himself. Within an hour or two, of course, the cold truth was known, but the demonstrators were at first reluctant to believe it. One may well suppose that the rumour was deliberately inspired by enemy agents. Certainly the ultimate result was to depress still further the spirits of the Athenians, and from about this time may be noted the emergence of certain defeatist elements in the capital, though the population as a whole stood firm as a rock.

German tanks and armoured cars were now racing down the broad and easy corridor of the Vardar towards Salonika, delayed at first only by the small Greek 'motorized' division with its tragicomic assortment of vehicles. At Axioupolis, where the railway and road to Salonika cross the Vardar, British troops, on this day April 8th, made their first contact with the invader. A patrol of the 4th Hussars encountered some German carrier-borne troops and after an exchange of fire blew the bridges and withdrew westward. Other forward detachments of the Armoured Brigade did likewise, after carrying out demolitions on the roads leading towards the British position. In Salonika there was time to destroy the oil stocks, installations and stores, the task of a special detachment of Canadian Royal Engineers known as the Kent Corps Troops. The vanguard of the German advance penetrated the outskirts of Salonika that night, and occupied the city at dawn the following morning, April 9th.

In eastern Macedonia, where several of the forts still resisted, the evacuation of the rear echelons of the divisions holding the Metaxas Line had begun from the ports of the Aegean coast.

After the opening of hostilities our main force stood awaiting attack for four days, an anxious and fretful period with little rest for either commanders or troops.

On April 6th reports of German progress made it tolerably certain that some enemy columns were heading for Monastir, while the thrust down the Vardar seemed bound to develop into an advance across the plain against the Aliakmon position. Our troops were still so thin on the ground that a characteristic German punch by the Twelfth Army would have broken the line anywhere; and the commander of the Australian Corps was in favour of pulling back the New Zealanders to the line of the passes without delay. General Wilson, however, considered that time was needed to clear stores and other impedimenta from the Katerini railhead but authorized a bigger allocation of labour to the Olympus positions.

The detachments of the 1st Armoured Brigade in the Vardar plain still expected to advance eastward to fight. At the Verria Pass the 16th Australian Brigade, fresh from the Western Desert, did not welcome the change of scene and climate. The three battalions were approaching positions 3,000 feet above sea-level; they had little protection from the bitter cold; and nearly all their gear required to be man-handled, for only a few pack donkeys were procurable and nothing on wheels could negotiate the steep mountain tracks. The relief of the Greek 12th Division promised to be a long and arduous affair. When the other two brigades of the 6th Australian Division should arrive Wilson intended to concentrate them near Kozani ready to reinforce either the main front or the Amyntaion position as the need arose.

First blood in the air operations went to the British. In a fighter sweep over the Beles-Rupel area a patrol of twelve Hurricanes met thirty ME 109's and shot down five of them without loss to themselves. The weather grew worse and after the first day the German advance was carried out under chilly grey skies and frequently in thick mist and through pelting storms of rain and sleet; but, although our own air reconnaissance and fighter and bomber attacks were hampered, we certainly gained more than we lost under these conditions. Once the skies cleared the *Luftwaffe,* in overwhelming strength, made short work of the task of establishing total air supremacy.

Early on the morning of the 8th a British motor patrol pushed across the Yugoslav frontier to Monastir which it found almost empty. There were no troops in the vicinity and no arrangements had been made to carry out systematic demolitions. The local police chief was in charge of the town and it appeared most unlikely that any resistance would be offered. The British patrol arranged for the demolition of the bridge across the Crna some miles to the north on the Prilep road and then withdrew, bringing back three Yugoslav tanks and four anti-aircraft guns.

That day a number of officers of the Yugoslav General Staff arrived over the Greek frontier in Florina. The news of the breakdown in southern Yugoslavia was confirmed. It was learned that three Yugoslav divisions had capitulated in the south and that the Germans were likely to be in Monastir by nightfall.

General Wilson came forward in the morning to confer with Generals Blamey, the corps commander, and Mackay, commanding the 6th Australian Division which was still arriving. On his way Wilson met the streams of Greek and Yugoslav refugees, military and civilians, in flight from the frontier regions. They were mainly on foot, but also on donkeys, in ox-carts, in antiquated buses and ramshackle cars, the vehicles covered with a medley of bedding, furniture and pots and pans lashed to roofs, mudguards and running-boards. This tragic exodus—one all too common in war—had already continued for several days and nights; and the Allies had no means of checking and organizing these pitiful crowds which might yet contain enemy agents, fifth columnists and other undesirables.

As the result of the conference at which Greek staff officers were present the decision was taken to withdraw from the Aliakmon Line to a position defined as Olympus—Servia—mountains west of the Kozani-Amyntaion valley. This course had the approval of General Papagos. It was imperative to defend the Monastir Gap with adequate forces, and orders had already been issued for the detachments of the 1st Armoured Brigade who were operating in the Vardar plain and to the northward of lakes Vegorritis and Petersko to fall back that night to the area Vevi-Kozani. These units were to reinforce the Amyntaion detachment which on expansion would be commanded by Major-General Mackay with the incomplete 19th Australian Brigade added to the force. Of this brigade the 2/4th Battalion was arriving; the 2/8th had been directed to the Verria region; the 2/11th was still on the sea.

It would be necessary for Mackay to hold on at Vevi, selected as a suitable position for the defence of the Monastir Gap, for two, probably three, days, in order to allow time for the withdrawal of the two Greek divisions, the 12th and the 20th, in the mountains between Verria and Edessa to the heights between Servia and Kastoria. So far as could be judged General Papagos was not yet reconciled to giving up the Albanian fruits of victory; but he was sending some support to the British left flank where a cavalry division and an infantry brigade from Albania were to link up with Mackay's command.

General Mackay reached Sotir—headquarters of Brigadier Lee who commanded the original Amyntaion detachment— shortly before midnight, April 8th/9th. No troops had yet arrived on the Vevi position for most of the 1st Armoured Brigade were driving westward by way of Edessa and Verria in fitful moonlight and rain, over roads greasy with mud and stony tracks running with water, all routes congested by Greek horsed transport, pack animals, bullock wagons, marching men and refugees. By dawn of the 9th, however, the troops were beginning to take up their positions in the Vevi Pass,' one of the first arrivals being the 64th Medium Regiment R.A. which had come from the Kelli area.

At Vevi the valley is at its narrowest, and the Monastir-Florina road follows a winding course through a pass which varies in width between 100 and 500 yards. The 1st Rangers, now included in Brigadier G.A. Vasey's 19th Australian Brigade in place of its missing battalion, had two companies at the top of the slope north-east of Vevi village and one in the foothills north-west of the highway which it thus bestrode. On the left of the Rangers the 2/4th Australian Battalion, which lacked one company, was given a four-mile front along the hills, linking up with Greek infantry on the eastern slopes of the eminence called Hill 1001. On the other flank the 2/8th Australian Battalion did not arrive from Verria until the morning of the 10th, officers and men having suffered considerably during the bitter cold night following the lack of opportunity for sleep while on their way to the front. The 2/8th linked up with the Rangers; and on the right of the Australians a Greek unit, the Dodecanese Regiment, came into position at the lakes.

The New Zealand machine-gunners were to support the 2/8th and the Rangers. The 1st Australian Anti-Tank Regiment put guns in forward positions with good observation of the road. In front of the Rangers the 2/1st Australian Field Company completed the laying of a minefield. Artillery support was supplied by the 2nd R.H.A., the 2/3rd Australian Field Regiment and the 64th Medium Regiment.

As a reserve in the region of Perdhika were collected the remainder of the 1st Armoured Brigade: 4th Hussars, 3rd R. Tank Regiment, and 102nd Anti-Tank Regiment (Northumberland Hussars).

April 9th was a day of great activity and preparation in the Vevi position which extended for nearly twelve miles, far too great a frontage for the three infantry battalions to hold, although the support of three artillery regiments might compensate, in some measure for the thin line. Lateral communication was difficult to maintain across the steep hillsides, and the position of the anti-tank guns, sited on the forward slopes and inadequately camouflaged, gave cause for some concern. Greek troops and refugees were still passing through our position, and in Vevi village, just in advance of our line were some unorganized soldiery among whom the presence of Germans in Greek uniform was suspected.

Fortunately the German advance was not so swift as had been anticipated. The hostile columns appeared to have been held up by the Crna demolition, for they did not enter Monastir until five o'clock on this afternoon. This extra respite was of great value not only to Mackay's force but to the whole of our troops and those of our Greek ally. The New Zealand Division was pulling back gradually from the Aliakmon mouth to the Olympus and Servia passes, where the defensive positions were strengthened. There was general regret that so much material had been used on the Aliakmon Line, for wire, sandbags, battle stores of all kinds, were not to be had in abundance.

Our forces were nowhere strong enough for the defensive tasks to which they had been committed. On the right the New Zealand Division holding the Olympus passes, the 16th Australian Brigade and the Greek 12th Division in the region of Verria, were under General Blamey; next on the left, the Greek 20th Division which occupied the wooded heights beyond and whose Dodecanese Regiment linked with Mackay west of the lakes, was the command of the Greek General Kotulas, superseded on the morning of April 9th by General Korassos; and Mackay's force was also directly under Wilson. Wilson who commanded this Anglo-Greek army had, of course, to fight his war under the strategic direction of General Papagos, Greek Commander-in-Chief, although, if occasion arose, he could appeal to General Wavell, Commander-in-Chief Middle East. Advanced G.H.Q. were near Elasson, not far from General Blamey. Rear G.H.Q. remained in Athens, 200 miles away.

MAP No.2.
THE WESTERN FLANK

SCALE   MILES

Monastir

YUGOSLAVIA

Kenali

M.Kaymakchalan

Pisodherion

Sitaria   Lofoi   Kelli

Florina   Vevi

L. Petersko   L. Vegorritis   Edessa

Hill 1001   Pandeleimon

Amyntaion

Sotir

Perdhika

Kastoria

Klisoura   Ptolemais

Proastion

Ardhassa

Mavropiyi   Komanos

Argos

Mavrodendri

Kozani

Siatista

Metamorfosis

Pass

Grevena

Venetikos R.

Aliakmon R.

Servia

CHAPTER V

The Western Flank

I

At the Monastir Gap

SNOW fell during the night of April 9th/10th and the bitter cold persisted. At 6.15 a.m., before daylight came, two armoured car patrols—one of the 4th Hussars and one of the New Zealand divisional cavalry regiment, each accompanied by a sapper detachment— drove forward from the Vevi position to reconnoitre. If possible, they were also to carry out more demolitions. They saw the heads of German columns about six miles away, and returned after an exchange of shots. The stream of refugees was thinning and no more Greek troops were expected to pass through, so, at 10 a.m., the Rangers blew up the road in front of the minefield. The Germans were now advancing steadily, and from noon onward the British and Australian gunners indulged in long-range shooting at the enemy vehicles. One of the first rounds fired by the 64th Medium Regiment put a German tank out of action and further casualties were inflicted as the hostile infantry and armour sought cover behind the ridge which runs between Lofoi and Sitaria. This ridge was some three miles beyond our forward positions.

It was obvious that the German artillery was not yet up, so no serious attack was to be expected until next day. Soon after four o'clock in the evening a German aircraft flew low over some of our batteries.

During the night German patrols crept forward up the slopes held by the 2/8th Australian Battalion and the Rangers. In the murk it was hard to distinguish friend from foe and some of the enemy took the Australians unawares by hailing them in English. Four Australians and six of the Rangers were captured, but when daylight came no hostile infantry could be seen.

At 6.a.m. on April 11th the 64th Medium Battery fired on Vevi village where lights and movements had been reported.

Snow lay heavy on the mountains, but the morning was fine in the valley; the bitter cold persisted, and in the afternoon rain and snow hampered our gunners in their search for targets. A few German tanks appeared, one, and then another coming to grief at the minefield in front of the Rangers. Later our artillery shelled the road leading to Kelli where German infantry were reported to be digging.

The German artillery came into action about noon, but our troops were more concerned with the mortar and machine-gun fire which began to open from Vevi village and from behind the Lofoi ridge. Movement between the forward posts became difficult and the infantry and the Australian anti-tank gunners began to lose men. Some of the German machine-gun posts were engaged effectively by the Ranger's small-arms fire; but the company on the immediate left of the Australians withdrew for 400 yards in order to shorten the line which was woefully thin.

As the light began to fail, about two battalions of German infantry attacked astride the road but were soon checked by the fire of our artillery. On the left the enemy was more persistant, his infantry advance against the 2/4th Australian Battalion making slow but steady progress despite the accurate shooting of the R.H.A. By 10 p.m. the Germans were digging in on the lower slopes about 300 yards away. At this time German infantry were dribbling forward between the posts of the 2/8th Australian Battalion and as the result of several encounters two prisoners were sent back. They proved to be hardy and well trained young soldiers of the SS Adolf Hitler Division.

In the early afternoon a report had been received that German tanks from Kelli were attacking the Greek troops between the Vegorritis and Petersko lakes where a break-through would carry the enemy down to Amyntaion and Sotir behind the Vevi position. To deal with this serious threat, a squadron of the 3rd Royal Tank Regiment and a troop of the 102nd Anti-Tank Regiment (Northumberland Hussars) were hurried across from Amyntaion to Pandeleimon, moving in snow and sleet over eight miles of ploughed vineyards. It seems that the Germans did not press their advance after losing one tank, and our troops were not engaged at all; but the occasion threw into relief the principal weakness of our armoured force. Six of the cruisers broke their tracks and were permanently out of action; another broke down through mechanical defects. We were notably deficient in tank repair facilities and, as a consequence, in the course of the campaign our armour wasted away.

On this day, April 11th, the 6th New Zealand Brigade completed the withdrawal from the lower Aliakmon in the coastal sector, passing through the 5th New Zealand Brigade which held the Olympus Pass, with one battalion detached to cover the Platamon tunnel corridor where the railway runs between the mountain and the sea. Meanwhile the 4th New Zealand Brigade consolidated its position around Servia. A cavalry screen of Bren carriers and armoured cars was left watching the crossings of the lower Aliakmon to the north.

And meanwhile General Bakopoulos had surrendered on behalf of his army in eastern Macedonia. Since the fall of Salonika these troops had been completely cut off from the rest of the Anglo-Greek forces, but even after their commander had capitulated the men in the frontier forts and some of the field troops continued to battle on. About 17,000 were made prisoners by the Germans, and some thousands were killed or wounded; but it may well be that, as the result of the resistance maintained by the forts of the Metaxas Line, half the total number of Greek troops between the Vardar and the Turkish frontier were able to escape by sea. The three lost divisions contained some of the finest fighting material in the Greek Army, and it was the more unfortunate that they had not been used in a sector where their courage and skill would have been of real profit to the Allies.

With the Germans in Florina General Papagos could not fail to see the threat to the right flank of his forces in Albania. Early on the morning of the 11th he made known his proposal to disengage in northern Albania and said that by so doing he would be able to provide a whole corps for the protection of the British left flank; but he asked for an assurance that our armoured brigade would carry out a diversionary operation towards Florina to cover the Greek movements. This assurance was given by our Rear Headquarters in Athens, although ignorant of the situation at the front where the 1st Armoured Brigade was hardly in a position to carry out any such task. In any case Wilson had issued his orders at 3.45 a.m., the withdrawal of the two Greek divisions, 12th and 20th, from their Verria-Edessa position to start first. Our troops at Vevi were to withdraw gradually during April 12th: the Rangers would cover the movement and come away during the night.

General agreement was reached by the British and Greek commanders when they met at Pharsala later in the day. Yet General Wilson was only too well aware of the problems which remained to be solved. The immediate one was to move back over the same roads a force consisting partly of mechanized troops with a high proportion of motor transport and partly of Greek infantry dependent upon bullock-wagons and mules. General Karassos had stressed the importance and the fighting quality of the Dodecanese Regiment which was posted in the area of Lake Petersko, and urged that every effort should be made to bring it safely back. We were prepared to move some troops with such transport as could be spared, but it was clear that the rate of retreat would be very uneven and that the slower-moving units might not get away at all.

And whatever might befall, Wilson saw his troops committed to tasks which they had not the numbers to fulfil. Every position they occupied would be too thinly held, with few or no reserves. There was no hope of further reinforcements from Egypt. General Wavell had arrived in Athens in the course of the day and, after conferring with General Blamey, confirmed his decision that the 7th Australian Division and the Polish Brigade, previously ear-marked for Greece should go to the Western Desert. There they were sorely needed, for the Germans, after retaking El Agheila, Benghazi and Derna, were already approaching Tobruk and Bardia. Wavell's decision was unavoidable, for the safety of Egypt and the Nile Delta mattered more than all.

Already there were signs that the next German thrust would develop at the junction of the British and Greek forces; if the enemy could reach Kastoria he would be in the rear of the Army of Western Macedonia, and the capture of Yanina would put him right across the line of retreat of the Army of Epirus. And that would bring down the curtain on the epic of the Albanian campaign. Wilson had already determined that his left flank must provide its own protection: when Mackay withdrew, the 1st Armoured Brigade would act as flankguard, moving via Kozani and the Siatista defile.

The course of events next day, Saturday, April 12th, seems to have determined the trend of the whole campaign. It would hardly be true to say that nothing went well, but a part of our forces suffered severe loss, and serious doubts arose as to the military capacity of our Ally. General Wilson was soon led to the conclusion that even the Olympus Line could only be held as a stage in our general withdrawal; and the loss of Olympus would involve the abandonment of the Larissa plain where our forward airfields lay.

Opinions differ as to the degree of disintegration which set in during the retreat of the Greek 12th and 20th Divisions from the Verria-Edessa heights to their mountain positions between Servia and Kastoria. The movement was bound to be a difficult one as its direction, roughly from east to west, crossed the line of communication and eventual withdrawal of Mackay Force; but it is seldom safe to judge foreign troops by our own standards. The Greeks, like the soldiery of many other nationalities, do not move with our formality and precision. Their withdrawal would, naturally, be carried out in small groups bearing little semblance of purpose and order even if they were ready and willing to respond to the next call for action. The primitive and varied types of transport was bound to slow down the march, causing traffic blocks and delay. The state of these two divisions, at least, may not have been so bad as some of our observers believed. Certain it is that the language difficulty caused misunderstandings and annoyance, while the Greek staff work proved to be of indifferent quality. Also it may be significant that Papagos asked us to assist in the defence of the new positions to which the two Greek divisions were directed, the Siatista and Klisoura passes.

Here a word must be said for the Greek cavalry division holding the Pisodherion Pass, west of Florina, where for several days the Germans had been able to make no headway.

We had promised to do what we could to get the Dodecanese Regiment out intact, but these troops were fully 50 per cent more numerous than had been estimated. They were lent thirty 3-ton lorries which were used mostly for the sick and wounded and they thinned out steadily during the day from their position on the right of the 2/8th Australian Battalion.

The withdrawal of the Greek armies in Albania formed the larger and more important issue, which was as much a psychological as an administrative one. The Greek commander-in-chief, who, before the German attack was launched, had been so reluctant to withdraw his troops from Thrace and eastern Macedonia could hardly bring himself to order the abandonment of the gains made with so much glory and at so much cost in Albania. He knew the limitations of his transport, and he knew also the moral effect of such a withdrawal upon his troops. This reluctance to abandon the tangible fruits of victory in the face of the despised and defeated Italians was not limited to the men in the front line. Several of the divisional commanders were showing themselves unwilling to withdraw; the Chief of Staff of the Army of Epirus had stated with a sublime disregard for strategy that he would go back no further than the Greek frontier; and the Bishop of Yanina, an extremely politically-minded prelate, was exhorting the troops in the same sense.

Yet withdrawal from Albania there must be, or the western flank of Mackay Force, and therefore of the entire British force in Greece would be placed in great jeopardy. Even now when General Papagos was about to act it might be too late.

2

The Action of Vevi

THE conditions under which fighting proceeded during these days are described by an Australian correspondent as follows:

Temperature has dropped to ten degrees below freezing point during this cold snap....Since the Germans began to invade Greece our men have been fighting in the snow, sleeping huddled together, wrapped in one or two blankets which they were able to carry. It is perishingly cold, though some young veterans say that it is no colder than the night winds of Libya in January and December. The bright side of the picture is that rain has evidently bogged the Bulgarian aerodromes. Few German aircraft have been going overhead; on the other hand our bombers have been going over in waves throughout the whole day.

Libya was like a billiard table compared with the terrifying ranges and yawning ravines. The roads which thread the mountains are narrow and tortuous... I set out to visit different sectors of the front early this morning. The going was fairly slow because of the endless line of army traffic on the roads—supply wagons, carriers, and guns moving up between the precipitous walls of the passes. The wind was cruel. It was blowing off the new snowfields formed on the mountain tops by the falls of last night. Truck drivers clung to their steering wheels with numb fingers. Their faces were blue with cold. I saw many groups of Greek soldiers swinging along on foot with their rifles slung over their shoulders.

I passed a battery of light guns drawn along by teams of shaggy mountain ponies...I met knots of refugees upon the road...I found men of an Australian battalion deep in the mountains. They were watering their donkeys at a stone trough fed from a spring. The country in which these troops are deployed is too craggy and precipitous for motor transport, and they are hauling up their food, ammunition and other supplies on the backs of donkeys. Some units of the Allied troops are living under very trying conditions on the snowclad ridges. Their only protection against the cold is provided by shelters which they erect in stony hollows with the aid of ground sheets. They have not been worried yet by enemy aircraft. The heavy banks of cloud hanging low over the mountains make bombing difficult.

At Vevi, to avoid any repetition of the infiltrations into our line which had proved so effective on the previous night, the commanding officer of the 2/8th Australian Battalion had given orders that between 9.30 p.m. and 5 a.m. all troops would remain in their rifle pits and fire at any movement observed or heard. His message read:

You may be tired. You may be uncomfortable. But you are doing a job important to the rest of our forces. Therefore you will continue to do that job unless otherwise ordered.

The morning of the 12th dawned with further falls of snow which had ceased by 8.30 a.m. when German infantry came forward to deliver another attack upon the Vevi position. The corps commander had at first favoured a double envelopment, but perhaps doubting the ability of his troops to carry this out over the difficult country on either flank he eventually agreed to allow the SS Division a further chance to force the position by frontal assault. This division was now supported by the whole of its own artillery and by a battalion of corps heavy artillery. The balance in fire-power had therefore swung over to the enemy since the previous day.

General Mackay had given precise orders for our withdrawal. The Australian battalions on the flanks were to thin out gradually and be in their trucks ready to depart by 8 p.m., the Rangers, astride the road through the pass, would act as rearguard and not retire until the early hours of next morning. The bulk of the 1st Armoured Brigade, in its capacity as left flank guard to our whole force, was to occupy two positions by nightfall of the 12th: one through Sotir, facing north-west, and one further back at Proastion about three miles south of Ptolemais.

Supported not only by artillery but by mortar and machine-gun fire the Germans came in steadily through the Vevi pass, the main thrust being east of the road and at the junction—weakly held because we were so few in numbers—between the rangers and the 2/8th Australians. Our artillery was able to inflict considerable loss upon the attackers but before 11 a.m. the platoon of the 2/8th on the extreme left of that battalion was overrun. To the Rangers it seemed that the Australians had withdrawn, though such was not the case. They were themselves so hard pressed that by noon they were forced to give ground and reorganize in the neighbourhood of the railway station. Casualties were mounting, some groups being cut off and lost, and it soon appeared to be a question of breaking off the action without further delay if complete disaster were to be avoided. The Bren gunners were organized as a rearguard while the remainder of the Rangers was collected and ferried back in the available transport to Amyntaion.

The 2/8th Australian Battalion hung on grimly all the afternoon, being able to bring some enfilade fire to bear upon the German tank and infantry advance; and one local counter-attack regained some ground. By 5 p.m., however, the Greeks (Dodecanese Regiment) on the right of the 2/8th had nearly all gone, touch had long since been lost with the Rangers on the other flank, and the Australians were in grave danger of being cut off altogether. They had to get out quickly as best they could and the only way of retreat was south-eastward and then down the road to Sotir. In this direction the survivors made their escape, most of them too exhausted to carry anything, so equipment and even arms had to be discarded. By 9 a.m. about 200 officers and men had reached Sotir, a large proportion bearing no weapons of any kind. During the night they were taken south by lorry to Servia.

On the left flank the 2/4th Australian Battalion was ordered to withdraw in the middle of the afternoon but, with a shortage of telephone wire and breakages to cable caused by hostile shell-fire, orders to the companies and platoons were difficult to transmit. When runners had to carry messages across the snow-covered hillsides one could not be sure when they would arrive or if they would arrive at all. Eventually the battalion came back piece-meal in the dark when the German infantry were almost among them. Small wonder that most of one of the rifle companies was cut off and captured: it was a great achievement to bring away what could still be reckoned a fighting force fit for further action.

٠. Much credit must go to the artillery, the 2nd R.H.A., the 2/3rd Australian Field Regiment, the 64th Medium Regiment and such Australian anti-tank guns as had not been overwhelmed in the German advance. Until darkness fell our gunners maintained an effective fire, although in some cases no infantry remained in front of them. The R.H.A. withdrew with the utmost coolness under small-arms fire at 400 yards range.

One may say that we were hustled out of the Vevi position as soon as the Germans were able to develop their full strength. But our troops had done all that was possible, bearing in mind the lack of numbers which condemned them to hold a far too extended position with little chance for mutual support, and no reserves. The bitter weather had probably borne more hardly upon our own men than on their antagonists. Considerable loss had been inflicted upon the Germans but only at a cost that we could ill afford, for all three infantry battalions had suffered severely and had lost arms and equipment. The Australian field regiment lost two guns which became hopelessly ditched during the withdrawal and had to be destroyed; the 64th Medium Regiment lost one gun and a tractor in the same fashion. The 1st Australian Anti-Tank Regiment lost 16 guns, ten of them when a whole battery was cut off by a premature road demolition and captured. A troop of the Northumberland Hussars, with the Greeks, had to abandon three of its anti-tank guns, also cut off by a demolition, but the gunners brought away the breech-blocks. In the 3rd R. Tank Regiment one squadron was now reduced to six cruisers and another to only four, repairs being impossible owing to the lack of track plates and pins, and engine spare parts. Patrols of the regiment had covered the withdrawal of some of the infantry to the Sotir position.

Here a certain amount of work had been done on the defences, Sotir being the responsibility of the 1st Armoured Brigade under Brigadier Charrington. At Amyntaion a demolition squadron under the command of Major Peter Fleming, the well-known explorer, had destroyed 20 locomotives and about 100 railway coaches, which must otherwise have fallen into German hands. Mackay Force had ceased to exist as such, its 19th Australian Brigade and other Australian troops being under orders to rejoin General Blamey's command which from this day forth was known as the Anzac Corps, thus reviving the old memories of a quarter of a century ago.

3

The Actions of Sotir and Proastion

AT Sotir Brigadier Charrington had at his disposal the reserve company of the Rangers and, being so short of infantry, he obtained permission to retain the two rifle companies which remained of the 2/4th Australian Battalion. His other troops comprised an anti-tank battery of the Northumberland Hussars, the 3rd Royal Tank Regiment (less one squadron), a platoon of the New Zealand machine-gunners, and a detachment of the 3rd (Cheshire) Field Squadron R.E. for demolition and minefield work. The 2nd R.H.A. came in during the night. Its task was to cover the whole front.

Back at the Proastion position were assembling the remainder of the 1st Armoured Brigade, the Rangers and New Zealand machine-gunners from Vevi being expected to arrive during the early hours of the morning. The 64th Medium Regiment arrived at Perdhika during the evening of the 12th, and at 7.30 p.m. was sent off to a village south of Servia to come under the Anzac Corps.

The Germans were not slow in following up our retreat, for some of their motor-cyclists were seen on the road in front of the Sotir position before nightfall on April 12th. They advanced to the assault next morning—Easter Sunday in the Western Calendar—with the weather turning fine and warm. The British position, which extended for some five miles along a ridge between Lake Vegorritis and a swamp south-west of Sotir, was partly protected from tank assault by a stream running diagonally across the front.

Driving forward in their trucks until they were well within field-gun range, the hostile infantry alighted near Amyntaion in full view of our forward troops and came on in short rushes despite the fire of the R.H.A. and of the Bren guns of the Rangers. They crossed the stream and tried to close but their threat to the right of the Rangers' company was warded off by our tanks firing from hull-down positions; and one squadron came into action on the forward slope, opening with all its weapons on German infantry and vehicles. This bold performance appears to have deceived the enemy as to our intentions. Some German reports describe the British tanks as moving forward with infantry clinging to them and running beside them, implying that a counter-attack was delivered; the German divisional commander is stated to have been consumed with anxiety, and to have ordered his anti-tank guns forward with the utmost speed, while the infantry prepared to defend themselves in fox-holes with hand-grenades and blocks of T.N.T. against an armoured attack.

Later, the German artillery began to come into action with air observation, sending over an aircraft which took the opportunity of opening machine-gun fire on the tanks in their exposed position. By this time the withdrawal had begun. First to go was the 2/4th Australian Battalion which travelled in trucks to join its own brigade. The Rangers followed about 10 a.m., the infantry retirement being well covered by the R.H.A. who, in their turn, came out of action while tanks and anti-tank guns maintained their fire. The whole movement was nicely judged—one battery of the R.H.A. pulled out just as howitzer shells began to fall about its position—and executed, but the troubles of the 1st Armoured Brigade were by no means over for the day. The brigade had received orders to hold off the German pursuit as long as possible, so that the Greek 12th and 20th Divisions might have more time to reach their new positions and reorganize. Most of the Sotir force was sent back to Mavrodendri, six miles beyond the next rearguard position at Proastion where the three companies of Rangers had arrived at 6.30 a.m.

At Proastion the road to Kozani passes through a mile-wide gorge which, while providing a natural defensive position, allowed sufficient room under cover for transport vehicles to be parked well forward, an obvious advantage when a rearguard action is to be fought. As at Sotir a stream served the purpose of an anti-tank ditch: it ran across the front some 300 yards in advance of our forward posts. The Rangers had two companies astride the road and one in reserve, with carriers well ahead to watch the line of the stream.

The Germans lost no time in covering the dozen miles from Sotir, and when they appeared it was seen that tanks and armoured troop carriers were now leading the way, with engineer detachments at hand. These were not our familiar opponents of the Adolf Hitler Division, but troops of the 9th Panzer Division which had been passed through to lend fresh impetus to the advance. German aircraft were already overhead, for after a week of bad weather the skies had cleared and the *Luftwaffe* was quick to take advantage of favourable conditions to exert its superior strength. Henceforth enemy air attacks were a real and constant hazard to be undergone alike by fighting troops and transport, communications, bases and ports.

A dive-bombing attack on our infantry and battery positions soon compelled the withdrawal of some of our forward guns to less conspicuous positions. The R.H.A., however, scored a hit on the leading vehicle of a motor column emerging from Ptolemais and the traffic jam which resulted seemed to hinder the development of the frontal attack. German tanks and infantry then started an out-flanking movement on our right where the Rangers were hard pressed but held on with the support of our tank and anti-tank guns. Next, the left forward company of the Rangers, under heavy fire from artillery and mortars, and machine-gunned repeatedly from the air, was pressed back so that the anti-tank guns of the Northumberland Hussars were left in action without infantry protection and the New Zealand machine-gunners seemed liable to be cut off. Yet our artillery fire held the Germans at bay and continued to do so until after darkness fell.

Meanwhile a column of enemy tanks and carrier-borne infantry had taken the Ardhassa track which leads westward, and then made for the left rear of our position. In the gathering dusk about thirty light and medium tanks, followed by infantry, approached Mavropiyi, not much more than a mile from the main road and 1st Armoured Brigade Headquarters at Komanos. The movement had not gone undetected: part of the 4th Hussars and a troop of anti-tank guns had been hurried across from our front positions and were there to meet them. A spirited combat ensued. The light tank of the 4th Hussars was no match for the heavier German type, but the troop of Northumberland Hussars anti-tank guns under Lieutenant A.W. Trippier was so swiftly and ably handled that the first crisis safely passed. Driven boldly in to effective range these anti-tank two-pounders, firing from their portées, took the enemy by surprise. A number of his tanks were manoevred into a ravine north-west of Mavropiyi and six were knocked out. As the fight continued two more were destroyed.

But the Germans were pressing on towards the main road. There, a squadron of the 3rd Royal Tank Regiment arrived and came into action at 800 yards range, hull-down behind a ridge above brigade headquarters. The fire of these tanks—there were only four of them—enabled the Northumberland Hussars to disengage and accounted for at least two more of the enemy tanks. The men of brigade headquarters were in action with rifles and Bren guns and some of the New Zealand machine-gunners withdrawing from Proastion assisted to shoot it out in the after-glow of the sunset.

The Germans drew off into the gathering darkness. From their own reports it seems that almost all their surviving tanks were out of ammunition and many were down to their last litre of fuel. They betray a rueful appreciation of the skill and courage of our anti-tank gunners, and pay the troops who fought at Komanos the compliment of describing them as a 'British tank division'.

The firing had hardly died away when the Rangers drove down the road past Komanos, withdrawing from the Proastion position on their way to Kozani. Our troops at Proastion sustained by admirable artillery support, had been able to break contact at their own time; and their actual withdrawal, under a smoke-screen laid down by the guns of the 4th Hussars and 3rd R. Tank Regiment, was carried out unperceived by the enemy who continued to shell the empty positions for half an hour or more.

Brigadier Charrington was withdrawing down the main road as far as Kozani and thence by a secondary road which leads south-westward to Grevena beyond the upper Aliakmon. From Kozani his way passed through the position of the Greek 20th Division around Siatista, but those of our Allies who were encountered seemed bent only upon retreat. Three of our cruiser tanks halted at Kozani until the whole column was through the town and, as the march proceeded, companies of the Rangers were dropped to hold delaying positions in case the pursuit should be pressed. At Mavrodendri German motor-cyclists and troop carriers made contact with the Rangers detachment and then withdrew: it seemed that the 1st Armoured Brigade had hit the enemy so hard that no trouble was to be expected from him at the moment.

Near the village of Siatista at the Metamorfosis Pass the column passed through the remaining battery of the 102nd (Northumberland Hussars) Anti-Tank Regiment which had followed the unit to Greece, and was in action for the first time. The pass was one of the positions which the Greek 12th Division was expected to hold, but the Greek divisional headquarters, established at Siatista, could provide no Greek infantry to supplement the anti-tank defence. However, two good machine-gun detachments were sent and, later, a horsed battery of Greek artillery arrived.

The 1st Armoured Brigade, very tired but still in good heart, reached Grevena in the early hours of April 14th but the brigade was now a brigade in name only and its chief losses were in armour. The 3rd Royal Tank Regiment, organized as one squadron, had only 13 cruisers left, most of the casualties being from broken tracks and other defects, not from enemy action. The 4th Hussars was reduced to 40 tanks fit for service and the Northumberland Hussars had lost six anti-tanks guns: in the affray near Komanos, however, Lieutenant Trippier's troop had lost only one gun, one portée and one truck. The 1st Rangers could now muster about half its original fighting strength, and was short of weapons and equipment, The 2nd R.H.A., after three days' fighting, reported two men wounded, an expenditure of 3,100 rounds of ammunition, and four vehicles and one motorcycle abandoned in the retreat. Observers had spoken with admiration of the splendid order in which the regiment came out of action after the most gruelling time.

It will be remembered that the 64th Medium Regiment R.A. had been sent to Servia to support the Australian division. Directed to the Portas Pass, south of Servia, the regiment found nearly all the available positions occupied by the 7th Medium Regiment, comparatively late arrivals in Greece who had only reached the forward area on April 11th. At first only two troops of the 64th could come into action, but reconnaissance for other positions began without delay.

As we knew the 4th New Zealand Brigade was established at Servia and the 19th Australian Brigade, whose two battalions had lost so heavily at Vevi, was taking up positions opposite Servia on the western side of the Aliakmon. Since there was no bridge in their rear to enable them to be supplied and reinforced or, if necessary, withdrawn, across the river, they began to construct two light bridges. Servia and the road junction about three miles beyond were of vital importance, for penetration here would place the enemy in rear of the whole Olympus position on the main road to the plain of Thessaly and Larissa. General Blamey therefore strengthened the defence by bringing across the 26th New Zealand Battalion from the coastal sector to take up a position on the right of the 19th Australian Brigade west of the river. Here the New Zealanders were in visual contact with their own 4th Brigade on the opposite bank.

In the mountains between the 4th New Zealand Brigade above Servia and the 5th at Olympus was the 16th Australian Brigade which had arrived from Verria. Its position seemed immune from attack except by the hardiest of mountaineers but the problem of supply was a difficult one: no motor transport could be used and only a few mules and donkeys were to be obtained.

On the morning of April 13th a German mountain division was reported to be arriving at Verria, and the enemy's advance towards the lower Aliakmon was now developing. The road bridge and the railway bridge between Guida and the sea had been blown, and the New Zealand cavalry (armoured cars, carriers and motor-cycles) watched the crossings. They had the close support of a troop of the 5th New Zealand Field Regiment. During the afternoon of April 12th some German motor-cyclists who approached this road bridge were scattered by the fire of Bren guns; a column of vehicles further in rear was engaged by the New Zealand gunners at dusk. Next morning the enemy came on in some strength. The fire of the New Zealand cavalry was concentrated upon infantry near the road, and the admirable, well-controlled shooting of the 25-pounders checked German progress for a time. The river was 100 yards wide and the infantry found it difficult to make the passage in rubber boats, but, after becoming exposed to the fire of tanks and artillery, our thin cavalry screen was withdrawn early in the afternoon. At night the New Zealanders were in position behind a tank-ditch ten miles south of the river crossings.

4

Retreat in Albania; Our Need to Withdraw

ON April 13th the Greek retreat from Albania had begun in earnest and Koritsa, the first great prize of the autumn victories, was evacuated. This movement was carried out without the slightest interference from the Italians who were actually unaware of the departure of the Greeks until twenty-four hours later. But, as had been feared, the beginning of the withdrawal from these gloriously won positions was fatal to the staying power of the Greek armies. They had shown that they could resist and overcome an enemy offensive and maintain with spirit and enterprise an offensive of their own. They could cope with bitter weather and some of the most uninviting terrain in Europe. But to retreat from an enemy they had beaten, along a single road packed with transport vehicles of every kind and swarms of refugees, constantly dive-bombed and machine-gunned from the air, and to maintain their cohesion and fighting spirit through it all was not to be expected.

The breakdown of the armies retreating from Albania undoubtedly affected the morale of the Central Macedonian Army as the Greek 12th and 20th Divisions were termed. As we know, these divisions had never been much more than brigades in strength, and had always lacked supporting arms and adequate transport. Their new position was on the left of the 1st Armoured Brigade, linking up with the armies now drawing back across the Albanian frontier, but whether they were capable of holding it was another matter. If the Germans could thrust down through Kastoria they might outflank the 1st Armoured Brigade at Grevena, but this danger does not seem to have been imminent. However, General Wilson believed that the western portion of the Anglo-Greek front extending from Mount Olympus to the Albanian frontier was unlikely to hold in face of a serious attack, even if it were not already on the point of dissolving. He conferred with General Blamey on the evening of the 13th, and then decided to withdraw to the Thermopylae position, a distance of over one hundred miles.

Looking south at central Greece from the direction of Macedonia all roads appear to converge upon Larissa which stands in the centre of the plain of Thessaly. If the Germans could once push their armoured forces—superior both in quantity and quality—through the crust of mountains into the 'soft' country beyond, before General Wilson's forces had made good their withdrawal from the Olympus line, the whole Anglo-Greek army would be in danger of destruction. The supreme achievement in war, the achievement which makes Cannae, Tannenberg and Tunis classic masterpieces of battle, is the defeat and annihilation of the enemy where he stands. On the morning of April 14th the possibility of such a victory may well have occurred to the German Command.

Of the roads which lead down from the north to Larissa that from Kozani crosses the Aliakmon river near Servia and reaches Elasson by way of the Portas pass. This is the only one which can be dignified by the name of a modern road. The route from the Aliakmon mouth and Katerini over the Olympus pass to Elasson is very inferior. And, east of the mountain, the coastal route which follows the railway and turns inland through the vale of Tempe to reach Larissa from the north-east is no better. Each of these routes passes through, on the mountain barrier, a natural defensive position against which there would be difficulty in deploying large numbers, whether of troops or armoured vehicles. The attacker could count upon no swift penetration.

But there was the fourth possibility which General Wilson had in mind. A road reaches Larissa from the west by Trikkala, which is linked with Kalabaka, on the fringe of the plain; and Kalabaka is connected by an indifferent but possible road with Grevena, thirty miles to the north. Von List might well decide upon an advance through and beyond Grevena where resistance might be expected to be of no great strength. Such an advance, although it would set a considerable administrative problem, possessed further advantages for the Germans. By coming south down the road from Kastoria to Grevena their forces would soon be in rear of the Greek front in Albania. Clearly a concentrated effort west of the Olympus mountain passes offered the prospect of big results.

CHAPTER VI

The Olympus Position

I

Left Flank Guard

IN the course of the morning of April 14th, columns of enemy transport were observed moving westward from Amyntaion and Ptolemais towards Klisoura which was in German hands before noon. In the better weather R.A.F. Blenheims and Hurricanes were employed to bomb and machine-gun these columns and certainly helped to delay their progress. Three Greek battalions were relied upon to be the next German objective. Meanwhile we despatched as many lorries as could be spared to Yanina to help in the evacuation of the ten Greek divisions still in southern Albania.

The 1st Armoured Brigade harboured at Grevena on the 14th, the only troops north of the Aliakmon being the battery of Northumberland Hussars who held the Metamorfosis Pass with their anti-tank guns. The battery was attacked in the afternoon, German infantry advancing with the support of mortar fire, but the Hussars, ably assisted by the Greek machine-gunners and field battery, held their own. At nightfall, however, the Germans began to occupy an unfinished anti-tank ditch near the mouth of the pass. The defenders then pulled out and retreated to Grevena, the rickety bridge over the Aliakmon being blown by the 3rd (Cheshire) Field Squadron as soon as they had crossed.

During the day the 1st Armoured Brigade in the Grevena region had been heavily attacked from the air. The transport, closely concentrated in a gorge a little way to the south, presented, as was said by one who was present, 'the best bombing target the Germans can have enjoyed since France'. Our only defence was provided by the 155th Light A.A. Battery, and it is therefore not surprising that considerable damage was done by the bombs and machine-guns of the *Luftwaffe*.

The 1st Armoured Brigade was not well placed at Grevena to fight a rearguard action and its powers of resistance were so diminished that General Wilson was obliged to take further measures to safeguard his left flank. Brigadier Charrington received orders to withdraw to the line of the Venetikos river—a tributary of the Aliakmon about five miles further south, the movement to begin at midnight. The 17th Australian Brigade, which had now arrived in Greece, was to concentrate in the Kalabaka area in a reserve position. The brigade was commanded by Brigadier S.G. Savige and consisted of the 2/5th, 2/6th and 2/7th Battalions: to it would be attached a battery of the 64th Medium Regiment R.A., some anti-tank guns, seven cruisers of the 3rd R. Tank Regiment, and an Australian machine-gun company. As it happened, transport difficulties had delayed the arrival of the troops at Larissa. Owing to break-down on the railway from Athens, neither the 2/6th nor 2/7th Battalions arrived until April 16th, and by that time were urgently required elsewhere. So the 2/11th Battalion from the 19th Australian Brigade was added to make up, in part, for this deficiency. When Brigadier Savige arrived at Kalabaka at 11.30 p.m. on April 14th most of 'Savige Force', as finally constituted, was present.

2

At the Passes

AT the Servia position the 4th New Zealand Brigade was dug in on a line from the village of Kastania to Rimnion, part of the front presenting an almost clear view of Servia village, the Aliakmon crossings, and the road from Kozani along which the German armour must come. Behind the New Zealanders the road, turning south-east through the Portas Pass, ran for nearly eight miles between rocky walls nearby 4,000 feet high.

On the left beyond the Aliakmon the 19th Australian Brigade had in position the 2/4th and 2/8th Battalions, both very weak in numbers and the 26th New Zealand Battalion. Its 2/11th Battalion

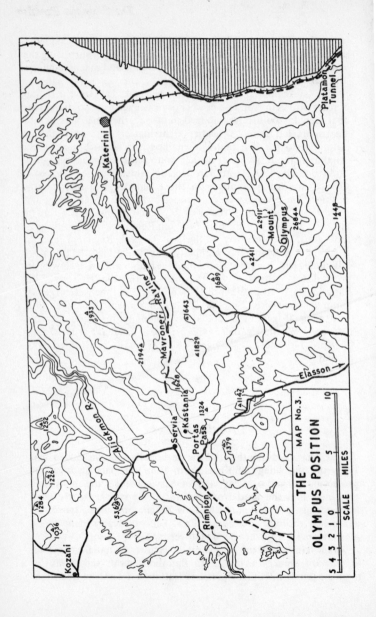

THE
MAP No.3.
OLYMPUS POSITION

SCALE   MILES
5 4 3 2 1 0   5   10

had been taken for Savige Force. In the mountains to the right of the New Zealanders was the 16th Australian Brigade.

The Servia area was heavily bombed from the air at intervals during the 14th, but the damage inflicted was slight. In the morning the 9th Panzer Division entered Kozani and moved south-eastward towards the Aliakmon crossing at Servia. The distance from Kozani to the river was little more than ten miles, but the German advance proved to be unexpectedly slow—a tribute, perhaps, to the effectiveness of our demolitions. Towards evening the head of the column approached the river where the bridge had been blown by the New Zealand engineers, and came to a halt. The hostile artillery had opened in reply to ours, but the firing died down as darkness fell.

Further to the east the 5th New Zealand Brigade which held the Olympus passes was also in contact with the enemy. The New Zealand cavalry regiment, retiring before a force of all arms, came in during the afternoon, having lost two troopers killed, one motorcycle destroyed, and one carrier abandoned through a mechanical defect. German aircraft had made little attempt to interfere with the movements of the regiment.

The demolitions at the entrance to the main Olympus pass which carries the Katerini-Elasson road were blown as soon as the New Zealand cavalry had passed through. Two hours later, about 5 p.m., forward posts of the 22nd New Zealand Battalion saw the head of a German column which was not fired on and soon disappeared from view. A number of enemy aircraft flew over to reconnoitre before darkness fell. Then, about 11 p.m., some motor-cyclists rode boldly up the road and, when they had almost reached the edge of the demolitions, the New Zealanders opened fire. Next morning five wrecked motor-cycles were found in front of the position—but no Germans. The remainder of the night was enlivened by bursts of machine-gun fire to which the defenders did not reply.

On the seaward side of Mount Olympus runs the road which is the shortest way to Larissa: the classic avenue of approach for invading armies. Here the railway passes through the Platamon tunnel. Demolitions had been prepared in order to wreck both road and railway though it was not to be expected that the enemy would be checked for long by these measures. Unfortunately the work of destruction had to be confided to an Army Troops company of New Zealand sappers which was short of its proper equipment. For making an impression in solid rock a pickaxe is a sorry substitute for a pneumatic drill. Before nightfall the 21st New Zealand Battalion which was defending the pass reported the advance of some 80 tanks and 150 other vehicles along the coastal road. Thereupon the demolitions were blown. A series of explosions blew away the face of the ravine and completely blocked the road, but the attempts upon the tunnel were not so successful. The first brought down the brick lining but did little damage to the rock and the second produced better but not very effective results. Throughout the night the heavy rumble of battle traffic could be heard in the New Zealand posts, and it seemed almost certain that with the coming of daylight a heavy attack would be delivered along the coast.

On the evening of this day General Papagos issued a directive which defined a new defensive position running from sea to sea: Mount Olympus passes—Servia—southern bank of the Venetikos river—Mount Smolikas—Greco-Albanian frontier—sea south of Santi Quaranta. It is difficult to understand the purpose of the Greek Commander-in-Chief who at this time was not credited by us with so optimistic a view of the Allied situation. At British Headquarters where, so far as was known, Greek resistance south of Kastoria was crumbling away; there were no illusions regarding the state of the Greek armies. No one believed that the Allies could stand upon the line described above. General Wilson, as we know, had already decided that a retreat to the Thermopylae position was the only course, and, as a preliminary measure, the Royal Air Force was instructed to evacuate its airfields around Larissa and to move back to the southern fringe of the Thessalian plain. It was accepted that the base at Larissa could not be cleared of heavy stores and equipment, since all available transport would be needed for the movement of the troops.

It was on this day, too, that the Joint Planning Staff in Cairo began to prepare a scheme for the evacuation of General Wilson's force from Greece, although evacuation had not yet been mentioned to General Wilson, either by the Greeks or by Middle East Command.

As though it had read the minds of the Allied Commanders the German propaganda machine seized upon the probability of a British evacuation, and on April 15th proceeded to capitalize it with some skill. Following an early morning report on the Swiss radio to the effect that the evacuation of General Wilkson's force was beginning, Dr. Goebbels's chorus got to work. The theme was developed on the lines that the British had, as usual, stirred up a small people to fight their battles for them; and now, after sending an insignificant force to Greece, they were preparing to run away, leaving the Greek troops to protect them from the righteous wrath of the German Army. The attitude towards the Greeks was one more of sorrow than of anger, and it was generally implied that if they saw fit to speed, or at any rate dissociate themselves from, the parting guest all might yet be forgiven and forgotten. But for the British retribution would be swift and sure.

3

Attack from the Air

ON this day, April 15th, communications from the front began to fail, and little news was received from the localities where our forces were in contact with the Germans. Even less was known of the situation of the Greeks on the western flank. Actually we held our own at the passes, but the day was an unfortunate one owing to the crippling losses suffered by the R.A.F.

During the bad weather which had accompanied the first week of the German offensive R.A.F. aircraft had been repeatedly in action, on several days having the skies to themselves and flying in weather in which the *Luftwaffe* did not attempt to take the air. The first day's action, when twelve Hurricanes were reported to have shot down five ME 109's out of a flight of twenty without loss to themselves, was most encouraging, and on the following days our bombers repeatedly attacked the main line of the German advance, first of all in the Strumitsa pass and later along the Prilep-Monastir road in southern Yugoslavia. But the second week opened with clear skies. On Easter Sunday, April 13th, when the Armoured Brigade fought its tank action at Proastion, a formation of six Blenheims of No. 211 Squadron, which had carried out the first raid of the war in the Middle East ten months earlier, set out with the task of holding up the German advance by a bombing attack on the road through the Monastir gap. None of them returned. As they emerged from dense cloud on the way to their target a number of ME 109's attacked them and destroyed every one. It was a tragic foretaste of what was in store.

The disaster of April 15th was of a different nature. Our advanced airfields had been distributed over the broad Thessalian plain, now . drying after the winter rains. At dawn the German aircraft swept out of the northern sky. The observer system which had been arranged in liaison with the Greeks had now broken down and out aircraft were caught on the ground. They were insufficiently camouflaged and too closely concentrated, and the A.A. defence was quite inadequate.

Every one of the 16 Blenheims at the Niamata satellite airfield was destroyed on the ground, as were 14 Hurricanes at Larissa aerodrome. It was a grievous loss. Air Vice-Marshal D'Albiac, who was at Larissa at the time, promptly ordered all R.A.F. units back to the airfields in the neighbourhood of Athens—a decision which, in any case, could not have been postponed more than a few hours in view of the imminence of the retreat of our ground forces. And, as a consequence, it was no longer practicable for the air force to provide any assistance to the army except some measure of fighter defence in the back areas. A second unfortunate result of the withdrawal would be the concentration of our remaining aircraft upon the two or three airfields available, thereby offering some tempting targets to the German attackers.

Throughout the day enemy aircraft, freed for the time being from all fear of interruption by our fighters, continued remorselessly to bomb Larissa, whence the railway workers fled. The wretched town, already wrecked by an earthquake in March, was suffering now from its unfortunate position as a nodal point of numerous roads along which the British must retreat. The more the Germans could crater the streets and block them with rubble, the greater would be the delay that they might expect to impose upon our wheeled traffic and therefore the brighter their prospect of throwing our forces into a state of chaos and destroying them before ever they made good their withdrawal to the Thermopylae position.

On our western flank the 1st Armoured Brigade had left the area of Grevena at midnight, April 14th/15th, to gain the line of the Venetikos river. This withdrawal was not molested by the German ground forces and the distance to be covered did not amount to more than six or seven miles; yet it took the column sixteen hours to reach its new position. The road was appalling. South of Grevena a narrow gorge could only take one line of traffic, and the whole route was encumbered by Greek and Yugoslav transport and marching men, dead horses, broken wagons and debris of all kinds, for the *Luftwaffe* had already been busy here, and our own vehicles had suffered equally with those of our Allies. As day broke and the long column emerged from the gorge on to high exposed ground the German dive-bombers came again. Fortunately they were attracted chiefly by the bridge over the Venetikos and had departed by the time the brigade made the winding descent to the river and crossed to the southern bank. Few casualties and little damage had been sustained, though the sorely over-worked 155th was the only anti-aircraft battery in action.

The position on the Venetikos was held by the Rangers with two companies and one in reserve, supported by the New Zealand machine-gunners, the 2nd R.H.A., and the Northumberland Hussars with their anti-tank guns. The 4th Hussars, which had been acting as rearguard, came back through the rain at nightfall to report that the Germans had not yet approached Grevena.

It was now evident that the Central Macedonian Army was incapable of organized resistance and Brigadier Charrington reported as much to G.H.Q. But his own brigade was officially described as having 'ceased to exist as an aggressive fighting formation'. Certainly, as an armoured force it could hardly be said to exist, for it was shedding broken-down tanks with every movement it made. The attached artillery was in much better case for the 102nd Anti-Tank Regiment (Northumberland Hussars) had lost only six guns, and the R.H.A. was said to be 'as good as ever.'

Savige Force was now moving into position near Kalabaka, and for the moment, at least, there appeared to be an easement of the pressure against Wilson's western flank. As will presently be seen, the chief danger was to come from the east.

In the morning was issued the formal order for withdrawal to the Thermopylae position which would be conducted by General Blamey, commanding the Anzac Corps, leaving General Wilson free to confer upon questions of policy with the Greek Commander-in-Chief and the Greek Government. The first phase was to begin that same evening—the evening of April 15th—when the 19th Australian Brigade and the 6th New Zealand Brigade, the reserve to its own New Zealand Division, were to move back to covering positions.

This Australian brigade, which comprised only two weak battalions, with the 26th New Zealand Battalion attached, was not in contact with the Germans during the day although, from its position on the high ground beyond the Aliakmon on the left of the New Zealand Division, it had seen some enemy movement. It came back at night over the improvised bridges which had been constructed in its rear, but there was no suitable bridge for the passage of the eleven guns of the 1st Australian Anti-Tank Regiment, which had fought with the brigade at Vevi. These weapons had to be destroyed on the spot.

The ultimate destination of the 19th Australian Brigade was Dhomokos, on the southern edge of the Thessalian plain, where a strong rearguard was to be assembled under the command of Brigadier J.E. Lee. This force would include the 2/4th and 2/8th Battalions (19th Australian Brigade); the newly arrived 2/6th and 2/7th Battalions belonging to Savige's 17th Australian Brigade; and the 2/1st Australian Field Regiment which had not yet been in action. It was April 17th before all these troops arrived.

The New Zealand divisional cavalry was already guarding the Elasson-Dhiskata road against enemy movement eastward from Grevena. Enemy aircraft bombed and machine-gunned the area without much effect. The 6th New Zealand Brigade went back to the Elasson area to come into position covering the two roads south of the town.

4

The Fighting at the Passes

AT the Servia Pass the 4th New Zealand Brigade was engaged with the 9th Panzer Division whose infantry had crossed the Aliakmon river during the night, presumably in readily portable assault boats. Before dawn of the 15th a party of Germans came up the road in loose formation after the manner of Greek soldiery for whom they were at first mistaken. Some got by the New Zealand advanced posts before the 19th Battalion opened fire and, with the support of its own mortars and the Australian machine-guns, settled the affair. Repeated attacks by dive-bombers followed and the German artillery pounded away, but all with no avail. At noon and again at 5.45 p.m. infantry assaults were repulsed, some of the enemy choosing to wave white flags from their positions on the rocky hill-sides rather than to withdraw under fire. Thus the New Zealanders were able to collect about two hundred prisoners, some of them wounded, and the German total losses were reckoned at four hundred. Two New Zealanders were killed and six wounded.

As close support for the infantry attacks the German bombers had failed comletely, and the German artillery had made little impression. On the other hand, the accurate and well-controlled fire of the New Zealand field guns and British medium batteries had hampered the enemy's artillery and prevented the bridging of the Aliakmon. All that the Germans gained by their efforts on this was possession of the village of Servia which, although on our side of the river, was well outside our defences.

Next on the right, among the mountains between the Servia Pass and the Olympus Pass, the 16th Australian Brigade was not engaged. It had orders to move to Zarkhon where it would cover the line of retreat of the 1st Armoured Brigade and Savige Force which were expected to move back through Kalabaka and Trikkala as the withdrawal proceeded.

At the centre, or main, pass of the Olympus mountain, the fighting started soon after dawn with artillery registration by the New Zealand gunners and then quick bursts of fire on enemy vehicles and infantry assembling in front of the 22nd New Zealand Battalion which was astride the road. German tanks then sought a covered approach to the position by turning up a track which brought them under the fire of mortars and machine-guns supporting the 28th (Maori) Battalion holding the mountain slopes further to the left. Later in the morning other vehicles were seen to leave the main road and disperse, but no serious attack developed against the 5th New Zealand Brigade. The German guns which opened at about 4.30 p.m. killed two men of the 22nd Battalion but otherwise produced little effect.

At the Platamon tunnel the 21st (Auckland) Battalion was subjected to something of an ordeal, for the Germans had been preparing throughout the night for an attack on the morning of April 15th. In the open plain which lay in front of the New Zealand position fresh enemy forces continued to assemble, and our outposts could see the flash of moving lights (the enemy could afford to ignore the possibilities of air attack) and even in some cases hear the guttural shouting of orders. The situation of the defenders was by no means satisfactory. Although they had done everything that was possible the tunnel was not seriously damaged, and the enemy appeared to be mustering in great strength for the assault against one solitary battalion. However, the New Zealanders enjoyed the advantage of excellent observation posts and of ground which would limit the number of armoured vehicles which could be deployed against them.

Daybreak brought the opening of a German artillery bombardment, to which the New Zealand guns replied. Then tanks and infantry began to move forward. It was estimated that as many as 150 tanks were seen in the course of the day, but despite this weight of armour the German attacks met with practically no success. There is little doubt that on this occasion the enemy was over-encumbered with armoured fighting vehicles, which could not be deployed on a broad front; and, when they were knocked out or broke down, they hampered the movements and limited the area of manœuvre of the columns which followed.

So the New Zealanders were able to hold all attacks, with few casualities to themselves. Only on the left did the Germans succeed in gaining some ground, infiltrating in small bodies up into the foothills of Olympus and temporarily occupying a village which was within our defences. A counter-attack expelled them before darkness set in, but the night promised to be another anxious one.

To avert disaster it was essential that our forces should make good their retreat through Larissa and cross the open plain with as little delay as possible to Lamia. This was the main route to the Thermopylae position. General Blamey, however, hoped that some of his forces would be able to by-pass Larissa by making use of two secondary roads, one on the west which led south-eastwards from Trikkala by Kharditsa to Pharsala; and one on the eastern flank, by Volos and then down the coast. Every effort was to be made to keep all routes clear of Greek troops, since congestion was likely to be bad enough in any case; and it was, of course, understood that the Thermopylae position would be held by our forces alone.

The dispositions for safeguarding the left flank were as complete as they could be; but the two brigades of the New Zealand Division holding the Olympus passes would be obliged to accept battle on the morrow and the day after. Then, on the night of April 17th/18th they must break contact with the enemy and come away with all speed. They were expected to retire through Larissa and thence by the road to Volos and so down the coast, but a reconnaissance by a New Zealand staff officer subsequently revealed that this road was not good enough for the 'shuttle service' of trucks required to get the two brigades away. So, plans had to be redrafted hurriedly. There was nothing for it but that the New Zealanders must be committed to the main Lamia road, to swell the stream of battle traffic in retreat. On this afternoon German aircraft carried out a heavy raid on Volos and did much damage.

On April 16th the only heavy fighting occurred at the Platamon tunnel where, perhaps, we had over-estimated the strength of our position and under-estimated the fighting quality of the German mountain troops. Certainly a single battalion could not be expected to hold this gap indefinitely, although it was reckoned that no more troops could be spared for the task.

The left flank of the 21st New Zealand Battalion had been heavily engaged by a strong German patrol during the night, and shortly after dawn the enemy attacked in this quarter with a battalion of infantry supported by mortar and artillery fire. After holding on for three hours the left company of the New Zealanders was forced to give ground, which resulted in the withdrawal of the centre and right companies to a reserve position south of the tunnel. Even so it became more and more difficult to prevent parts of the thin line from being over-run or cut off. All movement was harassed by artillery fire and by the attacks of tanks which were driven boldly up the steep hillsides. Soon after 10 a.m. Lieut-Colonel N.L. Macky, the battalion commander, signalled to the Corps that his position was untenable, and, in reply, was told to fall back towards the river Pinios, demolishing the road as he went.

The intention was to occupy for a time a ridge about a mile south of the tunnel, but the German pressure was too great. While the carriers kept the enemy infantry at bay with Bren gun fire the retreat was continued until the battalion was beyond the range of the German artillery. The four guns of the 27th New Zealand Field Battery came safely out of action. At length Macky's command reached the gorge where the Pinios river emerges from the mountains to flow into the sea.[1] Here a bridge had been destroyed, but a ferry was in use—a flat-bottomed barge pulled to and fro by handropes. The banks of the river were between twenty and thirty feet high, so light vehicles and guns could only be embarked and landed with great difficulty. The artillery tractors and limbers were driven over the undecked railway bridge after sleepers had been closely placed side by side across the rails. When all had crossed, extensive demolitions were carried out on road and railway. The ferry was sunk, 'but not before a large flock of sheep and goats and their two shepherdesses had been ferried across'.

Despite the enemy's efforts to smash his way through, the New

[1]See Map 4.

Zealanders had got back in comparatively good order from Platamon. Although much equipment had been abandoned the little force had brought away all its guns and had lost only one officer and thirty-five men.

During the passage of the river, Brigadier C. A. Clowes, commanding the Corps artillery, had arrived. He was sent by General Blamey to see what could be done to protect our coastal flank where a German penetration would jeopardize the whole plan of withdrawal. Already reinforcements had been bespoken. They were to come from the 16th Australian Brigade, which had begun to withdraw from the mountains between Olympus and Servia, its destination the western flank. When the leading battalion, the 2/2nd, reached Elasson it was diverted eastward to the Pinios gorge. Other units were to follow, for, whatever else happened, the western end of the gorge must be held.

In darkness and drizzling rain the 21st New Zealand Battalion moved up the gorge which is known as the Vale of Tempe. It is about five miles in length with steep banks rising on either side, the Pinios river, deep and flowing swiftly, being about thrity-five yards wide. Battalion headquarters was established at the village of Tempe. One company covered the road three miles forward in the gorge.

At the Olympus pass the men in the forward posts of the 22nd New Zealand Battalion, which was astride the main road, heard Germans calling out in English during the night. It was thought that by this means the enemy hoped to draw fire, so no action was taken; but next morning came the discovery that the shouts were a ruse to distract attention from the cutting of wire and the lifting of mines. The 22nd was attacked soon after dawn, but when our mortars, and the guns of the 5th New Zealand Field Regiment opened fire the enemy withdrew. Tanks and other vehicles were seen to be advancing, the demonstration—it was hardly more than that—covering the forward movement of mortars and infantry guns. These weapons, cleverly sited, soon became troublesome. Their fire appeared to herald the launching of another infantry attack up the rocky hillsides. Far back towards Katerini, the road was thickly crowded with battle traffic, and German tanks turned off right and left wherever the ground semed favourable for movement. There were many targets for our guns on the fronts of the 22nd and of the 28th (Maori) Battalion which held the left of the brigade position, and about a dozen German vehicles were hit. Tanks which opened upon one of our infantry posts at a range of 400 yards were driven back by the fire of our artillery and mortars.

By eleven o'clock rain shrouded the hillsides and half an hour later a luminous mist had reduced visibility to 300 yards. This by no means favoured the defence, for the enemy infantry took advantage of the obscurity to work their way forward along the whole front. About 3 p.m. the mist lifted for a while on the left, and the Maoris saw parties of Germans entering the Mavroneri ravine with the intention of moving along it round the left of the brigade line. Bren gun fire at 1,200 yards produced little effect. On the right the 23rd Battalion lost a post near a small village, but another thrust was not successful and cost the Germans twenty killed. On the extreme right in very broken country they worked round the flank almost unseen; and although a counter-attack succeeded, the New Zealanders found that their opponents were not shaken off.

Orders had been received for the brigade to withdraw to the top of the pass at night, for such a movement, while giving little away to the Germans, would greatly facilitate the main withdrawal when the time came. The Maoris began to carry back part of their impedimenta late in the afternoon. Their left company, in mist and falling rain, could see little of the scrub-covered hillsides below them, but managed to check by fire the advance of German mountain troops who had thrust forward in some strength. Covered by machine-gun and mortar fire the enemy attacked and overran one section post, but the Maori counter-attack was successful. Owing to these exchanges the withdrawal of the battalion, over a difficult route, was somewhat delayed and a number of men did not get back. The Maoris lost four killed and eighteen missing on this day but inflicted many casualties on the Germans.

The other two battalions had less difficulty in breaking contact except on the extreme right flank where the Germans were so close. Coming back over the shoulder of Mount Olympus the 23rd had to climb to 2,000 feet over narrow tracks slippery with mud and slush. Nine anti-tank 2-pdr. guns had to be tipped over the cliff; also ten of the battalion carriers and twenty trucks could not be brought away. The men of the brigade struggled on for most of the night, only discarding equipment when they could carry it no longer; but arms and ammunition were retained and the tracks and roads behind them were blown in. It had been an anxious day with artillery and tanks playing a diminishing part as the weather closed down, while the well-trained German infantry sought to exploit conditions which favoured an unseen advance. Yet the 5th New Zealand Brigade still held the pass.

CHAPTER VII

Retreat to Thermopylae

I

The First Two Days

AT the Servia pass the battalions of the 4th New Zealand Brigade made some alterations in their dispositions. An artillery duel continued throughout April 16th across the Aliakmon, but only a single German patrol made any attempt to approach the New Zealand posts. Late in the day the battery of the 64th Medium Regiment pulled out of action: owing to the rain and the mud and the difficult exits from the gun positions this business occupied nearly eight hours.

In case his New Zealanders in the Olympus positions should be pressed hard by armoured forces when their retreat began, General Freyberg gave orders for a covering detachment to occupy a position at Elevtherokhori where the main road from Olympus meets that from Servia. At this important junction were assembled in the evening three platoons of New Zealand carriers, some anti-tank guns and some machine-guns under the command of Lieut.-Colonel C.S.J. Duff of the 7th New Zealand Anti-Tank Regiment.

As for the western flank, Brigadier Savige had made his dispositions near Kalabaka where he waited for the 1st Armoured Brigade to come through. His chief trouble arose from the stream of Greek soldiery, mostly unarmed and in no sort of order, which filled the roads and caused a certain amount of disturbance in Kalabaka where some looting occurred. Yet it is said that these Greeks were, on the whole, 'a good humoured lot'

At daybreak the 1st Armoured Brigade had started off on its march from the Venetikos to Kalabaka. It proved to be a slow and difficult journey. The road, optimistically described on the ordnance map as 'motor, under construction', proved to be little more than a mud track winding through mountain country. Under any circumstances it would have proved almost impassable to a mechanized force; and the cratering caused by the previous day's bombing, in addition to the burned-out wrecks of Greek lorries and our own second-echelon transport, helped further to slow down progress. From the Venetikos to Kalabaka is only thirty miles, perhaps a good day's march for a fully motorized column. Yet by midnight, after something like eighteen hours on the road the head of the brigade had only advanced twelve miles, the rear only five miles. Progress would naturally be faster once the column got its head out of the mountains on to the straighter, clearer and better surfaced road across the plain; but the time lost in the course of the day might prove a serious matter if the New Zealand defence at the passes were to cave in against overwhelming attack.

Yet to the men engaged in the retreat it was a blissful day, for it poured with rain the whole time with very low clouds, which prevented any road 'straffing' on the part of the *Luftwaffe*. The German aircraft were, in fact, able to get into the air, but had to content themselves with bombing known targets such as Larissa.

After his original check at the Olympus passes von List seems to have decided to exploit the western route to the Thessalian plain by way of Kalabaka and Trikkala, advancing on the heels of the 1st Armoured Brigade. But this decision could not at once be put into effect. The 9th Panzer Division after its losses at Proastion was in no condition to undertake an energetic pursuit, so the 5th Panzer Division, which had taken part in the original breakthrough into Yugoslavia, was moved south to carry out the operation. This imposed a delay which destroyed all prospect of cutting off any part of the British force. It was not until April 15th that the bulk of the division began to move down the road to the south. Not until April 16th, when the British were moving towards Kalabaka, did the Germans reach Grevena more than thirty miles to the north. And south of Grevena the going appeared so bad, after British demolitions and the bombing of the *Luftwaffe* had reinforced the work of nature, that German military engineers were in some doubt as to whether the passage could be attempted at all.

Enemy accounts take considerable credit for the march that

followed. The road was no doubt in much worse condition than when our 1st Armoured Brigade passed over it a day or two earlier, and the German reports described it as the worst that the 5th Panzer Division had encountered. The engineers managed to throw up bridges of a sort, and every man who could be spared from the wheel of a vehicle aided in widening and otherwise improving the surface of the road. Tanks and tractors were used to pull the lorries over the worst spots, and the whole operation was carried out with characteristic German thoroughness and vigour. But it took the German division three nights and two days to cover something under forty miles from the Grevena district to Kalabaka. And from the point of view of its effect upon the campaign the whole effort was a useless expenditure of energy and ingenuity, for by the time that the head of the German column emerged on the western fringe of the plain of Thessaly the British force was well on its way to Thermopylae more than a hundred miles distant.

Any satisfaction that might have derived from the successful defensive fighting at Olympus and the freedom from interference by the German air and ground forces of our troops in retreat was more than counter-balanced by the dismal developments on the Greek front to the west. The Greeks and the British were now hopelessly split asunder and retreating along divergent lines. The Army of Central Macedonia, like the Army of Thrace, had ceased to exist, and all the Greek divisions north of Grevena had disintegrated and were scattering through the mountains. There remained only the Army of Epirus under General Tsolakoglou, and that was in very low water. Its ammunition was running short. Its commander had little heart left for the fight. There was only one route of supply for the troops and that was the road from the south through Yanina; and once the British withdrawal to Thermopylae was completed that too would be at the mercy of the Germans. That influential figure in Greek politics, the Bishop of Yanina, was pressing the Prime Minister to abandon the hopeless struggle.

On the morning of April 16th General Wilson had met General Papagos in conference at Lamia. The Greek Commander-in-Chief had nothing good to report, and at the end of the meeting suggested that the time had come when, in order to avoid the devastation of the country, the evacuation of the British Commonwealth forces from Greece might be considered. Naturally, General Wilson lost no time in reporting this suggestion to General Wavell in Cairo.

The rain and the mist which had preserved our troops from air attack during the withdrawal on the previous day again came to our assistance on the morning of Thursday, April 17th. Later in the day, however, the skies cleared in some localities, and the *Luftwaffe* were again in evidence, though the damage they did was small.

Not since the first clash at Vevi was there so little fighting on our front, a testimony to the fashion in which our troops had broken contact with the enemy and delayed his advance. For the retreat was now in full swing, at the moment not greatly menaced by the German ground forces except on the eastern flank where it seemed that the enemy was about to make his attempt to break out from the Vale of Tempe and advance in force down the road to Larissa.

The Vale of Tempe, a shady cleft parting the giants Olympus and Ossa, is the Arcadia of northern Greece. In a land of treeless, sun-dried hills Tempe is a veritable paradise of abundant foliage and cool flowing water. It caught the imagination of antiquity and to the classical Greeks it was the 'happy valley' of pastoral tranquillity and innocence, where the Gods themselves sported carelessly and it was always the Golden Age.

The description of Pliny, translated into the gracious Elizabethan language of Philemon Holland, will not easily be matched:

> ...the most famous river Peneus, which arising near Gomphi, runneth for five hundred stadia in a woodie dale between Ossa and Olympus, and halfe that way is navigable. In this course of his are the places called Tempe, five miles in length, and almost an acre and a half [*sic*] broad, where on both hands the hills arise by a gentle ascent above the reach of man's sight. Within-forth glideth Peneus by, in a fresh green grove, clear as crystal glasse over the gravelly stones; pleasant to behold for the grasse upon the bankes, and resounding again with the melodious concert of the birds.

Yet this pastoral scene has often witnessed the tramp of armed forces, and it was here that the Greeks under Leonidas had planned to make their first stand against the Persian hordes of Xerxes: planned but failed to execute, for the position could be turned by a force coming over the Olympus Pass, where the Germans came and the New Zealanders stood in 1941.

During the night of the 16th/17th the whole of the 16th Australian Brigade was moving down from the mountains. The 2/2nd Battalion arrived at the Vale of Tempe before dawn, but the 2/3rd, which was following, did not reach the gorge until the afternoon of the 17th. The 2/1st was too far in rear to be collected in time, although Allen, the brigade commander who was to command at Tempe, spent half the night trying to get in touch with it. He did not receive his orders until 2 a.m.

The two Australian battalions which did arrive were very tired. They had had a harassing march before they were picked up by their transport, and their route to Tempe was then by way of poor bombed Larissa where the traffic congestion was considerable and some of the roads were blocked by the rubble of wrecked buildings. Brigadier Allen arrived soon after midday by which time defence positions were already being occupied.[1] Covering the western end of the gorge the New Zealand companies were on the lower slopes of Mount Ossa, east of Tempe. One company was responsible for the road. The 2/2nd Australian Battalion protected the road and railway on the left flank against attack across the river from Gonnos, the Australian positions being on the western slopes of Mount Ossa near the village of Evangeliamos. Later, one company was placed on the high ground west of the road; and when the 2/3rd Battalion came up the position was extended still further to the west, the flank then resting south of Parapotamos. But most of the 2/3rd was kept in reserve. Seven anti-tank guns, Australian and New Zealand, and three troops of New Zealand field artillery were in support of the infantry.

In the afternoon German patrols appeared. Troops and pack animals were seen on the ridge above Gonnos, and in the evening the enemy entered the village. That they had done so was verified by an Australian patrol which crossed the river in a punt after dark: later there was a brush with some Germans at the river passage.

On the New Zealand front a German tank was seen to come along the railway in the gorge until stopped by a blocked tunnel. Towards dusk fire from this tank and from German infantry caused casualties to an Australian patrol. Poor radio reception, due to the mountainous country delayed our gunners in engaging targets, but the 26th New Zealand Battery kept the road and railway demolitions under harassing fire during the night, and expended a number of rounds on Gonnos where the enemy was showing lights. The German artillery was not yet in action.

[1] See Map 4.

As the Germans in the Vale of Tempe were in the right rear of the 5th New Zealand Brigade at the head of the Olympus Pass it was judged necessary to withdraw this brigade without further delay. The movement was carried out during the afternoon, the only interference coming from German mountain troops who pressed the 23rd Battalion rather hard and had to be held at bay by machine-gun fire while the companies dribbled back. In mist and rain the brigade was conveyed in trucks to join the general retreat through Larissa and along the Lamia road.

At the Servia pass the German artillery continued to bombard the New Zealand positions, and when the mist lifted aircraft attacked. But our guns were pulled out during daylight, and at 8 p.m. the infantry began to withdraw. Before daylight of the 18th the brigade convoys were well on their road south, a rearguard supplied by the 20th Battalion, with a detachment of New Zealand sappers, being left to complete the demolitions.

On their way back the 5th and then the 4th New Zealand Brigades passed through the New Zealand cavalry posted at Elevtherokhori; but the regiment had left some carriers in the Dhiskata region and sent some armoured cars to Allen Force. Duff Force, now no longer needed, was disbanded, while the 6th New Zealand Brigade, south of Elasson, made ready its demolitions and prepared to retreat when orders to do so should be received. This brigade had been joined during the day by detachments of the 5th New Zealand Field Regiment from the Olympus pass, and of the 7th Medium Regiment from Servia. The 26th New Zealand Battalion, which had parted company from the 19th Australian Brigade, came through and spent the night in rear of the 6th Brigade.

The retreat of the 1st Armoured Brigade had continued. Kalabaka was reached during the morning, and here some misunderstanding seems to have arisen. According to the orders of the Anzac Corps the 1st Armoured Brigade was to cover Savige's withdrawal, but Charrington had received orders from G.H.Q. to go into reserve forthwith at Ata Lanti, 170 miles away, behind the Thermopylae position. Leaving a small detachment—Rangers and anti-tank guns—to act as rearguard to Savige Force, the 1st Armoured Brigade proceeded on its way through Trikkala, where it refuelled, and towards Larissa. West of Larissa the premature destruction of a bridge over the Pinios river compelled a detour over a track slippery with mud; but despite this delay and another caused by an air-raid, the column passed into the main stream of traffic at

Larissa about nightfall. Driving on through the darkness with blazing headlights—it was our experience that the German dive-bombers never operated at night—the head of the brigade reached Pharsala by midnight: Pharsala where Caesar had overthrown Pompey and the forces of the Roman Senate in one of the greatest battles of antiquity. The 4th Hussars still had about thirty light tanks left, but the cruisers of the 3rd Rôyal Tank Regiment had been reduced to four as the result of more losses through broken tracks.

Savige Force was left nearest to the enemy on the western flank after the 1st Armoured Brigade had passed through Kalabaka. As we know, the Germans were still some distance away, and, on receipt of fresh orders, Brigadier Savige made preparations to withdraw during the night. It seemed that his chief problem would be a traffic problem.

As the British and Greek armies continued to withdraw along diverging routes with an hourly widening gap between them, no further co-operation was possible between the two Allies. The difficulties of command were manifest. General Wilson was, in theory, under the orders of the Greek Commander-in-Chief, but he had a right of appeal to Middle East Command and a certain indefinable responsibility regarding the use to which he committed the Australian and New Zealand troops in his force. It is probable too, that General Papagos exercised a rather looser control, and hesitated to express his views with quite the emphasis which he would have used in addressing a commander of his own nation. Difficult as it is to ensure the smooth working of such a command when all is going well, the task is immeasurably more difficult when that command has been hastily improvised to fight a delaying action against desperate odds on the territory of one of the participants.

It was on this day that the remnants of the Yugoslav armies surrendered at Sarajevo, depressing news for British and Greek alike. But if the Greek morale was beginning to waver, it was not among the fighting troops nor yet among the common people of city and countryside that there was any sign of weakening.

The present writer, who passed the whole of this period in Athens and its neighbourhood, had some opportunity of seeing the subtle corrosive of defeatism at work. Athens, which remains as distinguished for the mercurial effervescence of its population now as in the days of Saint Paul or Pericles, had begun to buzz with rumours early in the week. The Ministry of Press and Propaganda, while restraining all Press comment on the military situation, proved singularly unsuccessful in discouraging the stories that were being disseminated from day to day to the effect that the German forces had shattered the Olympus position, that the British were already making plans for a speedy withdrawal of all their forces, and that they had requested the Greeks to cover their evacuation with their army and fleet.

Wednesday, April 16th, and Thursday, April 17th, were among the worst days in respect of defeatist rumours. It was said that the British line had been fatally broken on the Olympus front, that the Australian Division had been cut to pieces and that the Germans were swarming over the Larissa plain. So far was this from the truth that at this time no German troops had yet broken through to the plain, the withdrawal was being conducted in good order and only one of the three Australian brigades had suffered at all severely.

Athens was badly rattled during these days. One symptom of the spirit now abroad was the tearing down of anti-German posters. On the first day of the German attack a number of these had appeared, the most effective being one which depicted Hitler as a butcher leading to slaughter a number of fat pigs—Poland, Denmark, Norway, Holland, Belgium, France, Rumania and Bulgaria, and calling out for more blood. Between nightfall on April 17th and dawn on April 18th every one of these had disappeared from walls and hoardings. It was never discovered who was responsible for this significant gesture.

The tension in the capital was much heightened during these last days by the appearance of slow-marching armed police who patrolled, in groups of half a dozen as a rule, up and down the Athens streets. This certainly did nothing to calm the general anxiety. Their somewhat sinister presence suggested that the Government feared an impending Germanophile *coup d'état.* There were actually rumours of some such stroke on the Thursday and the names of the leading members of the Government that was to seize power were bandied about.

In truth, there was now an urge, both in the Government and in the Army Command to prepare for the inevitable, acting without sanction of King or Premier, the former a loyal friend of Britain, the latter a sick and disheartened man.

Papademas, Minister of War, was responsible on April 17th for the issue of an order declaring further resistance impossible and giving a free hand to the Generals to behave as they saw fit. The same day an Army Order was published, releasing for a period of two months' leave all those classes which were just about to be called up for military service. This latter order was the first to become known, and nothing did more to convince the nation that the Government considered that the game was up. Still more reprehensible was the conduct of Oeconomou, Minister of Communications, who took it upon himself to issue instructions that, to prevent unnecessary loss of life, the remaining Greek aircraft should be grounded and the petrol dumps at Tatoi and Elevsis destroyed. The British Military Mission fortunately received early news of this intention and was quick to inform the King, who promptly secured the revocation of the order, and British ground staff at the aerodromes succeeded in preventing the intended sabotage; but Oeconomou's proposal is an indication of the lengths to which some defeatists were prepared to go in order to bring the struggle in Greece to an abrupt end. The surrender of Bakopoulos in eastern Macedonia at a time when his troops were still fighting bravely in the frontier forts may be regarded either as premature, or as displaying a realistic view of the fate of Greece. There were known to be other commanders who felt that a sufficient gesture had been made in the face of the overwhelming strength of the invaders, and that the Army should accept the situation and make the best terms it could.

2

The Rearguard Actions: Tempe—Elasson

FRIDAY, April 18th, a fine sparkling spring day, saw another crisis pass. Our forces, though under constant air attack, were on their way back across the plain of Thessaly, and were beginning to arrive upon the Thermopylae position, their hazardous withdrawal through the bottle-neck of Larissa being made possible by the stout resistance and self-sacrifice of the rearguards.

At the Vale of Tempe the Australians and New Zealanders comprising Allen Force had orders to hold the German armour at the exits from the gorge until nightfall. The German guns opened as soon as it was light enough to see, shelling the positions of the 21st New Zealand Battalion at the end of the defile and on the hillsides to the east. German mortars opened from the other side of the river and were engaged by the 26th New Zealand Field Battery.

About 7 a.m. German infantry moved down to the river from Gonnos, and about a battalion was seen on the tracks leading west from Gonnos towards the Elasson-Tirnavos road. An enemy advance near Parapotamos came under our artillery fire but the left of the 2/2nd Australian Battalion was threatened, and Australian carriers protecting this flank suffered loss from the German mortars.

Before noon the 21st New Zealand Battalion became heavily engaged, the enemy clearing away the road block in front of the forward company. Tanks came through and knocked out an anti-tank gun; then supported by infantry they sprayed the forward slopes of the Ossa *massif* with their fire. Other anti-tank guns claimed two or three tanks before they were over-run as the New Zealand infantry began to lose ground. The battalion began its retirement platoon by platoon in a direction which was mainly eastward, past the village of Ambelakia, the movement being covered by the fire of the field guns which kept the tanks in check for a time. Unfortunately, the New Zealanders found it impossible to reform or reorganize among the maze of gullies on the upper slopes of Ossa, and they were now out of touch with the Australian battalions in the centre and on the left. Comparatively few had succeeded in joining the Australians.

About 3 p.m. the Germans made a fresh effort, after Allen's head-quarters on the railway had been bombed by about thirty-five aircraft. While tanks advanced down the Larissa road from Tempe, infantry, covered by machine-gun fire, waded the Pinios and crossed it on rafts. Australian mortars and Bren guns checked this movement and killed a fair number of Germans, but the tanks, now followed by infantry, pressed on. Meanwhile the enemy were round the left flank of the 2/2nd Australian Battalion and digging in south of the village of Parapotamos. Covered by the fire from a number of carriers, the left company of the 2/2nd with a company of the 2/3rd in position on its left rear, were able to get back to the village of Makrikhori whence a further withdrawal was made in trucks.

These two companies joined brigade headquarters, another company of the 2/3rd Battalion, some carriers, and some armoured cars of the New Zealand cavalry, at a defile some six miles S.S.W. of Tempe where road and railway crossed.

German tanks and infantry were now fanning out in the valley near Evangeliamos, and the remnants of the 2/2nd Battalion were forced back into the hills to the east. The carriers and armoured cars

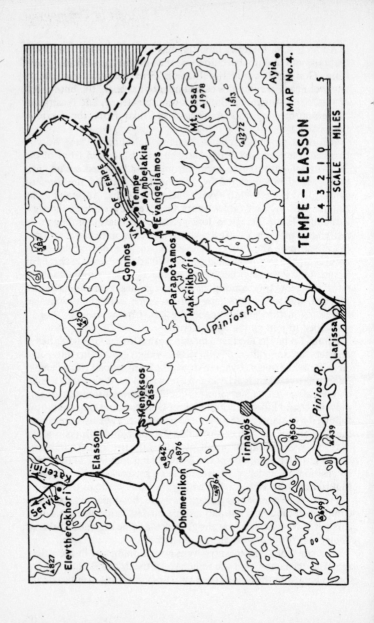

TEMPE — ELASSON

MAP No.4.

SCALE — MILES

5 4 3 2 1 0   5

Ayia

Mt. Ossa ▲1978

▲1513

▲1272

Ambelakia

Tempe

Evangeljamos

VALE OF TEMPE

Gonnos

Parapotamos

Makrikhori

Pinios R.

▲1420

Meneksos Pass

Larissa

Pinios R.

Elasson

Katerini

Servia

Elevtherokhori

▲1827

Dhomenikon

▲842 ▲876

▲664

Tirnavos

▲506

▲439

▲699

and the New Zealand field guns engaged the enemy armour till nightfall, covering the withdrawal of the infantry who were near brigade headquarters and enabling them to gain their trucks. The German advance along the road stopped when darkness fell, though hostile infantry were still in motion in the hills. Away to the east small parties of New Zealanders and Australians were making painful progress across the mountain ridges of Ossa towards the bomb-wrecked port of Volos.

Allen Force—it was only a 'brigade group'—had done its duty. The German advance, made by the 2nd Panzer Division and the 6th Mountain Division, from the Vale of Tempe down the road to Larissa had been held. Now all that remained of Allen Force, in carriers, trucks and armoured cars, drove back cautiously through the darkness with no lights showing towards Larissa. Less than three miles north of the town the leading trucks came under fire from the railway-crossing: a detachment of German Alpine troops had moved wide round the western flank of Allen Force during the afternoon and now blocked the road at this point. It seemed to our men, watching the tracer bullets and flares, that Larissa must be in enemy hands, so most of the column turned back. Then in the darkness groups of vehicles made off eastwards over farm tracks and sodden fields in an endeavour to reach the port of Volos.

They arrived at Aiya which was found to be a dead end, a mountainside village from which only goat-tracks led southwards. Some of the troops returned in the direction of Larissa, others took to the hills and made their way as best they could towards the coast. Helped by Greek peasants and fisher folk, some reached the sea-shore, acquired caiques and fishing smacks, and, sailing down the coast, rejoined their units further south. Others crossed into the island of Euboea and thence back to the mainland. Others, again, after lying hid for days in the hills eventually arrived in Crete long after the evacuation of Greece had been completed. But Allen Force which had fought so finely at Tempe against heavy odds of numbers and firepower had ceased to exist.

The scene now shifts westward to Elevtherokhori, on the main road twenty-five miles north of Larissa where the road from Katerini through the Olympus Pass comes in. This junction was protected by two squadrons of New Zealand cavalry and two troops of New Zealand anti-tank guns.

Out in front, coming back from Servia, was Lieut.-Colonel H.K. Kippenberger and a few Bren carriers of the 20th New Zealand

Battalion. As we have seen, this unit had been acting as rearguard of the 4th New Zealand Brigade, but Colonel Kippenberger had been thinning out his force as he retired until only this small detachment remained with him. As he moved towards Elevtherokhori he stopped at each road demolition while the charge was blown, so that he could bring along the sapper parties.

In the early morning the New Zealand cavalry were surprised to hear sounds of traffic on the road coming down from the Olympus Pass: it had been thought that our demolitions would have delayed an enemy advance by this route for some considerable time. Soon the Elevtherokhori rearguard was engaged with German tanks, two of which were hit, and motor-cyclists who also suffered loss. But one of our anti-tank guns became bogged and had to be abandoned as the rearguard, in the face of superior forces, drew back south of the road junction behind the bridge which was now blown up.

Kippenberger's party stumbled into this engagement and, being fired on by tanks at close range, could not get through. Sappers and infantry took to the hills whence the colonel led out later one small party on foot. Meanwhile the rearguard took toll of tanks, infantry, armoured cars and lorries before German mortars, opening at short range, settled the issue. The rearguard came back through Elasson which was being bombed from the air and then through Barraclough's 6th New Zealand Brigade in position to the south.

The brigade covered the two roads which led, respectively, southeast and almost due south from Elasson and united at Tirnavos. On the former road, which led over the Meneksos Pass, was the 24th New Zealand Battalion; on the latter, traversing easier country, the 25th Battalion was in position, well supported by the 2/3rd Australian Field Regiment and a troop of the 64th Medium Regiment, with two troops of New Zealand field guns further in rear. The 26th Battalion and a number of New Zealand anti-tank guns were in reserve at Dhomenikon, and an additional New Zealand field battery was also available if needed. We had no tanks. When battle was joined in this pleasant valley, Australian, New Zealand and British guns opposed German armour.

At first our shell-fire hit several of the tanks and kept them in check, while the German counter-battery work was of little avail. So the enemy attack was delayed until later in the day, although our medium artillery ran out of ammunition early in the afternoon. Brigadier Barraclough took the opportunity to thin out his artillery and infantry, the 26th New Zealand Battalion being taken back in trucks to Larissa to entrain for the south. Then, just before dusk, the Germans put down a heavy bombardment under cover of which they attacked the 24th New Zealand Battalion at the Meneksos Pass. Here the leading tanks hit land-mines, and the Australian guns shelled the remainder of the assault column; but as the German armour pulled back the infantry pressed on over the demolitions which no vehicle could pass. Yet they failed to close and only delayed for a little the withdrawal of the battalion when it sought to break off the action and obey the orders to go.

On the other road, where the batteries pulled out troop by troop as the New Zealand infantry retired, the rear parties held on until 11.30 p.m. and then drove hurriedly away, blowing culverts as they came, to reach Larissa about 3 a.m. on the morning of April 19th. From Larissa the 6th New Zealand Brigade—with the exception of the 26th Battalion which had already departed—was directed towards Volos with order to take up a covering positon in that vicinity. The Volos road, after being condemned as unusable, was now considered fit for traffic, thanks to the exertions of the sappers and to the effect of the hot April sun.

Savige had begun his retreat from Kalabaka, according to orders received, during the night of April 17th/18th, protected by a small rearguard of infantry, tanks, artillery and machine-guns. He was not worried by the enemy and the last of his vehicles had passed through Larissa early in the morning. His engineers had blown a large number of the bridges which carry the road across the streams of the Thessalian plain.

The 1st Armoured Brigade continued on its way to Ata Lanti, where it would be in reserve behind the Thermopylae position, and its units began to reach their destination before nightfall. The air attacks made upon them while passing through Larissa and crossing the plain had done little damage; but at the northern end of the Lamia pass Lieut.-Colonel R. L. Syer, commanding the 64th Medium Regiment R.A. which was under orders for Molos, received a wound from a bomb splinter and died a little later.

Puttick's 4th New Zealand Brigade began to reach its destination, Molos, by noon. Instead of continuing southwards to Lamia, Hargest's 5th Brigade turned east to reach Volos by way of Almiros, its operation order having, by mistake, substituted Volos for Molos. In consequence the brigade did not reach its destination before dark.

3

Air Attacks Continue

DURING the daylight hours, the column of motor transport which crowded the road from Larissa to Lamia and beyond underwent a trying ordeal for, with improved weather conditions, the *Luftwaffe* was out in force. Our vehicles could never move faster than the modest rate of ten to fifteen miles an hour on account of the congestion; and in the absence of any anti-aircraft batteries the German bombers had it all their own way. They would circle overhead, select a target, and then dive. Sirens screaming, they swooped down amid a rattle of ineffectual small-arms fire from the ground. A crash or thud as bomb after bomb burst about the road was followed by the roar of the approaching fighters who swept along the column to machine-gun their all-too-visible targets. Yet the procession crept on by fits and starts: damaged vehicles were pushed aside, blazing wrecks avoided, detours made where the road had been destroyed. Even when no bombs had fallen the surface, broken by the effect of winter rains followed by the unaccustomed traffic which it had been called upon to carry, was now turning to mud in this flat and marshy plain. All day long the Anzac engineers toiled at the tasks of reinforcement and repair, using any materials which came to hand.

It was fortunate that no direct hits were made upon any of the important bridges during the course of this phase of the retreat, but an ammunition truck was hit quite early in the day just as it was approaching a little north of Pharsala. This consequent explosion badly damaged the embankment north of the bridge and the engineers went to work to make a diversion, but the ground was so soft and yielding, after the recent rain, that the job took four hours to complete. And during all this time, while the close-packed vehicles waited, by great good fortune the German bombing was both inaccurate and unintelligent. The pilots might have concentrated on hitting the leading vehicles and thereby still further extending the road-block and the consequent delay. It would have been worth much more to the enemy than the aircraft which might have been lost in the process.

As it happened, the column was able to start again by 1.30 p.m. and push on towards Thermopylae with only insignificant loss and damage. Indeed, as the hours passed, it became evident that, in spite of the nerve-racking noise and the smoke and the fumes, and the spatter of machine-gun bullets, the German airmen were doing comparatively little harm either to troops or vehicles. If among Australians, New Zealanders and British there was little sign of loss of morale they owed something to the splendid example set by their divisional commanders and other senior officers who were determined to regard the German air attacks as nothing but a nuisance. Yet British fighters in the sky would have been a heartening sight. Twice during the day General Blamey, commanding the Anzac Corps, made urgent requests for fighter protection, but only two sorties, each of one hour, for fifteen miles on either side of Lamia was all that could be given him, for this and the following day.

And now let us spare a thought to Larissa, the ruined unhappy town through which guns and trucks and fighting vehicles were passing in long procession throughout the day and night. Confusion there was bound to be in the debris-strewn streets; but though halts were frequent and traffic tangles had to be sorted out the flow never stopped for long. Rumours of many kinds were rife. Some parties of troops turned aside to seek fresh routes towards the south, believing that the Germans were in possession of the town. This was not so: neither was it true, though the story has persisted, that enterprising Germans wearing Australian uniforms had slipped into Larissa and were directing—or rather mis-directing—our columns as they converged upon the place from the north. Although the ambush on the Tempe road prevented the remnants of Allen Force from going through, all other routes remained open, and belated New Zealanders testify that a British military policeman was seen calmly directing the traffic at about 4 a.m. on April 19th. It was after that hour that the bridge over the Pinios was blown, and there is no doubt that our traffic police, Australian and British, remained in full control until this demolition was carried out. We know now that, according to their own reports, the Germans—tanks and infantry from the Tempe gorge—did not enter Larissa until 7 a.m.

4

Political Crisis

ON this day, April 18th, General Papagos, the Greek Commander-in-Chief, delivered an exceedingly depressing report on the military situation to the King and the Cabinet. It is unlikely that this came as any particular surprise to those who enjoyed any degree of inside information: despite the guarded nature of the Greek official communiqués it was already becoming clear that the army in Albania had delayed its withdrawal too long. In fact, von List was already preparing its *coup de grâce*. Just as he had thrust a wedge between Greeks and Yugoslavs during the first days of the campaign and had then proceeded to isolate and destroy the latter, so, now that the British and Greek forces had been widely separated, he could prepare for the final advance on Yanina and the cutting of the last line of retreat of the Greek Army.

The Cabinet meeting was followed later in the day by the death of M. Koryzis, the Greek Premier. Himself wholly loyal to the alliance but harassed by the defeatists in his own Cabinet, unable to determine in his own mind whether the moment had come for the evacuation of the seat of Government to Crete, and appalled by the magnitude and imminence of the disaster which loomed over his country, he took his own life.

The King himself now became Premier, and a few days later in a broadcast to the nation announced his intention of fighting to the finish. A succession of Vice-Premiers followed one another until, at the time of the removal of the Government to Crete, the post was taken over by M. Tsuderos, a moderate Venizelist and a former Governor of the Bank of Greece; and an admirable 'compromise' Minister, with the additional advantage of being himself a Cretan.

By this time the question of the evacuation of our forces from Greece was due and over-due for settlement. When, in March, the troops had been packed into warships and despatched with all speed from Egypt to the port of Piraeus, it had been present in the minds of many senior naval officers that the need might arise to bring the soldiers back again. On April 15th Wavell had conferred with Longmore and Cunningham, his air and naval colleagues, and the three Commanders-in-Chief had come to the conclusion that preparations for evacuation must be made. Consequently a section of the Joint Planning Staff under Rear-Admiral H.T. Baillie-Grohman was sent from Cairo to examine the problem of withdrawal and to formulate preliminary plans. This party had arrived on April 17th.

The news from Greece brought Wavell to Athens on April 19th, and his first act was to discuss evacuation with Wilson. To go or not to go! Primarily the Commander-in-Chief had to consider his position in North Africa in the light of reverses suffered and his present means of defence. Certainly no more troops would be available for the Greek adventure. It was true that, so long as we maintained a footing in Europe we might delay the execution of whatever plans the enemy had made for a summer campaign. Further reinforcement of German troops in Libya might be regarded as unlikely while we remained in Greece.

Again, there could be no question but that yet another evacuation might gravely affect our prestige and also the morale of our troops. We might have to leave many behind; many ships might be lost in the process of evacuation; quite certainly there would be a grave loss of heavy equipment. We were still so overmatched in respect of war material that a further sacrifice could not be lightly regarded.

But to attempt to hold on—not on the planned line of defence but upon a new and improvised line—would necessarily involve further reinforcement. More troops implied more shipping both for maintaining our force in action and for feeding the civil population, the latter being now wholly cut off from all European sources of supply. Since the shattering early raids on Piraeus our only major port was partially out of commission, and there was scarcely even a secondary port available since we were now in the process of evacuating Volos. Above all, we could not maintain ourselves without a great strengthening of our air forces. In the clear Mediterranean spring weather the convoys would require adequate air protection to avoid heavy losses from dive-bombers, and the fighting power of the troops would be worn down by the *Luftwaffe* unless we could meet the Germans in the air. We had not the aircraft to carry out these tasks neither did we possess the airfields and air bases.

So it seemed that we could not contemplate an indefinite defence of a bridge-head—it would not be more than that—in Greece because it would not be possible to supply our forces, seeing that we had not got the means to maintain the struggle in the air.

It will be remarked that these considerations took no account of the Greek Army as a fighting force: there was, indeed, no hope that the Greeks would continue to resist for more than a day or two longer. As already related, the suggestion that we should leave Greece had first been expressed by the Greek Commander-in-Chief.

The British commanders were well aware that political purpose had yet to be reconciled with good military counsel when, on the same day, they attended a conference called by the King of the

107

Hellenes at his palace at Tatoi, outside Athens. Wavell assured King and Cabinet that our army would fight so long as the Greek Army continued to resist; yet, if the Greek Government so desired, we were prepared to go. He pressed for an early decision. Papagos painted a gloomy picture of the condition of his armies, and feared that continued resistance might result in the total devastation of his country. After renewed British assurances that both our ground and air forces would make every sacrifice to fight on if required to do so, Greek military opinion expressed itself in favour of British evacuation. It remained for the British Minister, Sir Michael Palairet, to read a telegram from our own Prime Minister which clearly stated that we would only leave Greece with the full agreement of King and Government. King and Government then gave their unqualified approval of the evacuation of the British forces.

We were faced with an unwelcome and very difficult task. Baillie-Grohman's first report was not encouraging, and the Commander-in-Chief was left with the impression—happily much too pessimistic a one as events were to prove—that we should be lucky if we embarked as many as 30 per cent of the troops. There was little hope of getting away any of the guns and transport that had been so hardly spared from Africa. Piraeus, being much damaged already and under constant air attack, could not be used; and as no other port was available the embarkation would have to be from open beaches and on as wide a front as possible. Any troops who found it impossible, for one reason or another, to reach the embarkation points would be expected to make for the Peloponnesus, whence they might be rescued later.

Wavell still hoped that, unless unforeseen events compelled a more hurried departure, it would be possible to hold on at Thermopylae for a little time; and every day that our troops maintained their positions in Greece meant a day gained for organizing the defences of Crete and Egypt. April 28th was selected as a provisional date for the embarkation to begin. There would be a new moon on the 26th.

At Thermopylae

WHILE General Wilson and Admiral Baillie-Grohman continued at work on evacuation plans, General Wavell left Athens at night for Levadia where, at Anzac Corps headquarters he saw General Blamey on the early morning of April 20th. The Corps commander was not unsatisfied at the progress of the retreat. On April 19th the bulk of our forces had won clear of the plain of Thessaly, and were beginning to take up their positions on the Thermopylae line. The scenes of the previous day had been re-enacted, for the *Luftwaffe* was as active as ever, bombing roads, railways, and suspected areas of troop concentration in rear of Thermopylae. Despite their ordeal by air-attack, their lack of sleep, and the feeling of frustration which was induced by their continuous retreat, the morale of the fighting troops was still high.

Long columns of German troops were reported on the 19th to be converging upon Larissa from the Olympus Pass and from Servia; but by nightfall the enemy was still not in contact with Lee Force at Dhomokos. All stragglers and belated parties of our troops appeared to have passed through Lee's position which had been under heavy but ineffective air attack at times, so Lee was ordered to blow his demolitions and withdraw. This he did, two New Zealand anti-tank guns being cut off in the process by a premature explosion. Two companies of Australian infantry, with detachments of machine-guns and anti-tank guns, and five cruiser tanks, were left to hold the pass ten miles south of Dhomokos.

Having fulfilled its purpose the 6th New Zealand Brigade had come in from the Almiros—Volos area, via Lamia where it half-expected to clash with the advancing Germans. Before withdrawing the New Zealanders had gathered in a number of parties who had fought at Tempe. The Navy had been asked to provide patrols so that others who might appear on the coast could be brought away by sea.

On April 9th a German force of about a hundred Stukas, with fighter protection, made a concentrated attack upon our airfields in the Athens area. All the remaining serviceable British fighters, fifteen Hurricanes, took off to intercept them. For the last time over Greece the R.A.F. David was able to challenge the German Goliath.

In terms of heroism in the face of odds, the pilots of those fifteen fighters deserve to rank with the heroes of the Battle of Britain. They destroyed twenty-two enemy aircraft, perhaps eight more, but in the action they lost a third of their number. And that indeed constituted a Pyrrhic victory.

During April 20th great progress was made in sorting out the troops and placing them under their proper commands. By the evening the retreat could be regarded as ended, although there was still much to do to remedy the confusion which had been caused by the traffic congestion on the roads. Battle casualties, except in the few battalions which had borne the brunt at Vevi and at Tempe gorge were not heavy, but several convoys had lost direction during the retreat, and many groups of men seeking to make their way back on foot across the hills had failed to rejoin their units. An official summary of the situation, dated April 20th, states that 'a measure of control had been lost'; but after a short breathing space the combatant units could be expected to give a good account of themselves whenever the Germans should again attack. The loss of guns, fighting vehicles, transport, and other arms and equipment was, however, a serious matter.

The only fighting on this day occurred at the pass on the Dhomokos-Lamia road where Lee's rearguard under an Australian major was posted. At 11.0 a.m. German vehicles were seen coming down the slopes from Dhomokos, but the first clash did not occur until after two o'clock in the afternoon when some German motor-cyclists rode into our well-concealed positions and were killed. A little later the fire of one of our cruisers destroyed a German armoured car, but under cover of a rainstorm enemy mortars came into action. Their fire was silenced for a time by the Australian machine-guns; then at 4.30 p.m. Lee informed the rearguard commander that he could withdraw when he liked, all Australian and New Zealand convoys being clear of Lamia. The withdrawal was carried out in some confusion under heavy fire from artillery and mortars, but the anti-tank guns were got away, two cruiser tanks helping to cover the whole movement.

Some of the Australian infantry who were cut off made their own way back to Thermopylae during the night.

Both Force Headquarters at Thebes and Corps headquarters at Levadia were persistently bombed from the air, and the telephone system was destroyed. Our shortage of radio equipment was an additional handicap to commanders and staff officers striving to reassemble battalions, batteries and brigades, to guide troops to new and unfamiliar positions, and to deal with problems of supply.

The name of Thermopylae conjures up visions of a narrow mountain pass held by a tiny band of heroes against a horde of invaders. Every schoolboy (at any rate every schoolboy of a generation or two ago) has heard of the dramatic resistance of Leonidas and his three hundred Spartans—the seven hundred Thespians who also died there are for some reason nearly always ignored in history and anecdote—against the tens of thousands of Persians under Xerxes, the prototype of all Oriental tyrants. It seemed fitting that what might be the final stand in Europe against the new tyrant of the West should be made at this historic pass.

But however alluring the prospect of history repeating itself may have seemed to those enjoying a sense of historical fitness, together with a comfortable physical remoteness, the value of Thermopylae as a defensive position at the present day is considerably decreased by the fact that the sea has receded in the course of centuries. Instead of the narrow road only wide enough for a single chariot to pass at a time, there is now a plain some three miles broad between mountain face and the water.[1] Nor is it the only, or even the best, route by which an army nowadays can approach Athens from the north. The main motor road from Larissa and Lamia runs to the south through the high pass of Brallos and thence by way of Thebes to the Greek capital. And any German force which might come down on the Gulf of Corinth from Epirus would have the road through Delphi at its disposal.

Thermopylae itself, and the marshy ground south of the Sperkhios river, was to be covered by the New Zealand Division, its 5th Brigade taking up the whole front from the sea near Molos to the mountain face. Coastal patrols, to watch for a possible enemy landing from Euboea, were furnished by the 4th Brigade, a reconnaissance of the island being carried out and a number of craft on the beaches destroyed. In reserve was the 6th Brigade which had fought the rearguard action at Elasson on April 18th.

On the evening of the 20th a report, which proved to be false, that German armour was moving south from Lamia caused the demolition of the bridge which carried the Lamia-Molos road over the Sperkhios river.

[1] See Map 5.

Brallos Pass was the responsibility of the Australians, their 19th Brigade, which had been with Lee, arriving from Dhomokos to occupy positions astride the road. On the left the 17th Brigade—Savige's battalions being now re-united—was drawn back to cover the appoach along the railway. The 16th Brigade was in divisional reserve: it only disposed of two battalions, both very weak in numbers after the action at Tempe, the 2/1st Battalion being now with the 19th Brigade. This was the first occasion during the campaign when General Mackay had all three brigades of his division under his own command.

The 1st Armoured Brigade had almost ceased to exist as such. When the 3rd Royal Tank Regiment eventually collected itself south of Thermopylae only one of its 52 cruiser tanks was in running order. Few of the others had been lost in battle; mechanical and steering troubles and damage to tracks had accounted for most of them. One is reminded of the solitary elephant that survived Hannibal's crossing of the Alps and Apennines. The tanks sent out from England in the winter of 1940-1 were as unfit to negotiate the Greek countryside as were Hannibal's unfortunate quadrupeds to cope with the rigours of an Alpine winter. So the 3rd Royal Tank Regiment was ordered to the Athens area to give protection against possible parachutist attack.

The light tanks of the 4th Hussars had stood up to the earlier ordeals better than had the cruiser tanks; but during the retreat from Grevena they, too, began to suffer severely from mechanical breakdowns. They were reduced to 30 runners by the time they reached Pharsala, and 17 more failed at the pass of Lamia. With its remaining 13 tanks the regiment was regrouped around Thebes, available for reconnaissance purposes or, in an emergency, to counter-attack against an infantry penetration.

The infantry battalion, the Rangers, had suffered considerable loss in action and during the long retreat from Vevi, and a great deal of equipment had been left behind. What remained of the unit was posted near Force Headquarters at Thebes in an anti-parachutist rôle.

The advantages of the Thermopylae position were obvious enough. As reconnaissance proceeded, however, a number of serious handicaps began to be apparent to the harassed commanders of the force while their men rested, and bathed in the warm sulphur springs at Thermopylae as the Spartans of Leonidas had bathed twenty-five centuries ago.

The two weakened divisions were manifestly insufficient to defend the whole thirty miles of front. For an effective defence it was estimated that a full division would be required at each of the two major approaches, Thermopylae and Brallos, apart from the forces needed to cover the hill-tracks which trained mountain troops might well be able to negotiate.

The right flank in the plain of the Sperkhios could be enfiladed across the Gulf of Maliaic.

There was the practical certainty that the Germans would rapidly establish themselves in the island of Euboea which lay parallel to the Greek coast for many miles to the rear of our position. A proportion of our force must therefore be permanently employed patrolling the coast all the way back to Khalkis and beyond; and at the latter town, where the strait was little more than fifty yards wide, special precautions must be taken to prevent a crossing. A detachment of the Rangers was therefore sent to Khalkis.

The plain of Thebes, now our Headquarters area, provided the enemy with excellent conditions for airbone landings with which we were singularly ill-equipped to deal. Very few troops could be spared, and those who were available were rendered almost static by our losses in tanks and transport during the withdrawal. At best we could only hope to organize a few platoons of Bren carriers as mobile detachments in this wide area.

Troops had yet to be found to defend the road through Delphi by which an enemy advance from Epirus would turn the whole position. Such an advance might be expected to follow quickly upon the collapse of Greek resistance.

6

Greek Surrender

EVEN now the final scene of the tragedy of the Greek Army of Epirus was being enacted. The word tragedy is not lightly employed in this connection. Contemplating the sudden and total dissolution of this brave and long-enduring force, never defeated in six months of constant battle, one experiences a genuine Aristotelian *katharsis,* an awe-inspiring sense of the futility of all human effort and all human courage when pitted against the will of the Gods. That is of of the very essence of the tragedy of classical Greece and of the tragedy of contemporary Greece during these April days.

It was on April 19th that von List put into operation the movement designed to inflict the *coup de grâce* upon the Greek forces in southern Albania, the last intact army possessed by our Ally. It was then slowly falling back in fairly good order towards the Greek frontier, the Italians still following up with extreme caution and making little attempt to interfere. But the collapse of the Central Macedonian Army and the British retreat to Thermopylae had uncovered a route across the Pindus mountains by which the Germans might take the Greeks in flank and rear.

Von List wanted to clear the way to Yanina and thence to the Gulf of Corinth for subsquent operations, if necessary, in the Peloponnesus; and he presumably still doubted the capacity of the Italian troops to cope with the Greeks unaided. At all events, he committed the SS Adolf Hitler Division, which had already been engaged by our forces at Vevi and Sotir, to hasten a consummation which would otherwise have been brought about by the *Luftwaffe*, by the Greek lack of transport, by the Greek roads and —perhaps—by the Italians.

The task assigned to the SS Adolf Hitler Division on the morning of Saturday, April 19th, was to push through to Yanina in order to cut the last supply line of the Greek forces in Albania and precipitate their capitulation. To reach Yanina the division had to cross the pass at Metsovo. General Papagos had rushed a force there as fast as marching men could go, in a last forlorn effort to stave off the inevitable. The Greek troops reached Metsovo, but not in time to dig themselves in before the enemy arrived. The pass could not be held in the face of a German motorized division and though the Greeks fought with the utmost courage, the high ridge of the Pindus was crossed by the enemy who occupied Yanina on the following morning.

How complete had become the lack of contact between the British Headquarters in Athens and the Greek forces may be shown from the following anecdote:

> Our General in command of the mission at Athens had decided to go direct to Yanina to see exactly what the situation was. He had taken the precaution of having a message sent to the Greek staff there, and the reply had come in German—'Hier is das deutsche Heer'—or words to that effect. There is nothing like asking the enemy precisely where he is.[1]

[1] Casson, *Greece Against the Axis.*

With von Stumme's advanced guard in possession of Yanina and von Boehme's troops all over the plain of Thessaly the end of this disastrous week meant the end of Greek resistance. On the following day, April 21st, General Tsolakoglou, commander of the Greek Army of Epirus, offered his surrender to the Germans. The General acted without authorization from his Commander-in-Chief, General Papagos, but in accordance with the instructions issued by M. Papademas, Minister of War, three days earlier, giving Generals a free hand to behave as they saw fit.

Looking at the situation purely from a military point of view it is difficult to see what purpose could have been served by further resistance. With Yanina taken by the German forces who had come down on his rear, Tsolakoglou had no hope of getting his army away, even had he possessed the transport to attempt a quick break-through to the south. It should be noted that the surrender of Tsolakoglou did not affect the strategic position of his Ally. General Wilson's force was already completely out of contact with all the main Greek formations when the surrender occurred and had made good its retreat to the Thermopylae line, so its position was in no way immediately worsened by the surrender in Epirus. Had the British aimed at fighting a rearguard action all the way down to the southernmost point of the Peloponnesus irrespective of losses, then the enemy forces released by Tsolakoglou's surrender might have been employed with great effect. But the British decision to evacuate Greece had already been taken, and the chosen points of embarkation were comparatively close at hand.

Tsolakoglou had made his original offer of surrender to the Germans on April 21st, but it was not until 2.45 in the afternoon of the 23rd that the surrender was formally concluded at Salonika. General Jodl who, four years later, was to put his signature to a considerably more momentous document in a school-house at Reims, signed for the German Army, General Ferraro for the Italian. The original terms proposed by the Germans had been almost suspiciously generous. The Greek victory in Albania was recognized; their armies were required only to withdraw as far as the Greek frontier in places where they had not already done so; the Germans were prepared to undertake to prevent any attempt by the Italians to cross the frontier; Greek officers were to be allowed to retain their equipment, while the soldiers, after surrendering their arms, would be free to return home.

No doubt, the Germans could, had they chose, have exacted much harsher terms from the unfortunate Tsolakoglou, but there was no particular need to do so. The agreement to capitulate once being extracted, the Germans were quick to repudiate it, on the grounds that the King's 'fight to the end' broadcast made on April 22nd nullified the terms on which the armistice had been arranged. This excuse served as well as any other. As finally signed, the capitulation provided that all Greek equipment should be handed over to the Germans and all Greek soldiers become prisoners of war, though the latter condition was never, in fact, brought into force. And the Italians, of course, were enabled to advance into the country as conquerors.

CHAPTER VIII

Evacuation

I

Plans and Difficulties

IT is true that there were fewer troops to be withdrawn and that we still controlled a wide extent of coastline and were not bottled up around a single port; but the conditions of evacuation from Greece were, in some respects, more formidable than they had been at Dunkirk. The distance to be traversed to Egypt (600 miles) and even to the intermediate stopping point of Crete (160 miles) was very much greater than the width of the Channel. The Saronic Gulf, which is the natural route of evacuation from the Athens area, had been heavily mined by enemy aircraft. The much-bombed port of Piraeus could only accommodate a limited proportion of its customary tonnage, owing to the damage done, more particularly in the first disastrous German raid.[1] The Germans might, at any time, seize the isthmus of Corinth with paratroops, which would effectively prevent any evacuation from the ports of the Peloponnesus. R.A.F. fighter defence was almost non-existent as a result of the repeated low-level bombing attacks upon our landing-grounds; indeed, within a day or two it was to be altogether eliminated. And, finally, we could not on this occasion depend upon a great rally of the little ships. To those of us who were in Greece at the time it looked an exceedingly bleak prospect.

[1] In the opinion of the present writer the damage done to the port of Piraeus has been somewhat exaggerated in accounts written from second-hand. Large numbers of civilians were evacuated from this port on April 18th/19th and also on April 22nd/23rd.

Our command was faced with the unenviable alternatives of an evacuation by night, which, though ensuring relative safety from air attack during the actual period of embarkation, meant that most of the voyage to Crete would take place in daylight with enemy dive-bombers swooping down on our convoys; or a day evacuation, with all the attendant disadvantages which embarkation under observation of the enemy would imply. The former was considered to represent, on the balance, the lesser evil. April 28th had been the original date provisionally selected for the beginning of the evacuation; after that a waxing moon would have progressively discounted the advantages of a night embarkation. The news of the Greek surrender in Epirus, however, determined Wavell to advance the date by four days. Evacuation would now begin on April 24th/25th and be spread over that night and the two successive nights. The small beaches on the eastern coast of Attica, also those around Megara and towards the isthmus and the port of Navplion in the Peloponnesus would be the principal points of embarkation. In order to ensure a quick turn round of the shipping, a good proportion of the troops would be evacuated in the first instance to Crete for subsequent transference to Egypt.

It seemed that the Germans were aware of our approaching departure. The *Luftwaffe* was making determined attacks upon the railways in our areas, leaving most of the tracks and equipment in a condition beyond our capacity to repair during these last few days. Perhaps from our point of view, it was not worth while to do so, for railway staffs had, for the most part, dispersed and what ammunition was required for the forward dumps could be sent by road at no greater risk. Coastal shipping suffered in the same fashion as the railways. The Royal Navy reported twenty-three vessels sunk by air attack in Greek waters during the 21st and 22nd; and, although some of these craft were small, the total included a Greek destroyer and two hospital ships. This could be taken as a hint of what we might expect when embarkation began.

On April 22nd evacuation orders were issued, and the intention to depart was made known to the troops. Wounded and convalescents; nursing sisters; signals, ordnance workshop and survey personnel: these would be among the first to go. Rifles, light machine-guns, anti-tank rifles, gun sights, and such items of signal equipment as could be man-handled were all to be brought away by the troops concerned. Motor vehicles were to be destroyed by smashing radiators and batteries and breaking engine casings with sledgehammers, and all tools and tyres were to be made unserviceable. Explosions and fires were to be avoided as far as possible. Horses would be shot, mules handed over to the Greeks. These instructions make melancholy reading; to carry them out was a melancholy task.

The oil stocks in the neighbourhood of Athens were, fortunately, not large; for the King had requested that they should not be fired so as to cause danger to the civil population, and the Greeks who had taken charge were opposed to their destruction. Under these circumstances it was judged better to leave the oil stores intact.

The King of the Hellenes, with members of his Government and the British Minister left Greece on April 23rd by Sunderland flying-boat for Crete and landed at Suda Bay.

The localities selected for embarkation, four in Attica and one in the Peloponnesus, were all open beaches. The troops would go first to 'collection areas', thence to 'assembly areas', and so to the beaches as their turn came to embark. Owing to the menace from the air it was important that no time be lost whenever a vessel closed the coast to take troops aboard: even a concentration of shipping so far away as Suda Bay—in Crete—was held to be a dangerous risk. One need not be surprised that General Wilson asked for fighter protection round the coast.

It had been intended that our embarkation should be covered by the few Hurricanes that still remained serviceable. This we could not do. After the destruction of a large number of our Blenheims and Hurricanes on their landing-grounds in the dawn attack of April 15th, the remains of the British air force in Greece had been hastily evacuated to the airfields in the neighbourhood of Athens. It had been the only practicable decision under the circumstances, and in any case the ground forces were on the very point of themselves withdrawing across the plain to Thermopylae. There were no satisfactory landing-grounds immediately behind Thermopylae, though a Greek Gladiator squadron and a British army co-operation squadron of Hurricanes were temporarily based upon Amphiklia in the plain of Boeotia until the Greek unit was caught on the ground and destroyed. Thereupon the Hurricanes were hastily withdrawn to Attica.

Air Vice-Marshal D'Albiac draws attention in his despatch to the dilemma in which he found himself with his scanty number of aircraft and inadequate airfields.

The constant lack of intermediary aerodromes made it inevitable that, if our fighters were placed on an aerodrome from which they could give protection to our troops, they were in imminent danger of destruction as soon as they were on the ground. If, on the other hand, they were placed beyond the range of air attack when grounded, they were unable to protect our troops and the tightly packed columns of M.T. withdrawing along the roads. The utmost efforts had been made to give protection to our much harassed ground forces, and pilots went again and again into the air to work at extreme range and against immeasurable odds.

With the preparations for evacuation now well advanced, D'Albiac withdrew his remaining fighters to the tiny airfield at Argos to cover the embarkation of the troops. It was here that on April 23rd in an evening attack the *Luftwaffe* shot up and destroyed on the ground all our remaining Hurricanes, including a number newly arrived from Egypt.[1]

That was the end of any hopes of air protection for the evacuation. Moreover, it became necessary to modify certain of the plans for embarkation.[2] It was now decided that we could not afford to make so much use of the beaches of Attica, which lay dangerously exposed to air attack, and must place more reliance on the ports of the Peloponnesus. More use would be made of destroyers in order to speed up the process of evacuation, and the revised embarkation programme was now worked out as under:

	Rafina	Porto Rafti	Megara	Navplion	Tolo	Kalamata	Yithion & Plytra
April 24th/25th		5 N.Z. Bde. (4,000)		H.Q. Anzac Corps. Base details RAF (5,000)			
April 25th/26th		19 Aus. Bde. (4,000) 1 Armoured Bde. details (500) wounded (1,000)					
April 26th/27th	6 N.Z. Bde (3,000)	6 N.Z. Bde. (3,000) 1 Armoured Bde. (400)	4 N.Z. Bde. (4,000)	Base details 3 R.T.R. 4 Hussars (6,000)	Base L of C (2,000)	16 & 17 Aus.Bde. (4,000) Base details (4,000)	Stragglers advised to use

In addition there were about 2,000 Yugoslav refugees who would be embarked from the tiny beach of Theodhoroi midway between Megara and the Corinth isthmus.

The programme was not ideally balanced, for while it allowed for an embarkation rate of 9,000 on the first and 5,500 on the second night, an estimated total of over 26,000 would have to be embarked on the final night. Nor do the actual figures themselves appear to have been very accurately estimated, for even after two serious mishaps in the latter part of the evacuation we were still able to withdraw a larger number of troops than had been allowed for in the programme.

The section of embarkation beaches showed a desire to achieve a greater degree of dispersal on either side of the Isthmus. At the same time, in view of the probability of a German airborne landing at the Isthmus itself, it was perhaps unfortunate that arrangements were not made for a larger proportion of embarkations from ports and beaches rather more remote from that marked danger spot. It would have involved longer drives by daylight under the observation of the *Luftwaffe,* but in the event the choice of so many beaches in the neighbourhood of the Isthmus proved a little unfortunate.

[1]There is a considerable amount of discrepancy between the various figures for the actual number of aircraft destroyed on this occasion. D'Albiac gives no numbers. Longmore says 13. Wilson in his report says 'only about 9'. The heavy A.A. Battery posted at the isthmus gives the figure of 21. The late Lieut.-Colonel Stanley Casson, Intelligence Officer at British Headquarters, who drove through Argos on the following day was told by an anti-aircraft officer there that 'the previous dawn [sic] a swarm of German fighters had descended on the airground and shot up some forty newly-arrived British aircraft'. (Casson, *Greece Against the Axis,* p. 182.) That the total, whatever it was, included new Hurricanes from Egypt seems clear from the evidence of T.H. Wisdom (*Wings Over Olympus,* p. 199) who was R.A.F. Press Officer in Greece at the time.

[2]See Maps 6 and 7.

2

The Covering Forces

IT was as well that the German follow-up to Thermopylae was not so speedy as to threaten any danger of our troops being 'bounced' from the position before full arrangements for the evacuation had been completed. Our force was back behind the Sperkhios and at the Brallos Pass by the evening of April 20th, though defensive preparations had yet to be completed: it was not until the 24th that the enemy attacked.

Not that the pursuit was sluggish; but the combination of stout resistance by our rearguards with the natural difficulties of the country and our effective demolitions made swift movement impossible. These conditions must have been foreseen by the Germans for von List had his transport aircraft in readiness. Just as they had been used to land troops on the Kozani plateau, so now JU 52's carrying both infantry and light field guns began to descend, at first in the meadow country north of Lamia and then still closer to our front. Parties of the enemy reached the line of the Sperkhios river on April 21st, and the repair of the bridges appeared to have been taken in hand. Enemy aircraft were active in reconnaissance and attacked our infantry and battery positions. As a precaution, New Zealand carriers patrolled as far as the river bank at night.

That there was no threat of envelopment from Epirus in the form of a German advance southward, and then eastward to the Delphi pass, can be attributed to the fact, unknown to us at the time, that the SS Adolf Hitler Division did not move from Yanina until April 25th. On the 21st the Delphi pass was still unguarded by us, a state of affairs which could not be allowed to continue, for once the Germans were through the defile they would have a clear run through to Corps or even Force Headquarters.[1] Scarcely less dangerous to our prospects of embarkation would be the existence of a roving German column at large in the Peloponnesus. Somehow, therefore, troops had to be found to cover the open flank, extending our defensive positions so that we held some sort of a front from sea to sea: from the Maliaic Gulf beyond Thermopylae to the Gulf of Corinth in the neighbourhood of Delphi.

Accordingly, on April 22nd, the 19th Battalion was withdrawn from the 4th New Zealand Brigade on the coast of the Maliaic Gulf

[1] See Map 6.

and sent to the Delphi pass under Corps command. Then, on the following day, the 2/5th Battalion from the 17th Australian Brigade, holding the left sector of the Brallos position, was added to the Delphi detachment together with a machine-gun company and a troop of field guns. Some Greek troops and anti-tank guns were pushed forward to Navpaktos to deepen the defence, and at both places demolitions were set in hand. Major Fleming's unit, which had already distinguished itself at Amyntaion and subsequently during the retreat, arrived at Navpaktos on the morning of April 23rd and the same evening, after it was estimated that all that was left of the Greek forces from Agrinion and the west had passed through our lines, blew the road at a point about eleven miles east of Navpaktos. Twenty or thirty yards of road were carried away by the explosion, and the damage done was such that, at a conservative estimate, it would take forty-eight hours to repair. Further back, at Delphi, the New Zealanders were engaged in rolling down rocks to block the gorge, thereby repeating the classical legend; for the tale goes that at the time of the Persian invasion the Delphic Oracle had been saved from violation through the action of the god Apollo who dispersed the advanced parties of barbarians by hurling down rocks upon them in protection of his sanctuary.

Precautions had also to be taken against a German advance into the Peloponnesus after crossing the Gulf of Corinth at its narrow entry near Navpaktos. A Greek infantry battalion which was available was despatched to Patras, while the 4th Hussars, whom we left on the look-out for parachutists around Force Headquarters, were sent, with their remaining twelve tanks, organized into four squadrons of three each, with 'rifle troops' added, to patrol the road along the southern shore of the Gulf from Patras to Corinth. At the Isthmus was gathered a troop of heavy A.A. guns and the headquarters squadron of the Hussars, forming the embryo of Isthmus Force which was to protect that vital point against airborne attack. Finally, the 3rd R. Tank Regiment was set to work upon road blocks and local defence in the Athens area.

It was the best that could be done. All units were weak in numbers and short of arms and of every sort of equipment; and their only protection against attack from the air would be an inadequate number of anti-aircraft guns.

And still the German attack hung fire, while our preparations to embark were pushed forward and the defenders of the Thermopylae

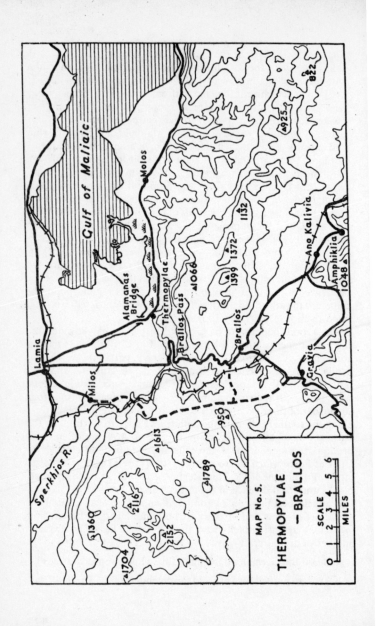

Gulf of Maliaic

Lamia

Sperkhios R.

Milos

Alamanas Bridge

Thermopylae

Brallos Pass

Brallos

Molos

△1066

1399 1372

1152

△925

822

Ano Kalivia

Amphikila 1048

Gravia

△1613

△950

△1789

△1360

△2116

△2152

△1704

MAP No. 5.

THERMOPYLAE — BRALLOS

SCALE

0 1 2 3 4 5 6

MILES

position were thinned out. On April 22nd the 6th New Zealand Brigade took over the whole divisional front, while the 5th Brigade, having spent the day unostentatiously destroying such of its equipment as could not be taken away, moved back towards the beaches after dark. The withdrawal of the 5th Brigade meant loss of contact with the Australians at the Brallos Pass, but the mountainous country which intervened was practically impassable.

Brigadier Barraclough, commanding the 6th New Zealand Brigade, placed the 24th Battalion on the right, facing north-west from the sea-coast to a point on the main road opposite the northward turn of the stream beyond the marshes. The 25th Battalion continued this line westward in the foothills well south of the road, the left flank resting about a mile and a half short of Thermopylae village and twice that distance from the Alamanas bridge where the main road crosses the river. The 26th Battalion was kept in reserve.

Once across the Sperkhios river the German armour would be able to move freely on a broad front over the drying marshes, so our artillery dispositions were planned to repel a southward attack, with many of the batteries well forward, and some 25-pdrs. in an anti-tank rôle. Two troops of the 5th New Zealand Field Regiment and the 7th New Zealand Anti-Tank Regiment were actually emplaced beyond the most advanced infantry posts and protected by special patrols at night. Indeed the infantry were so thin on the ground that the defence mainly depended upon the artillery which consisted of one medium regiment (the 64th Medium Regiment R.A.), four field regiments (three New Zealand and one R.H.A.), two anti-tank regiments (one New Zealand and our Northumberland Hussars), and the 155th Light A.A. Battery R.A.

Further to the left at the Brallos Pass the thinning-out process had left Brigadier Vasey of the 19th Australian Brigade with the 2/1st, 2/4th and 2/11th Battalions, all weak in numbers, two companies of the 2/8th, and the 2/2nd Field Regiment. Detachments were maintained at the crest of the pass well forward of the Brallos position. The Australian gunners had some difficulty in finding battery positions which gave crest clearance; but two guns which came into action on a mountain ledge with good observation over the plain, did considerable execution before being shelled to destruction in their precarious position.

To the men waiting in the Pass of Leonidas for the assault to open, these days preceding the German attack may well have been among the most trying in the campaign. The suspense was bound to be rendered more uncomfortable by the depressing foreknowledge of the overwhelming advantage in striking power which the enemy possessed both on the ground and in the air. From their eyries among the mountains the Anzacs could observe the rhythm of enemy preparations developing often in full view. They watched the German artillerymen digging their gun pits in the plain, and at night they could see the undimmed lights of the German transport proceeding serenely along the roads as the enemy infantry dispositions were taken up just out of range of our guns. The hot sunshine was drying the earth. Every day, enemy aircraft could be seen touching their wheels down to test the surface of the landing grounds. The Germans were 'winding up their tail' by means of their transport planes, which were being used to bring troops and supplies forward to the area of deployment for battle. Though to the anxious watchers at Thermopylae they may have appeared to show no signs of particular hurry it is most unlikely that the German war-machine was wasting any time.

Bombardment and counter-bombardment continued all through the 22nd and 23rd, the Germans shelling our positions as a preliminary to launching their assault, the Australians and New Zealanders firing with the determination to expend as much ammunition as possible upon their targets before the order came to go.

German air co-operation continued to be close and effective. 'Spotter' planes were constantly overhead, locating our gun sites or signalling back the fall of the German shells, while dive-bombers made sporadic attacks upon our positions, difficult though it was for them to secure direct hits in this mountainous country. Perhaps the Germans were using the dive-bombers more for the moral effect; for the dive-bomber was something of a spell-binder. It was not a strikingly accurate means of attack, but it could be an exceedingly alarming one to any but well-trained and experienced troops.

In the course of Wednesday the 23rd, German landings were reported on Euboea, but these proved to be only on a very modest scale. It was judged prudent, however, to withdraw the company of the Rangers which had been posted on the Euboea side at Khalkis and to blow up the bridge across the narrow strait. Khalkis had been heavily bombed by the Germans for some days for it appears that the enemy, quite wrongly, regarded the town as playing an important part in our evacuation plans. These certainly did not involve any embarkation at Khalkis.

During the night the 4th New Zealand Brigade with the 2/3rd Australian Field Regiment, the 106th Light A.A. Battery, an Australian anti-tank battery, and some machine-gunners and sappers, occupied a covering position at Kriekouki on the Thebes road.

3

The Action of Thermopylae

At dawn of the 24th on the New Zealand front our patrols discovered that the enemy was repairing the bridges over the Sperkhios river. The artillery duel continued with great intensity throughout the morning, and German dive-bombers repeatedly attacked our battery positions, albeit with little success. The enemy did not attempt to come to grips until the early afternoon.

Then, about 2 p.m., tanks were observed moving forward over the marshy ground in front of the 25th Battalion. Two tanks were knocked out by the fire of our field guns, and then the main attack developed down the main road from dead ground near the Thermopylae cliff face, well beyond the left flank of the 6th New Zealand Brigade. A group of cyclist and motor-cyclists came on at a fast pace, followed by a number of tanks, while infantry took to the hills in an endeavour, which promised to be only too successful, to envelop the flank of the 25th Battalion.

Along the road repeated attacks of the German armour ended in a triumph for the defending artillery. As the tanks pressed eastward across the front of the 25th Battalion they were exposed to heavy shell-fire which wrought great destruction. Although a few tanks eventually succeeded in approaching battalion headquarters they were effectively disposed of by a troop of New Zealand 25-pdrs., and a six-mile stretch of the road was afterwards described by the New Zealanders as a 'graveyard of German tanks'. The credit belongs equally to the New Zealand and British gunners. At least fifteen tanks were destroyed during the day and many others damaged. Finally, Brigadier R. Miles, commanding the New Zealand divisional artillery, ordered a concentration to be put down on the road near Thermopylae village by three field regiments, to discourage a renewal of the German effort. This had the desired effect. On the right flank a counter-battery shoot at extreme range had silenced German guns in action beyond the Maliaic Gulf.

After dark, when the withdrawal was about to the begin, it was possible to send vehicles forward past the burnt-out tanks along the road and collect the forward gun-detachments, some of whom had beeen engaged at close quarters with German infantry in the course of the fight.

On the left flank, however, the Germans had climbed higher into the hills, aiming, on precisely the same ground, at the identical flanking manœuvre which had been employed by Mardonius when he sent the Immortals on their night march to take Leonidas and his force in the rear.

The historic tactics were being repeated, but the chance which made accomplishment possible was due to a technical breakdown on our side for which a parallel cannot readily be found in the days of Xerxes. The turning movement had of course been observed by our artillery observers in the hills, but they were unable to inform the batteries because their field telephone lines had been cut by enemy fire. The German infantry continued to creep from boulder to boulder each bound forward making more hazardous the situation of the 25th Battalion and perhaps of the whole brigade. And if the brigade position were overrun that afternoon, the German tanks might well be swarming over the plain of Boeotia around Thebes by evening, perhaps to throw the whole scheme of evacuation due to begin that night into tragic confusion.

The company holding the left of the line was pulled back, but suffered severely from enemy fire during the process of getting clear. And when the withdrawal began it was necessary to send a company from each of the other battalions and two carrier platoons to enable the 25th Battalion to break off the action and depart.

Even after dark the enemy infantry continued to probe forward, and the artillery duel continued until 9.30 pm. By this time, when the Germans seemed to call a halt, the New Zealand infantry were boarding their trucks which had been so late in coming up that arrangements had been made to take both infantry and gunners away in the artillery vehicles; for the medium and field guns were due for destruction, the last battery remaining in action being one of the 2nd Regiment R.H.A., which did not cease fire till nearly midnight. By this hour the New Zealand convoys were clear of Molos and driving, first along the coast road and then southward through Thebes, to Kriekouki. Further south the troops were to be dispersed and hidden until, forty-eight hours later, they could expect to be embarked.

Thus the main effort of the enemy to break through the Thermopylae position ended in failure with considerable loss to his armoured forces.

In the morning Australian observers on the forward crests near the Brallos road had seen the Germans cross the Sperkhios in the plain below and concentrate for their attack eastward against the New Zealand position. On the Australian left, men of the advanced companies of the 2/1st Battalion watched German mountain troops scaling the hillsides out of range. At intervals throughout the morning the battery positions were under attack by dive-bombers, but the 2/2nd Field Regiment, which had moved most of its guns to rear positions before dawn, suffered little loss. At 11.30 a.m. the machine-gunners with the 2/11th Battalion in the centre engaged German infantry advancing along the railway, and the afternoon wore on without the enemy making much progress. Suddenly a heavy mortar bombardment opened upon one company of the 2/11th which suffered considerably, and then, just before 5 p.m. a determined attack by German infantry caused the two forward companies of the battalion to fall slowly back through the support companies on the edge of Brallos village. The fire of the Australian machine-guns covered this movement, and made possible the rescue of many of the wounded who were carried back and then sent away in the battalion transport. Later, orders were given for the 2/11th to hold a line west of Ano Kalivia until 9 p.m.

The two companies of the 2/1st Battalion holding the left of the forward position had been withdrawn from the top of the pass at noon. At Brallos they were deployed to cover the mountain track along which they had retreated. Brigadier Vasey sent another company of this battalion to watch the road from Gravia and at dusk, near the village, fire was exchanged with German infantry. Enemy pressure was maintained, the detachment of the 2/8th Battalion east of Brallos coming under attack, until nearly 8.0 p.m. and then the fighting died down. Rather unexpectedly the Australians, who had been watching the southward road leading into Ano Kalivia, were able to board their trucks and withdraw without interference. The tail of the column moved off about 10.15 p.m. First ordered to destroy their guns, the 2/2nd Field Regiment was told, later, to bring them away and did so, with the scanty supply of ammunition that remained. Driving through the night, mostly with headlights on, Vasey's troops passed through Mandhra and at about 8.0 a.m. on April 25th—Anzac Day—arrived at Megara.

4

First Embarkations

AFTER the Greek surrender there was no longer a Commander-in-Chief, but the Greek staff continued to do their best to assist our embarkation. Thus Greek troops were kept clear of the main roads so that there should be less chance of congestion as our traffic moved to and fro between the forward positions and the areas of concentration near the beaches. The Greek people were now well aware that we were on the point of departure, but, for the most part, their friendliness was no less than when they had welcomed us as allies, and perhaps deliverers, little more than a month before. They called their thanks, tendered small gifts and cried 'come back again!' as the fighting men in their battered vehicles drove through Athens towards the sea.

Anzac Corps headquarters had moved from Levadia to Elevsis during the previous night and closed at 2 p.m. on April 24th. General Blamey visited General Wilson in Athens during the morning and, later, was flown to Egypt where his presence was much desired.[1] At Alexandria he saw Admiral Cunningham and emphasized the need to speed up the evacuation.

Some revision of the programme was made in order to embark still more troops from the furthermost beaches of the Peloponnesus, localities which were deemed less liable to air attack. To protect the isthmus of Corinth from the assault of airborne forces 'Isthmus Force' was formed under Brigadier Lee. His troops consisted of a company of the 19th New Zealand Battalion, the 6th New Zealand Field Company, and a section of the 122nd Light A.A Battery; his orders were to keep the Megara road open, but to make preparations for the destruction of the road and railway bridge over the Corinth canal as soon as the last of our troops had passed. Here a conflict of loyalties arose, for the Greek commander at Corinth insisted that he was in sole charge of the bridge and responsible for its protection.

With the fall of darkness our trucks began to move back along the roads converging upon the beaches where the embarkation was to take place. Elaborate plans had been made to conceal our intentions

[1]He was appointed, forthwith, Deputy Commander-in-Chief, Middle East.

from the enemy up to the last possible moment. During the stand at Thermopylae all day-movement of road convoys towards the rear had been forbidden, so as to give as little appearance as possible to the roving aircraft of the *Luftwaffe* that withdrawal was being planned. Now, during the period of embarkation, all night-movement of convoys forward was prohibited, in order to allow unimpeded movement to the columns of vehicles making their way towards the beaches. Strict road discipline was maintained and vehicles were forbidden to overtake, but driving with side-lights was permitted to ensure the maximum practicable speed. The traffic control of the withdrawal, at any rate at this early stage, compared favourably with some of the subsequent desert 'flaps', when our increased power to give air protection to retreating troops had led to the gradual adoption of more free and easy methods on the road. Now and again a vehicle would break down en route. Unless it was due to a minor failing that could promptly be remedied, it was pushed off the road and jettisoned, and its occupants distributed themselves among the succeeding trucks. For traffic blocks and delays of any sort during the hours of darkness had to be avoided at all costs, and the loss of a few more vehicles was of no importance when all would have to be sacrificed in the end.

The 16th and 17th Australian Brigades—moving as one group—drove from the Mandhra region into the Peloponnesus and harboured near the small fishing village of Myloi.

And so the troops moved by night and lay hid in the thickly-planted olive groves or in the mountain ravines by day, enduring that queer boredom of enforced inactivity while great events are moving—a type of boredom that bears no relation to any other form of that misfortune. They kept as still as could be during the daylight hours—and prayed that the *Luftwaffe* would fail to observe them.

The Germans attempted no night bombing of the embarkation beaches; but during April 24th they had attacked Athens and Piraeus. In the evening they set on fire and sank with great loss of life the Greek steamer *Hellas* which carried wounded, R.A. and Pioneer Corps personnel, and civilians.

Aided by a calm sea, on this first night of evacuation, the estimate of troops who could be embarked was exceeded. At Porto Rafti, much favoured by Athens bathers in times of peace, about 5,200 men, mostly of the 5th New Zealand Brigade Group, were taken on board H.M.S. *Calcutta* and s.s. *Glengyle* by means of various types of landing-craft, and sailed for Crete. At Navplion occurred the first

131

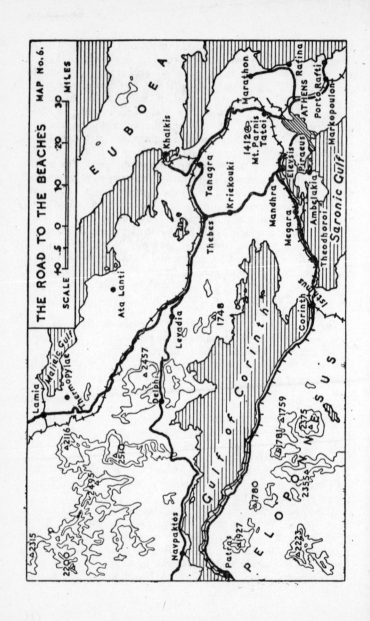

of many mishaps that were to befall the force during the next few days, s.s. *Ulster Prince* ran aground at the entrance to the harbour, was refloated, and ran aground again. She had been allotted a contigent of 2,000 men who would now have to wait until the following night: nevertheless at least 5,500 troops—mostly of Corps headquarters, Australian Division headquarters, the 4th Survey Regiment, 16th Heavy A.A. Battery and 'base details', with about 150 Australian and New Zealand nursing sisters, were taken off in the s.s. *Glenearn,* the cruiser *Phoebe,* the destroyers *Voyager* and *Stuart,* and a corvette. This convoy, also, was for Crete.

In addition to recalling General Blamey to Egypt, orders were issued on this day for the departure of the two divisional commanders. Major-General Mackay was flown direct to Crete early on April 25th. Major-General Freyberg, whose troops were heavily engaged at Thermopylae and also holding the covering position at Kriekouki, received from Force Headquarters in Athens an order to depart which he could not well obey. Actually he continued in command until the end.

All concerned may take pride in the success with which contact was broken with the Germans after the fighting at Thermopylae and Brallos. Almost our entire force was withdrawn to the Athens area or beyond. By daybreak of April 25th the only troops remaining north of Athens were the rearguard consisting of the 4th New Zealand Brigade at Kriekouki, south of Thebes, and the skeleton of the 1st Armoured Brigade on the southern fringe of Mount Parnis with a strong detachment forward at Khalkis. Thus the two principal approaches to Athens from the north were still covered.

There was in fact no close pursuit during the day. The Germans duly entered the abandoned Thermopylae position, and finding that they had failed to trap any part of the British force published a somewhat imaginative account of the operation. The German communiqué proclaimed that Thermopylae was captured 'by a pincer attack, by which the enemy were thrown out of a particularly strong and long fortified defensive position'. In fact, the fighting on the previous day justifies the belief that Thermopylae could have been held for days longer if the general plan had demanded it. The perhaps understandable pride in the 'ejection' of the British force could scarcely be reconciled with statements already being broadcast by Dr. Goebbels that the bulk of the British troops had gone and that only a small covering force still remained in Greece.

Behind Thermopylae on the main road to Athens the sappers had done one of the best demolition jobs of the campaign. The road was so thoroughly cratered and wrecked that the German engineers, after taking a look at it, ruefully reported that they could not guarantee a speedy repair, and the enemy tanks, which should have been bowling along towards Levadia and Thebes, had to be diverted on to side roads and mountain tracks which had never seen a motor vehicle before; and then to make their slow and difficult way as best they could in a generally south-easterly direction. At nightfall, they were still far from Thebes.

The decision to abandon the main road was perhaps only in part conditioned by the work of destruction carried out by our sappers. Though the enemy aircraft failed to locate the New Zealanders at Kriekouki, it seems that they believed in the likelihood of our making a further stand where the mountains begin to rise south of Thebes, dividing the plain of Boeotia from Attica. It was from these mountains that Pausanias had watched the Persian forces in the year after Thermopylae, until he descended into the plain and destroyed them at Plataea.

It may be that von List had read his Herodotus and realized the potential dangers of an incautious advance; but what is more surprising is that the Germans were so far from wanting to engage and destroy our rearguard that their movements were designed definitely to avoid action and to approach Athens by a more devious route. Whatever Dr. Goebbels may have been saying over the radio, it seems that the German Intelligence, with its habitual inaccuracy, considerably overestimated the strength of our troops in the Thebes area.

Apart from the now uninterrupted air activity of the ubiquitous *Luftwaffe*, which was systematically combing the whole hinterland in search of our places of concealment, the day passed quietly over the area that had ceased to be 'the front'. Perhaps the most noteworthy incident was the demise of the last of our cruiser tanks when it fouled the bridge at Tanagra as our rearguard withdrew from Khalkis.

This same day the Germans, following the occupation of Samothrake, Thasos and Skiros, landed troops on Lemnos. The island had been regarded as of key importance to the general defensive system in the eastern Mediterranean should the Germans invade Turkey; and, in view of this, a British battalion had been landed there from Palestine on April 4th, two days before the German attack on Greece. With Turkey left unmolested and the enemy in possession of the coast of Greek Thrace, there was no point in our retaining a garrison on the island. It had been withdrawn on April 12th.

On the mainland it was a comparatively quiet day but anxiety was felt for the isthmus of Corinth, Brigadier Lee's troops being neither equipped nor organized to repel an airborne attack. During the day reinforcements in the shape of three companies of the 2/6th Australian Battalion and a squadron of New Zealand cavalry were received. Then, in the evening, a bombing raid silenced nearly all the anti-aircraft guns in the canal area. It was an ominous portent for the morrow.

An order issued by Force Headquarters placed General Freyberg in command of all troops in the Peloponnesus as soon as he should arrive there from Attica. At night General Wilson left Athens for the Peloponnesus, and early next morning his headquarters were established in an olive grove near Myloi. Here General Freyberg and his headquarters arrived, having also moved down during the night. Near Tripolis, a rather ugly modern town in the heart of ancient Arcadia, was the 6th New Zealand Brigade which, coming from Attica, had crossed the Corinth bridge before daylight of the 26th. The brigade had impressed all beholders by its admirable discipline and the calm and confident air of all ranks; it was still well equipped and eminently battleworthy.

The 16th/17th Australian Brigade Group moved on this night from the Myloi area to the vicinity of Kalamata where it was to be embarked.

The night's embarkations had comprised the 19th Australian Brigade Group, a party of nursing sisters, and some wounded and other troops. These were taken on board from two beaches at Megara to the number of 4,700. The ships had to put to sea by 3 a.m. in order to be sufficiently far out by daylight to escape serious danger of dive-bombing attacks; as a result 500 men were left behind. Knowing that the Germans might arrive at almost any time, these troops tried to get together transport to convey them to the Peloponnesus whither the remainder of the Australian Division (the 16th/17th Brigade Group) had proceeded with the beach at Kalamata as its objective. For reasons soon to be related they were unable to get through the Isthmus next day. Many made their way north to join the New Zealanders near Porto Rafti beach, but a party of about two hundred embarked in a Greek schooner and were picked up on the way to Crete by one of our destroyers.

With nearly 15,000 troops embarked and at sea, the rate of evacuation was well up to the programme laid down, and, despite the accidents on each night, all appeared to be running as smoothly as could be expected. The next day was to tell a different and much more unfortunate tale.

5

Airborne Attack

It was now, when fully a quarter of our forces was already safely at sea and a good proportion of the remainder was either already through to the Peloponnesus or in the neighbourhood of their embarkation beaches, that von List executed the manœuvre which, had it been made earlier, might have produced disastrous results. He attacked the isthmus of Corinth with airborne troops.

Saturday, April 26th, dawned clear, still and bright—perfect weather for an enterprise of this type. The tactics employed by the Germans are of particular interest, since the operation was in the nature of a rehearsal for the full-scale airborne attack made upon Crete in the following month. The day opened with a high-level bombing attack upon the canal area at about 6 a.m. aimed at locating the positions of our anti-aircraft guns. In this the attackers proved all too successful, and when the next wave arrived—twenty or thirty dive-bombers, escorted by from eighty to a hundred ME 110's—the guns were most effectively silenced. The JU 87's swooped down and dropped their bombs on or around our gun positions, and what they failed to hit was largely accounted for by the machine-gun and cannon fire of the fighters. For half an hour there was nothing to be heard but the whine and crash of falling bombs and shells and the chatter of machine-guns; and then, when every man in the neighbourhood of the canal had his head well down in a slit-trench or was under cover of some kind, the troop-carriers began to appear. Arriving usually in formations of three, practically wing tip to wing tip, they approached, flying quite slowly (or so it appeared to eyewitnesses on the ground) at a height of not much more than 200 feet. It looked like an exercise in field manœuvres, for there was not an R.A.F. fighter to be seen and there was not an anti-aircraft gun to be heard.

Then the parachutists began to emerge, dropping through the clear almost windless air and descending on both sides of the canal.

The outer aircraft of each formation of three dropped men, the inner ones, by means of different coloured parachutes, dropped supplies. And while this was happening the German fighters were machine-gunning the approach roads from north and south in an endeavour to seal off the canal area which it was the task of the parachutists to seize, preserving the bridge intact.

Two battalions of the German No. 2 Parachute Rifle Regiment with supporting arms were used for the action, a force amounting to not less that 800 men.

Isthmus Force had a wide area to cover, and the troops actually in position close to the canal were not numerous. They consisted chiefly of a company of the 19th New Zealand Battalion and a squadron of New Zealand cavalry, and on them fell the first weight of the assault. Many Germans were killed in the air, and others fell into the canal; but as more and still more arrived our men were overwhelmed. The defenders inflicted many casualties but suffered severely themselves, and after some confused fighting the bridge over the canal was seized intact. This was a matter of importance to the enemy if his ground troops were to advance speedily into the Peloponnesus. Promptly the paratroop-engineers, who had been among the very first to drop, set about tearing up the fuse wires and removing the charges, congratulating themselves upon another bridge, the most important of all, taken intact. Suddenly there was a loud explosion.

Two young officers, Captain J.F. Phillips (Devonshire Regiment) and Lieutenant J.T. Tyson (Royal Engineers) had both taken cover at a point about two hundred yards south of the bridge when the parachutists completed their mopping up task in the immediate neighbourhood.

> As...they saw the possibility of their retreat being cut off, they decided to divide the German forces by the width of the canal. With admirable coolness one of them took a rifle and, although already seen and fired at by the Germans, took steady aim at the charge they had fixed to the bridge. The first shot missed, but the second detonated the charge with a violent explosion, just as a dozen parachutists were crossing to round them up. Down crashed the bridge, the hundred and fifty feet into the waters of the canal, taking the Germans with it. The two boys escaped and reached Navplion, where they were taken off.[1]

[1]Casson, *Greece Against the Axis,* p.196.

The headquarters squadron of the 4th Hussars had been stationed at the Isthmus, and the three light tanks that they still possessed might have been of value against the parachutists, who seem to have been short of anti-tank weapons; for a German account stresses the fact that they were ordered to salvage all abandoned British anti-tank guns and rifles to meet an expected counter-attack with tanks. This they proceeded to do.

> The guns and ammunition were piled into a captured car and taken up ahead to where one Captain S. was waiting. This officer had the guns set up immediately and it looked for a moment as if immediately would be none too soon. For about that time one of the light tanks did appear across a field. The gunners drew a bead and got ready to fire, but something about the tank looked phoney: it would start and then stop, and when under way it travelled jerkily. Just in time Captain S. hit upon the thought that this was a British tank now being operated by a couple of his parachutists. This turned out to be true.[2]

In fact, the headquarters squadron of the 4th Hussars had been overrun almost at the start and we were never able to get any of the tanks into action against the parachutists.

By 8 a.m. the action round the canal was practically over. The Germans held both banks; the bridge had gone, but it was quickly replaced by an emergency bridge. Corinth itself was entered a little later without opposition by a party using a captured British car driven by a German war correspondent who had been dropped with the parachutists. Four or five paratroopers hung on to the running-boards or clung to the car with one hand while holding a grenade or a machine-pistol in the other. This car was followed by the captured British tank. Just as they entered the town from one side a German aircraft touched down in a field a few hundred yards away on the other.

From it there emerged—an interpreter. He proceeded sedately into Corinth and in excellent modern Greek relieved the mayor of his responsibilities.

German thoroughness!

Isthmus Force now disintegrated. Many had been killed or captured, and the survivors were split into two bodies by the German paratroopers solidly established between them. Some of

[2]Major Paul W. Thompson, *Modern Battle,*

our men went north to find the 4th New Zealand Brigade, but only two appear to have done so; others, by various means, eventually arrived in Egypt. Parties on the south side of the canal made for Tripolis to join the 6th New Zealand Brigade.

Those who made contact with this brigade brought news of the airborne attack but not of the destruction of the bridge. Accordingly two companies of the 26th Battalion were sent north to counter-attack in order to re-open the route for the withdrawal of the rest of the force from Attica. The operation would have to be carried out without artillery support of any kind and even without mortars; in addition, the New Zealanders were subjected to heavy attack from the air as they approached Corinth. Nevertheless, they had gone into action against the new firmly established paratroops when news of the destruction of the bridge was at last received. There being no object now to be gained by the attack, contact with the enemy was broken off, and companies fell back upon the remainder of the 26th Battalion, which was being organized to cover the Navplion embarkation points by holding a defensive position at the highest point on the road between Corinth and Navplion. The ascent is gentle and easy from the direction of Corinth; on the southern side the ground drops away more steeply, and the crags to the east, where stand the massive remains of Agamemnon's palace of Mycenae, look out over the open plain of Argos.

It was not a position that could have been held for any length of time, but fortunately it soon became clear that the German force at the Isthmus had no further objective for the day than the capture of the canal area and the town of Corinth. No attempt was made to advance southward; it seemed that the enemy's main object had been to bottle up our troops to the north.

Fortunately for us most of the troops who had still to be embarked were now in the Peloponnesus, and the remainder had access to an adequate number of beaches in eastern Attica.

Therefore, despite its spectacular quality, despite its profound tactical significance, the airborne landing had accomplished remarkably little except to inflict upon us considerable loss. The Germans claimed 21 officers and 900 other ranks as prisoners from the fighting around the Isthmus, also 1,450 Greeks including the commander of the 'Army of the Peloponnesus'. Their own reported losses in killed, wounded and missing, were no more than 237. The attack had practically wiped out our small and ill-equipped force; but although it had given our Command added anxiety regarding the fate of our troops further to the north, it had not decided their fate.

There was one other significant German move during the day. The vanguard of the SS Adolf Hitler Division, which had taken Yanina six days earlier and had since been moving south by Arta and Agrinion, crossed the Gulf of Corinth during the afternoon and landed in the Peloponnesus just south-west of Patras. The three squadrons of light tanks of the 4th Hussars—nine tanks in all—had been withdrawn earlier in the day in the direction of Kalamata, and there was nothing left to oppose the crossing or to prevent the Germans from making contact with their paratroops at the Isthmus. They promptly took possession of the brand-new airfield at Araxos in the immediate neighbourhood. It had been slowly constructed under British supervision during the long winter months—just in time to be ready for the Germans when they arrived.

Brigadier Lee had already been dispatched with a small force of Australians and New Zealanders and a few guns to prepare a last ditch defence in front of Monemvasia in the extreme south-east of the Peloponnesus. In view of the presence of German troops at both Corinth and Patras, more use would now have to be made of this port and of Kalamata in the final evacuations.

The largest formation still remaining north of the Isthmus was the 4th New Zealand Brigade. Already for two days by the artful use of camouflage it had succeeded in laying hidden from air observation and attack in the gullies and olive groves south of Thebes. But the German ground forces were in Thebes early on this Saturday morning, and a reconnaissance patrol pushed through between eight and nine o'clock almost to the New Zealand outposts. The New Zealanders—they had the 2/3rd Australian Field Regiment in support—gave no sign of movement, and the patrol returned evidently quite satisfied that the road through the hills into Attica was undefended.

Just before noon a column of about 100 trucks filled with infantry, preceded by motor-cyclists and a solitary tank, drove confidently up the road. Not until the tail of the column was within range did the Australian gunners open fire. Hit after hit was scored, and the German force withdrew in some confusion.

The enemy, it appeared, was anxious to avoid direct contact with a rearguard which he presumed to be a good deal stronger than it actually was. There had been none of his customary rapid deployment to either flank which normally followed the opening of fire by our defenders. In the afternoon the New Zealanders observed a much stronger column consisting of about 500 vehicles moving eastward from Thebes, towards the coast road. This was the main spearhead of the advance against Athens, moving at right angles to our line of retreat to the beaches east of Athens. Therein lay a danger for the following day.

The planned withdrawal of the brigade to the Peloponnesus had had to be abandoned when news was received of the paratroop landing at Corinth. General Wilson's headquarters had no means of communication with Brigadier Puttick, but General Freyberg's high-powered wireless set managed to call up the last remaining set of the 1st Armoured Brigade near the Marathon beaches. A message was transmitted 'in clear', but in sufficiently disguised phraseology, instructing the 4th New Zealand Brigade to make for the Porto Rafti area during the night, and to prepare for embarkation on the night of April 27th/28th. This message was carried from Marathon by two officers to Brigadier Puttick. It seems that Brigadier R. Miles, commanding the New Zealand artillery, picked up the message at Porto Rafti and also sent it on; so the brigade commander must have received this important order in duplicate.

The 4th New Zealand Brigade was therefore condemned to another twenty-four hours on the mainland north of the Isthmus, and the evacuation, of necessity, was spaced over a fourth night. It was certainly the best arrangement which could be made, under the circumstances, and offered good prospects of the rescue of Puttick's fine battalions at the eleventh hour. The withdrawal began at dusk, the 20th Battalion covering the movement. Demolitions were blown without interference from the enemy and the brigade reached its bivouac area near Porto Rafti in the early hours of next morning.

6

Last Days at the Beaches

THIS Saturday night was to have seen the major part of the evacuation accomplished, but things went amiss and performance could not keep pace with programme.

From the Attica beaches the intention was to embark 6,000 men at Porto Rafti and Rafina. The Porto Rafti lift was safely accomplished, the 64th Medium Regiment R.A., the 5th New .

Zealand Field Regiment, the 27th New Zealand Machine-Gun Battalion, the 7th New Zealand Field Company, and other troops being taken aboard the s.s. *Salween* for Alexandria and H.M. ships *Carlisle* and *Kandahar* for Crete. At Rafina, where the s.s. *Glengyle* had to lay a mile and a half out to sea owing to the heavy swell, and each boat trip from shore to ship and back again took over sixty minutes, the sailing hour had to be advanced to 2 a.m. In consequence about 2,600 men were taken and 1,000 left, the latter including 1st Armoured Brigade headquarters and parties of the Rangers, R.H.A., Northumberland Hussars, 6th New Zealand Field Regiment, New Zealand cavalry, and anti-aircraft gunners. The Hussars destroyed their anti-tank guns on the beach when it became obvious that these weapons could not be embarked.

The ships from Porto Rafti and Rafina were dive-bombed at sea amd suffered some casualties, but no vessel was sunk or seriously damaged.

From Myloi General Wilson departed in a Sunderland flying-boat for Crete leaving General Freyberg in command of all our troops remaining in Greece, a command which even so fine a soldier found difficult if not impossible to exercise; for some of the detachments waiting to embark were cut off from all communication, and their numbers, whereabouts, and condition could not now be ascertained.

The Navplion area was likely to become untenable by Sunday night, so every effort had to be made to evacuate the troops gathered near. The stranded *Ulster Prince*, however, was a decided obstruction; reduced to a mere hulk by dive-bombing her position made the approaches to the quayside so difficult to negotiate that the whole business of evacuation was slowed down.

Here is the account of the embarkation as given to a special correspondent by the captain of H.M.S. *Calcutta*, who had been present at the Aandalsnes evacuation and also subsequently at Dunkirk:

> The whole thing was different from Dunkirk in this—the task of transporting the men from shore to ship was slower as they were heavily laden with all their equipment. But they were not exhausted. Most of them had been resting under trees, waiting for us to pick them up when darkness fell. All these operations were carried out without a single light, and as far as I know not a life was lost accidentally.
>
> I took three merchantmen with me, and made for Navplion. The rest of the ships in my convoy, with the escorting destroyers,

went to Porto Rafti and another fishing port, Rafina. At four that afternoon, after we had separated, we had a sharp attack from eighteen JU 87's and 88's attacking in two waves of nine machines. They hit one of my transports[1] in the engine room, disablig her, while a second vessel was hit by a small bomb but not badly damaged. When it was over I ordered the destroyer *Griffin* to stand by the crippled transport, which was towed into port. With the other two I arrived at Navplion about ten o'clock. I took 960 men on board while the destroyers *Hotspur* and *Isis* took 500 and 400. So far the weather had been perfect, but that night the wind got up with a choppy sea, which made boat work most difficult. The cruisers *Orion* and *Perth,* with the destroyer *Stuart,* appeared before midnight and embarked men from Tolo. These ships took on about 2,500 men.... I was anxious to be going, as the Germans had occupied the aerodrome at Argos, a few miles north of Navplion.

From Navplion and Tolo together, therefore, a total of about 4,360—including men of the 3rd Royal Tank Regiment, with some of Force Headquarters—was taken on board during the night. But the Germans were now very much on the *qui vive* and from earliest dawn their reconnaissance planes were roving the southern Aegean in search of the convoys, whose route they could, after all, clearly predict.

The captain continues:

At seven o'clock in the morning of April 27th, bombers came over and did not leave us until 10 a.m. We were shooting so accurately that again and again we put them off. About 7.15 one transport was hit and began sinking. I ordered the *Diamond* alongside to take off the troops, and about 9 a.m. three more destroyers, the *Wryneck, Vampire* and *Voyager,* joined us in the battle with the dive-bombers, so I detached the *Wryneck* to help with the rescue work. In that three hours the *Calcutta* fired about 1,200 round of four-inch shells and many thousand rounds of pom-pom and machine-gun ammunition.

H.M.S. *Calcutta* eventually got away safely to Port Said. The s.s. *Slamat* was the transport sailing in company which was sunk by bombing on the way, but all the survivors were taken off. The destroyers *Diamond* and *Wryneck* were less fortunate. They were hunted by dive-bombers throughout the morning, and both were sunk about midday. A few survivors were picked up by the destroyer

[1] *s.s. Glenearn.*

143

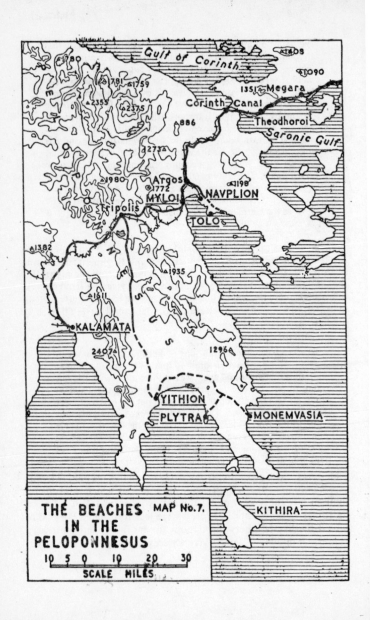

THE BEACHES
IN THE
PELOPONNESUS

MAP No. 7.

10 5 0   10   20   30
SCALE MILES

Griffin but in addition to the crews over 500 of the troops on board were drowned.

The choppy waters in the bay had slowed down the turn-around of the boats to such an extent that, when the hour came for the ships to depart 2,200 men had to be left behind at Navplion and Tolo. Of these, some 400 moved off down the coast in a landing craft which was subsequently bombed and sunk by the enemy.

Kalamata had been designated as the embarkation point for the 16th and 17th Australian Brigades, both very weak in numbers and therefore organized in one group. This group formed by far the most coherent part of a miscellaneous force of about 15,000 which had arrived by evening; nearly double the number that had been allowed for when the decision was first taken to use Kalamata as a place of evacuation. The total had been swollen by stragglers who had made their way south after the news of the German airborne descent on the Isthmus. The cruiser *Phoebe,* with the transports *Dilwara, City of London* and *Costa Rica,* duly arrived to embark the troops, but it was clear that the few hours of darkness at their disposal would not allow them to take off all those who were waiting to leave. They managed to get 8,000 troops on board, mostly from the two Australian brigades, before it was time to set sail. Although the *Costa Rica* was bombed and sunk on the way to Egypt, the troops were taken off and landed in Crete.

Two caiques left Yithion, the ancient port of Sparta, that night, bound for Crete, but there were 7,000 men waiting on shore at Kalamata when dawn broke on Sunday.

This night of Saturday/Sunday should have seen over 26,000 men embarked. The total of troops who were actually taken off amounted to approximately 17,300 (Rafina 2,600; Porto Rafti 2,400; Navplion 1,800; Tolo 2,500; Kalamata 8,000).

Apart from the stragglers scattered over Attica and the Peloponnesus there remained four main groups still waiting to be embarked. Of these, the 4th New Zealand Brigade and the remnants of the 1st Armoured Brigade were moving towards the neighbourhood of the beaches of eastern Attica. There was a concentration from many units at the head of the Navplion gulf. Another group was formed by the 6th New Zealand Brigade, strung out along the road from the neighbourhood of Argos back to Tripolis. And finally, there were the troops at Kalamata. Of these four groups, only the two New Zealand brigades were still capable of a prolonged resistance. They were as good as ever.

April 27th, Sunday morning in Athens. It was exactly three weeks from that Sunday when Germany had launched her attack upon Greece. Throughout the previous evening British, Australian and New Zealand troops, cut off from their units or prevented by the enemy movements from making their way to their assigned embarkation points, were trickling through the Greek capital. To the last they met with friendliness and assistance. 'We know you will return' was the prevailing sentiment with which the Greeks bade farewell. To the last the cry of '*Nike! Nike!*' (Victory! Victory!) could be heard, while girls tossed flowers to the weary dusty transients as they made their way on foot or in the few remaining lorries through the streets of Athens, and civilians of all ages made the 'thumbs up' sign, widely believed on the Continent of Europe to be the customary British form of greeting.

Here may be related the story of a small party of New Zealanders who found themselves stranded at Megara and, early on Sunday morning, took a bus into Athens whence they travelled by taxi-cab to Rafina—an unconventional retreat under the circumstances, and one made possible only by Greek goodwill.

At 9.30 a.m. on this calm and beautiful Sunday morning there was no sound of approaching battle. No German bombers swept over the city. But down the road that approaches Athens from the gay, garden cities of Kephissia and Amaroussi, down the broad Queen Sophia Avenue passing the large pale pink building which had been the house of Venizelos and was and is the British Embassy, appeared a reptilian swarm of motor-cyclists. They moved on towards the heart of Athens, looking neither to right nor left, like automatons of some evil Wellsian fantasy. At the great Square of the Constitution they swung left, past the Royal Palace and the tomb of the Unknown Warrior, and up the winding road that leads to the Acropolis. And on the flagstaff at the summit of the rock that has stirred the imaginations of thirty centuries, on the hill of Athene and Poseidon, their leader hoisted his flag. Then came the armoured cars and the tanks and the lorried infantry. Athens had fallen.

Now let us look at the 4th New Zealand Brigade, a fighting force still capable of returning blow for blow. The battalions had driven back from their well-guarded lair above Thebes during the night, back through Athens, and on the morning of the 27th they moved into position just beyond the village of Markopoulon. Here they deployed for action for the last time in Greece, the 18th and 20th Battalions forward, the 19th in reserve. Throughout the day they must hold the final beach-head in front of Porto Rafti. They had still Australian field artillery in support, and to the north of them around Rafina lay a remnant of the 1st Armoured Brigade—headquarters troops, some of the Rangers, and a handful of artillerymen—too weak to offer effective opposition if the Germans should discover their hiding place.

Was there to be a last-ditch fight in front of Porto Rafti? A flight of twenty or more Messerschmitts came over in the course of the morning, sweeping down upon the cornfields and vines and olive groves while some of the New Zealanders were still taking up their battle positions. Men among the ripening corn saw their cover sprayed with incendiary bullets and were compelled to display themselves in the open. Worse still, the German planes were seeking out the guns which had so often during the past fortnight saved our infantry against tank assault. Of the small number of pieces still serviceable they destroyed one 25-pounder and six anti-tank guns. It seemed the certain prelude to an attack in strength by the German ground forces.

Yet noon passed by, and the sun began to descend towards the ridge of hills behing Athens, and still the enemy tarried. Then armoured vehicles and lorries were seen moving forward along the road into Markopoulon. Our gunners engaged them and the infantry opened up with mortars; but the reluctance of German vanguards during these last days to push home attacks against a resolute resistance again served the defenders well. The Germans, who lacked artillery support, began to draw back out of range, but not before they had suffered considerable losses. Bombing and machine-gunning of the New Zealand positions from the air was then resumed and continued intermittently until dusk.

After dark the brigade pulled back to the beaches at Porto Rafti, where H.M. ships *Ajax, Kimberley* and *Kingston* had arrived to take them off. Some losses had been suffered by attack during this final uncovenanted day ashore, but on the whole things had gone better than could have been expected. The brigade group, to the strength of 3,400, embarked without incident and sailed for Crete at 3 a.m. on the morning of the 28th.

At Rafina the destroyer *Havoc* took off a party of New Zealand cavalry and what was left of the 1st Armoured Brigade.

But these were the only troops embarked from Greece that night, for no shipping had been available for a fourth night's evacuation from the Peloponnesus. There were still about 1,700 men, mainly base details, around Navplion, many of them now without rations, all anxiously aware that Sunday night would probably provide their last opportunity of escape. For the Germans were said to have reached Argos and there was nothing now to prevent them advancing to Navplion and Tolo, gathering in all the men who remained at the beaches.

The 7,000 left behind at Kalamata after the previous night's evacuation were joined in the course of Sunday by 300 men of the 4th Hussars who had made their way down, by bad mountain roads, from their last patrolling position on the southern shore of the Gulf of Corinth. Brigadier Parrington, as the senior officer on the spot, deployed the Hussars as a covering force for defence of the beachhead while instructing the remainder to disperse and take cover. He estimated that he possessed about two days rations for the whole force, but, as more than half of the 7,000 men under his command had no arms and the fighting value of many was, in any case, questionable, the actual capacity for resistance of his force bore little relation to its size. Nevertheless, the greatest part of the New Zealand Reinforcement Battalion was present, and a contingent of Australian reinforcements, while the 4th Hussars was, of course, a good, well-trained regiment.

Between the small force at Navplion and the much larger one at Kalamata was the 6th New Zealand Brigade which, at daybreak, was strung along the road from the Gulf of Navplion back to Tripolis. The 26th Battalion, breaking the custom which had prevailed throughout the period of withdrawal, took the risk of moving by day, despite the omnipresence of the *Luftwaffe*. This policy proved fully justified, and though the column was repeatedly attacked by German aircraft as it made its way back over the bad roads of the Peloponnesus to Monemvasia in the extreme south-east, it actually suffered only three casualties. The other two battalions followed after dark, and travelling all night by unfamiliar and ill-mapped roads, reached Monemvasia just as dawn was breaking on Monday, April 28th.

Here Brigadier Lee had organized a defensive perimeter and sappers had prepared the approach roads for demolition, using, in default of other explosives, depth charges taken from Greek destroyers stranded in the harbour.

As at Kalamata, there had been no opportunity for evacuation during the night. But Colonel Blunt, British military attaché in Athens, and Colonel Quilliam, Deputy Director of Military

Intelligence, Middle East Command, had been busy gathering caiques in the neighbourhood with a view to the possibility of 'island hopping' during the ensuing night, if no shipping arrived.

On Monday, April 28th, the German vanguard came down upon Navplion and Tolo in the course of the morning, and by noon the beaches were under fire. Some sporadic resistance was offered, but by evening all was quiet. A few of the 1,700 escaped in small boats to one or other of the neighbouring islands or started to work down the coast towards Monemvasia. A few more got away on foot inland. But the bulk of the force, short of food and arms and including many non-fighting personnel, was gathered in by the Germans in the course of the day.

At Monemvasia the evacuation on the whole went with astonishing smoothness. There were about 4,000 troops assembled, mainly consisting of the 6th New Zealand Brigade which covered the land approaches, and then withdrew to the beaches after dark. The ships were late in arriving and little had been done by midnight. Later, the destroyers *Isis, Hotspur* and *Griffin* were joined by H.M. cruiser *Ajax,* and the tempo began to speed up in astonishing fashion. At 3 a.m., the normal hour for the ships' departure, Admiral Baillie-Grohman decided to risk another hour in order to get the remainder of the men away. The gamble proved fully justified, and by 4 a.m. the entire force had been embarked, the last boatload carrying the Admiral himself and General Freyberg. All the four thousand troops were evacuated without loss that night from Monemvasia.

General Freyberg had watched with satisfaction the orderly and business-like departure of his New Zealand battalions who had come away fully armed and equipped. So far as he knew no more of our troops, apart from the inevitable stragglers, remained on Greek soil. He had no knowledge of the fact that thousands of men were waiting—and waiting in vain—to be taken off the beaches of Kalamata.

At Kalamata occurred the tragedy of the night.

The total of 7,000 left behind after the previous night's evacuation had swollen to about 10,000 in the course of Monday. The latest arrivals included fully 2,000 Yugoslav soldiers and civilians, numbers of Greek civilians, and Cypriots and Palestinians of the pioneer companies. The Germans were well aware that a force of some size was assembed in the neighbourhood of the port, and while their troops hastened forward along the mountain roads of the

Peloponnesus their aircraft bombed and machine-gunned the neighbourhood during the day.

Nevertheless, the embarkation promised to go well. A strong force of cruisers and destroyers was coming to take the troops off. The whole assembly, representing so many nations and so many units, had been organized in four detachments: each would begin to arrive at its own control post, ready to enter the boats, at 9 p.m.

After dark, when the troops were moving down to the sea, the German vanguard broke into the town. Their armoured cars accompanied by lorried infantry and self-propelled guns had succeeded in over-running the weak covering screen formed by the 4th Hussars; and, shooting their way through, they raced on to the quayside, where they captured the beachmaster, the only naval officer ashore.

At 9 p.m. the ships were reported to be lying off the harbour: the cruisers *Perth* and *Phoebe,* the destroyers *Nubian, Defender, Havoc, Hero, Hereward, Decoy* and *Hasty,* and three merchant vessels. Confused fighting was still in progress on shore, and the news was flashed by hand-torch to the ships: they were informed that attempts were being made to clear the quay and they were asked to stand by and to send a boat. A naval officer was promptly landed. He met Brigadier Parrington and returned to his ship with the brigadier's evacuation plans.

Now came another turn of Fortune's Wheel and, for the moment, the situation was saved. We still had men apt and ready for the counter-attack. Sergeant J. D. Hinton, a New Zealander, crying 'To hell with this, who'll come with me?' ran forward to within a few yards of the nearest German gun which fired and missed him. He hurled two grenades at the gun detachment and wiped them out. Then, with bayonet fixed, he led a rush of New Zealanders which caused the Germans to abandon their guns and take refuge in two houses. Smashing in doors and windows, Hinton and his men settled the issue with the steel.

Elsewhere officers had rallied small parties of men and were attacking the Germans wherever encountered. By 11.30 p.m. Kalamata was practically clear of the enemy who had lost a dozen lorries, two guns, two armoured cars, and about 150 prisoners; and the little victory seemed to promise salvation. An 'all well' message was flashed to the ships.

But the Fates were against our unfortunate and much-tried men. Only a little later a naval officer came ashore to announce a terrible disappointment. Orders had just been received from the Commander-in-Chief for all ships to rejoin the Fleet without delay, as the Italian fleet was reported to be at sea. There was no alternative. Orders had to be obeyed, even though they were practically tantamount to a sentence of captivity for the duration of the war for the 10,000 men at Kalamata. Only a few boats were available and there was no time to embark more than a few wounded and 400 troops before the ships sailed.

It was obvious that Kalamata could not be held for long. Already the Germans were beginning to work their way back and firing had again broken out in the northern outskirts of the town. The gallant Sergeant Hinton was wounded at this time and was subsequently captured. Months later, in a German prison camp, he learned that he had been awarded the Victoria Cross.

Brigadier Parrington reviewed the situation. Although one German attack had been repulsed there was no hope of prolonging the resistance. His men lacked support weapons and there was a shortage even of rifles and small-arms ammunition. There was no means of reply if enemy artillery should bombard the town and harbour. The wounded were many. Little food was left. After a conference with some of his senior officers the brigadier determined on surrender and despatched a representative, together with an English-speaking German officer prisoner, to inform the enemy that no resistance would be offered after 5.30 a.m.

And so, on the morning of Tuesday, April 29th, the Germans took Kalamata and some seven thousand prisoners.[1] The pity of it was that the report concerning the Italian fleet proved to be unfounded. With this surrender the British campaign on the mainland of Greece came to an end. About 300 of the troops got away to the south-east and some of them were picked up later. Destroyers which came in close to the Kalamata beaches on the night of the 29th took off 16 officers and 19 others. Numbers of stragglers had got away, during the course of the previous day or two, to Kithira, making the short voyage in every sort of craft, seaworthy and otherwise, an *Embarquement pour Cythère* never dreamed of by Watteau.

[1] This is the figure claimed by the Germans themselves. It appears entirely congruous with the number known to be in and around the town under Parrington's command at that time. The balance of something over 2,000 (after allowance is made for the number evacuated and those killed in the night's action) may be assumed to have dispersed into the hills.

In the end Colonel Blunt had as many as 850 under his command on the island and they were successfully evacuated to Alexandria. About 600 more got away by caique to Milos and thence to Crete and Egypt.

For days and weeks after, survivors continued to trickle through to Crete, to Chios and the islands of the eastern Aegean and to the coast of Asia Minor; and the total number evacuated after the actual close of operations is estimated to have been as high as 1,400.

Because of the variety of methods and times of evacuation, it is difficult to achieve an exact estimate of the total number of our troops evacuated from Greece. Figures from official sources vary slightly, one with another, but the discrepancies are of no great significance.

Revised official figures of the strength of the Army in Greece, casualties sustained and numbers evacuated are as follow:

	British	*Australian*	*New Zealand*	*Total*
Strength at beginning of campaign	24,206[1]	17,125	16,720	58,051
Evacuated	13,700[2]	14,157	14,454	42,311
Losses	10,506	2,968	2,266	15,740

Our battle casualties may be reckoned at about 3,000, a by no means heavy figure, and among the 'missing' counted in the losses are a considerable number of men who remained at large in Greece after our departure. Some of these managed to rejoin Middle East Command later in the year.

The Germans, by their own computation, lost 5,000 officers and men.

The much greater proportion of British losses to those of the Commonwealth troops is accounted for by the fact that the lines of communication and base troops were supplied entirely by the British. It should be remembered that the maintenance, supply and general administrative services had been calculated for the requirements of a combatant force almost double the strength of that which actually went through the campaign. As we know, the crisis in Egypt prevented our sending additional fighting formations to Greece.

[2] Includes 5,000 Palestinians and Cypriots.
[1] Includes 1,100 Palestinians and Cypriots.

Grievous to relate, there had been yet another mass abandonment of equipment, not on the Dunkirk scale—for the forces involved were so much smaller—but on a scale quite sufficient to embarrass General Wavell, who had so many fronts to provide for. Practically none of our artillery, heavy equipment or motor transport could be brought away. At least 8,000 vehicles of all kinds were abandoned or destroyed. With certain notable exceptions the troops who returned from Greece were short of machine-guns, mortars, ammunition and even rifles. Some detachments were without blankets, cooking gear, or personal possessions of any sort. Such signal equipment and close-support weapons as the units still retained had been smuggled aboard the ships, for the Navy, in order to facilitate quick loading, insisted that nothing of any bulk or weight be brought away. Men were, indeed, more important than material. So there was great need of re-equipment, reorganization, and reinforcing drafts before most of the troops who fought in Greece could do themselves justice in battle again.

Epilogue

SO all was over. Australians, New Zealanders, men from the British Isles, had fought a good fight. As soldiers they had shown themselves equal, more than equal, to their well trained, better equipped, and far more numerous German adversaries. They had endured a harassing, if brief campaign which from the start had offered little hope of clean-cut victory; and their departure from the scene had been achieved at considerable price. That that price was not bigger is to the credit of the Royal Navy who risked ships and men day after day and night after night to bring the troops to safety.

The resolve to send this expedition to Greece has been the subject of much argument. Of all the decisions which rested solely with the British War Cabinet none has given rise to more speculation and debate.

Let is consider the issues.

It had been urged that the original pledge of aid to Greece had been given at a time when France was our ally and the balance of power in the Mediterranean was utterly different and immeasurably more favourable to us. Such a pledge was conditioned by the over-all war situation; and just as William Pitt had conquered Canada on the plains of Germany, so Greece might have been aided best by victory in the desert of Libya.

But our obligation to Greece was a direct and genuine one. We were in honour bound to do our utmost to assist an ally who, while engaged in an heroic struggle with one of our common enemies, was threatened by the other. We could have pleaded, and no doubt obtained, remission of our guarantee of aid, in view of our mainifold commitments elsewhere; but to do so would, in the words of the New Zealand Government, have destroyed the moral basis of our cause. There are some transactions that must be carried through, even though the ledgers show a loss.

Again, it has been contended that, although the enlistment of American sympathy and therefore of American aid was essential for the cause of liberty in Europe, a further gesture of the lines of the Norwegian expedition, by displaying our limitations in land-fighting against Germany, could do nothing but harm: failures, even gallant failures, are not calculated to bring neutrals to the help of a nation at war.

Nevertheless, at the beginning of 1941 we could only count upon victory in so far as we could rely upon aid from the United States; our failure to give corresponding help to a small ally would have produced a most unfavourable effect upon the Americans. It was not really to be contemplated that, at a time when the Roosevelt administration was pushing through 'Lease-Lend' to Britain, we should have taken no steps to pass on what aid we could to Greece. And if we were to fail, failure was likely to bring home to the American public the magnitude of our task. Defeat in Greece, after we had committed all we could spare to the campaign, might well increase American awareness of the aggressive strength and expansionist tendencies of Nazi Germany.

When the campaign was over President Roosevelt used these words in a telegram to our Prime Minister: 'You have done not only heroic but very useful work in Greece...you have fought a wholly justified delaying action....'[1]

Then there is the argument—very ably put—that the forces we employed in the Greek campaign could have been used to complete General Wavell's conquests in North Africa. The Italian forces were, at the time, quite incapable of effective resistance and the *Afrika Korps* was only beginning to arrive: Wavell's vanguards might have been on the frontier of French North Africa before the end of March: the problems of maintenance, admittedly difficult, could have been solved.

Yet here we should take account of the weakness of Wavell's forces: he had so few formations which were battleworthy, and, in his own judgement, was not ready for an offensive. Having regard, also, to the difficulties of supply it would seem that only a small force could have been pushed forward quickly. Such a force might have occupied the port of Tripoli. To have maintained it there would have

[1]Churchill, *The Second World War*, Vol. III,

[2]By Major-General Sir F. de Guingand in *Operation Victory*.

been difficult in the extreme; and it would have been exposed to the German attack. Truly the prospect of completing our conquest of North Africa does not appear to have been so bright after all.

Possibly, if the troops we sent to Greece had been available in the Desert when Rommel advanced, the German success might not have been so great. One can say no more than that.

We do know, however, that Hitler's decision to occupy Yugoslavia and Greece and to reach the eastern Mediterranean caused him to postpone the invasion of Russia for a month. It is true that we failed in our efforts to create a defensive front by rallying Yugoslavia, Turkey and Greece, but our military expedition to Greece may be regarded as one of the reasons why Germany devoted larger forces and more time that she had intended to the solution of her Balkan problem.

The time question is perhaps the more important. Russia was to be crushed by a quick campaign and Hitler required all preparations to be completed by May 15th, 1941; it was not, however, until June 22nd that the Germans attacked. So two questions arise, neither of which is easy to answer. Is the whole delay to be attributed to events in the Balkans? And did the loss of less than six weeks of good weather make just the difference between German success and failure in Russia?

Now to examine the actual military prospects of our Greek venture, which in General Wavell's phrase was 'a gamble with the dice loaded against us'. It is quite wrong to suppose that the British Cabinet and those who advised them underrated the difficulties. They were well aware of the power of the German Army and recognized that a German penetration of the Balkan States would threaten our position in the Middle East and bring us no strategic advantage. They appreciated that our chief dangers lay in the enemy's superiority in the air, the uncertainty of the Yugoslav attitude, and the risks to our shipping in the narrow waters of the Aegean. These were major matters—the problem of air defence, the problem of establishing effective defensive positions in Greek territory, and the problem of maintenance and supply.

And to the certainties that we were bound to be overmatched in numbers and equipment, that we could not compete with our adversary in the air, that the defence of Greek territory was in reality a Balkan problem hard to solve, and that the Royal Navy had more than enough to do already, may be added other risks and difficulties. There was the danger that Germany might strike before our full strength—such as it was—could be deployed, and the length and inadequacy of our land communications in Greece was a handicap hard to overcome.

Unfortunately there was nothing novel in our situation. It was not the first instalment, nor yet the last, of the penalty we had to pay for our unpreparedness for war. We should have been no more justified in declining battle on this occasion than in refusing to enter the War in September 1939 or in giving up the struggle after Dunkirk. Past policy condemned us to face the odds, and for many weary months to come dictated the offensive-defensive policy described in the opening pages of this book. It was our inevitable rôle to engage in delaying actions which would win us the precious time we needed to develop our armed might and, as it happened, to rally the forces of liberty to our side. Failure and losses there were bound to be, for at this stage our armed forces were, in a very special sense, the scapegoats of a policy which had failed.[1].

In common with most campaigns, the planning of the campaign in Greece and the way in which it was conducted offer some grounds for criticism—not all unfavourable. Before discussing our preliminary dispositions it is as well to consider the circumstances under which our troops arrived to take their part in the defence of Greece. We were, of course, at a great disadvantage in having to fit our contingent into the framework of the Greek defensive dispositions. So long as Greece was fighting we were dependent in more or less degree upon the policy of her High Command and, indeed, the quality of her troops. It may be that some our commanders were inclined to expect too much of the Greeks. Co-operation did not prove to be easy—there was always the language difficulty and the military customs and outlook of our ally were so different from our own—in spite of the goodwill displayed by both sides. How regrettable was the misunderstanding which left three good Greek divisions isolated in the Metaxas forts when we expected them to be available for the Aliakmon line!

The strength and merits of the Aliakmon line have been the subject of some discussion. It was obvious that a German drive through Yugoslavia had to be taken into account; hence it followed that the position was liable to be turned by an advance through the Mónastir Gap. This contingency could have been met if sufficient forces had been at our disposal: actually we were not strong enough to do other than fight a delaying action at the main position. Our

[1]See Eric Linklater's *The Campaign in Italy*, p.1

men were too thin on the ground and there was no depth in the defence. The Greek troops under General Wilson's command were ill-equipped for modern warfare and were woefully deficient in artillery. It is true that the Germans struck before our deployment was much more than half completed, but in the upshot we were not perhaps much the worse for that. Our forward troops fought well and were well handled. What we needed was not the arrival of the rest of the Anzac Corps, but at least another corps, and armour as well.

The larger the force in the field the greater demand upon the services of transport and supply. The weakness of our line of communication so vulnerable to air attack is obvious: it crossed six hundred miles of sea and then followed a single railway and a single road for three hundred miles. As it happened we were at no time, during the three weeks' campaign, faced with a maintenance problem, and this may fairly be regarded as a considerable achievement. Even so, if we had been required to maintain very much larger forces for a longer period the task might well have proved impossible, for the power of the *Luftwaffe* grew day by day to the time of evacuation.

Again, more troops without a corresponding increase in air power would have paid no dividends. Perhaps, in some respects, we were too considerate of Greek feelings: we might have been more insistent upon the preparation of the airfields we so urgently needed. The prompt provision of the necessary materials and a great effort by civilian labour were needed to give our air squadrons adequate ground protection and facilities for dispersion. Not that such measures would have done more than delay the inevitable, for we lacked, and were bound to lack, the numbers to challenge the enemy in the air.

When the Greek resistance weakened and collapsed, withdrawal and evacuation became our only course. The withdrawal was well conducted, our infantry fought very stoutly, and time after time we matched artillery against armour with considerable success. This is true even to the last action before our departure; and the losses we sustained at or near the beaches and on the high seas were again the result of the German command of the air.

THE BATTLE FOR
CRETE

BRITISH TROOPS ARRIVING AT PIRAEUS

A BRITISH GUN PASSING THROUGH LAMIA

NEW ZEALAND IN GREECE

TRANSPORT OLD AND NEW ON A GREEK MOUNTAIN ROAD

MOUNT OLYMPUS

THE PASS AT THERMOPYLAE

Photo: Exclusive News Agency Ltd.

WAY TO THE BEACHES, AUSTRALIAN INTERLUDE

SUDA BAY UNDER ATTACK

CRETAN COUNTRYSIDE

Photo: Imperial War Museum

THE KING OF THE HELLENES AND 2nd-LIEUT. RYAN

A GERMAN TROOP-CARRIER   *Photo: Imperial War Museum*

GENERAL FREYBERG

CRETAN AIR-RAID REFUGE NEAR THE BEACH

TROPHIES FROM CRETE

CHAPTER 1

The Island

1

Base or Outpost?

THE evacuation of the last of our troops from the mainland of Greece at the end of April 1941, and the occupation of the Aegean Islands by German forces, left Crete as our outpost in the eastern Mediterranean. So also had Rommel's practically simultaneous sweep across the Cyrenaican desert to the frontier of Egypt left Tobruk 'islanded'. Crete and Tobruk, at the beginning of the month of May represented two forward positions which, so long as they continued to be held by us, hampered the completion of the German victories. The possession of these two outposts would have a defensive value for Germany: at the same time they were of potential offensive value—each as an advanced base—in the event of any further development of enemy operations in the Middle East.

In particular the Germans required Crete as a means of barring the access of British warships to the Aegean Sea.

The strategic importance of Crete to Britain and France had been realized from the first: in enemy possession the island would constitute a threat to our seaborne communications in the eastern Mediterranean. It has been explained earlier in this volume that as far back as May 1940 an agreement had been reached with the Greek Government by which the two Powers might immediately land troops at any point in the island in the event of war developing between Greece and Italy. The tragic developments of the succeeding month, involving the defeat of France, meant that our role in the Mediterranean must for some time remain essentially

161

defensive, and had Italy delivered an attack upon Greece and Crete as early as June, the position, in view of the extreme paucity of Wavell's resources, must have become acutely embarrassing. At that time he did not consider that he could spare even one brigade to garrison Crete. Yet the importance of Crete was not forgotten by any of the Services, and the Navy in particular considered it essential that the admirable harbour of Suda Bay, on the north coast of the island and near its western end, should be available as a refuelling base for our ships and thereby denied to the Italians.

With the intensification of the Italian threat against Greece, military conversations had been initiated with the Metaxas Government in mid-October regarding the defence of Crete in the now probable event of aggression by the Fascist State in the near future. Following the outbreak of war with Italy at the end of the month the Greek Government gave us the most complete freedom of action. They assured us that they would welcome the presence of our troops, and that they did not require to be asked for permission to land them but merely to be informed of our intentions.

We now proceeded to establish a naval refuelling base in Crete and to send for defensive purposes what troops and armament could be spared. The naval part was accomplished without incident; and on October 31st—Greece having rejected the Italian ultimatum on the 28th—the 2nd York and Lancaster Regiment was sent by Wavell to Suda Bay to come, temporarily, under the naval command. The battalion landed safely on November 1st, although Suda and Canea were bombed twice by enemy aircraft during the day and again on the morrow. The most pressing question was that of maintenance. Little food was to be obtained locally, so that a considerable reserve of supplies required to be built up by shipment from Egypt.

On November 6th another contingent arrived at Suda Bay. Brigadier O.H. Tidbury, commanding the 14th Brigade, brought with him his own headquarters, the 151st Heavy Anti-Aircraft Battery, the 156th Light Anti-Aircraft Battery, and the 42nd Field Company R.E. His orders were to take command of all British troops in Crete; to keep close contact with the Greek military commander; to defend the naval refuelling base; and, in co-operation with the Greek forces, to prevent and defeat any attempt at invasion by hostile forces.

The geographical aspect of Crete could scarcely have been worse from the point of view of organizing its defence against attack from the north. The island is 170 miles long (the equivalent of the distance from Dover to Poole harbour), but practically the only major road was that which followed the north coast. This road, on which were situated the two principal towns, Canea and Heraklion, was narrow at many parts; some of its bridges were too weak to take the strain of heavy military traffic; and long stretches lay open to attack from the sea. Yet it was to constitute both our line of communication and our 'front line'.

There were no railways.

To the south of the road, and running almost the whole length of the island, is a ridge of mountains rising to about 8,000 feet. These mountains fall very steeply to the southern coast where access to the few small, shallow, cliff-girt beaches is difficult. Thus the shipping required to supply our garrison, not to speak of the civil population which amounted to nearly 400,000 was committed to the use of the ports on the northern coast facing the direction from which invasion would come. Our convoys must pass either through the narrow channel between Kithira—where the Germans after their occupation of the Peloponnesus were quick to construct a landing-ground—and the western extremity of Crete, or through the still narrower Caso channel between the Italian-held Dodecanese and the eastern end of the island. Crete could not be supplied or reinforced unless our ships were at all times prepared to run the gauntlet of attack by watchful enemy aircraft.

Unfortunately the ports on the northern coast, all subject to air attack, offered very limited facilities for the prompt discharge of cargoes, or disembarkation of troops. Suda Bay is a capacious harbour, but only two ships at a time could be unloaded at the jetty. Heraklion could berth four ships, up to 3,000 tons, at the main jetty, and three or four could tie up inside its long breakwater; but Canea could only discharge ships by lighter. Retimo affords little shelter in stormy weather and under favourable conditions it was only possible to discharge one ship at a time, and that by lighter.

Before the war Crete possessed only one airfield, situated near Heraklion. The concrete runway measured 1,000 yards by 800: there were no hangars.

Brigadier Tidbury sent in his first report on November 10th. Transport and labour were scarce and road conditions difficult, especially after rain; but anti-aircraft and coastal defences were being organized in co-operation with the Navy. Some of the anti-aircraft armament had been allotted to the defence of a new airfield under construction at Maleme. 'Creforce'—the code-name for the

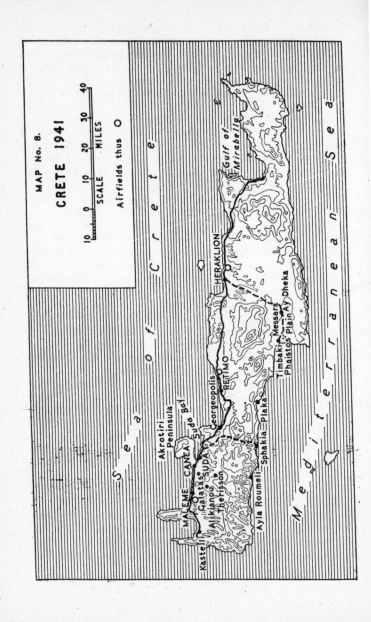

MAP No. 8.

CRETE 1941

SCALE   MILES

10   0   10   20   30   40

Airfields thus O

Sea   of   Crete

Mediterranean   Sea

Akrotiri
Peninsula

Suda Bay

Georgeopolis

MALEME — CANEA
Galatas   SUDA
Alikianos
Therisson

Kastelli

Ayia Roumeli — Sphakia — Plaka

RETIMO

HERAKLION

Timbaki   Messara
Phaistos Plain O Dheka

Gulf of
Mirabella

British military forces in Crete—could, at most, prepare to resist landings in the western half of the island and protect outlying defence works for a time. More artillery was urgently needed.

The Greeks were anxious that we should take over entire responsibility for the defence of Crete, in order to release their own troops for action in Albania. We were prepared, though reluctantly, in view of our numerous other commitments, to undertake the defence, in conjuction with such local levies as could be raised. As early as mid-November 1940, however, the British Chiefs of Staff had come to the conclusion that, in the event of the mainland of Greece being overrun our use of the island would be conditioned by the extent of the enemy's air power and by the weight of attack that could be brought to bear from the mainland. Air defence was indeed the vital factor if we were to retain control of Crete.

General Wavell visited the island on November 13th. He accepted—indeed he could hardly do otherwise—the withdrawal of the Greek troops, and he had another battalion of the 14th Brigade, the 2nd Black Watch, sent from Egypt. No. 50 Middle East Commando followed. It was considered that in Crete this unit would be well placed to carry out raids on the North African coast or the Dodecanese islands. At the moment no more infantry could be found by the Middle East Command, but an increase in the anti-aircraft armament was more important, and this was realized in Egypt as well as at Home. Mr. Churchill expressed the view that, despite the many claims upon our anti-aircraft batteries, a further definite allotment should be made to Crete. There seemed little possibility of doing so. General Wavell had urgent commitments in the Western Desert of Egypt, in the Sudan and East Africa. He had to take measures for the protection of the Suez Canal and to keep a watchful eye on our defences in Palestine and on the possibility of a threat to the Persian Gulf by way of Iraq. And early in 1941 he had to find the troops for the expedition to Greece. Under these circumstances it was not to be supposed that Crete could receive a very high priority of material for defence. Nor would it have been either wise or possible to have locked up larger forces there so long as the island was not actually in the 'front line'. Moreover, if more troops were eventually to be allotted to the defence of Crete measures must be taken to accommodate them. Middle East Command considered that the pressure of events—say the over-running by our enemies of the Greek mainland—might compel us to bring the garrison of the island up to the strength of at least one division: the immediate need was to plan for the necessary installations and camps.

Thus, in the period from November 1940 to May 1941, Crete served its purpose as an advanced naval base, and transit camp for naval and R.A.F. personnel. Cruisers and destroyers refuelled in Suda Bay, although it was not wise for ships to anchor for long periods because of the danger of air attack and the lack of a net defence against torpedoes. And the Army devoted the labour, transport, material and tools at its disposal primarily to the preparations for the establishment of a military base: roads, light railways, water supply, petrol pits, huts for storage and workshops. Accommodation for additional troops—camps, hospitals and the like—was planned. There was never any prospect of turning Crete into a 'fortress'.

2

Defence Problems

SO far nothing has been said of the part which the R.A.F. was expected to play in the defence of the island. At the beginning of January 1941 the Chief of the Air Staff had considered that strong air forces established in Crete should be able to delay the German advance southward through Greece, and would also be well placed to give aid to Turkey at need. Strategically this was sound enough, but the necessary aircraft to operate from this new and supplementary base simply did not exist. We sent what air forces we could spare to Greece, and it was not until the evacuation of the mainland was imminent that any aircraft, other than those of the Fleet Air Arm, were available for Crete.

Since the island lies over 400 miles from the coast of Egypt it would have to be self-supporting so far as the operations of defending aircraft were concerned, for no fighter cover could be given from North Africa. The airfields consisted of the original one at Heraklion, the new one put in hand at Maleme, ten miles west of Canea, and a third to be constructed at Retimo, some thirty miles to the east of the capital. A fourth, which was begun at Kastelli, in the extreme west of the island, was afterwards abandoned and the site ploughed up as we possessed neither the armament for its defence nor the aircraft to operate from it. At Suda there was a base for flying-boats and another in the Gulf of Mirabella but both were dangerous in heavy weather and unsuitable for use at night.

Local fighter forces were thus confined to three airfields—Heraklion, Maleme, Retimo—which were neither well situated nor sufficient in number for our purpose. There would be the constant risk that our squadrons might be neutralized, or even destroyed, by the concentrated attacks of superior air forces based on the mainland of Greece and in the Dodecanese. We knew by bitter experience in Greece and Norway that in a struggle against a stronger air power safety must be sought in dispersal: the eggs should be in many baskets.

An attempt was made, during the battle which ensued, to overcome the problem of air cover by fitting Hurricanes with extra tanks to enable them to make the distance from Africa and back and to permit them up to half-an-hour's patrolling and fighting over the island. But the experiment was not successful; the hampering effect upon the speed and operational efficiency of the machines proved too great.

During these months there is no doubt that Crete suffered from the frequent changes in command. Brigadier Tidbury, who arrived in November 1940, had begun to tackle the defence problem. He urged a policy of night and day digging of infantry positions and the preparation of gun-sites; but shortage of labour and transport hampered the initiation of the work. As early as mid-December the Brigadier had drawn up a remarkably accurate appreciation of the form which an enemy attack would take. He forecast an airborne assault with the primary object of taking possession of the naval base of Suda Bay, the attacking troops being dropped at the three landing-grounds: Maleme to the west, Retimo to the east and Heraklion (Candia) still further to the east of the port. He therefore recommended the concentration of the main defence position around Suda Bay.

On January 10th, 1941, Tidbury was succeeded by Major-General M.D. Gambier-Parry, former military head of the British Inter-Services Mission to Greece. Gambier-Perry's tenure lasted only three weeks, for at the beginning of February he was appointed to the command of the 2nd Armoured Division then arriving in Egypt. Lieut.-Colonel H.D. Mather, officer commanding the anti-aircraft artillery, then took over temporarily until Brigadier A. Galloway was given command on February 19th with the specific tasks of defending the Suda Bay base in co-operation with the Greeks;

preparing for the reception of reinforcements up to the strength of one division; and controlling such operations as might be initiated against the Dodecanese islands. The small and remote island of Castelrosso off the coast of Asia Minor—it is over 200 miles northeast of the eastern extremity of Crete—was occupied for a few days at the end of the month by No. 50 Middle East Commando who destroyed the wireless signal station and then withdrew in the face of a strong Italian counter-assault. The commando was then recalled to Egypt, but the 1st Welch Regiment (the third battalion of the 14th Brigade) arrived to replace it on February 17th.

Brigadier Galloway left in his turn to become Chief of Staff to General Wilson commanding the expedition to Greece, Colonel Mather again taking over at the beginning of March. Then it was the turn of Brigadier B.H. Chappel who arrived on March 19th 'to assume command of the garrison' but with no definite directive as to the extent of his authority and 'in some doubt as to whether he should include the defence of Heraklion in his commitments'.

Within ten days of Brigadier Chappel's arrival yet another officer was informed that he would be appointed to command Creforce. This was Major-General E.C. Weston, Royal Marines, who was despatched early in April to carry out a thorough reconnaissance of the island. The advent of General Weston was consequent upon the decision to develop the refuelling station at Suda into a properly equipped naval base, and to send to Crete the Mobile Naval Base Defence Organization (M.N.B.D.O.). This self-contained 'organization'—there seems to be no other word for it—was, or had been, lavishly equipped for its purpose. It consisted of an underwater group, a sea patrol, and a land group which contained a searchlight regiment of anti-aircraft artillery. In October and November 1940 the land group was merged in the anti-aircraft defences of Britain. It was the only portion of the M.N.B.D.O. which was eventually sent to Crete and it did not begin to arrive until May 10th, 1941.

On April 15th General Weston submitted a report which recommended the independent defence of the two vital areas, Suda and Heraklion each to be allotted a brigade group; the construction of 'full scale operational aerodromes'; and the provision of more anti-aircraft batteries and defence stores. This report was followed by a paper prepared by the Middle East Joint Planning Staff which held much the same views as to what was required and agreed with General Weston that the 16,000 Italian prisoners then in Crete should be removed. These men were, of course, the prisoners of the

Greeks. General Wilson, who arrived from Greece on April 27th also reported on the defence requirements of the island. He thought that the Navy would find it difficult to interfere with a seaborne expedition covered by strong forces of shore-based aircraft, so he expected that the German invasion would be by air and sea; we required more troops, more searchlights, more anti-aircraft batteries.

Plans and dispositions for the defence of the island were bound to be complicated by the decision to use Crete as a transit camp in the evacuation of our forces from Greece. By landing troops in the island the necessary quick 'turn round' of the ships was ensured; but the reception, reorganization and maintenance of the different units as they arrived affected and hindered our preparations to resist a German assault. It was never intended that the men from Greece should play a leading part in such resistance—they were to be taken on to Egypt and Palestine and the garrison reinforced by fresh troops—but lack of shipping facilities ruled otherwise.

On April 30th General Wavell visited Crete. The very last of our troops were being picked off the southern coast of the Peloponnesus that night, and an attack upon Crete was expected after an interval of about three weeks.

The Commander-in-Chief held a conference of senior officers, those present including Lieut.-General Wilson, Major-General Freyberg, Major-General Weston, Wing Commander Beamish who was senior air officer in Crete, and Air Vice-Marshal D'Albiac, late commanding the R.A.F. in Greece. Sir Michael Palairet, British Minister to Greece, was also there. General Wavell pointed out that a combined airborne and seaborne attack was to be expected, but in view of our extreme shortage of fighter aircraft he doubted whether any further air support could be supplied. He appointed General Freyberg to command Creforce with orders 'to deny the enemy the use of air bases in Crete'.

Freyberg had reached Crete on the previous day when his 6th New Zealand Brigade, practically intact, had also arrived from Greece. This brigade, under naval orders, left Suda Bay for Alexandria but Freyberg had come to see his 4th and 5th Brigades which had already landed in the island. To the Commander-in-Chief he expressed his desire to go on to Egypt, there to reorganize the New Zealand forces who were his peculiar responsibility, but Wavell called him aside and said, 'It is your duty to stay'. This was enough. Certainly no better choice of a commander could have been made.

3

The Men and the Means

THE troops in Crete at this time may be divided into three main categories. There was the permanent garrison, equipped and armed for the defence of the island; there were the men who had been brought away from Greece; and there were the Greek forces.

The permanent British garrison at the beginning of May, when the evacuation of Greece was completed, consisted, exclusive of artillery, of the three battalions (2nd York and Lancaster, 2nd Black Watch, 1st Welch Regiment) forming the 14th Brigade. These were reinforced on May 16th by the 2nd Leicestershire; and on May 19th, the day before the assault began, the 1st Argyll and Sutherland Highlanders arrived at Timbaki on the south coast.

The troops from Greece were much more numerous. Of these the organized and disciplined fighting units which had proved their mettle in the campaign on the mainland were a valuable asset, even though nearly all their heavier armament and much of their equipment had been jettisoned by superior order. But the presence on the island of certain elements, base and line-of-communication troops of various nationalities, was a distinct liability. General Freyberg reported that his preparations were hampered by 10,000 'other ranks' without arms and with little or no employment other than getting into trouble with the civilian population. There was a danger, he considered, that our hitherto excellent relations with the Greeks would be imperilled unless we could get rid of these men.

Subsequently the majority of them were shipped back to Egypt.

The Greek forces in Crete, which at one time during the winter had been reduced to as low a figure as 750, in order to provide battalions for service in Albania, now amounted to about 15,000 organized in a number of units, each about 1,000 strong. This total was made up of 11,000 of the Army, 2,800 gendarmes, 300 cadets from the Greek Military Academy and 800 from the Greek Air Force Academy. They were most inadequately armed, even those who possessed rifles having on an average less than 30 rounds per man, and in the opinion of General Weston could only be used for guerrilla fighting, for counter-action against parachutists in the less-important districts and for providing information.[1] However, the

[1]In fact, some fought with extreme courage and tenacity.

eastern end of the island, where landing was not anticipated and did not in fact occur until our troops were actually in the process of evacuation, was eventually allotted to them for defence. Some of the better-armed battalions were posted in the neighbourhood of Suda and at Retimo.

Although the retention of Crete had at an early stage been recognized as depending upon air defence and (in view of the difficulty of operating fighters) especially upon anti-aircraft guns, it had never been possible to supply these in large quantities. At the time of the evacuation of Greece there were only 16 heavy and 36 light anti-aircraft guns on the island, and one-third of the latter could not be described as mobile. This total was absolutely inadequate to defend the three airfields and the base area around Suda, and it was officially estimated that our minimum additional requirments were another 40 heavy and another 12 light anti-aircraft guns, as well as 72 searchlights. It proved impossible to supply them, simply because we did not possess such a surplus in the Middle East at the time. When the month of May arrived and attack was known to be imminent the only anti-craft reinforcement in sight was that to be provided for the defence of the Suda area by the Mobile Naval Base Defence Organization—one searchlight regiment and sixteen heavy and twelve light guns.

On May 20th the first day of the assault, the garrison in Crete was made up approximately as follows:

	Original 'Creforce'	Arrived from Greece and remained	Reinforcements from Egypt	Total
British	5,200	6,399	3,464	15,063
Australians . . .		6,451		6,451
New Zealanders .		7,100		7,100
TOTAL . .	5,200	19,950	3,464	28,614

To strenghten the defence and to provide an effective means of counter-attack, a few tanks had been sent by Middle East Command. They arrived on May 14th–sixteen light tanks of the 3rd Hussars and seven 'infantry' tanks of the 7th Royal Tank Regiment. There was a promise of more to come.

After the disastrous German attacks upon our airfields in mid-April the remnants of our squadrons in Greece were hastily evacuated to Crete. There was not much left of them. The famous No. 211 Bomber Squadron had been wiped out on April 13th and many of our fighters, including some newly arrived Hurricanes, had been shot up and destroyed on the ground. The R.A.F. brought back from Greece fourteen Blenheims, only half of which were serviceable, fourteen Gladiators, only six serviceable, and six Hurricanes. These were all that were left of Nos. 30, 33, 80 and 112 Squadrons. In addition nine Blenheims of No. 203 Squadron had arrived from Egypt. Most of these aircraft now began to operate from Heraklion, the remainder from Maleme. Retimo was, as yet, little more than an emergency landing-strip.

The total at one time in May reached the not very formidable figure of 36 aircraft, scarcely any of them in really satisfactory condition. These, it was understood, would have to cope with an attack from over 300 long-range bombers, between 200 and 300 dive bombers, and over 300 fighters. No more puny David ever faced a well-accoutred and confident Goliath.

Allusion has already been made to the presence on the island of the 16,000 Italian prisoners of war captured during the Italian campaign. We had been anxious to have these removed to the greater security of Egypt, but the Greek Government had shown itself reluctant to agree, fearing that such an action would be regarded as contrary to international law. It was not until just before the attack opened that we obtained their consent, with the result that it proved too late by that time to organize the evacuation of the prisoners—we soon had another and more urgent evacuation to consider—and though we succeeded in carrying off the officer prisoners to Egypt, practically all the remainder were subsequently freed by their German allies. Although these men can hardly be considered a significant accession to Axis strength it is regrettable that arrangements were not made to convey them to Egypt weeks before, when our transports were returning empty from conveying troops to Greece.

4

The Plans

GENERAL Freyberg was under no illusions about the formidable nature of the task which had been allotted to him. At the beginning of May he pointed out to the Middle East Command, and also to the New Zealand Government—as was his right and duty—the inadequacy of the means at his disposal for meeting an attack. Only numerically would his men be sufficient to cope with an airborne assault: in all other respects his resources fell short of the necessary minimum. Besides our weakness in the air and the difficulty our naval forces would experience in repelling a seaborne attack, artillery, entrenching tools, transport, and reserve supplies of every sort were lacking. Therefore he urged that the decision to hold Crete be reconsidered if it were not possible to send adequate reinforcement.

By way of reply General Wavell could only endorse Freyberg's impression of the gravity of the position; but in view of the definite instructions from the War Cabinet that Crete must be held, he had no choice in the matter; and even if the question were re-considered it was doubtful now if the island could be evacuated before the Germans attacked. Admiral Cunningham would give the fullest possible support by sea. Air support would be more difficult, for we were going through a very lean period as regards fighter aircraft in the Middle East, but every effort would be made to obtain further reinforcements from home.

'I fully realize', wrote General Wavell, 'the difficulties and dangers of your situation. . . We have very anxious times ahead in the Middle East for the next few weeks.'

It was true enough. A victorious Rommel lay on the frontier of Egypt, with little between him and the supreme prize of the Nile Delta. Iraq was in revolt and there were ugly mutterings and indications of German activity in Syria. Only in Abyssinia, where Addis Ababa had been entered on May 5th and where the enemy resistance was fast folding up, was the military situation in the least encouraging. Indeed, the period of six weeks covering the month of May and the first half of June 1941 was, for Britain, among the most critical of the whole war. Wavell had scraped the bottom of the barrel to provide the necessary minimum of manpower and material for his many fronts. He had spread his meagre resources to plug the most urgent cracks—and there was simply not enough to go round. Somewhere—Crete, Libya, Iraq, or Syria—a crack would widen and the German flood pour in.

Faced with a regretful *non possumus* General Freyberg continued to organize his defence as best he could with the limited resources at his disposal. Whatever shortcomings may be found with the planning or execution of the defence of Crete, Military Intelligence is not among them. The preliminary forecasts of the time, place and method of the German attack proved remarkably accurate and were confirmed by last-minute information from captured enemy airmen. It was not that we were lacking in information or made any serious misjudgments regarding the coming attack (the important misjudgments were all on the enemy side), but that we lacked the resources with which to counter the invasion.

Freyberg and his improvised staff realized that the assault would be delivered in a series of phases. First, an intensive air attack for several days in succession upon the landing-grounds and their vicinity. Then, the dropping of paratroops on or around the airfields. Thirdly, the arrival of troop-carrying aircraft, so soon as the airfields had been cleared by parachutists. Fourthly, the follow-up with seaborne landings on the beaches in the neighbourhood of the airfields and a seaborne attack directed against Suda Bay itself.

Since it would have been quite impractical to have attempted a thin 'cordon' defence of the whole coast, and since all the indications suggested four areas of especial danger, Freyberg organized his forces in four commands to protect respectively Heraklion town and airfield; the landing-ground at Retimo; the port of Suda Bay with the adjacent town of Canea; and, fourthly, the airfield of Maleme.

At Heraklion, under Brigadier B.H. Chappel, were stationed two battalions of the 14th Brigade (2nd York and Lancaster and 2nd Black Watch); the 2/4th Australian Battalion supported by the 7th Medium Regiment R.A. organized and armed as infantry; the 156th Light A.A Battery; one troop and one section of the 7th Australian Light A.A. Battery; one section of the 15th Coast Regiment, R.A.; and six light and two infantry ('I') tanks. Two Greek battalions were to be added, also the 2nd Leicestershire Regiment when it arrived on May 16th.

At Retimo Brigadier G.A. Vasey was in command with his own 19th Australian Brigade forming the core of the defence. The brigade had been reformed since Greece and now consisted of the 2/1st, 2/7th and 2/11th Battalions, with the 2/8th Battalion only two companies strong. An Australian machine-gun company and two Greek battalions were also in this sector, which contained two localities particularly favourable for a landing from the sea. One of these was between Retimo town and the landing-ground, situated close to the shore and about five miles to the east; the other was the flat, open beach of Georgeopolis, dozen miles west of Retimo.

Vasey accordingly divided his force, setting up his headquarters at Georgeopolis with two of his Australian battalions (2/7th and 2/8th). The remainder, consisting of the 2/1st and 2/11th Australian Battalions, the two Greek battalions, some supporting artillery and two Infantry tanks, was detached to form an eastern force under Colonel I. R. Campbell, Commanding the 2/1st Battalion. It was considered likely that the eastern and western parts of the Retimo command would have to act independently of one another once operations started. This indeed proved to be the case.

No anti-aircraft guns were available for the protection of Retimo landing-ground; but two 'I' tanks were dug in, one at either end of the ground.

At Suda-Canea Major General Weston directed the defence. His ground forces were practically limited to the personnel of the Mobile Naval Base Defence Organization; the Northumberland Hussars (102nd Anti-Tank Regiment) who were posted with rifles to defend the isthmus leading to the Akrotiri peninsula; the 16th and 17th composite Australian battalions, together totalling little more than 600 men, on the coast east of Suda; and a Greek battalion. But much of the anti-aircraft armament was concentrated here: the 151st and 234th Heavy A.A. Batteries, the 129th Light A.A. Battery, the 7th Australian Light A.A. Battery less two troops and one section, the 304th Searchlight Battery, and the 15th Coast Regiment less one section.

Ten miles west of Canea along the coast road was the newly constructed airfield of Maleme. Here the defence was mainly entrusted to the New Zealanders lately returned from Greece. General Freyberg being in command of the whole garrison of Crete, Brigadier E. Puttick was acting commander of the division. Covering Maleme airfields was the 5th New Zealand Brigade (21st, 22nd and 23rd Battalions and 28th Maori Battalion), under Brigadier J. Hargest, supported by a composite battalion of New Zealanders, known at that time as Oakes Force but later to be brigaded with the New Zealand divisional cavalry, the 20th New Zealand Battalion and two Greek battalions to form the 10th New Zealand Brigade under Colonel H. K. Kippenberger. The particular task of the brigade was to hold a defensive position covering the village of Galatas from the west and also a stretch of coast west of Canea.

There were also available three Greek battalions, two troops of the 156th Light A.A. Battery and a troop of the 7th Australian Light A.A. Battery.

As at Retimo and Heraklion, two 'I' tanks covered the airfield. Three more 'I' tanks were on the way, and the remaining ten light tanks were also allotted to this sector.

So our forces were disposed in order to defend four—or rather five—localities stretched along more than 70 miles of coast and connected by one coastal road. Where to place reserves for prompt counter-attack was not easy to decide. Judging that the crucial sector was situated between Suda Bay and Maleme, Freyberg concentrated both the 1st Welch Regiment and the 4th New Zealand Brigade (less the 20th Battalion) of Brigadier L. M. Inglis, in this area. The former was designated to operate towards Suda, the latter towards Maleme, but both were to remain in touch with Force Headquarters and one another, ready to move in any direction that seemed immediately threatened.

Force Headquarters were in dugouts on the south-eastern side of Canea.

These dispositions, however, give a decidedly false impression of the actual strength and power of our forces in each sector. The units that had returned from Greece were weak in numbers and were very short of equipment, though Freyberg had done his best to ensure that every man possessed at least a minimum power of self-defence, by retaining a proportion of rifles from all units that we had been able to re-ship to Egypt. But apart from a few light automatics there was an acute lack of other infantry weapons. The Cypriot and Palestinian troops who ran into several hundreds were largely unarmed.

Some units consisted of artillerymen without their guns; and apart from the anti-aircraft batteries the only guns we possessed at the beginning of May were a number of captured Italian pieces and a very few British 3.7-inch howitzers for static defence.

The troops who had been brought from Greece possessed little more than what they stood up in. By a redistribution of blankets it was found possible to provide almost every man with one, but the lack of cooking utensils and mess tins was a matter of practical inconvenience. Worse still was the shortage of entrenching tools. There had never been enough in Crete to undertake the large-scale defence works necessary for the protection of the island. Now, with the garrison suddenly swollen to five times its previous size, there were nothing like enough, and some men were to be reduced to the primitive expedient of digging trenches by scooping out the earth with their steel helmets. This lack of entrenching tools led to heavy casualties in our counter-attacks, since our troops often had not the means to dig in quickly and consolidate the ground they gained.

In view of the makeshift way in which the force had been built up it was natural that there should be an acute shortage of transport. None had been brought out of Greece, and naturally in an island so poor as Crete there was little that could be commandeered locally. Even brigadiers found themselves without cars, and a battalion which possessed as much as one truck and one staff car to serve all purposes considered itself lucky. Too much importance however, can be attached to this lack of vehicles, for road convoys could scarcely have moved by day, owing to the complete domination of the air by the enemy; also, distances were short, and the troops had little to carry. Yet an adequate supply of trucks would have been invaluable when we were faced with the necessity of speedy concentration in order to deliver a counter-attack while it was still dark.

The general policy of the defence was to dispose about one-third of the total force allotted to each locality on, or in the immediate neighbourhood of the airfield. These men would bear the brunt of the first assault. The remaining two-thirds were so located that they would be outside the probable area of parachute and troop-carrier landings. Thus our infantry defence would form, in effect, an inner and an outer ring. The inner ring would get to grips at the start, the outer would be available for a speedy counter-attack. The necessity of covering the probable landing-beaches from a seaborne attack involved a further commitment for many of the troops.

It has been suggested that a risk might have been taken with the beaches, on the assumption that the Navy could be left to take care of the sea invasion, and that the maximum strength could have been concentrated in the neighbourhood of the airfields. This would have been a totally unjustified gamble. The seas are wide—an elementary fact not always realized by amateur strategists—and whatever the vigilance of the Royal Navy there could clearly be no guarantee against small forces slipping through at night. Freyberg could not possibly have taken such a risk. Also he was afterwards of opinion that the Germans made an inexplicable mistake in not attempting seaborne landings by day. They could have provided ample air cover against attacks by the Royal Navy, and there were many suitable beaches.

Since the airfields were in use by our own aircraft to within twenty-four hours of the German attack, the policy of defence depended rather upon shooting down the enemy in the air than on rendering the landing-strips unusable through extensive demolitions. Consequently the Bofors guns of our light anti-aircraft batteries were sited well forward towards the edge of the airfields in positions where concealment was extremely difficult and sometimes impossible. It was a real tactical dilemma. Place your Bofors close enough to deal with low-flying troop-carriers, and they are liable to be destroyed by the preliminary bombing from the air; place them further back where they can be effectively concealed, and their capacity for dealing with the enemy aircrafts is gravely, perhaps fatally diminished. The only satisfactory solution lay in adopting concealed and camouflaged positions as close to the airfield as possible, in shifting the guns repeatedly and at the same time providing numbers of dummy anti-aircraft guns to mislead the attacking aircraft. But this could not be done on an effective scale except by consistent effort over an extended period: the frequent changes of command and the lack of sufficient labour, tools and material were fatal to the realization of such a scheme of defence.

At each landing-ground the 'I' tanks were dug in with a view to sweeping the field with fire as the German airborne troops arrived. These tanks could hardly be employed in a more mobile role, for their engines were mostly worn and unreliable. The light tanks, such as were available, were to be used as the spearhead for counter-attacks.

Fire from all but the anti-aircraft guns was to be withheld until the preliminary bombardment was over. Infantry might open fire when parachutists began to descend, but the field guns and tanks would, in principle, only open up when troop-carrying aircraft started to land. Otherwise there was a danger of gun sites and infantry positions being prematurely revealed to the enemy and severely dealt with by his air forces. Some Bofors were ordered to remain silent during the first stage of the attack.

5

The Enemy

WHILE Freyberg was improvising his makeshift defence, organizing a staff out of regimental officers gathered in almost literally from the highways and hedges, forming composite infantry units of 'gunners who had lost their guns, sappers who had lost their tools and R.A.S.C. drivers who had lost their cars', arranging for the digging of defensive positions which should have been initiated six months earlier, a few score miles away across the straits of Kithira the German Command, in a very different spirit and with the confidence which comes from a knowledge of greatly superior power, an almost perfected battle technique and the prestige of continuous victory, was meticulously preparing for a unique enterprise.

There was every reason to suppose that the attack on Crete represented the first move in a general all-out offensive against the British position in the Middle East, that offensive which had been the dream of Hermann Goering and the nightmare of every responsible British commander. The invasion of Crete seemed to link up naturally with the German-incited revolt in Iraq, with the highly equivocal conduct of General Dentz who held Syria for Vichy France, and with Rommel's offensive across Cyrenaica. It appeared to be the logical preliminary to a further airborne operation against Cyprus which would help to create a band of Axis-controlled territory—Crete, the Dodecanese, Cyprus, Syria, Iraq, perhaps Persia—across the Middle East, shutting off General Wavell's forces from their vital sources of oil and completing the operation by means of a gigantic double envelopment or 'pincer' (the hackneyed word is occasionally also the *mot juste*) movement against the Nile Delta.

Here it is appropriate to notice a Directive issued by the Führer's Headquarters on May 23rd, 1941, three days after the German attack on Crete had begun and we were already occupied in restoring the situation in Iraq. This Directive runs:

> The Arab Freedom Movement is, in the Middle East, our natural ally against England. In this connection, the raising of rebellion in Iraq is of special importance. Such rebellion will extend across the Iraq frontiers to strengthen the forces which are hostile to England in the Middle East, intercept the English lines of communication and tie down both English troops and English shipping space at the expense of other theatres of war. For these reasons I have decided to push the development of operations in the Middle East by going to the support of Iraq. Whether, and in what way it may later be possible to wreck finally the English position between the Mediterranean and the Persian Gulf, in conjunction with an offensive against the Suez Canal, is still in the lap of the Gods....

179

The decision to occupy Crete, stated as 'for the purpose of using the island as an air base against Britain', was not actually taken until April 21st, but preparations for the attack thereafter developed concurrently with the last stage of the Greek campaign; and while our forces were embarking from the ports of southern Greece the German engineers were already at work upon the landing-grounds to be employed by the fighters, dive-bombers and transport aircraft. In some cases, as for example at Araxos, they found airfields just completed and awaiting their occupation, but elsewhere they got straight away to work, commandeering local labour and sparing neither their serfs nor themselves. Making all allowances for the more satisfactory weather, the sureness with which they selected their sites and the rapidity with which they constructed or improved upon existing installations almost takes one's breath away. Their ground troops arrived at Myloi near Navplion in the last days of April; within a week an airfield had been constructed and was already in use. On the west flank of Crete a forward landing-ground was rapidly constructed upon Aphrodite's island of Kithira; on the eastern flank the landing-ground at Scarpanto was improved and enlarged. Milos was not occupied by German troops until May 10th; but May 13th a landing-ground was already in use: the survey party started work while fighting was still in progress on the island, and the enemy did not scruple to employ the forced labour of British prisoners. On the mainland local labour was conscripted quite ruthlessly. By contrast with British usage which, in consideration for the susceptibilities of our ally, refrained from the conscription of available labour either in Greece or Crete, the Germans took what they wanted—and they certainly showed results. By mid-May they had a ring of forward landing-grounds on the most advanced islands, from which single-engine fighters could operate. Dive-bombers and twin-engine fighters were to use the three aerodromes round Athens (Menidi, Hassani, Elevsis), and also Corinth and Argos; the transport places would work from the Athens airfields, from the Isthmus and from Tanagra, back on the plain of Boeotia; while the heavier bombers would be based mainly upon the airfields of Macedonia, southern Bulgaria and Rhodes.

The troops selected for the first wave of the attack on Crete were drawn from the IX Air Corps of General Student, who had been in charge of the parachutist operations in the Low Countries a year earlier and who was to end the war in command of the Parachute Army, fighting as infantry in the last retreat from the Rhine to

Hamburg. The full strength of the 7th Air Division was to be employed, together with the glider-borne 1st Assault Regiment, and in support the 5th Mountain Division. Of the Air Division about 8,000 men would be used in parachute attacks, the remaining 2,000 going by sea with the heavy equipment; at least two-thirds of the mountain division would be conveyed directly to battle in troop-carriers; the remainder, two battalions strong, would follow by sea.

The air component was drawn from General von Richtofen's VIII Air Corps which could provide about 600 troop-carriers (JU 52), capable of transporting several thousand fully equipped men with light support weapons, and also supplies. These would be supported by 280 bombers (JU 88, ME 111, DO 17), 150 divebombers (JU 87), 90 twin-engine fighters (ME 110) and a further 90 single-engine fighters (ME 109) and about 40 reonnaissance planes.

The troops allotted to 'Operation Mercury', the seizure of Crete, were therefore made up as follows:

Glider troops . .	750
Paratroops. . . .	10,000
Airlanding troops .	5,000
Seaborne troops.	7,000
TOTAL	22,750

These forces were to be divided into a Centre Group (Major-General Süsmann) consisting of the bulk of the 7th Air Division (less one regiment and one battalion), to be reinforced on the following day by a rifle regiment of the 5th Mountain Division; a Western Group (Major-General Meindl) composed of the glider-borne Assault Regiment (a part of which was to be dropped by parachute) and another rifle regiment of the 5th Mountain Division; and an Eastern Group (Colonel Brauer), which had one parachutist regiment and one airborne mountain regiment.

The same astronomical terminology which had given the code name of Mercury to the whole operation was maintained in the nomenclature of the groups, which were known as 'Mars' (Centre), 'Komet' (West) and 'Orion' (East).

The task of Mars was to land a little to the west and south of Canea; clear the country as far west as Galatas, as far south as the mountain spine of Crete and as far east as Suda Bay; and take the town of Canea. A sub-section would be landed at Retimo in the afternoon and, having captured the town and airstrip, would proceed west in captured transport to link up with the main body near Suda. A further sub-section, under Colonel Heidrich (afterwards to achieve fame as commander of the 1st Parachute Division in defence of Cassino in 1944) would clear the area south-east of Canea on the Canea-Alikianou road, deepening the 'bridgehead' and getting into position for the attack upon Suda, which was to take place on the following day.

In the west, Group Komet had the task of capturing Maleme airfield and the road and sea approaches, after which it was to link up with Mars on the Canea road.

Group Orion had the similarly straightforward role of taking the town and airfield of Heraklion, following a landing at 3.15 p.m. that same afternoon.

Thus, it was intended that by the end of the first day of the battle the assault troops should be in possession of all three airfields, the town of Canea, the town and port of Heraklion, and the town of Retimo, while they should have neutralized Suda Bay and be in a position to take control of the harbour early on the morrow. Their western and centre groups, it was estimated, should already have made contact with one another, and practically the whole of the coast from Maleme to Retimo would be in German hands. On the second day Suda would be attacked and taken and further reinforcements, with the heavy weapons, would arrive by sea.

The remaining pockets of resistance would be cleared up on the third day.

Two concentrations of ships were available, mainly composed of commandeered Greek vessels. They were primarily to carry the heavy weapons, motor transport and supplies necessary to ensure that the positions gained by the assault could be successfully maintained. On the second day of the battle one convoy would make for the open coast west of Maleme while the destination of the other would be the coast east of Heraklion. Each of these two 'fleets' carried a further rifle battalion of the 5th Mountain Division, as an additional guarantee that the assault would be adequately reinforced even if the landing of troop-carriers on the three airfields were delayed by our destruction of the runways.

It was known that our Mediterranean Fleet was at sea, scouring the waters to intercept just such a seaborne operation as this; but the Germans reckoned that the all-powerful *Luftwaffe* would be equal to the task of defending the invasion flotillas. They were quite ready to match their dive-bombers against the anti-aircraft armament of our warships.

The whole operation had been prepared with that elaborate care and method characteristic of the German military mind. The reconnaissance work was generally admirable, though the value of the German air photography was diminished by the fact that, in some sectors at any rate, no photographs had been taken during the last week before the attack, during which time various changes in our dispositions had been made. It is particularly remarkable that the field hospital on the little peninsula about two miles west of Canea was marked on German maps merely as 'tented encampment' and that the attackers who were launched upon it were clearly unprepared to find no one but doctors, hospital orderlies, nurses and wounded there. Moreover, the habitual inaccuracy of their Military Intelligence, which was one of the major phenomena of the whole war, led to a dangerous misjudgement of the strength of the defending forces. The organization of Admiral Canaris had reported that there were no Greek troops on Crete and the total of the British forces amounted to about 5,000 men.[1] The British, Australian and New Zealand troops, quite apart from the Greeks, amounted to more than five times that number.

In consequence, it was reckoned that an assaulting force of approximately 23,000 men would be more than adequate to obtain possession of Crete, and it was intended, as we have seen, that the whole affair should be completed in three days. With astonishing naïveté the Germans believed that the Cretans, anxious to enjoy (in the words of the official German appreciation of the situation before the attack) 'the favourable terms which had been arranged on the mainland with the German forces', would actively assist, or at the very least would not hinder the invaders. This strange assumption would appear to be based on the knowledge that the people of Crete, being Venizelists almost to a man, had been widely out of sympathy with the internal policy of the Metaxas dictatorship; that *a fortiori* they were convinced democrats, and therefore profoundly opposed to the Totalitarian Monster, and that, above all, they were patriots does not seem to have penetrated the German mind.

[1] Estimates from German XII Army Intelligence sources were more nearly correct. They placed our strength at two British infantry brigades and one brigade of artillery. But they too were inclined to ignore the number of troops brought from Greece.

With this degree of misinformation, both numerical and psychological, it is not surprising that General Lohr who directed the battle from his headquarters in Athens, should have considered two highly trained and well equipped divisions quite sufficient to carry through Operation Mercury. As a further insurance, however, the 6th Mountain Division was held in reserve in the Athens area in case it should be required.

It was, indeed, required.

6

Prelude to Assault

THE May days drifted by over Crete in brilliant sunshine and cloudless skies, and the slender sickle of the moon swelled nightly towards the full circle as the men under General Freyberg's command prepared their hasty and improvised defences, struggling to achieve, in a few days and with wholly inadequate means, a degree of strength and a capacity for resistance for which the six months that the locust had eaten—those months of untroubled occupation—had been so unsatisfactory a preparation.

No one could doubt that the attack was coming. British Intelligence forecast it, Lord Haw-Haw on the German radio gloated almost nightly over the prospect, the *Drang nach Osten* of German strategy seemed to demand it. The first reports suggested that it might be launched even as early as May 1st or May 2nd. Then, when the days passed and the invasion tarried, there seemed good reason to believe that the 15th or 16th would be the chosen date. That at all events gave some respite, and Freyberg took from it what advantage he was able. His sense of realism was undiminished, but it was matched and exceeded by his greatness of heart and the Homeric gusto with which he welcomed situations of exceptional hazard. Driving round the island from one position to another, he managed to infuse something of his own dynamic spirit into the defenders, to such an extent that by May 16th he was able to report 'all ranks are fit and morale is now high....I feel at least that we will give a good account of ourselves. With the help of the Royal Navy I trust that Crete will be held.'

But it was bombers' weather during these bright, still, cloudless days. From the beginning of the month the buzz of their engines was repeatedly audible overhead. At first they concentrated mainly against the ships approaching or lying off the island bringing the much-needed supplies and equipment to the garrison. As there were no ports on the south coast that could be used, and no adequate means of transferring the supplies across the island even if there had been ports, the convoys, as we know, had to run the gauntlet of the channel between Crete and Krithia or between Crete and the Dodecanese.

The majority of the cargoes were unloaded at Suda Bay, with repeated interruption from the *Luftwaffe*. Shipping losses steadily increased until by May 19th there were no less than 13 damaged, sunk or partially submerged hulls in Suda harbour, and it was becoming clear that, with a continuation of bombing on this scale, the entrance to the port would be effectively and perhaps permanently blocked.

Day after day a black pall of smoke from the burning petrol stores in ships bombed by the Germans hung over Suda Bay. The losses were growing very serious and supply was dropping further and further behind our needs in terms of rations, while our build-up of arms, ammunition and transport vehicles was developing only very slowly. Half the guns and more than half the R.E. stores despatched between May 1st and May 20th were sunk en route or in harbour.

But during this period the garrison did receive certain important reinforcements: the Royal Marines of the Mobile Naval Base Defence Organization with their anti-aircraft batteries and searchlights; the 2nd Leicestershire; the tanks of the 3rd Hussars and the 7th R. Tank Regiment; and the 1st Argyll and Sutherland Highlanders. General Freyberg also received forty-six field guns with three hundred rounds per gun. Ammunition had been brought up to the total of 1,450 tons, enough for several days' operations if it could be effectively distributed; but that, in view of the difficulty of transport and communications, was almost impossible to do.

Daily the Germans came over Suda, bombing almost at leisure and at will, though not always without loss. Under these conditions it had been decided to run in supplies only at night in ships fast enough to unload, turn round and be well away from port before dawn. This practically limited the number of vessels available to the faster warships of the Royal Navy. At the same time the constant air raids notably diminished the quantity and reliability of civilian labour. Despite the losses en route, the rate of unloading and disposal of the cargoes failed to keep pace with the rate of arrival of the ships. Ships had to hang about off Suda quay in imminent danger from enemy bombing, or put to sea again without discharging; at best, the cargo was liable to be hastily unloaded and then left about on the quayside.

To meet this emergency volunteers, preferably with previous experience as dockers, were requested from the Australian and New Zealand troops stationed around Suda. About 400 offered themselves and were organized in shifts. Through the short and perilous nights these men put in a tremendous job: they worked in constant and deadly danger, for the German bombers were over night after night. It made no difference to the effort of these stalwart volunteers from the Dominions.

'You can dive over the side if the ship you are on is hit by a bomb,' the officer commanding the Australians told them. 'Otherwise, you must keep right on with the job, even if the bombs are falling all round you.'

So it was usually possible to unload at least 500 or 600 tons nightly. During the whole period between April 29th and May 20th some 15,000 tons of stores were landed at Suda. It represented something like 70 per cent of the estimated current total required to feed and maintain the troops and the civilian population in Crete.

On May 13th the main bombing effort shifted to the airfields and to the anit-aircraft positions around them. The purpose was plain enough. The Germans aimed at destroying the three dozen R.A.F. aircraft operating in Crete and knocking out the anti-aircraft guns which might subsequently oppose their own landings. It was what the *Luftwaffe* had attempted and so signally failed to do at the beginning of the Battle of Britain. But in Crete our serviceable aircraft were a mere handful, our airfields were only three in number, and there was no reserve of machines, of manpower or of space that could serve the defence.

The few damaged Hurricanes or obsolete Gladiators that remained fought gamely to the last. They shot down during this period a number estimated as 23 enemy aircraft with another nine 'probables' and a further eleven damaged. But having to engage repeatedly in action with quite insufficient periods for re-servicing, they gradually dropped out of the air if they were not shot up on the ground. By May 19th only three Hurricanes and three Gladiators were left. This tiny force had no means of providing its own cover and represented only a further commitment, since it was necessary to keep an aerodrome in readiness and ground staff available.

And so on Mondany, May 19th, these six aircraft were flown away to Egypt and orders were given to render the airfields useless. It was too late. There was not time now to carry out demolitions, for the German airborne attack came in on the morning after our remaining aircraft were withdrawn. Earlier in the month, while we were still conducting air operations from Maleme, Major F. M. Hanson of the New Zealand Royal Engineers had asked permission to mine or crater the airfield. Authority was not granted. Our aircraft, who were to continue their reconnaissance flights for as long as possible, could not be moved to Retimo or Heraklion because no transport was available to transfer their ground crews and equipment.

After the loss of the island much stress was laid upon the importance of the German capture of Maleme, the only airfield the enemy succeeded in taking by his airborne assaults. One critic has written:

> It was indispensable to the Germans to capture an airfield in Crete. They tried and failed to capture Retimo and Heraklion. The airfield they did capture was Maleme. And it was the possession of Maleme that enabled them to reinforce their ground troops and operate their aircraft from Crete. It is little wonder that Hanson, in a report on the Crete operations, wrote with some bitterness:
> 'I still feel that a major mistake was made in not making the (Maleme) aerodrome unsuitable for landing planes'.[1]

Yet while one must sympathize with Major Hanson's views, it can hardly be contended that the failure adequately to wreck Maleme was itself of decisive significance. Even before they obtained control of the airfield itself the Germans were landing their troop-carriers in the bed of the Tavronitis on its western side; and at Heraklion on a plateau far from the airfield. There seems litte doubt that they would have continued to come in, accepting the consequent losses, and used any place where an aircraft could make a landing.

From May 14th onwards the German air attacks were concentrated against the anti-aircraft guns and the men in the slit trenches around them. The bombers pin-pointed their targets at leisure. The fighters, finding that there was little occasion to concern themselves with warding off attacks on the bombers they were escorting, were diverted, day after day, to attack on their own account the defence positions among the olive groves.

[1] Hetherington, *Airborne Invasion*,

It was a grim experience for the men who crouched in their slit trenches under orders not to fire at the German aircraft until the attack by airborne troops actually opened, for fear of giving away their positions. Supplies reached them fitfully by night, for the roads were under almost constant air attack during the day.

The astonishing thing is that so little harm was done by these almost unopposed bombing attacks and these 'ground-straffings' carried out by fighters often coming down as low as fifty feet from the ground. The selection and digging of gun-positions had, it is true, been one of the few defensive precautions taken in hand at an early stage of the occupation, some hard work had been put in on camouflage, and slit trenches among olive groves are in any case extraordinarily difficult to detect from the air. In some respects high-level bombing from an unseen enemy is the harder to endure: both the dive-bombers and the low-flying machine-gunning fighter are always a good deal more dangerous in appearance than in reality to trained troops. Even on May 19th, when the airfield raids reached a crescendo of intensity—sure sign of an impending attack—no direct hit was scored upon any of the guns around Maleme. Some slight mechanical damage was done to the predictors and heightfinders by 'near misses', but that was all. Our casualties that day from air attacks on Maleme amounted to one man killed and three wounded.

For the whole period of a week during which the enemy aircraft worked to 'soften up' our powers of resistance the total losses among our anti-aircraft troops were only six killed and eleven wounded. And in two companies of the Black Watch the total casualties during eight days amounted to three.

But whether by accident or design there is little doubt that the German tactics which forced the defenders to keep their heads down made them slow to observe the approach of the first troop-carriers. What happens in the first minutes of an airborne assault often decides the issue between success and failure. It is in those first minutes, while his enemy is still in the air, or on his way to the ground, or has but just landed, that the defender enjoys the advantage and has his best chance of wiping out the attack.

Far away to the north at Hildesheim in the heart of Germany the crack Assault Regiment that was to make the initial landing by glider had been assembled, and had been brought down by train to the Salonika area in the first days of May. Paratroop units were moving from Bulgaria and converging upon northern Greece at the same time. An air of intense mystery distinguished the preparations for the attack, in remarkable contrast with the gloating forewarnings of Dr. Goebbels and William Joyce over the radio. No pains were spared to ensure the utmost secrecy of movement to the concentration areas. The troops were instructed to remove their parachute badges; their special equipment was kept under lock and key; their vehicles, when they moved by road, had the identification marks painted out; paybooks were exchanged for identity cards which gave no indication of the bearer's unit; the strictest censorship was enforced upon private mail; the men entrained under cover of darkness; and even the singing of parachute songs was strictly forbidden during the journey.

Three years later the most meticulous precautions were taken to ensure secrecy among the forces preparing for the assault landing in Normandy, but it is doubtful whether even the detailed and effective security measures employed by the Anglo-American Command on that occasion exceeded in thoroughness the restrictions applied among General Student's men for an operation of which the probability, locale and timing had been so accurately forecast by our Intelligence.

That the private soldier was not taken into the confidence of the command as much as might have been expected, and as would certainly have been the custom before an operation of a similar type in our own Army during the later part of the war, seems established from the fact that the majority were not informed of their destination until an hour or two before the aircraft took off, and some not until after they were in the air. Many had little idea of the names of the positions they were to attack, though it appears to have been impressed upon all of them that the first objectives were to be taken within forty minutes of landing. As if to balance these deficiencies in information, special phrase-books were issued, of the type usually supplied to foreign tourists, containing sentences considered likely to be useful to the invaders translated into (phoenetic) English, such as the following: 'If yu lei yu uill be schott!'

The speed with which this highly complex undertaking had been laid on necessarily involved certain hitches in the organization. To mount an operation involving the employment of some twelve hundred aircraft of various types was a colossal undertaking. To base it on the barren, poor and ill-provided territory of the Greek peninsula was bound to multiply the difficulties. The small and sparsely-equipped airfields of Attica and its neighbourhood were over-burdened with the number of squadrons that were detailed to operate from them. The official report of XI Air Corps, published after the battle, complains ruefully of the lack of ground organization and supply services. Owing to the destruction of bridges on the single railway line from the north and the damage done to the roads by our demolitions, practically all the supplies required had to come by sea to Corinth and Piraeus. Our minefields and the activities of our submarines helped to delay the arrival of the ships and throw the timetable out of gear. And when the ships did reach the ports the unloading of the cargoes at the blitzed quaysides, with local labour inadequate and unwilling, proved slow and difficult.

The date for the attack had originally been fixed for May 15th. But delays in the arrival of the supply ships, combined with the difficulty of providing adequate quantities of petrol for the many airfields that were in use, caused a postponement until May 18th and then again until May 20th.

Our Intelligence had been well informed when it forecast May 15-16th as the most probable dates. Then, on May 18th two German airmen, who had baled out after their aircraft had been hit, were fished out of the sea off the coast of Crete. To their Cretan captors, whom they oddly supposed would be in sympathy with the 'liberating' German forces, they frankly admitted that the invasion was timed to take place soon after dawn on May 20th. The information was duly conveyed to General Freyberg.

Freyberg had done all that he could within the straitened limits of his resources and in the brief time allowed to him. Neither he nor Wavell was under any illusion about the dangers that beset Crete, and the deficiencies of its garrison. He had had a bare three weeks of desperate improvisation in which to set his defences in order. Now he faced the very *élite* of an army which could choose its own time for such an occasion as this, an occasion for the employment of great resources, immense technical skill, tactical ingenuity and unquestioned human courage of a high order.

CHAPTER II

The First Day

I

Airborne Invasion

TUESDAY, May 20th, dawned in glorious summer weather. Scarcely a wind disturbed a serenely cloudless sky, and in the clear Mediterranean air the watcher on the island could see a full twenty miles out to sea.

Over came the German aircraft. To the men who shook themselves shivering from their single blankets (the nights were still astonishingly cold) it was just the customary early morning 'hate', and they dived for the slit-trenches with what was now becoming the speed born of habit. The long whine and thud of the falling bomb, the increasing buzz and roar of the dive-bomber, the quick rattle of machine-gun fire from the accompanying fighters—they had heard it all before, every day for the past week. And despite the information which had reached the Command no general order had yet informed the troop that this Tuesday was 'The Day'.

It was at 6.30 a.m. that the air attack had begun, and when, after an hour of bombing and 'ground-straffing', the bombardment was clearly intensifying rather than diminishing in scale the Headquarters of Suda Area decided that this was indeed the grand attack, and Operations Room, Canea, issued warnings to all anti-aircraft positions.

While the gunners were being pinned to earth by the bombardment the first German transport aircraft were approaching across the southern Aegean, moving over the western extremity of the island and approaching Maleme and Canea from the south-west, the landward side.

This is how it appeared to an eye-witness:

At about 7.30 a.m. some of the other officers and I were standing near the mess tent, chatting and waiting for breakfast to be served, when suddenly without any warning there was a terrific outburst of ack-ack fire. We all sprang into the slit-trenches, thinking that this was just another of the ordinary raids we had got so used to lately. But this time it was something very different. Before we knew what was happening, the skies were full of Germans planes which had apparently sprung from no-where. There seemed to be hundreds of them, diving, zooming and criss-crossing as they bombed and machine-gunned all over the place. Then a flight of large silvery machines passed low down over our heads, coming from the south-west and making for Canea. They passed as silently as ghosts with just a swishing sound instead of the usual roar, and their wings were very long and tapering. It was only then I understood that these were *gliders* and that an airborne attack on Crete had begun in grim earnest.

Shells from our ack-ack batteries were bursting all around the gliders and their accompanying planes, but these were so many and our guns so pitifully few that little damage seemed to be caused. I saw one glider twist sideways with a jerk and come down behind the trees at a very steep slant, and I guessed that it must have crashed, but most of the others—about thirty, I esti-mated—slid serenely on and descended in the direction of Canea. They were going much slower than an ordinary plane and I re-flected what a hash a few of our Hurricanes would have made of them if only they had been there.

From the gliders which made their landing sprang armed men with mortars, machine-guns, tommy-guns, and hand-grenades. All were ready for instant action, and could move at once in compact groups as they had arrived.

To some the first intimation of the invasion came when, relieved at the temporary cessation of bombing and low level machine-gun fire, they heard the steady uninterrupted hum of approaching aircraft and, looking up, perceived the slow-moving JU 52's overhead. A British regimental officer who was at Heraklion afterwards wrote:

I must say the Nazis have little to learn about effect! The troop carriers are huge black beasts with yellow noses. They fly slowly and alomost sluggishly and with a wealth of experience and confidence in their very appearance. It is, of course, just too easy for them when they have local (I hope temporary) air superiority. Even one Hurricane could have done tremendous execution.

From the underside of the German aircraft white puffs appeared, tiny clouds that settled and then drifted rapidly down towards the earth. In a moment tiny figures could be seen attached to the parachutes, yellow, green, blue or black. These carried arms and ammunition, medical supplies and food. Some parachutes seemed to descend in groups of three; these carried down light field and anti-tank guns, most of which were dropped in separate pieces, which could be rapidly assembled and put together; but there were cases of the 20-mm. anti-tank gun being dropped complete and ready for immediate use.

Nothing seemed to have been forgotten in the equipment of the men who landed by parachute. Besides their personal arms (automatic pistol and jack-knife) they carried two or three days rations, including the specially-prepared Wittler bread sliced and wrapped in cellophane or silver paper (it was supposed to last indefinitely until unwrapped, but in fact did not); processed chocolate and rusks; tartaric acid, sugar, biscuits and thirst quenchers; cigarettes and contraceptives. They wore camouflaged overalls and crash-helmets. Their wrists and ankles were bandaged, as a rule, to lessen the risk of sprains or breaks. With their packs they carried blankets, stoves and utensils for boiling water. Doctors arrived by parachute with complete sets of surgical instruments, bandages, cotton wool, quinine and a variety of different types of drugs. To quote our regimental officer again:

> Without any exception their [the parachutists'] equipment was first-class and brand new. Their clothing is most practical and well designed and very light. For instance they have a big inside turnup to their trousers and in this they keep a spare pair of socks, vest, pants, etc. In some sort of sling pockets on the waist they had odd bits of food—small hard biscuits, sausages, etc., and their dope... and the prisoners I took complained it made them very thirsty.

It is curious to discover that a German regimental report afterwards complained that the paratroopers' uniform had proved 'quite unsuitable in this hot climate'. Quick movement was said to be impossible and many officers and men suffered from heat-stroke during the subsequent operations; the British uniform (most of our men wore battle-dress, though some fought in shirts and shorts) was considered to be superior.

At all events our antagonists displayed such energy during the struggle that the question arose as to whether special drugs were employed to maintain an abnormal degree of alertness and resistance to fatigue. It seems clear enough now, however, that the parachutists did not go into action doped in the generally accepted sense of the term. But they were supplied with tablets such as energen or pervitin, akin to benzedrine, calculated to produce energy and wakefulness, to be taken under orders or at discretion. Further than this, some at least, of the paratroops were issued with hypodermic syringes and a special preparation with which they were instructed to inject themselves or one another if subjected to prolonged fatigue.

Dr. Brett Day of Cairo told John Hetherington, the Australian war correspondent:

> Curiosity led me to investigate this matter, and as I was seeing profesionally many officers of the various units serving in the Middle East, I was ultimately able to obtain several hypodermic equipments. I have one compact taken from a German parachutist shot down in Crete. It is three and a half inches long and one inch wide. The small hypodermic syringe is of the all-glass type, fitted with a steel needle one inch long. A spare needle is in the box. The ampoules, of which there are two in each box, contain caffein-sodium salicylate. Each ampoule is of one cubic centimetre in 2 gm. solution.
>
> The therapeutic effect of this combination would be to stimulate the nervous system, particularly the higher mental faculties. The special senses, hearing, vision, smell, etc. become more perceptive. Reflexes are heightened. The use of the drug is not followed by depression. Functional increase of muscles is another consequence of its injection, and one of its outstanding effects is prevention of fatigue, both mental and physical. It is most notably a first-class agent for the prevention of sleep.
>
> I have shown one of these packet equipments to several wounded German prisoners of Rommel's Afrika Korps who were under treatment in a Cairo hospital, professing my ignorance of the usage. They told me that all their shock troops, parachutists, tank and glider, were injected with one ampoule of the solution before going into action. Immediately following the injection, they were given a glass of lemonade to drink. There is an incompatibility between caffein preparations and acid fruit juices which would theoretically increase the kick of the solution.

Our regimental officer has something to say regarding the men themselves:

> They do not run to form at all. Some were so tough that they just never gave in, and having assembled in small parties, fought on hopelessly until we killed them. Others appeared to be very resentful of the reception they had had on the way down (they had been told to expect no opposition) and after wandering helplessly for 48 hours, more or less gave themselves up with cries of 'give me water'. I could write a book about these paratroops! Such odd creatures!

Many of those who saw the descent of the parachutists agree that there was something hypnotic in the spectacle of the slow-moving aircraft spewing out their cargo of paratroops like handfuls of confetti in the bright sunlight.

This paralysis was only a matter of seconds. But the first moments are of the utmost importance in countering an airborne attack. For the parachutists were being dropped from remarkably low levels, from 600, 300, even 200 feet, and were only in the air for a matter of seconds. During those seconds they were easy targets for a cool infantryman on the ground with rifle, Bren-gun or machine-gun.

Men seized their arms and fired as the parachutists descended. Many were hit and died before they reached the ground.

'Suddenly you'd see one go limp, then give a kick and kind of straighten up with a jerk, and then go limp again, and you knew he was done for,' was one description given of the manner in which these men died in the air.

Some fired to hit with incendiaries the parachutes themselves. Bullets were seen to tear the bellying silk, setting it on fire. The men suspended from these parachutes fell heavily, breaking legs or ribs. Elsewhere parachutes were becoming entangled in the branches of trees and the men hung suspended like Absalom, waiting until some Joab arrived to put paid to their account.

That the Germans lost very heavily during this phase of the operations is clear, but it is equally clear that their losses varied greatly between one sector and another. Thus one account states that out of ten 'sample' parachutists, who jumped from a height of about 300 feet, one was killed through the failure of his 'chute' to open; one was picked off by the defending riflemen as he descended; one was put out of action by breaking a wrist or ankle on alighting; and the others 'spouted about helplessly with tommy-guns' only to be 'picked off with rifles at 600 or 700 yards distance'. Another account stated that it was impossible to hit a descending parachutist with a pistol and almost impossible with a rifle; but that it was 'easy enough with a captured German tommy-gun if you can get close enough'. On the other hand, the present writer was told by troops leaving Crete that the picking off of paratroops in the air was comparatively simple for the alert riflemen. It was asserted that the descent took as much as twenty seconds and that during this time they were extremely vulnerable.

'We fire at their feet and we can be almost certain of getting them in that way' was the summing up of these men.

A relatively small number of troops had been allocated to the glider operation, only 750 in all. But the parachutists were descending in far greater numbers, fifteen from each transport aircraft, and because the nature of their descent tended to disperse them, they appeared even more numerous than they were. Though many were killed before they reached earth and many more were so badly shaken that they were easily rounded up as prisoners, yet the speed which those who arrived uninjured rallied to their formations was most remarkable. Some of the paratroopers, though not all, carried tommy-guns and even fired them at random as they descended. The remainder, being armed only with jack-knives and pistols, collected their weapons from the containers that fell among them. Troops in the first wave carried hand-grenades, sometimes as many as four.

The first move of the parachutist after detaching himself from his cords was to seek cover. His second was to rally towards an N.C.O. or officer. Cover was abundant. Not only did the dense plantations of olive trees and vines provide shelter from view, while the deep gullies gave temporary protection from fire as well, but there was a good deal of thick undergrowth. Concealment therefore was not difficult for those who reached the ground alive and out of close range of the defenders' small-arms fire.

Those first ten minutes were the vital period: the few seconds while the paratrooper was swinging helplessly in the air; the second or two while he was sorting himself out and releasing himself from his parachute; the few minutes while he was still an isolated individual detached from other members of his unit, alone or almost alone in a jungle where men on all sides would try to kill him and where little quarter could be expected. Among the prisoners were some who seemed to be under the impression that the defence would have been obliterated by the preliminary air attacks and that they would have little to do expect 'mop up'. There was indeed a great deal of 'mopping up' done all through the day; but the active rôle was more often assumed by the British, Anzac and Greek troops than by the German invaders.

During the first hours the wildest confusion prevailed upon both sides. Such confusion is inevitable at the beginning of any paratroop battle much more so in this which remains one of the greatest and most formidable airborne operations in history. Men stalked one another among the olive groves and the thickly planted country around Canea and Maleme. It was kill or be killed. Neither side could afford to take prisoners, for there was no means of effectively securing them and few could know for certain whether they were surrounding the enemy or were themselves surrounded.

Gradually the Germans—those of them who were still alive—coalesced into groups holding certain areas of ground. The parachutes of officers or of those charged with leading a particular formation were of a distinctive colour, so that they served as provisional rallying points at the start. As information trickled back to the various British headquarters and anxious staff officers marked with blue circles on the talc covers of their maps the enemy positions, it was seen that the airborne troops were appearing in two main areas, one around Maleme airfield, the other in what was known as the Prison Valley, about four miles W.S.W. of Canea. Further landings were noted to the west and south of Canea and on the Akrotiri peninsula. The enemy was clearly fulfilling expectations by aiming at the Maleme airfield, Canea the principal town in western Crete, and the naval base at Suda.

2

Maleme

JUST to what extent the anti-aircraft defence at Maleme failed to do itself justice on that grim and fateful Tuesday morning can never now be accurately determined. Too many of the men who fought are dead. It is possible that the cry of 'Wolf! Wolf'!' had been repeated too often and that in consequence the gunners were reluctant to believe that the real airborne attack, for which everything else was a preliminary, had actually begun. It appears that some of the gun detachments were driven from their guns during the vital period.

Certainly the Bofors gunners at Maleme had an unenviable task. They had, of necessity, to be sited well forward on the edge of the airfield where concealment was practically impossible; and yet their vision was obliterated by the clouds of dust and smoke arising from the bursting bombs. In any case, the Bofors had been located, for the most part, to deal with an attack coming in from the sea; it was difficult to bring fire to bear when the German aircraft approached from the south-west. Of the heavier artillery, one section of 3-inch guns, on a ridge south of Maleme, was about 500 feet above sea-level; when the enemy flew in at heights of from 600 to 300 feet our gunners were at a manifest disadvantage.

The first German gliders drifted down and began to discharge their cargoes of armed men in the dry river-bed of the Tavronitis to the west of Maleme airfield. This was an admirable rallying point, concealed from the observation of the defenders and sufficiently close to the airfield to put that important objective in grave danger. The time was about eight o'clock. Twenty minutes later the parachutists began to arrive, some five hundred being dropped in this locality. Those who fell to the west were the more fortunate, since they were largely out of range of the defence, and were in any case protected by the covering fire of the troops who had previously been landed in the river bed by glider. They constituted what was probably the largest group of the Assault Regiment allocated to the attack on Maleme, but others were landing on the higher ground about a thousand yards south of the airfield; close to the spur known as Hill 107; and in the neighbourhood of a bridge over the Tavronitis bed south-west of the airfield, near which a group of R.A.F. buildings had been previously noted from the air by the German observers.

Groups of paratroopers came down in and near Maleme village. Those who landed in the narrow streets and on the flat roof-tops were promptly attacked by men of the headquarters company of the 22nd New Zealand Battalion—two platoons of drivers and storemen—armed with rifles and Bren guns. The Germans had the advantage in automatic weapons and the New Zealand effort to clear Maleme and its approaches was not completely successful although most of the enemy were killed. Here Cretan civilians joined the fray. There were few able-bodied men who were not already under arms, but old men, boys, even women, used knives and staves and ancient rifles which had perhaps seen service against the Turks half a century before.

Not far away, near the coast, a German company descended upon a New Zealand engineer unit whose commander, when asked if he required assistance, replied on the telephone, 'They'll all be dead before you can get a man here.' These words hardly exceeded the facts. A captured company roll found in the pocket of a German officer showed 126 names; within three hours the New Zealander sappers, who were fighting as infantry, had accounted for 112 of them.

To the east of the airfield the Germans dropped a battalion, nearly 600 strong, of the Assault Regiment. It had originally been intended that it should land along the beach between Maleme and Platanias. But in order to avoid the danger of any of the parachutists being dropped into the sea, and because their information told them that this stretch of country both along the coast and inland was undefended, the battalion was put down in the foothills south of the coastal road.

The result was disastrous—for the attackers. They descended slap into the prepared positions of the 23rd and a part of the 22nd New Zealand Battalion. Many were killed or wounded in the air or caught up in the trees, and most of the containers, in which all but the personal arms were stored, fell into New Zealand hands. Every officer with the battalion was either killed or wounded. Here and there a handful of men held out until the following day or even until the day after that, and a few eventually fought their way through westwards to the main body in the Tavronitis river-bed. But the battalion was completely destroyed as a fighting unit.

The enemy's aim was to capture the anti-aircraft battery at the mouth of this broad and sandy river bed;[1] secure the Maleme airfield; and establish a perimeter defence beyond the airfield. He had not yet succeeded. Losses had been severe, and included General Meindl himself who had landed with the first wave of attackers and received a wound in the chest. Next day he was succeeded by Colonel Ramcke.

By 10.a.m., however, several hundred troops had been landed by glider and parachute and were rallying in small groups for local defence, at the same time preparing to take the offensive supported

[1]Thus German Intelligence. Actually the guns were high up on the western slopes of Hill 107, about a mile from the coast.

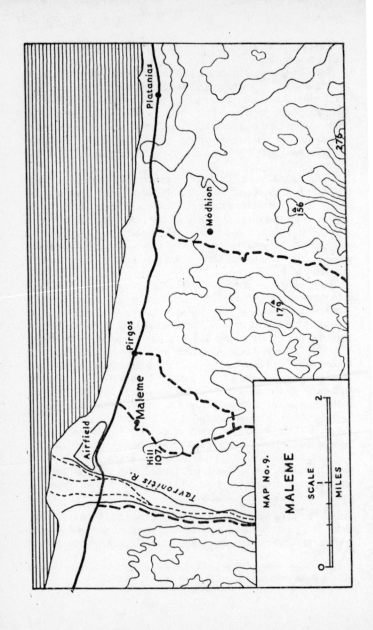

MAP No. 9.

MALEME

SCALE

MILES

Platanias

Mòdhion

276

156

179

Pirgos

Maleme

Airfield

Hill 107

Tavronitis R.

by the mortars and light guns which had been dropped in special containers. And the parachute landings were being followed up by the arrival of troop carriers, about twenty of these craft having already made crash landings on the beaches east and west of Maleme. Clearly a fresh German effort would not be long delayed; and the 22nd New Zealand Battalion (Lieut.-Colonel L. W. Andrew, V.C.), which Brigadier Hargest had made responsible for the defence of the airfield and its approaches from land and sea, was faced with no easy task.

As our anti-aircraft artillery had inflicted comparatively little damage upon the airborne Germans the New Zealanders had to deal with a heavier weight of attack than had been anticipated. Our signal cables had suffered great damage in the preliminary air bombardment and the paratroopers had been taught to seek for and cut field telephone lines as one of their first duties. So the separate companies of the 22nd New Zealand Battalion soon found themselves engaged in isolated action with little means of communicating with each other or with battalion headquarters save by the very slow and uncertain method of employing runners.

The broad gulley of the Tavronitis became at an early stage a rallying point for the Germans. The main body of the Assault Regiment which had descended in this neighbourhood, soon secured intact the long bridge which spans the gulley. Further south an attempt was made against Hill 107. A few R.A.F. ground-staff were captured from the camp near the foot of the hill, but the report, widely circulated at the time that these men were used as a screen behind which the Germans advanced to the attack, cannot be substantiated. Two attacks appear to have been made against the hill, but neither was pressed home in strength and neither was successful.

Meanwhile a further battalion of the Assault Regiment had been landed south of Kolimvari (a coastal village more than two miles west of the Tavronitis) to provide protection against a possible counter-attack from this side. The drop was made without interference, for we had no Regular troops available for holding the coast so far west,[1] and the Germans promptly began to push along the road in a south-westerly direction towards Kastelli. Their progress was opposed by Cretan guerrillas who had been organized

[1] The German account published by XI Air Corps attributed much of the success achieved on the first day to our failure to occupy positions between the Tavronitis and Kolimvari.

by British and New Zealand officers, and one platoon of Germans which had landed still further to the west was completely wiped out. The enemy, apprehensive of a counter-attack in strength, pushed ahead to secure a high pass five miles down the road to Kastelli. This was reached by evening.

By noon the position around Maleme was that the Germans to the east of the airfield had largely been 'mopped up', while the attempts to exploit southwards on to the high ground, where a part of the 22nd New Zealand Battalion was stationed, had hitherto met with no success. But to the west they were strengthening their postion in the dry river bed of the Tavronitis, and the hard-pressed isolated platoon of the 22nd Battalion on the western fringe of the airfield could not be succoured or reinforced, since the enemy was bringing powerful crossfire to bear on the airfield itself. And meanwhile troop-carrying aircraft continued to land on the beaches. Nearly forty had come in by midday. The men they brought, arriving simultaneously and ready for action, constituted a far more menacing reinforcement than a corresponding number of paratroopers would have done.

At the start the Germans were concerned chiefly to deny the use of the airfield to our troops, since they could not be certain that we were not in a position to use it to fly in reinforcements on our own account. During the morning, therefore, this flat coverless field was a death-trap for the troops on either side. It became clear from an early stage that it was to some extent the key to the whole situation in this part of Crete, perhaps the key to the possession of Crete itself, and it was realized that the Germans would make the most strenuous efforts to secure it for their own use.

Throughout the afternoon the position grew worse. Had communication between our units been swifter and easier, had we possessed more transport, had we possessed even vestigial air cover, it might have been possible to mount a prompt counter-attack against the enemy concentration near Maleme airfield before it had been reinforced to any great extent by further airborne troops. But the German air power proved of decisive importance during this crucial period. The co-operation between ground troops and air forces was of a high order. A most effective system of signalling was used by the parachutists to indicate their own whereabouts, the location of our troops, the development of the action and their own immediate needs. A few white or yellow strips laid out in any open space in a series of simple diagrammatic patterns proved easy of recognition by the low-flying German aircraft. Did a unit wish to indicate that it was surrounded, that the enemy was about to attack, that it require medical supplies, mortar ammunition, anti-tank ammunition, smoke bombs, or ground reinforcement, the appropriate signal could readily be made. Indeed, the German fighter aircraft swooping down at will over the field of battle in Crete could report the progress of the struggle and the requirements of the ground forces to General Lohr's Headquarters in Athens in less time than it took some of our isolated company commanders to communicate with their battalion headquarters by the tedious and uncertain method of runners.

The ubiquity of the German air force during this day and the following days and its unchallenged and unchallengeable supremacy meant in the first case that, from Force Headquarters downwards, the passing of information, and of orders consequent upon that information, was virtually suspended or slowed down to such an extent as to surrender the initiative wholly to the enemy. It is difficult to think of any instance in the history of warfare where one force has been so pinned down and paralysed *at every level,* from the rifleman in his slit-trench fifty yards from the enemy to the staff officer at Force Headquarters waiting for information that does not arrive or planning movements that will not be carried out because the orders will never get through or only when the situation has so changed as to render them completely obsolete and irrelevant.

Even when it proved possible to make some sort of counter-move, launch some form of counter-attack, the signs of preparation by our forces were all too patent to the enemy. The inevitable low-flying, dive-bombing or machine-gunning air attack followed as surely as the hounds of spring upon winter's traces. It paralysed movement, it blinded observation, it shook morale. One may well ask what chance had the defence under such conditions as these?

Yet it may be that the chief danger had not yet been adequately realized. The parachute obsession was great, had been so ever since the days of the Netherlands campaign, and there was a tendency to regard these troops as constituting the major threat, whereas they only served as an advanced guard to the main body landed by troop carrier during succeeding days. The parachutist of today does not correspond so much to the shock trooper but rather to the light skirmisher of nineteenth-century warfare. This, perhaps, was not at first appreciated, partly because it was difficult to realize the extent to which the enemy was prepared to go on landing troops on an airfield still under fire or in crash-landing carriers on the beaches or elsewhere. That is why it is uncertain whether, even had we succeeded in keeping our grip on Maleme airfield, we could have prevented the enemy from landing troops on a large scale and gradually passing to the offensive with an ever-increasing weight of numbers and firepower. We might have made him pay even more dearly for his conquest of the island. We could hardly have prevented it.

The situation, as has been observed, grew worse during Tuesday afternoon. The enemy was clearly getting stronger, and he succeeded in establishing a grip upon the ridge south of Maleme airfield; but the main danger came from the west. It was in this direction that our first more or less co-ordinated counter-attack was delivered.

It will be remembered that two 'I' tanks had been allotted to the defence of Maleme airfield. These do not seem to have proved effective during the period of the first air-landings but they were well-suited to accompany and cover a counter-attack with infantry. Shortly after 5 p.m. an attempt was made to re-establish the position west of the airfield. Forty New Zealanders of the 22nd Battalion, assisted by a few Bofors guns and supported by the two tanks, advanced. The small number of infantry available is an indication of the extent to which the battalion had been deployed over the wide area, making it difficutlt for any but a small force to be concentrated for a counter-attack. Our men were moving forward against a force that might be anything up to ten times as numerous as themselves, but they possessed two potential trumps in the 'I' tanks for at no time did the enemy land any armoured fighting vehicles from the air; those that were subsequently observed to be operating against us were captured British tanks.

Supported by the two tanks, the troops made good progress and reached the further fringe of the airfield without loss. Then the mechanical inefficiency which seemed inseparable from British tanks during the Greek and Crete campaigns decided the issue. The 2-pounder gun, also apparently the machine-gun, of one of the tanks jammed hopelessly, and the tank, now a useless mobile metal box, was compelled to turn round and withdraw. Worse still, the engine of the second tank, which had penetrated as far as the edge of the Tavronitis gulley, broke down.

The Germans captured both the crew and the tank and very soon began to use its guns against our troops.

Lacking the covering fire of the tanks, the infantry had no

alternative but to withdraw rapidly, since they were far too weak in numbers to press on alone. In re-crossing the airfield they suffered so heavily from enemy fire that only three of those who managed to get back to their original starting point were unwounded.

Owing to the slowness and difficulty in transmitting messages the situation at Maleme airfield was only very imperfectly realized at 5th New Zealand Brigade headquarters. In fact, about mid-afternoon, a message was despatched to the commanders of the 21st and 23rd Battalions informing them that they would not yet be required to counter-attack. It was recognized, however, that the 22nd Battalion had been severely tried, and at dusk the Brigade ordered a company from the 23rd and a company from the 28th (Maori) Battalion, both of which were in position further to the east, to counter-attack.

It was at 9 p.m. that Lieut.-Colonel Andrew, commanding the 22nd New Zealand Battalion, came to the conclusion that he must withdraw from the immediate neighbourhood of the airfield. At this time he was in touch with only two of his five companies—A and B. Of the remaining three, C Company, which was directly concerned with the defence of the airfield, had been heavily engaged and was known to have suffered great loss; the headquarters company, which held the Pirgos and Maleme area to the east, had been out of contact since noon; D Company in the south at Hill 107 was known to have been hard pressed and one of its members who joined Colonel Andrew in the evening reported himself to be the only survivor. So far as the battalion commander knew, he had not many more than 200 men available to defend the whole area.

As a matter of fact, of the three outlying companies the headquarters company was firmly established around Maleme-Pirgos, where it had dealt with most of the parachutists who had been dropped in its midst; D Company was still holding its positions at Hill 107; and even C Company had one platoon almost intact and could rally survivors from the others.

However, these facts were not known to Colonel Andrew. He merely knew that the Germans were building up in strength from the west against what he supposed to be his only two remaining companies and that they were infiltrating, or appeared to be infiltrating, to the south and east.

Accordingly, after communicating by radio to brigade head-quarters, he dropped back, first to the south-east, where he concentrated A and B Companies, and then into line with the 21st Battalion holding an inland sector, and the 23rd Battalion whose area stretched through Pirgos to the coast line.

Of the two companies which had gone forward to counter-attack during the evening, the company of the 28th (Maori) Battalion got as far as the fringe of the airfield, which it reached at about midnight. Finding no New Zealand troops there it withdrew to its original position, 'mopping up' on the way isolated parties of German paratroopers to the number of about fifty. The company of the 23rd Battalion made contact with Colonel Andrew and assisted in covering his withdrawal.

The 'lost' companies, finding that their battalion had withdrawn, succeeded in making their way back, with the exception of one platoon of D Company, which remained on Hill 107 and was surrounded and captured next morning; and another platoon of the same company, which moved off into the mountains and eventually reached the south coast.

The evacuation of the airfield (which had not, in fact, been effectively in our hands since the morning) by the withdrawal of the 22nd New Zealand Battalion has been authoritatively described as 'probably the most decisive single step in the battle for Crete'. It is important, therefore, to give full consideration to the reasons that prompted this withdrawal. They are many.

Our combined forces in the neighbourhood, even if they had been fully equipped, were insufficient to hold an area with a perimeter some five miles in extent. All units were weak in numbers.

The weapons of our troops were very inferior, both in quality and in numbers to those of the enemy. Colonel Andrew had less than 60 per cent of his establishment of machine guns, and less than 30 per cent of mortars.

His battalion was short of officers. There had only been twenty on the morning of the German attack, and eight of these had become casualties in the course of the day.

Communications were poor owing to damaged cables and lack of signal equipment.

The tanks had failed. The one which broke down on the edge of the river-bed was already being used by the enemy as a pillbox from which to fire upon our most forward company.

There was a lack of artillery support due to bad communications, forward observation officers being almost invariably cut off from their batteries.

The multiplicity of command within the area hampered defensive action.

No proper counter-attack had been made. Instead, two companies had gone forward separately to deal with an almost unknown situation.

The anti-aircraft defence of the aerodrome had failed, partly through the siting of the Bofors guns in obvious and vulnerable positions, and also through our inability to provide additional concealed guns and guns which would only open fire when the German troop-carriers came in.

The policy adopted with regard to the airfield which might have been mined in advance of the German landing. Only temporary obstructions had been placed in position. Moreover, a great deal of petrol and many bombs and miscellaneous stores had been left intact in the neighbourhood.

The tremendous value of the close support given by the *Luftwaffe* to their ground forces.

Thus it may well be assumed that our positions at the airfield had become untenable. Lieut.-Colonel Andrew, a resolute commander, afterwards felt that 'looking back now and knowing more of the facts I am convinced that the withdrawal at that time was the only possible action to take'.

It is less easy to understand why the invaluable hours of darkness were not utilized to launch a vigorous counter-attack in the greatest force available. The other battalions of the 5th New Zealand Brigade had had a hard day, but there was no reason to doubt their energy and spirit. Probably the explanation is to be found in the inadequate signal communications which prevented commanders from obtaining promptly the information upon which successful action must be based. With this handicap in mind it has been suggested that brigade headquarters, near Platanias some four miles away from the airfield, were too far distant to control the fight.

3

Canea—Suda

LET us now transfer our attention to the second sector attacked on the morning of May 20th, the area of Canea and Suda Bay, main objective of the Centre (Mars) Group of the German assault. No. 3 Parachute Rifle Regiment and half a battalion from the Assault Regiment were employed in a widely dispersed drop all around

Canea, which was to be taken on the first day, the various British camps and troop concentrations being destroyed at the same time.

The operation opened badly for the Germans, for the glider carrying Major-General Süssmann, the commander of the Group, crashed on the island of Aiyina in full view of Athens, and the general and all his personal staff were killed.

For the most part the assault fell not upon the Canea-Suda garrison, but clashed with the 4th New Zealand Brigade, and attached troops in the area west and south-west of Canea which was under the command of the New Zealand Division.

This tract of country had been subjected to an air bombardment of great intensity between 7 and 8 a.m. and our guns were silenced. Four gliders are said to have landed in the vicinity of the prison, on the Canea—Alikianou road, but the main attack was made by paratroops who did not begin to descend until about 9.20 a.m.—an hour after the first wave had come down in the Maleme sector. Since Canea was the main objective and the landings were made roughly in a semi-circle around the town, it will be simplest to follow the fortunes of each main group from north-west to south-west around the perimeter.

On a small promontory on the coast two miles west of Canea stood No. 7 General Hospital, the principal British military hospital in western Crete. It consisted of a number of larger tents with beds for 500, many of which were already filled with men wounded in the air attacks of the past three weeks. It also obtained a few wounded German airmen.

The morning had witnessed a heavy bombing attack on the neighbourhood, where the ground was reasonably flat and therefore well suited to the dropping of parachutists. Some hospital tents had been set ablaze by the bombs while others had been ripped open by machine-gun fire. Those patients who could walk had made for the slit-trenches, but many had to remain helplessly in their beds with the burning camp around them. A number of wounded men were hit again by machine-gun bullets or bomb splinters.

An hour elapsed. The noise of bombing had long since died away, but a cloud of smoke still drifted from a blazing marquee. Down came the parachutists, a full company strong. Possession of the hospital peninsula besides providing a good dropping area would enable the attackers to cut the Canea—Maleme road and would give them a good starting point from which to launch an attack upon Canea itself.

Few of the patients or hospital staff appear to have seen the parachutes open. Almost before they realized what had happened they found paratroopers all around them. The men in the slit-trenches and the men in the hospital beds, all who were capable of standing, were abruptly ejected and rapidly rounded up. Though they were speeded with shots and hand grenades, it appears that in only one case was an unarmed man killed at this time. Lieut.-Colonel J. L. R. Plimmer, who commanded the 6th Field Ambulance, standing up on his slit-trench and having one arm in a sling, was immediately shot dead. Help was given to the paratroopers by some of the German wounded in the hospital who had leapt or crawled from their beds and were seen signalling with hand-mirrors.

By 11.a.m. the Germans were completely in control of the hospital and of the New Zealand dressing station, away on the southern side of the Canea road. They found, as was to be expected, one of their wounded who was quite ready to take charge of his fellow patients. He greeted the paratroops with the Nazi salute, demanded a tommy-gun and then took up a position watching those who were too weak to leave their beds.

The parachutists could now be seen dispersing among the trees, but about a dozen remained in charge of the walking wounded. About noon they began to move off to the south with a view to linking up with a battalion which had been observed dropping east of Galatas, possibly a mile distant. For the neighbourhood of the hospital looked like becoming decidedly unhealthy. A German aircraft had swooped down and fired upon the group, whereupon the guards had made one of the captive officers climb a tree and drape a white flag on top. And a light tank of the Hussars had come into view, hesitated and then withdrawn. Intermittent rifle fire, though in no great volume, was coming from the neighbouring trees.

So the party, about 300 strong with its dozen German guards, began to move off inland, the wounded men barefoot and in pyjamas, stumbling along as best they could. The ground was rough and broken and every kind of cover was provided by hillocks and ditches, by trees and bushes, and by an occasional low stone wall. From time to time a sniper's rifle barked out and one or two men were hit. It was difficult for the prisoners and their guards to know whether these shots came from friend or foe.

The straggling crocodile of prisoners had travelled about a mile, but there was no sign of the battalion of parachutists whom their

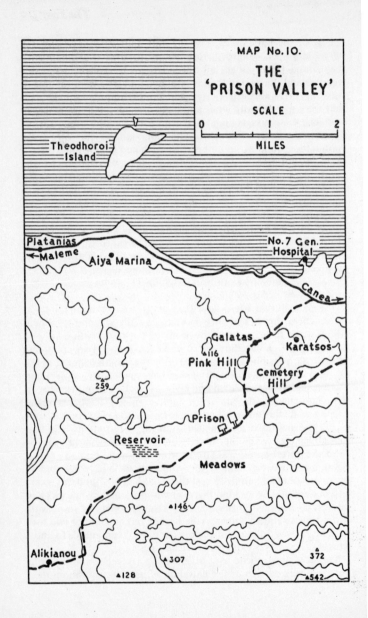

MAP No. 10.

THE 'PRISON VALLEY'

SCALE

0   1   2

MILES

Theodhoroi Island

Platanias
←Maleme
Aiya Marina

No. 7 Gen. Hospital

Canea→

Galatas

Karatsos

▲116
Pink Hill

Cemetery Hill

▲259

Prison

Reservoir

Meadows

▲146

Alikianou

▲307

▲372

▲128

▲542

guards hoped to join. In fact these troops had dropped into the defended area of the 19th New Zealand Battalion and had either been wiped out or driven off southwards. So the procession continued its painful progress, snipers being met with fire, while the prisoners themselves were from time to time urged on with shots.

In the early afternoon the column came to a halt on the brow of a hill which commanded fair observation. The guards deployed to left and right behind a low stone wall while the prisoners sank to the ground and tried to take cover as best they could.

Presently a New Zealand patrol from the 19th Battalion came into sight, working through a thick plantation of olive trees not more than a hundred yards distant. The prisoners were compelled to keep silent by the guns of their captors and had to watch the New Zealanders move straight across their front. One of them could be heard saying 'There are no bloody Huns down here'. Slowly the patrol moved out of sight, and the hopes of the prisoners vanished with them. But the guards did not dare to move from their position, and presently the New Zealanders could be heard returning. This time one of them fired a shot—apparently at random. It passed close to a *Luftwaffe* pilot who had attached himself to the parachutists. He fired back and the alarm was given.

The fight that followed lasted for perhaps half an hour, perhaps longer. The New Zealand patrol did not at first realize that there were some hundreds of our own wounded among the Germans. When they did, they acted with the utmost circumspection. A British captain, a Maori major and others afterwards paid tribute to the precautions which were taken. 'I cannot praise too highly', said the British officer, 'the way in which the New Zealand troops developed their attack with the utmost regard for our safety.'

With some help from the prisoners in directing the fire, the New Zealanders moved round to outflank the wall and one by one they picked off the paratroopers until only two remained. Greek troops, working in from the rear, helped to finish off the action.

A few of the wounded prisoners and medical staff had been hit during this action, but considering the circumstances they had been almost miraculously lucky. They were brought into the area held by the 19th Battalion.

At much the same time the hospital itself had been recaptured by a detachment of New Zealanders, with some assistance from the 3rd Hussars who had a few light tanks stationed in the Canea area, though none appear to have been engaged in this particular affair.

German losses in the whole engagement in this neighbourhood were very heavy. By their own account most of the company were killed in the course of the day's fighting. Our estimates put the number at nearly 200.[1]

Further south an untidy battle—or rather, a series of isolated fights—raged all day around Galatas and along the Canea—Alikianou road to the south-west. South of the road a strong force of parachutists came down all around a troop of 3.7-inch howitzers. The gunners were overwhelmed, but not before one of their number, on his own initiative and at grave personal risk, had succeeded in disabling three of the four guns so as to prevent them falling intact into enemy hands. There were nine light tanks of the 3rd Hussars in the rather close country between Canea, Galatas and the road from Canea to the prison and reservoir. Three of these, with a company from the 18th New Zealand Battalion, delivered an attack shortly before dusk against the hamlet of Galaria (a mile east of Karatsos) which for the time being had become one of the principal enemy strongpoints in the sector. The German parachutists were established in the houses with mortars and machine-guns and succeeded in driving off the attack; nevertheless, during the night, in obedience to orders received from their regimental headquarters, they quietly evacuated Galaria and wihdrew south-west to help form a defensive *bloc* in the area of the prison, where the main body of No. 3 Parachute Rifle Regiment was concentrating in expectation of a counter-attack on the following day.

The initial German assault had failed, largely because most of the 3rd Battalion of this regiment had dropped in or near the defence positions of the 19th New Zealand Battalion and No. 6 Greek Regiment. Attempting to carry out their role of attacking and taking Galatas, which was held by the Composite New Zealand Battalion, they were set upon from all sides and were reported to have been 'unquestionably annihilated in quick order'. Only a few survivors escaped southwards across the Canea—Alikianou road.

It was on either side of this road, in the area known to our troops as Prison Valley, that the main body of No. 3 Parachute Rifle Regiment had been dropped. For a good part of the eight-mile

[1]Many contradictory accounts have been given of the capture of the hospital and the subsequent alleged use of the wounded and medical staff as a screen for the advance of the parachutists. The author has largely followed the report of the New Zealand War History Branch which is based on a large number of narratives by eye-witnesses.

stretch to Alikianou the road traverses open meadow land, eminently suitable for the landing of paratroops. It had, however, the disadvantage that it was overlooked from the high ground immediately southeast of Galatas, and no force dropped in this valley could feel secure until this height, known to our men as Cemetery Hill, had been secured.

To meet the threat in this area we had No. 6 Greek Regiment, flanking the valley from the east from Galatas southward to the foothills, and No. 8 Greek Regiment covering the western exits and the approaches to Alikianou. Further north, in the same area but out of effective range of the landing, was the New Zealand divisional cavalry,[1] less than two hundred strong, fighting as infantry since their Bren carriers had been left in Greece.

[1] From May 22nd, after the divisional petrol company had been brought under command, this detachment was renamed Russell Force.

The parachutist descent was carried out more or less as planned but over a more widely dispersed area than had been intended, with the result that numbers of the enemy were easily picked off by rifle fire in the open country before they could find cover or give each other support. It was estimated that of the two battalions which were dropped here about one hundred were disposed of almost at once; the number may have been much higher, for a member of the 2nd Battalion afterwards stated that out of the 700 men of that unit who were dropped only 500 survived the landing and the initial forming-up period. But nearly three hundred men made successful landings on the slopes to the south-east of the road; and a more formidable force, over five hundred strong, came down in the prison valley astride the road, roughly midway between Canea and Alikianou. The two Greek battalions had had a fairly easy task in the first ten minutes or so, since the country afforded little cover for troops dropping from the sky. But No. 8 Greek Regiment, in the foothills, found itself cut off from the rest of our forces. From the sound of heavy rifle and mortar fire it seemed that the Greeks were engaging the Germans, and, though gradually driven southward they certainly prevented the enemy from making any important progress. When he launched an attack upon the village and bridge of Alikianou from the east it was decisively repulsed, women and even children turning out against the invader. The stout resistance of the battalion continued right up to the night of May 25th/26th, and prevented any wide German flanking movement south of Canea during these days.

No. 6 Greek Regiment was less successful. It had received a consignment of small-arms ammunition on the previous evening, but most unfortunately this had not yet been distributed, with the result that the men had only a few rounds apiece when the parachutists descended in the morning. After a brief resistance the Greeks dropped back north on Galatas and east on Perivolia. The New Zealand cavalry had been moved towards Galatas where they took up a position near the southern edge of the town.

The Germans, always quick on this vital opening day of the battle to exploit an advantage gained, followed up rapidly. Colonel Heidrich, who commanded No. 3 Parachute Rifle Regiment, and who was now commanding the 7th Airborne Division until a successor to Süssmann could be appointed, had arrived early on the scene in the neighbourhood of the prison. He promptly realized that the heights south of Galatas were the key to the whole situation. One of his three battalions had landed almost intact in the prison area, and advanced to the attack 'in classic style' (to use the words of the German official report). Despite flanking fire from the direction of Galatas it rushed Cemetery Hill and pushing east joined up with another force. The advance continued eastward upon the village of Mournies, scarcely more than three miles from Suda. Since the attack was being closely supported by low-flying aircraft, the situation began to look critical; but parties of No. 6 Greek Regiment, led by Lieutenant Forrester of the Queen's Regiment and a resolute Greek subaltern, helped to check the German effort.

But the enemy remained in control of the Prison Valley. Heidrich's 1st Battalion had taken Cemetery Hill and during the afternoon his 2nd Battalion, after one repulse, took Pink Hill immediately southwest of Galatas. Thereupon two companies of the 19th Battalion (4th New Zealand Brigade), together with a detachment of the 3rd Hussars which provided two light tanks, were ordered to counter-attack.

Unfortunately it took over two hours to launch the counter-attack after the order was given. When our men advanced at 8.30 p.m. the enemy's defence was fairly solidly established and although a number of casualties were inflicted the attack came to a halt, pinned down by fire, 600 yards from the starting line. Brigadier Puttick commanding the New Zealand Division, considered that there would be no chance of success when daylight came; so at dawn our troops were brought back to their original positions.

When darkness fell the Germans were still in possession of both

Cemetery Hill and Pink Hill, but owing to a misunderstanding the commander of the 2nd Battalion withdrew his troops from Pink Hill. Cemetery Hill continued to be held by the Germans until the morning of the 21st.

Following the perimeter of Canea round in an easterly direction we come to the second area of glider landings, where three independent companies of the Assault Regiment were detailed to land, one under Lieutenant Gentz, immediately south of Canea, where an anti-aircraft battery and the wireless transmitting station were to be attacked and captured; the other two companies to the north-east of the town on the Akrotiri peninsula. Here also an anti-aircraft battery formed the primary objective.

South of Canea Lieutenant Gentz's company, though losing one of its fifteen gliders during the approach flight, while three more landed at Canea itself, had the advantage of following up a highly successful air bombardment which had neutralized our guns and had scored a hit on a big ammunition dump just before the landing took place. Consequently the Germans met with little opposition except from a scattered splutter of light machine-fun fire. They overran the battery, killing or capturing the gun detachments, and then proceeded methodically to stalk and destroy the machine-guns with hand-grenades.

A scratch force of the Canea-Suda garrison, consisting of elements of the Rangers, the 1st Welch Regiment, Royal Marines, and No. 2 Greek Regiment came into action during the afternoon, moving out from Canea and the village of Mournies just to the south. They not only dislodged the Germans from their positions, but succeeded in recapturing two heavy anti-aircraft guns which, the more surprisingly, were found to be undamaged. With the guns they rescued 32 survivors of the detachments. By the end of the day Lieutenant Gentz's command had been reduced to a few dozen men, isolated and with little hope of holding out on the morrow. They were, however, in wireless communication with Colonel Heidrich in the prison area and received orders to break out to the south-west through the hills and thence to rejoin the main body. The route which they followed took them straight through a succession of our positions, but by dint of bluffing, Gentz, who spoke fluent English, succeeded in working, and occasionally shooting, his way back to the main body of the regiment which he rejoined early on the following morning with three officers and twenty-one men.

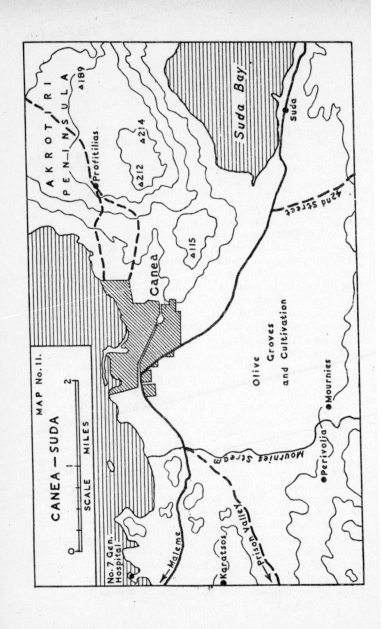

CANEA — SUDA

MAP No. 11.

SCALE   MILES

AKROTIRI PENINSULA

▲189

●Profitilias

▲214

▲212

Canea

▲115

Suda Bay

●Suda

42nd Street

No. 7 Gen. Hospital

Maleme

●Karatsos

Prison Valley

Olive Groves and Cultivation

Mournies Stream

●Perivolia

●Mournies

Still less fortunate were the two companies under Captain Altmann. It had been intended that they should land on the Akrotiri peninsula and immediately put our guns out of action. But the flight came under both heavy and light anti-aircraft fire and lost cohesion as it approached land. Out of fifteen gliders taking part in the operation four fell into the sea. That was the first misfortune that befell the enemy. The second was that our gun positions had been shifted since the last German air reconnaissance with the result that the troops in the gliders, who should have been landed close enough to overwhelm the guns at the first rush, found themselves put down in positions which gave them little chance against the defenders. They were not allowed the opportunity to give one another effective support; and, to add to their troubles, German aircraft action during the landing proved less effective here than elsewhere.

The effect of this German miscalculation and our own intelligent and alert defence soon showed how far even these picked assault troops were from being the supermen of fevered defeatist imagination. The Northumberland Hussars, who were stationed here with a view to dealing with an airborne landing, promptly attacked the glider-borne troops, many of whom had descended on our positions at the village of Profitilias. Some of the enemy, it seems, never had an opportunity of emerging from their aircraft and deploying. A large number, including Captain Altmann, were killed; others surrendered. By the end of the day, though there were still a few remaining to be 'winkled out' from the defensive positions they had taken up in the hills, all danger from this direction was at an end.

But what happened at Akrotiri provides an excellent example of the flexibility of German assault tactics. From the quality of the troops employed and the tactical importance of their objective (the neck of the peninsula close to Canea) it is reasonable to assume that this was regarded as one of the most important parts of the operation. But when it came so completely to grief the Germans made no further attempt either to reinforce it, to continue pressure from this side, or to extricate the men isolated there. General Lohr was intent upon pursuing the sound policy of reinforcing success. More and yet more troops would be poured in at Maleme, for at Maleme there was a possibility of successful exploitation. The operation at Akrotiri would be jettisoned and the surviving troops abandoned, for it had failed. 'To him that hath shall be given' is a maxim of more than scriptural application.

Generally speaking, the attack around Canea had misfired badly.

The various groups of parachutists and glider-borne troops should have linked up; they should have been in uninterrupted control of the coast from west of Canea to the approaches to Suda; Canea should have been taken. Instead, the various detachments had been isolated and largely rounded up. Only a few snipers—less than a dozen in all—actually penetrated into the town of Canea, and these had merely a nuisance value. Of the three battalions that formed Colonel Heidrich's Parachute Rifle Regiment, one had been completely dispersed and partially destroyed; the other two, heavily engaged all day, had accomplished much less than had been expected. In addition, the pioneer battalion had been engaged all day with the Greek forces towards Alikianou, had suffered severely and been compelled to fight its way through to the main body in the Prison Valley during the night. The assault groups of Altmann and Gentz, amounting to another half battalion, had been destroyed.

In only one sector, the Prison Valley, between four and five miles south-west of Canea, was there an enemy concentration that threatened serious trouble on the morrow. And even these troops were not in a position to contemplate serious offensive action. The balance of advantage remained with the defence.

4

Retimo

OUR forces defending Retimo were, as has been mentioned, divided into two parts. Two battalions of the 19th Australian Brigade were stationed, under the direct command of Brigadier G.A. Vasey, to cover the beach at Georgeopolis, a full dozen miles to the west of Retimo (a good deal further if the winding of the road is taken into account). At Georgeopolis a seaborne landing was considered a serious possibility. The other two battalions and some Greek troops covered the Retimo landing-strip (airfield by courtesy), which lay flush with the coast, something more than five miles east of the town.

The Germans had allocated No. 2 Parachute Rifle Regiment (Colonel Sturm) from the Centre (Mars) Group to carry out the capture of the town and airfield, after which it was to move west in such transport as it could lay hands on and join forces with the main body of Mars in the neighbourhood of Canea. Here, as at Heraklion, the drop was not to take place until 3.15 p.m. by which time it was to be assumed that the attention and perhaps most of the available resources of the defence would be concentrated upon the operations further west around Canea and Maleme.

The terrain at Retimo was, in its essential aspects, similar to that at Maleme. A narrow coastal strip, threaded by the main road, was overlooked by a series of steep-banked terraced ridges, here and there rising perpendicularly to a height of twenty feet. Visibility was limited by olive plantations and by vines in the coastal plain and on the seaward slopes of the ridges. Cover from view was therefore considerable both for attack and defence, and provided considerable opportunity for delaying action.

Colonel Campbell, in local command at Retimo, concentrated his force on two hills, known respectively as Hill A and Hill B, to cover the landing-ground from the east and south-west respectively. The 2/1st Australian Battalion was posted on and to the west of Hill A, with two companies on the fringe of the airfield and a third well forward to support them; the 2/11th Battalion on and around Hill B. Detachments were also stationed on an intermediate ridge running parallel to the sea coast. Most of the field guns (captured Italian pieces and four American '75's' all without sights) and most of the machine-guns were placed on one or other of the hills to ensure a prompt concentration of fire, if such should be needed, against the landing-ground.

Two 'I' tanks were stationed in a wadi a little south of the landing-ground. Gun ammunition was scarce, but there was plenty of small-arms ammunition.

The Greek contingent numbered about 2,300, organized in four battalions. These, however, had only ten rounds of ammunition per man, were mostly very young and inexperienced and were described as 'having little confidence in themselves'. One battalion was located in the centre between the two Australian battalions; the other three were in reserve south of the village of Piyi.

The timing and execution of the enemy's preliminary moves were by no means so successful as those of the morning attacks further west. The refuelling of the aircraft at the airfields in Greece had taken longer than was expected, and a dust haze had made the take-off difficult. However, the bombers arrived over their targets about 3.45 p.m. and proceeded to deliver a heavy but not very effective attack upon our supposed defences. The air photographs taken by the reconnaissance aircraft during the preceding days had been erroneously interpreted and little damage was done to our gun

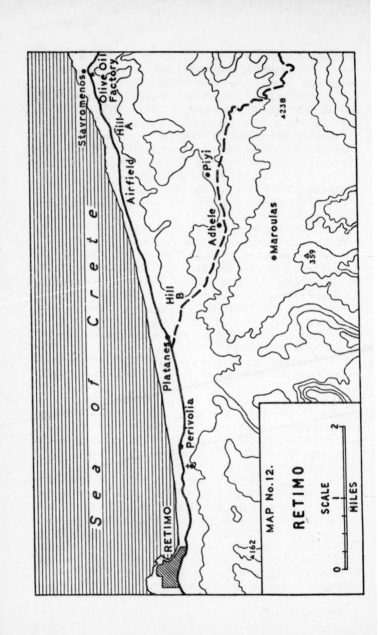

Sea of Crete

RETIMO
Perivolia
Platanes
Hill B
Stavromenós
Olive Oil Factory
Airfield
Hill A
Adhele
Piyi
Maroulas
▲238
▲359
▲162

MAP No. 12.

RETIMO

SCALE

0   1   2

MILES

positions; also, the bombers were half an hour in advance of the first paratroop-bearing aircraft, and the latter, instead of themselves arriving *en masse* and being able to put in a concentrated attack, kept appearing in successive waves. Four flights of about 25 aircraft each seem to have been used, their descent covering a period of fully half an hour.

As a result of these mistimings the defence was on the *qui vive,* and in better shape to deal with an airborne attack than had been the troops at Maleme that morning. It has been noted that no anti-aircraft guns were available for the defence, otherwise the whole operation might have foundered almost as badly as it did at Akrotiri. But with admirable coolness the infantry concentrated with small-arms fire against the troop-carriers. Nine of them were brought down by these means and a number of parachutists were killed or wounded in the course of their descent.

It may here be noted that some of the Germans, with that extraordinary mental obtuseness which characterizes them, took strong exception to our men firing upon 'helpless' parachutists in the air, regarding it as a breach of the often-invoked and highly elastic 'laws of war'. In this war it was the normally accepted practice to refrain from shooting at single airmen baling out by parachute from a damaged aircraft over enemy territory, the assumption being that such men were on their way to surrender. But there is of course no conceivable reason why armed paratroops dropping in their scores and hundreds, with most decidedly hostile intent, should be allowed a clear 'run in' without interference.

In all, about 1,200 paratroops were landed in the Retimo sector, to east, west and south of the airfield, during the afternoon of May 20th. They were quick to cut the coastal road and sever communications with bridgade headquarters at Georgeopolis, but their losses were severe. The Greek battalion in the centre had started to disperse southward towards the hills when the air attack began, but, rallied by some Australian non-commissioned officers, these men returned to their positions and fought bravely. The early fighting was necessarily of the same 'kill or be killed' character that we have seen elsewhere. Enemy losses were far higher than our own, and the 2/11th Battalion, which suffered only forty permanent casualties during the day's fighting, reported that next day it buried 400 Germans. The remainder of the enemy on this western flank, 400 in number, withdrew into Perivolia village on the coast a mile and a half east of Retimo and there fortified themselves and began to infiltrate eastwards during the night. An attempt to penetrate into Retimo town was driven back by a force of armed Cretan police who greatly outnumbered the attackers.

Things had not gone quite so well for us on the eastern flank. Most of the paratroops who landed opposite the airfield defence companies of the 2/1st Australian Battalion or opposite No. 4 Greek Regiment were overwhelmed, but the two 'I' tanks on being sent against the enemy concentrations to the west of the airfield became ditched, and the Germans began to develop a dangerous attack against Hill A. Moreover, overcoming their customary reluctance to undertake unplanned night operations, they worked up to the eastern edge of the airfield after darkness fell and captured the crews of the two ditched tanks and drove the machines off before dawn. At Maleme they had employed a broken-down tank as a pillbox; here they showed themselves more apt at re-starting our own tanks than we were ourselves.

Nevertheless, the balance of the fighting in the Retimo sector was decidedly in our favour. The enemy had captured neither airfield nor town and had suffered very heavy losses. His force had been split into two widely separated parts, and for the following morning Colonel Campbell planned two dawn attacks to clear his threatened flanks. The enemy was to be driven from the neighbourhood of Hills A and B by the 2/1st and 2/11th Battalions repsectively, while the Greek forces in the centre would attack northwards to the coast to clear the ground between the two Australian battalions of isolated groups of snipers.

A request despatched to Force Headquarters asking for reinforcements had to be regretfully refused, since other sectors were making more urgent demands upon our slender reserves. The Retimo detachment would have to hold its own with what it possessed; and this it seemed quite capable of doing.

No attack developed at Georgeopolis during the day, and in the evening the 2/8th Australian Battalion—only two companies—was despatched to Canea to come under command of the Suda sector.

5

Heraklion

HERAKLION, the second town of Crete, is the best known to visitors from the west, an account of the vicinity of the vast and imposing ruins of the ancient Minoan palace at Knossos, excavated during the last century by Sir Arthur Evans. It was the objective of the German East ('Orion') Group, under Colonel Brauer, which was to be landed in the afternoon of May 20th with the task of taking the walled town and the airfield, two and a half miles to the east, and then preparing a beach-head for the landing of No. 85 Rifle Regiment from the 5th Mountain Division.

The defence here consisted of the bulk of the original British garrison troops with an Australian battalion and some Greeks. It was therefore a relatively well-equipped body, the troops were fresh and units up to establishment in numbers. It may be that General Freyberg anticipated that the main attack would be delivered against this sector; certainly he realized that the somewhat isolated position of Heraklion demanded a self-sufficient scheme of defence.

The area to be defended stretched from an open beach a mile or two beyond the airfield on the east to the town of Heraklion on the west. Brigadier Chappel had taken great pains to protect the airfield. Holding a hill overlooking the beach, a ridge south of the landing ground, and an intermediate gorge between the two positions was the 2nd Black Watch. Next to the Highlanders but south of the main road was the 2/4th Australian Battalion occupying a feature including two knolls near Aghiai Pandes but known to the Australians by the more homely name of 'Charlies'. Men of the 7th Medium Regiment R.A., now acting as infantry, were stationed near the sea in Nea Alikarnassos, a newly built village for Asia Minor refugees on the road between the airfield and Heraklion town. To the west of the Australians, and in the rear of the artillerymen, lay the 2nd Leicestershire as mobile reserve, ready to counter-attack in any direction but especially towards the airfield. The 2nd York and Lancaster, next to the Leicestershire, was immediately south-east of Heraklion. The town itself and its approaches from the south as well as some beaches to the west were held by a Greek garrison battalion

223

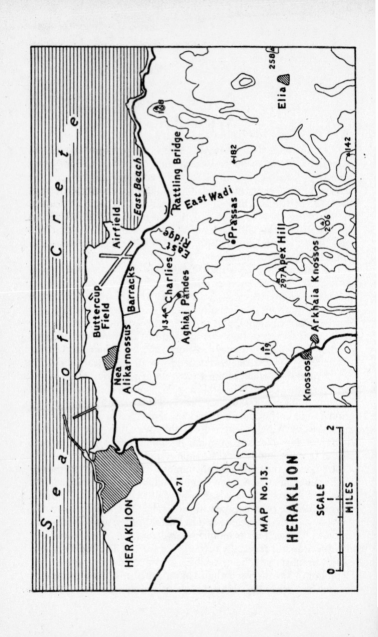

MAP No. 13.

HERAKLION

SCALE

0   1   2
MILES

and two Greek recruit battalions. Right outside the main defences on a ridge overlooking East Beach from the southeast, were posted a platoon of the Black Watch and two Greek reservist companies.

Another platoon of the Black Watch held a road-block at Knossos across the highway that runs inland to the central mountain ridge.

The airfield itself was well covered also by our guns. Two Bofors were sited on its fringe, and an 'I' tank was concealed at each end. Two troops of captured Italian field-guns were in position on the high ground to the south-west, and the remainder of the guns with six light tanks of the 3rd Hussars to the south-east. So provided a more formidable concentration both of troops and guns than had been possible in the somewhat makeshift arrangements at Maleme.

Here, as at Retimo, the Germans somewhat mistimed their attack. It had been intended that the descent of the parachutists should begin at 3.15 in the afternoon, when Colonel Brauer with No. 1 Parachute Regiment would land and seize the town and airfield of Heraklion, keeping the latter open for subsequent landings. But, though losses among the troop-carrying Junkers planes had been surprisingly few—according to the German official account only seven were lost out of over 500 employed in the morning's operations—a number had crashed on returning to their bases on the mainland. Their removal to clear the airfields took time, and, as already observed, there were delays over refuelling, and complications caused by the dust storms that swept the mainland airfields. Owing to the difficulties of telephonic communication between the various units, scattered all over southern Greece and the islands, no fresh common starting time could be planned. Accordingly, formations started in ragged order and 'incorrect tactical sequence'.

At 4 p.m. the preliminary bombing began. Our ground troops reported that as many as 750 aircraft took part in this bombardment, but this seems almost certainly an over-estimate. The attack continued from four until five o'clock. Then, nearly two hours behind schedule, the first troop-carriers came into view, and the anti-aircraft guns which had remained commendably silent during an hour's bombing opened up as the parachutists began to descend.

Owing to the delays, the drop, as at Retimo, was not concentrated into the shortest possible time. It spread over a period of about two hours, the troops descending in a series of waves as the carriers arrived, usually in groups of twelve, from the north-west.

The defence was ready, neither troops nor guns having suffered seriously from the preliminary air bombardment, and the anti-aircraft gunners worked with a will. Out of more than one hundred and fifty—there may have been two hundred—JU 52's employed in the operation fifteen were shot down in the air, and apart from the men in these aircraft a large number of parachutists were killed as they descended to earth.

One gunner said:

> I saw planes burst into flames, then the men inside feverishly leaping out like plums spilled from a burst bag. Some were burning as they dropped to earth. I saw one aircraft flying out to sea with six men trailing from it in the cords of their 'chutes. The 'chutes had become entangled with the fuselage. The pilot was bucketing the plane about in an effort to dislodge them.

There was no delay in launching the counter-attack. Every unit had received instructions to go straight in and annihilate the enemy, taking the fullest advantage of that brief favourable period before the parachutists had had time to establish themselves and while the ground situation was too confused to permit the *Luftwaffe* to intervene effectively from above.

The parachutists seem to have been quite taken by surprise. Prisoners·stated that they had been assured that the preliminary 'blitz' would obliterate the defenders, and they were utterly astonished to see men rising from the slit-trenches and greeting them with powerful and accurate fire.

First of all the airfield was cleared. The Germans had dropped an entire battalion here, one half to the east and one half to the west. It was practically annihilated before dark. A carrier platoon of the Leicestershire with a platoon of the York and Lancaster counter-attacked into 'Buttercup Field' on the western side and dealt with all the invaders within twenty minutes, while the Black Watch cleared the eastern approaches. Captain Burckardt, the only surviving officer from the whole battalion, managed to collect about 60 or 70 men in a gulley to the south-east of the airfield at nightfall, and a few snipers who had established themselves in the Greek barracks on the southern edge of the field continued to hold out. But the rest of the battalion had been destroyed. Five men escaped by showing considerable enterprise and endurance. They managed to reach the shore and, swimming along the coast, eventually rejoined regimental headquarters to whom they brought news of the disaster.

After the clearing up of this area, the Leicestershire were able to give assistance to the Australians in attending to the hill known as 'Charlies' and the country immediately east of Heraklion.

> Some Germans took refuge in a field of barley. The barley stood about three feet high and gave cover from view. From this position they sniped our troops who, unable to see them, could only fire back at random.
>
> 'Let's set the bloody barley on fire boys,' a soldier said.
>
> Men crawled out across the intervening ground with bullets flipping all round them. The barley was fairly dry and flared up as matches were touched to it. A brisk wind set the flames dancing through it at high speed, and the hidden Germans jumped up and ran like rabbits smoked out of their burrows. They were machine-gunned and picked off with rifles as they ran.[1]

Not pretty! Just war.

Things were going very badly for the Germans, and at about 7. 20 p.m. when it had become clear that the main objectives had not been achieved, the bombers came over again to attack our principal concentrations. Further parachutists were subsequently dropped, this time well to the east of East Beach, beyond even our most advanced outpost. These late arrivals knew nothing of the situation at the airfield, which they assumed to have been seized by this time. They endeavoured to push through and join hands with the battalion supposed to be in possession there, and were surprised to find themselves held up shortly before midnight by strong opposition on the edge of the airfield plateau.

The rather raw Greek troops in Heraklion, meanwhile, were undergoing a much greater ordeal at the hands of Germans who had forced their way in from the south and west. A confused and scrambling fight developed from dusk onwards in the steep and narrow streets running down to the harbour. The Germans, opposed by an odd medley of Greeks, Australians, York and Lancaster and Black Watch, gradually worked their way forward and between ten and eleven o'clock they reached the harbour itself.

A party of some thirty Australians and British, retreating before them, had been driven on to the long mole that juts out to sea, a relic of Venetian times. There was a gun at the end of the mole, but it had run out of ammunition.

[1] Hetherington. *Airborne Invasion,*

With the Germans at the landward end of the mole, sweeping its extremity in the moonless night with heavy but inaccurate fire, there was nothing for our troops to do but attempt to escape by boat. They were fortunate in finding four small rowing boats moored near the end of the mole, and the whole party managed to embark without loss of a single man. They rowed some little distance out to sea.

Then the dark outline of a ship loomed up close ahead. There was a hail in English.

'We're British!' was the reply.

'All right. Come on board!'

They had encountered a British destroyer which was searching the seas round Crete for the enemy invasion fleet.

6

The Balance

WHEN, in the light of the information available, the German Command reviewed the situation at the end of the first day there could have been little cause for satisfaction. It must have become clear that a bad miscalculation had been made regarding the strength of the Anglo-Greek forces in Crete; so far from having to deal with some 5,000 British troops there were about five times that number from Britain and the Dominions, besides the Greeks who amounted to 11,000. Against these the Germans had landed some 8,000 men.

At Heraklion they had launched 2,000 of whom half were already lost. Some of the attackers had got into the town; others were very much on the defensive in buildings to the south of the airfield; another detachment was established further to the east. The airfield itself had not been captured.

At Retimo, 1,200 men had been dropped and about half had become casualties. The remainder was separated into a eastern and western detachment, with almost the entire garrison of Australians and Greeks between them; and although the eastern force was still in a position to threaten the airfield it could scarcely be claimed that it held the initiative.

At Canea about 2,000 had been put down, but severe losses had been suffered and the attack on the town had failed. Only to the south-west along the Alikianou road (Prison Valley) was there any considerable force in being.

At Maleme rather more than 2,000 troops had been dropped, and here again losses were severe. The invaders had forced us off the airfield and controlled the western fringe themselves while our troops remained near to the eastern edge. The field itself was therefore a no-man's-land effectively held by neither side. It was not yet true to say that Maleme was 'taken'.

One may say that the German sacrifices—and in men and aircraft they were considerable—on the first day had gained certain opportunities rather than solid advantages.

The scale of losses was of course not yet known to the German Corps Command back in Athens. The first reports, following the morning air landings around Maleme and Canea, gave reason to suppose that all was going well and according to plan. Then, in the early afternoon, information was received that the attack upon Canea had been discontinued after heavy losses had been suffered: and about this time the news of the fatal accident to General Süssmann was reported.

Later came information from Group West describing heavy fighting and the wounding of General Meindl. Towards evening came a report, unconfirmed and as it happened inaccurate, that Maleme airfield had been captured.

No news had been received from Retimo since the attackers had found it impossible to establish any wireless communication. From Heraklion came news of heavy fighting to the east of the airfield. List and Student must have realized that days of more heavy fighting lay ahead.

It is unlikely that any serious consideration was given to the possibility of calling off the whole operation. In practice, there was no choice. The Germans were deeply committed, and to cut their losses meant writing off the picked troops who had been landed on the island that day. Nor was it the German method to throw in a hand so easily. More troops must be fed into the battle—therefore the decision was taken to commit the 5th Mountain Division in full. The seaborne support troops and weapons must be forthcoming on the following day, although no port had yet been won at which they could be landed. The ferrying of troops by air must continue—therefore every effort must be made to obtain quick possession of at least one airfield. Only at Maleme was there a possibility of obtaining an early grip—therefore the success already won there must be reinforced to the full. And meanwhile until an airfield could be effectively occupied, transport aircraft must be crash-landed wherever the nature of the ground allowed, and those troops who were established in reasonable strength in open country must set to work to prepare landing-strips.

Fresh forces had to be found at once to maintain the offensive at Maleme. Consideration was given to a proposal to evacuate the troops from Retimo and land them in the neighbourhood of Maleme; but it was realized that this could not be achieved with any speed, and the plan was abandoned. But two companies were available which should have landed on the west side of Heraklion during the previous afternoon, but had been kept back owing to the lateness of the hour. These could now be employed at Maleme, and the whole of the 5th Mountain Division (the 'follow-up' division) would now be landed there as well. That part of it which was to have gone by sea to Heraklion would now be diverted towards Maleme and Canea.

If the German Command was considerably dashed by the result of the first day's fighting, it cannot be pretended that the picture from our side was reassuring. The scale of the attack though not exceeding the expectations of the defenders on the island was greater than had been anticipated by the Middle East Command as it frankly admitted in General Wavell's despatch. Nevertheless, the result of the day's fighting was on the whole encouraging, since nowhere save at Maleme were the enemy achievements such as to cause undue disquiet. General Freyberg reported to Wavell that night:

> The day has been a hard one. We have been hard pressed. So
> far I think we hold Maleme, Heraklion and Retimo aerodromes
> and the two harbours. The margin by which we hold them is a bare
> one, and it would be wrong of me to paint an optimistic picture.

He added that communications were 'most difficult'. There was a shortage of supplies, particularly ammunition, in some sectors, and these could only be brought up henceforth by night and under an armed guard in view of the possibility of convoys being attacked by roaming bands of Germans.

An attempt was made, without delay, to satisfy Freyberg's request for more ammunition. This would have to be landed at Suda, and the only solution was to ask the Royal Navy for a warship which could make the trip and unload during the hours of darkness. Two destroyers were promised, to take fifty tons of ammunition between them on the following night.

The problems of transport and communication could not be solved. Had they been we might have held Crete longer and parted with it at a greater price. With inadequate wireless equipment, telephone lines destroyed by bomb attack or cut by enemy paratroopers, and no kind of vehicle which could be spared to carry a message, all that remained was the runner. The ingenuity of modern offensive war had reduced us to employing the methods of Pheidippides, who ran a hundred and fifty miles to carry the news of the battle of Marathon from Athens to Sparta. And so runners, or an occasional motorcycle despatch-rider, carried the bulk of the messages between the four sectors and between units in the same sectors. The impossibility of maintaining effective and punctual contact under such circumstances is apparent from a single example. On one occasion a runner was sent with a message from Retimo to Suda Bay. The distance was 45 miles. The messenger had to run the gauntlet of spasmodic fighting on the road, had to pass twice through enemy positions, wriggling through bushes on his stomach and sniped at if he dared to raise his head. He got through in the end. But it took him—just six days.

The communiqué issued on the afternoon of May 20th by G.H.Q., Middle East ran as follows:

> Early this morning German parachutists and airborne troops made an attempt to secure a footing on the island of Crete. A number have already been accounted for.

The communiqué of May 21st dealing with the fighting of the later part of the previous day, read:

> Throughout yesterday Crete was subjected to a series of intensive air attacks, in the intervals of which fresh waves of German parachute airborne troops were landed at various points.
>
> Heavy fighting continued throughout the day, in which the enemy sustained serious losses, while ours were comparatively light. At one point a German detachment which succeeded in penetrating into the outskirts of Canea was quickly surrounded and accounted for. Operations are continuing.

CHAPTER III

Royal Escape

MEANWHILE, as the battle swayed backwards and forwards around Maleme and Canea, outside Retimo and Heraklion, the day had witnessed the beginning of one of the most sensational and dramatic episodes of the war.

King George II of the Hellenes was regarded by the Germans as their chief enemy in Greece. They affected the view that his blind Anglophile prejudice had caused him to urge his country into conflict with the Axis (oblivious of the fact that it was Greece which had been wantonly attacked by Italy and Germany in turn) and that he was therefore the symbol of an obscurantist refusal to accept the blessings of the 'New Order'. He had been singled out by Hitler for special denunciation in the latter's speech on May 4th after the conclusion of the campaign in Greece.

On April 22nd King George had withdrawn with his Government to Crete and had there issued a proclamation announcing his determination to fight to the finish. It would therefore be not altogether surprising if an enemy airborne operation should aim at seizing the person of the King as a valuable hostage and as a sign that the long arm of Hitler could pluck even monarchs from under the protection of the British.

This danger had been fully realized, and plans had been made for an overland evacuation of the King and his entourage, if the situation seemed to demand it. According to the scheme worked out by Colonel J.S. Blunt, British military attaché in Greece, with the approval of Force Headquarters, the Royal party would move from the house where the King was then living near the village of Perivolia, a couple of miles from Canea, up across the central mountains and thence down to the village of Ayia Roumeli on the south coast, where a destroyer would be in readiness, two days after the start of the march, to convey the party to Egypt.[1]

It was on the morning of May 19th, following the customary bomber raid, that the King decided that it would be advisable to move from his own house, which lay more or less directly under the route of the dive-bombers, to that of his Prime Minister, M. Tsuderos, which was a mile or so further south and close to the foothills. Here, besides being less exposed to attacks, he would be better placed for assuring the retreat into the mountains, should the necessity arise. Accordingly, the move was made—very fortunately, as it turned out—that same afternoon.

Next morning, following the customary air bombardment, the gliders and troop-carriers could be seen flying serenely overhead. The imminence of a large-scale airborne attack was obvious, and even before the parachutists appeared Colonel Blunt had made his preliminary arrangements for the party to move towards the mountains.

Standing in the garden outside the Prime Minister's house, the King and his attendants were able to watch the parachutes open and the little dabs of silk, white, green and red, float down towards the earth. A landing in strength was being made around Perivolia, and between 150 and 200 men descended on every side of the villa so lately occupied by the King of the Hellenes. On the face of it, it seemed reasonable to assume that the Germans were accurately informed of the whereabouts of the Sovereign and that this particular party had received definite instructions to kill or capture him.[1].

Colonel Blunt accordingly ordered that, in view of the scale of the attack and its propinquity to the King's person (the nearest parachutists were less than half a mile away), the party should make a prompt withdrawal from the neighbourhood of Perivolia. It was so important to keep the King out of German hands that in view of the form which the attack had taken, the only course was to move

---

[1] See Map 8.

[1] This was not the case. The parachutists who landed around Perivolia were a company of the 3rd Battalion, No. 3 Parachute Rifle Regiment who should have been dropped in the neighbourhood of Galatas. They had no knowledge of the whereabouts of the King. Nevertheless, had he remained in his own house on the night of May 19th/20th he might well have been either killed or captured, next morning.

without delay right out of the battle area up into the central mountains.

For assuring the protection of the King one platoon of New Zealanders, from the 18th Battalion, under 2nd Lieut. W. H. Ryan had been provided by Force Headquarters; counting a number of Greek gendarmes, the whole party totalled less than forty. With the King was his cousin, Prince Peter, Colonel Levidis (Master of Ceremonies), M. Tsuderos, M. Varvaressos (Governor of the Bank of Greece) and one or two servants. By 9.30 a.m. the party had begun to move off through the foothills towards the high mountains that form the backbone of the island.

Almost at the start they ran into danger, for a dozen parachutists dropped very close to them but were driven off by the fire of Ryan's New Zealanders. A little later three groups of parachutists landed within a few hundred yards of the Royal party, but apparently they failed to see it, for they at once moved off from the foothills in the direction of the plain.

Again and again, however, the King and his escort had to drop flat on their faces among the rocks as hostile aircraft droned overhead. At times these came so low that the watchers on the ground could actually see the faces of the pilots. Since the King was wearing the uniform of a Greek general, covered with gold braid and medal ribbons, he was lucky not to have attracted any particular attention, and at length Ryan was constrained to request him to take his tunic off, for fear that some more observant German pilot should draw the correct conclusions regarding the identity of the party.

Actually the danger was greater from Greeks than from Germans. On that confused and hectic morning they were more than once fired at by a party of Cretans who had observed their progress up the mountain slopes.

'Can't you see we are Greeks?' called out Prince Peter.

'Germans also speak Greek and wear Greek uniforms', was the damnably logical reply; and the firing continued for some minutes longer before the men on the ridge above were finally reassured.

After five hours climbing the party reached a cave on the mountain side where it was possible to rest in safety and eat a meal from the rations which the troops carried. A number of mules were obtained here. After arranging for the King and his escort to continue on up into the hills, Colonel Blunt moved off down into the plain with a section of Ryan's New Zealand platoon to make contact with the nearest Allied formation and find out how the battle was going. At Mournies he met the New Zealand liaison officer of the Greek battalion holding the village and heard the story of the first few hours of fighting in the neighbourhood. He learned that there were Germans in strength between Mournies and Canea and that there was no prospect of getting through to Force Headquarters. A patrol which he had sent back to Perivolia to secure certain papers left behind by M. Tsuderos and certain valuables belonging to the King (including the insignia of the Order of the Garter) reported the Prime Minister's house occupied by the Germans. Colonel Blunt accordingly made his way back with his escort and rejoined the Royal party in the mountains.

That night, the King and his escort, going on ahead, reached the village of Therisson at the head of a mountain glen. It was almost deserted because all the able-bodied inhabitants had already set off for the valley to fight the invader. Though they had been climbing all day, so steep had been the mountain and so slow their progress that they were scarcely more than eight miles, as the crow flies, from Canea.

The headman of the village, who was far too old to fight, received the party in his house and provided them with a meal of bread, cheese and red wine. While they were settling down to sleep on the stone they heard a clamour of voices and then a heavy knocking at the door. Supposing that they had been tracked to this mountain fastness, they sprang up only to find a body of uncouth-looking Greeks on the threshold. They wore striped prison garb.

They were convicts from the prison on the Alikianou road in the valley below. The Germans had dropped around the building early in the day, occupied it, freed the prisoners, and were now setting up a military hosptial in the building.

Gratitude, however, for this unexpected release in no way overcame patriotism. The freed convicts took the first opportunity to make off to the hills where they hoped to find arms. And many of them afterwards fought bravely against their 'liberators'.

Next morning the Royal party woke to a clear view of the battlefield below. The red earth of the coastal plain and the fields of ripening corn were flecked and spattered with innumerable parachutes—white like patches of snow, sometimes red like patches of blood. Here and there the carcasses of disabled troop carriers could be seen, but there were more troop carriers moving in to dump their loads, and enemy bombers and fighters roamed at will the skies above the battle.

Colonel Blunt in the course of the previous evening had at last succeeded in getting through from the local telephone exchange to the senior naval officer at Suda Bay. The latter advised the party to continue across the island to the southern coast. It was estimated that the journey would take a further two days to accomplish, and he undertook to do his best to ensure evacuation on the night of Thursday, May 22nd.

The party resumed their climb. It proved less eventful than that of the previous day, but certainly no less tiring. By nightfall they were over 7,000 feet up and close to the crest of the central mountain ridge and were compelled to sleep out in the bitter cold. They cleared the snow that was still lying on these upper ridges, lit a fire and roasted a lean mountain sheep over the flames. The only shelter they were able to obtain during the night was by squeezing down among the rocks in the crevices of a mountain gulley. Some managed to sleep in this manner; others found it warmer to sit huddled around the fire all night. The New Zealanders, who had come from the heat of the coastal plain, had neither greatcoats nor blankets and were clad in regulation summer kit of thin shirts and shorts.

Next morning, awakened before dawn by the sound of naval gunfire from the north where Admiral Cunningham's Mediterranean Fleet was dealing faithfully with the enemy attempt at a seaborne invasion, they continued southwards. They were now beyond the crest of the mountain ridge and descending towards the sea, but the going was no easier, for they had to abandon the mules at an early stage, since even these animals were unable to keep their feet on the precipitous, rocky slopes. There was much actual climbing to be done in the course of this day, and the boots of almost everyone in the party were torn and ripped on the sharp crags. The novelty of the adventure had certainly worn off by this time, and everyone was feeling the effects of the past two strenuous days.

Early in the day Colonel Blunt found it advisable to divide the party into a fast-moving and a slow-moving group. The former consisted of the King, Prince Peter, members of the Royal Household and the troops, with whom was Colonel Blunt himself. The latter was composed chiefly of the civilian Ministers and the gendarmes.

M. Tsuderos subsequently said:

> During the whole of this fatiguing and heart-breaking march the King did not for the moment lose his smile. With a majestic simplicity he shared with us all dangers, all privations, all hardships. He slept for a

few hours on the cold ground, and shared with us the scant food and snow which the peasants used to bring to sustain us and quench our thirst in the absence of water.

Colonel Blunt's tribute was equally emphatic.

The bearing of everybody from His Majesty downwards was all that one could desire. His Majesty treated it like an outing and seemed bored at having to take cover from the planes.

With blistered, bleeding feet and tattered boots the party limped into the village of Samaria in the foothills, about half a dozen miles from the sea, in the early afternoon. They were regarded at first with suspicion and hostility by the villagers, who had heard stories of parachutists and were not at first reassured when the King spoke to them in Greek. However, the fugutives eventually succeeded in establishing their identity and were hospitably received. While they were resting, a Cretan messenger arrived. He carried a note from Major-General Heywood, who had been chief military representative of the British Inter-Service Mission to Greece. It stated that the General was at the rendezvous at the coastal village of Ayia Roumeli a few miles away. The King's party accordingly resumed their tramp. They had now to pass down a narrow, boulder-strewn gorge through which a stream ran to the sea, and for hundreds of yards at a time the way ran though the bed of the stream itself. A short time before they reached the coast a German air patrol passed overhead. It was a reminder that they were not yet wholly out of danger, but the aircraft were flying far too high to notice them.

General Heywood had left Canea the previous day and had done the last part of the journey by means of a small motor-boat. With him was Sir Michael Palairet, British Minister of Athens, Lady Palairet, Admiral Turle, British naval attaché and head of the Inter-Service Mission, and Mr. Harold Caccia, First Secretary at the British Legation. They had learned of the general direction taken by the King's party and had moved along the coast in the hope of meeting him.

After a meal cooked by Lady Palairet, one of the party went down to the seashore and for some hours continued to send S.O.S signals on the chance that they might be picked up by a firendly ship. Since the King's intention was known at Force Headquarters it was a reasonable assumption that some vessel of the Royal Navy would be patrolling the south-west coast of the island on the look-out for such a signal.

Not until 1 a.m. was there any reply, and then an answering flash was noted some miles out to sea. But the ship seemed reluctant to come in closer. During the evacuation from Greece the Germans had made use of S.O.S. signals to lure our warships into shore and then opened fire on them.

Eventually Admiral Turle and Mr. Caccia found a way out of the impasse. They volunteered to go out alone in the fishing boat to discover if the ship were indeed friendly.

It was a full hour before the watchers on the shore heard the throb of the engine once more and saw the fishing-boat loom out of the darkness.

'Our luck holds,' called a voice. 'It is H.M.S. *Decoy*.'

The party was speedily ferried out to the British warship, which sailed promptly to Egypt, setting them on shore late that night at Alexandria.[1]

---

[1]The facts concerning the King's escape and journey across Crete are compiled from information supplied to the author by M. Tsuderos and Colonel Blunt at Alexandria immediately after their arrival.

CHAPTER IV

The Days of Decision

1

Focus on Maleme

A REPORT received in the early morning of May 21st that the Germans had landed from the sea under cover of night near No. 7 General Hospital was soon discovered by New Zealand patrols to be false.[1]

Dawn had brought the customary, the inevitable German air attack, searching, though not very successfully, for our gun position. Then, a little after 9am., over came the troop carriers. It was a matter of sombre interest to the defenders to note whether the enemy were in a position to repeat the parachutist attack on the same scale as on the previous day. About sixty transport aircraft appeared, and these dropped something in the neighbourhood of 500 paratroops on to the positions already held by the enemy west of Maleme airfield.

Already yesterday's arrivals had renewed their attack against the airfield and against Hill 107, a mile to the south. Throughout the morning a ding-dong fire-fight continued across that bare open square mile; but with the help of their aircraft which, as so often before, played the part of a mobile artillery, the enemy was able to edge the defenders back.

The 250 men who were all that remained of the 22nd New Zealand Battalion were now divided between the 21st and 23rd Battalions, Colonel Andrew being charged with the task of co-ordinating the defence of Maleme and preventing the Germans from getting control of the airfield.

[1] See Map 9.

Then the troop carriers began to appear again.

At first they seemed content to effect crash-landings on the beaches or in the relatively safe bed of the Tavronitis. Then the defenders near the eastern fringe looking skywards saw the heavy and cumbersome JU 52's circling slowly over the airfield itself.

The airfield was still directly under fire from every weapon the New Zealanders could bring to bear—field guns, mortars, machine-guns and small arms.

> It could be nothing but a death-trap for Nazi planes attempting to land there. Nothing could live in that hell of fire. No man but a madman would send aircraft to destruction there. No man but a madman would obey an order to pilot an aircraft on to that steel-raked field.

That was the first reaction of the men on the ground . But the aircraft were circling overhead; and then they swooped down.

It seemed suicidal madness, and for the first men who landed in this manner it certainly was no less. The New Zealanders—nearly all the 5th Brigade was engaged by this time—were throwing all the metal they could at the enemy arriving overhead. It seemed to be 'money for old rope' to the men at the guns.

> Then the thing that couldn't occurred. One of the troop carriers touched down, rolled to a stop, unloaded its men and their equipment, lifted, and flew off again. It was down and away within seventy seconds.... The dark line of aircraft still streamed in from the Aegean. It seemed endless. And presently a second plane made a landing and got away then a third, then a fourth. More and more. Madness that counted not at all the cost in men's lives and shattered planes.[1]

Yet perhaps it was not really such madness. We had only eight guns available for firing on the airfield, and though contemporary reports, made in undoubted good faith, spoke of one after another of the troop carriers bursting into flames in the air or being shot to pieces by field guns and mortars before they had run to a halt, a sober examination of the facts does not support these stories. One reliable observer—the commander of a troop of artillery which was firing on Maleme—has stated that he did not see a single aircraft hit on the airfield before it came to a halt, though his troop certainly set some stationary planes on fire and caused losses to the men disembarking from the machines.

---

[1] This and the above passage are taken from the description given by Hetherington in *Airborne Invasion,* pp. 104-105.

But our guns were firing mostly with makeshift sights (in the case of one troop these were improvised from slivers of wood stuck on with chewing gum); not all of them were well emplaced for bringing direct fire to bear upon the airfield; there was repeated interruption from enemy fighters overhead; and by this time the spectre of an ammunition shortage was beginning to haunt the gunners, for a number of ammunition dumps had been destroyed by the hostile bombers.

The German Command, having made its decision to fling in the 5th Mountain Division at Maleme, was obviously prepared to accept losses on a formidable scale in order that these fresh troops might do what the parachutists had manifestly failed to do and secure the use of an airfield without delay. And that was why our persistent fire, though it caused the enemy heavy losses, particularly at the start, could not stop the landing of the troop carriers.

As more and more troops arrived in this manner the balance of fire-power began to tilt towards the enemy. Each aircraft was carrying up to forty men; the new-comers arrived fully armed and ready for instant action. They went quickly to ground, and began to put up a formidable small-arms fire. And as the afternoon lengthened the tempo of the arrivals quickened. By the end of the day enough German aircraft had touched down in the Maleme area (including the beaches and the Tavronitis bed) to bring in a considerable part of the 5th Mountain Division. How many of these hardy mountaineers had survived the experience is another question.

The landing of the troop carriers was accompanied throughout the day by a very heavy concentration of German fighter aircraft against our forward and rear positions—though in these conditions 'rear positions' is a misnomer when the defence of an area is concerned—and in particular against the routes of approach to the 5th New Zealand Brigade. It was clearly the German objective to seal off the battle area and prevent movement of any sort to or from it. For this reason the ground further east suffered as heavily during the day from low-flying attacks by Messerschmitts as did the troops near the airfield; and movement along the roads became a practical impossibility.

Believing that the bulk of the New Zealand forces had been drawn into the battle around Maleme, it seems that General Student determined to employ against the New Zealand communications the two parachute companies whose flight to Heraklion on the previous day had been cancelled owing to the lateness of the hour. These companies would be dropped along the supposedly open stretch of coast from Pirgos to Platanias and attack the 5th New Zealand Brigade near Maleme from the east, while the Assault Regiment on the airfield attacked simultaneously from the west. But once again German information was inaccurate. The two companies, who were dropped in the course of the afternoon, jumped straight into the positions held by New Zealand support troops or in full view of them. The majority had no chance of getting near their weapon containers and were speedily 'mopped up'. About eighty survivors fought their way west towards Pirgos and managed to establish themselves at a farm near the beach. Here and there over the area isolated groups collected for defence as night fell, but, viewed as an important offensive effort, the drop had failed completely.

Some Germans landed among the 'inmates' of the 5th New Zealand Brigade Punishment Centre, who gave them short shrift.

By this time our troops had captured a number of the coloured strips employed by the Germans to signal to their aircraft for supplies, as well as the code which was conveyed by a series of simple diagrams. They used these lucky finds to signal for supplies to the hostile aircraft overhead, and were rewarded by getting exactly what they asked for. Assuredly, the value of the parachutists was now proving subject to that 'law of diminishing returns' which seems inseparable from the employment of any novel weapon or novel method of warfare. On this, the second day of the battle, they were auxiliaries only and no longer the decisive arm.

The German Command had shown their recognition of the potentially decisive importance of Maleme by the heavy scale of their reinforcement there during this second day of the battle and by their comparative neglect of other sectors. Now to Freyberg came the realization that the clock was about to strike the vital hour; and the gravity of the situation and the odds arrayed against him called out the best of a man who had faced so many difficult and hazardous tasks. He knew that if the Germans were granted another day for the landing of troop-carrying aircraft on Maleme airfield they would have built up such strength that successful counter-attack would be impossible and the defence must progressively collapse. He knew that with the enemy in total and dominating control of the air above the battlefield by day the only time for a successful attack by our troops was the night. And it must be that night.

It must be that night; and it would demand every man, vehicle and gun that could be concentrated for the attack. But Freyberg knew that they might not be enough or that it might not be possible to concentrate sufficient strength in time.

All this Freyberg knew. He knew, also, that a seaborne landing was to be made—or at least attempted—that evening, and there could be no certainty that the Navy would intercept it.

The plan, as determined by General Freyberg after conferring with Brigadier Puttick, envisaged a counter-attack to retake Maleme airfield and the higher ground overlooking it, beginning with a night march to the points of concentration and developing with an assault launched just before the dawn of Thursday, May 22nd.

The whole of the 5th New Zealand Brigade would ultimately be committed. The three battalions, 21st, 22nd and 23rd, had been in action against the paratroops for two days, and the 22nd Battalion, in particular, which had borne the brunt of the fighting at Maleme on the first day, was, as we know, very much reduced in numbers and excessively tired. To lead the assault there would be available the 28th (Maori) Battalion, which had so far not been very heavily engaged, and the 20th Battalion, brought under the command of the 5th Brigade for this operation. Both were at present in technically rear areas which covered the coast line between Platanias and Canea. But since to move them up into position would leave an undefended gap along the coast which might be exploited by paratroops or by a seaborne landing, it was decided that the 2/7th Australian Battalion, which formed part of Brigadier Vasey's force watching the unassailed Georgeopolis Bay, should be moved across in motor transport to take over from the 20th New Zealand Battalion; and the latter was instructed not to begin its move forward until the Australians arrived. This was planned to occur at about 10 p.m.

There was another and more compelling reason for the delay, in that it would be necessary for the New Zealand Battalion to take over the transport vehicles from the Australians, since the first part of their move forward would be made in lorries along the main coastal road. They did not possess sufficient transport of their own. Otherwise Freyberg might have been prepared to risk leaving uncovered the coastal stretch between Platanias and Canea.

While the 20th New Zealand Battalion would advance along the coast road, with Pirgos, something over a mile short of the airfield, as its first objective, the Maoris would advance along a route parallel and to the south of the 20th to gain the high ground overlooking the objectives from the south. It was hoped that the two battalions would be able to take up positions from which the airfield could be brought under mortar and machine-gun fire. Then the final assault would go in.

The approach march from the Platanias area was to begin at 1 a.m. and the attack from the forward positions at Pirgos and to the south would open at 4 a.m. A troop of the 3rd Hussars, with its light tanks, was to lead the advance along the coast road. No 'I' tanks were available, but it appeared that the Germans lacked adequate anti-tank weapons.

Further support would be forthcoming from the R.A.F. operating from Egypt. They undertook to bomb the Maleme area from midnight onwards.

The supreme importance of the occasion was fully appreciated. All that planning could do had been done. The rest was in the lap of the gods.

Eastward, a few short miles away, the fighting on this second day of battle brought no great change to our fortunes round Canea and Suda.

As we have seen, the enemy was strongest in the Prison Valley south-west of Canea. Although the attack by the 19th New Zealand Battalion, which had started on the previous evening, had been called off, later in the morning a single company drove the Germans from Cemetery Hill, a position from which they could have enfiladed our troops further north towards Galatas and denied us artillery observation over their own concentration area.

Heidrich, who had now concentrated something like two battalions in the meadowland below, was apprehensive of an attack in force from our side, but Cemetery Hill being bare and exposed proved just as untenable by us and we were unable to exploit the advantage which its occupation had given us.

And so the ding-dong fighting went on in the restricted area between Galatas and the prison. The Germans continued to attack from the air, and their troops made an unavailing attempt to seize Cemetery Hill again. They were driven back by fire. During the day ammunition and supplies in very considerable quantities were dropped to them by air.

Elsewhere little change took place in the situation. There was, of course, little respite from the attacks of the German bombers and fighters. The Northumberland Hussars and a detachment of the Welch Regiment continued with the 'mopping up' of the Germans who had survived the ill-fated airborne landings on the Akrotiri peninsula. Canea itself was strengthened during the day by the arrival of the 2/8th Australian Battalion (400 men) from Georgeopolis and about 200 Australian gunners (from the 2/2nd Field Regiment) armed as infantry.

By the end of the day, though the enemy had gained no further ground, he had consolidated his position and strengthened his firepower in the Prison Valley, while his constant air attacks and the presence of numerous snipers within our lines continued to disrupt our communications. Moreover, the supply of small arms ammunition was running short among certain of our units, and the troops were showing ominous signs of fatigue.

On the evening of May 21st, the Headquarters of the XI Air Corps, following from Athens the development of the battle, reached the conclusion that the crisis of the attack upon Crete had been successfully surmounted. As the result of the day's fighting at Maleme, it was felt that the situation at the airfield was reasonably secure, for the landing of the troop-carriers had been effective, though entailing serious losses. It seemed to the German Command that our power to launch a counter-offensive here was exhausted. The New Zealanders had been repulsed when they attempted local counter-attacks; air reconnaissance reports of an advance in strength from the south, which at first caused some alarm, had proved to be groundless; and it was now clear that we had no forces in the Kastelli neighbourhood—that is in the extreme north-west of the island—which could deliver an attack from the west. Major-General Ringel, who now took over Group West at Maleme, hoped to be in a position to advance against Canea on the following day. Gradually the whole of the 5th Mountain Division would be fed into his sector, while the invaders at Retimo and Heraklion concentrated upon keeping the maximum number of our troops engaged and denying us the use of the airfields at those places.

And that night the invasion fleet, carrying the heavy supporting arms, motor transport, and two battalions of Ringel's 5th Mountain Division would arrive off shore.

2

Sea Venture

IT is the measure of the German failure during the first two days that, with the exception of Maleme, not one of the points that were to have been in their hands before the arrival of their sea expedition had yet been taken. They had not secured Canea—much less Suda, or Retimo and its airfield, or Heraklion and its airfield. The ships due to sail for Heraklion had been counter-ordered, and those destined for Maleme had had their departure twice postponed. But now their purpose was to put ashore the troops and arms as near Maleme as possible and if necessary to force a landing.

Our Mediterranean Fleet had been ready since May 15th for such an attempt. On May 20th the ships were widely deployed, screening the island from invasion by sea. The battleships *Warspite* and *Valiant* accompanied by six destroyers (Rear-Admiral H.B. Rawlings) were to the west of Crete to guard against the unlikely event of the reappearance of the Italian fleet.[1] The cruisers *Dido, Ajax* and *Orion,* with the destroyers *Isis, Kimberley, Imperial* and *Janus* (Rear-Admiral I. G.S. Glennie wearing his flag in the *Dido*) were to patrol the western half of Crete's north coast by night, with particular attention to Maleme-Canea-Suda. A third force, consisting of the cruisers *Naiad* and *Perth,* with the destroyers *Kandahar, Nubian, Kingston* and *Juno* (Rear-Admiral E. L. S. King wearing his flag in the *Naiad*) would simultaneously sweep the eastern half of the north coast, with particular attention to Heraklion.

These night sweeps were duly carried out, but apart from a few Italian motor-boats to the north-east of the island no hostile craft were observed. Meanwhile the destroyers *Jervis, Nizam* and *Ilex* bombarded the Italian aerodrome on Scarpanto in the Dodecanese with some success.

So far so good. But the perils to which the fleet would be exposed became only too apparent on the following day. Our ships were patrolling close to the enemy forward air bases and possessed no

---

[1] A renewed attempt had been made by the Germans on May 20th to persuade the Italian fleet to put to sea in order to draw off the British warships from Crete. It failed owing to the stubborn, and realistic, refusal of the authorities in Rome.

fighter protection of their own. Throughout May 21st they were attacked by German bombers, both of the dive-bomber and high level variety. These had the definite objective of sinking so many ships that the remainder would be compelled to withdraw in order to escape destruction, leaving the way clear for the German seaborne invasion. On May 21st, however, the enemy aircraft failed conspicuously in his task.

Over came the bombers again and again, while the ships below them zigzagged continually to avoid being hit and thundered back at the aircraft without pause. It was a grim experience, this trailing of the coast in front of the German Bomber Command, and to the men in the ships the long hours of daylight seemed interminable. All three squadrons were spotted by German reconnaisance planes and were bombed repeatedly, but the losses were far lighter on this day than might have been expected. *Juno* was hit soon after noon by a whole stick of bombs and quickly sank, and *Ajax* was damaged by near misses. But the fleet kept the sea unperturbed, and before nightfall the bombers were compelled to desist. The German invasion ships would have to take their chance, with the British Mediterranean Fleet still at sea very much on the alert to intercept them; and with land patrols covering the beaches round Suda, where searchlights and coastal guns were waiting in readiness to play their part in repelling the attack.

It was shortly before midnight that Admiral Glennie's force[1] picked up the first of the invasion convoys, consisting of small steamers and caiques, escorted by an Italian torpedo-boat, about eighteen miles north of Canea. Once the searchlights had illuminated them the rest was almost child's play. The boot was on the other foot now, and our ships were able to do much more than repay all they had suffered from the bombing during the day. The torpedo boat was heavily hit but not sunk, and then the British destroyers thrust grimly in among the light craft and destroyed many of them.[1] Some were rammed, others sunk by gunfire. In the restrained words of the Admiral, our ships 'conducted themselves with energy and zest'.

Destroyers *Hasty* and *Hereward* had now relieved *Isis* and *Imperial*.

According to a German account only a small portion of the flotilla was caught and destroyed. This *Luftwaffe* report adds: 'To avoid the risk of a similar fate overtaking the 2nd Motor Sailing Flotilla, then on its way to Crete, the admiral commanding South-Eastern Area ordered its immediate return to Piraeus, and the problem of supplying heavy arms and reinforcements by sea therefore remained unsolved.'

About 8.30 next morning a further section of the invasion fleet was encountered by *Naiad* and *Perth* with their attendant destroyers, now joined by the anti-aircraft cruisers *Calcutta* and *Carlisle* and the cruisers *Fiji* and *Gloucester*. Admiral King's powerful squadron promptly engaged the first ships visible. A caique was sunk, then a small merchant vessel. An enemy torpedo-boat was sighted and engaged, hits being scored on her; she then withdrew behind a smoke-screen which also helped to conceal a large number of caiques which were under her escort.

The enemy force was withdrawing rapidly northward in the direction of Milos, and under other circumstances would have been easy game for our ships. But in view of the fact that his anti-aircraft ammunition was already beginning to run low, and remembering his experience of the previous day, Admiral King decided against pursuing the destroyers and light craft of the invasion fleet any further northward.

Contact was therefore broken off, and the enemy force was enabled to withdraw in the direction of the ports from which it had emerged a few hours earlier. Nevertheless, these two actions did in fact practically mark the end of the danger of attack from the sea. Estimates of the number of trained mountain troops drowned or killed vary between two and four thousand. A few survivors, almost demented by their ordeal, eventually stumbled ashore near Canea. A large number were washed ashore dead during the next few days.

Yet our fleet had to remain at sea, for more enemy craft were known to be available for a further attempt. And it was during this day, May 22nd, that it suffered its most severe losses from bombing attacks, losses which exercised a great influence upon the course of the battle for Crete.

Admiral King's force of cruisers and destroyers, after dispersing the second portion of the German invasion fleet, was within easy reach of the German dive-bomber bases. At 10.a.m., on May 22nd, while, as will presently be seen, the land battle was swinging his way at Maleme, the enemy's aircraft resumed their attack upon our ships. Wednesday had been a supremely hazardous but under the circumstances not a costly day for the Mediterranean Fleet. They could scarcely hope to expect such good fortune a second time. The destroyer *Greyhound* was sunk early in the afternoon in the strait between Crete and Kithira. The cruiser *Gloucester* was hit and sunk in the same neighbourhood; and very late in the afternoon the cruiser *Fiji,* which had survived some twenty bombing attacks in the course of four hours, fell a victim to a single aircraft which swooped suddenly out of the clouds. Luckily, most of the crew were saved. *Warspite, Valiant* and *Carlisle* were also hit during the day, and *Naiad* was seriously damaged.

At 10.30 that night Admiral Cunningham received a signal from the commander of the Seventh Cruiser Squadron, from which it appeared, owing to a calligraphic error, that the battleships of the main force at sea had no pom-pom ammunition left. In fact they had plenty. Acting on this misinformation, however, Cunningham issued the order at four o'clock next morning, that all naval forces should withdraw forthwith to Alexandria.[1]

With the daylight the dive-bombers returned, and at about eight o'clock in the morning (May 23rd) the destroyers *Kelly* and *Kashmir,* which had arrived as part of a destroyer flotilla from Malta to join in the hunt, were hit and speedily sank. The remainder of the fleet continued its withdrawal. In the course of three days since the battle had started two cruisers and four destroyers had been sunk, while two battleships, two cruisers and four destroyers had been more or less seriously damaged. These losses clearly showed that it was impracticable for the fleet to continue to operate by daylight in the neighbourhood of Crete. They could only continue to navigate in reasonable safety if given overhead cover from fighter planes; and that was exactly what they could not be given, for the same reason that the troops who were being riddled by low-flying aircraft around Maleme could not be given it—because our bases were too distant. Crete lay a full two hundred miles too far to the north. Upon that simple geographical fact hinged the whole issue of the battle.

For if the fleet could not keep the seas around Crete there would be nothing to prevent seaborne reinforcements ultimately following up the airborne troops. The enemy henceforth could not put supplies and reinforcements by air and sea into Crete and could prevent us doing likewise. On that fateful May 22nd it was so clearly seen that it is not enough to command the seas unless one can command the air over the seas as well. Our air battle had been lost

[1] The withdrawal of the ships on the morning of May 23rd was not caused, as has been shown, by the losses incurred, but by the misinterpreted signal regarding the shortage of A.A. ammunition. The fleet did not, in fact, operate by daylight in the neighbourhood of Crete again. Reviewing the position on May 24th Admiral Cunningham decided that 'the scale of air attack now made it no longer possible for the Navy to operate in the Aegean or vicinity of Crete by day'.

from the start. Now the sea battle was lost, on the very day that the tide began to turn decisively against us on land. What remained could only be a delaying battle, a rearguard action, such as we had fought in Greece a month earlier, an action in which we must aim at inflicting the maximum losses upon the enemy and at saving what we could of our own forces from the wreck.

All this could not, of course, be immediately apparent to Freyberg and his subordinates, piecing together their information as it came in and improvising from one day to another, often from one hour to another, With the information now available, in the light of after events, we can see that from this day onwards the battle must follow a fixed and determinate course.

3

Maleme—Canea—Suda

THE hardest and most bitterly contested engagement of the battle for Crete began before the dawn of May 22nd paled the sky.[1] It was, perhaps, the decisive engagement of the whole ten days. It was decisive in the sense that unless we could drive out the Germans from Maleme airfield and its neighbourhood Crete was lost to us. On the other hand it is too much to assume that even victory at this stage could have kept the island for us.

The counter-attack, planned so carefully and delivered with as much strength as General Freyberg could commit, was, from the first, subject to the inevitable hazards of war. Its timing depended upon the punctual arrival of the 2/7th Australian Battalion which was to relieve the 20th New Zealand Battalion (Major J.T. Burrows) in the coastal area between Canea and Platanias. But the Australians were delayed in their move westward by a heavy air attack which pinned them down for some time, and coming through Suda they lost their guide. Only two companies had arrived at 1 a.m. when the whole battalion should have been present and ready to hand over its transport to the New Zealanders for their advance along the coastal road.

It was then decided that the New Zealanders should move off to the attack company by company as the Australians came in. This course was far from ideal, but to wait until the whole Australian

[1] See Map 9.

battalion had appeared would have resulted in the total loss of the invaluable hours of darkness.

Not until 3.30 a.m. was the whole of the New Zealand force in motion and advancing against its first objectives. Two and a half hours had been lost and dawn was very near, but until dawn the troops did very well.

Preceded by the three tanks of the 3rd Hussars the New Zealanders pressed on with the 20th Battalion on the road and the coastal strip, Lieut.-Colonel G. Dittmer's Maori battalion along the higher ground inland. In this area on the previous afternoon an unsuccessful parachutist landing had been made, but not all the enemy had been disposed of. So the number of isolated centres of resistance to be cleared—often by bayonet and grenade—proved greater than had been expected and consumed precious time. But, in any case, the advance could not be rapid: the darkness made it difficult for each platoon to keep touch with its neighbours and to recognize friend from foe. And as the New Zealanders pushed westward the German resistance increased and progress became slower still.

Commanding one of the leading platoons of the 20th was 2nd-Lieut C.H. Upham who, with pistol and grenade, subdued, almost single-handed, two machine-gun posts and, by tossing a grenade through the window of a house, enabled his men to destroy another. Later he was to go forward under heavy fire and guide back to the battalion position a company which had beome isolated during the advance. And all this was accomplished by a man who was weak from dysentery, in no state, one would have thought, to enter the battle at all. We shall hear of Charles Upham again.

With dawn at hand the New Zealanders approached their vital objectives—the airfield itself and the high ground overlooking it from the south. Maleme village was still in German hands and here the fire of anti-tank guns (so much for the theory that the enemy possessed no such weapons) hit a tank. The guns of the other two tanks jammed, and all three were then withdrawn, one of them being lost by air attack in the process.

On the extreme right some of the 20th Battalion had pushed forward along the beach to the edge of the airfield. Further they could not go. The left wing of the 20th was engaged in hand to hand conflict at Maleme. The Maoris had reached the near end of the ridges south of the airfield.

The New Zealanders had accomplished remarkable things. And

they had found that at close quarters the German infantryman possessed less actual battlecraft than themselves.

'They broke before bayonet charges and bunched badly in their flight' ran one official report. 'They also tended to bunch badly in cover and showed little knowledge of deployment. The impression was confirmed that the Germans were physically very fit and superbly armed, but that they showed a meagre knowledge of the finer points of soldiering.'

But with daylight the German aircraft began to take a hand in the battle, as had been all too accurately anticipated. With repeated low-flying attacks being made upon our troops it was clear that we could not hope to take the airfield. Nor could Maleme village be cleared without a heavier concentration of artillery fire than we could bring to bear upon it. Also, the positions that the forward troops had reached by daybreak were not suitable for defence against air attack.

Almost the whole of the 5th New Zealand Brigade was now committed, for the 21st and 23rd Battalions (between whom was divided the remnant of the 22nd) had joined in as the advance reached them.[1] One small detachment (men of the 22nd) actually got as far as the final objective, the Tavronitis valley. But the forward positions could not be held, and the decision was taken to withdraw the troops in the coastal plain southwards to try and consolidate on the higher ground won by the Maoris.

The counter-attack had indeed failed. It had, in the words of General Wavell's subsequent despatch, 'recaptured almost the whole of the ground lost', and in the process it had inflicted heavy casualties on the enemy; but at the decisive point it had failed, because we had not recovered possession of the airfield. The over-late start, the length of the opposed approach march, and the exposed nature of the positions which we had attained when the *Luftwaffe* intervened after daybreak were all factors contributing to the failure.

And our casualties, too, had been severe.

Oblivious of the losses they might still suffer, the Germans now began to employ a regular 'taxi' service to and from Maleme. The big JU 52's kept arriving, each with its complement of up to forty fully equipped men. At one time during the afternoon these planes were actually coming in at the rate of three to every five minutes. Circle around, spiral down, land, take off, was the regular drill.

---

[1] The share of the 23rd Battalion was limited to the employment of one company for 'mopping up' purposes after the attack had passed through.

To some observers it seemed a shade too speedy, a shade too regular. Could it be that the enemy, discouraged by his losses, was actually beginning to withdraw, and that the planes which appeared, landed and disappeared so rapidly were in reality taking men off the island and not bringing more to it? It seemed a theory worth testing, and strong fighting patrols were sent out during the afternoon to do so. They found the Germans well-armed and posted in strength across the routes of their reconnaissance and were forced to withdraw. These encounters scarcely supported the theory of an evacuation.

Evidence from enemy sources shows that such a possibility was never seriously considered. It is true that the German Command was very discouraged by the poor results achieved in the first forty-eight hours of the battle. The wise inaccuracy of their estimate of our strength in Crete had thrown the well-laid plans agley. How much longer they could have continued to reinforce by air, with the attendant losses involved, had they lost control of the airfield is an open question. But some comments on the British side seem somewhat to understress the use which the Germans were already making, and were presumably prepared to go on making, of the beaches and of the Tavronitis river bed. For that reason it can never be said with certainty that, even had the counter-attack in the early hours of May 22nd succeeded to the full, the Germans would have been unable to retain and subsequently extend their foothold on Crete. All that can be said with certainty is that we could certainly have rendered it more costly. There was, of course, a limit to the number of aircraft which the Germans could crash land, but even if this limit had been reached the enemy might still have exploited the possibilities of seaborne landings.

In the course of this critical May 22nd the Germans landed three mountain battalions, elements of a parachute artillery unit and a field hospital on the airfield at Maleme. Even allowing for the effectiveness of the enemy's use of aircraft for bombardment purposes, this was a remarkable achievement: the landing-ground was still within range of our field guns and was littered with broken-down and burning aircraft, but the debris was rapidly removed, with the help of tanks captured from us; and the strong measures taken by General Ringel, the new commander of Group West, restored discipline which was at one time badly shaken.

The number of new troops was quite sufficient to swing the balance of strength to the side of the enemy, and Ringel could now turn his attention to developing the offensive, instead of having to concentrate solely upon maintaining his foothold at Maleme. Under the new plan three battle groups were formed.

The first, two battalions strong, under Major Schaette, was detailed to protect Maleme from any possible counter-thrust from the south and west to which the Germans throughout these early days of the battle were peculiarly sensitive. The main body at Maleme would be placed under Colonel Ramcke, who had commanded the Group temporarily after the wounding of General Meindl. Reorganized, it would develop the attack eastwards towards Canea. A third body, consisting of the 1st Battalion of No. 85 Mountain Regiment (5th Mountain Division) under Colonel Utz, would begin an enveloping movement to the south.

The advance eastward upon Canea could not start before the following day, but Schaette began to move out to the west to clear the way to Kastelli. No. 1 Greek Regiment, with three New Zealand officers and ten N.C.O.s, about forty gendarmes and some Cretan guerrillas, the whole under the command of Major G. Bedding, offered a tenacious resistance, fighting—in the words of the German official account—'with the utmost cunning'; so that it was not until the morning of May 26th that Schaette completed his mission by the capture of Kastelli.

Despite its great exertions the 5th New Zealand Brigade was still to be reckoned with. Local counter-attacks by the 21st Battalion and the Maoris against a spur south of Pirgos were still developing during the afternoon, though the enemy had penetrated once more into Pirgos village. At five o'clock the indefatigable Freyberg ordered yet another counter-attack against the airfield, estimating that if Crete could be saved at Maleme, that evening provided the last desperate chance of doing so. The morrow would be too late. Brigadier Puttick, however, who had command of all the forces west of Canea, felt compelled to point out that enemy concentrations 'of considerable but undisclosed strength' were threatening an attack towards Galatas from the prison area and that these troops, who constituted a permanent threat to the communications between the two New Zealand brigades, should first be dealt with. To cap this, Brigadier Hargest, on behalf of the 5th Brigade, reported that his men were exhausted by the hard fighting of the day, following upon a night of intense activity, and were unfit for any immediate operation.

So it seemed that attack was impossible, and the positions

occupied after the counter-attack were unsuitable for defence. Brigadier Puttick therefore took the decision, which was reluctantly confirmed by General Freyberg, to withdraw the 5th New Zealand Brigade to a new concentration area on the coast to the rear of Platanias. The effect of this would be to echelon the brigade from Platanias to the neighbourhood of Canea. The Maori Battalion, which had been the rearmost of the four (in relation to Maleme) on the morning of the attack, would now in resuming its old position become the most forward battalion, the others taking up positions further to the east. This move would have the advantage of still preventing a link-up of the enemy's Maleme troops with the Prison Valley contingent and would give the divisional commander the option of employing his more closely concentrated brigade either for a counter-attack against the prison region, for consolidating a line from Platanias south-eastwards or, thirdly, for carrying out a measured withdrawal upon Canea.

Unfortunately, detailed instructions could not be issued to the battalions until the small hours of the following morning, and although the forward troops began the withdrawal before midnight, it was clear that the movement would still be in progress at daybreak.

None of the reserve rations could be brought away with the troops, and all the food which reached the brigade on this evening was in one half-loaded carrier. The hundreds of corpses which lay in the sun threatened to breed disease, and there was a probability that the village wells were becoming polluted. Attending to the wounded and getting them away was a well nigh impossible task, for every convoy needed an escort and every vehicle a constant guard.

The threatened attack towards Galatas mentioned by Brigadier Puttick was delivered about sunset when a force of some four hundred Germans advanced from the south. After gaining 500 yards the enemy was checked with considerable loss by the New Zealand divisional petrol company and a Greek detachment. Command in this area was then unified under Major Russell of the New Zealand cavalry, his force also containing the petrol company, a platoon of the 19th New Zealand Battalion, and some gunners.

Apart from the encounter related above, and a certain amount of patrolling and sniping by both sides during the day, there was little activity in the prison valley area. German aircraft had dropped supplies in the prison about 10.0 a.m., but no reinforcements had arrived. For the moment the position was one of stalemate.

And now, after three days fighting, the scene shifts eastward from Maleme airfield to where our troops are about to take up fresh dispositions in order to defend Canea. A line of sorts covering the town is taking shape from north-west to south-east, with the much tried 5th New Zealand Brigade at the western (coastal) end; the 4th New Zealand Brigade a little further east; the improvised 10th Brigade of Greeks and New Zealanders under Colonel Kippenberger holding the front as far as the Canea—Alikianou road; and Brigadier Vasey's 19th Australian Brigade (the 2/7th and 2/8th Battalions from Georgeopolis) south of the road. In the immediate vicinity of Canea a scratch defence force is being organized; it consists of the Australian gunners of the 2/2nd Field Regiment, now fighting as infantry, a company of the Rangers, and some Royal Marines.

At this juncture the decision was taken to evacuate the civil population from Canea, where the essential services had already collapsed, to the hill villages some miles to the south. The geographical position of the town, and its narrow winding streets rendered Canea a favourite target of the German bombers, and it was as well to get the people away in orderly fashion while there was opportunity to do so. Most of them left during the night. None was compelled to go.

Friday, Saturday and Sunday, May 23rd, 24th and 25th, represent the period during which the German forces in Crete progressively grew stronger and exerted an ever growing pressure, while our own position correspondingly weakened from day to day—less as the result of direct enemy attacks than on account of the increasing difficulties of supply, administration and command arising out of the lonely battle in which our ground forces were now engaged.

These were the days when the enemy was building up towards his major effort—days which saw the balance tilt over further against us. In addition to all the other handicaps under which our men were fighting, it must be remembered that they were practically without reinforcement or relief, so that dwindling units and troops growing ever more weary fought day after day against opponents who were fresh and newly arrived in battle.

During the night of May 22nd/23rd the withdrawal of the 5th New Zealand Brigade from the Maleme region had begun, but, as we have seen, the movement could not be completed under cover of darkness. In the last stages of the retreat, when it was light, German aircraft and German forward troops harassed our men considerably.

The enemy combined frontal pressure at Platanias with attempts to infiltrate through to the coast between the 5th and 4th Brigades. The latter movements were more easily held than the direct attack which came down the road and along the beach at Platanias. The German vanguard, driving captured R.A.F. lorries, seized a bridge across a river-bed which was to have ben held by the New Zealanders as part of their forward position, and then planted a captured Bofors gun to defend it. This attack developed in strength during the afternoon of the 23rd and threatened a direct breakthrough. Here were engaged some tanks of the 3rd Hussars, two companies of the 20th New Zealand Battalion, and a company of the Maoris which fought on the beach. The Bofors gun was recovered and at length the German effort died away.

It was clear that the 5th New Zealand Brigade, now enduring its fourth day of continuous battle, was no longer equal to maintaining the struggle without a temporary relief. The strain of fighting under such uniquely unfavourable conditions, the constant pounding from the air, the supreme trial of the previous night's attack, all these had contributed to produce a dangerous state of exhaustion. No troops in the world could have endured longer than these New Zealanders did. It seemed, both to Freyberg and Puttick that the limit had been reached. The brigade must be relieved and withdrawn into divisional reserve.

In that case the 4th New Zealand Brigade and the polyglot 10th Brigade would be obliged to take over the line—if line it can be called—and since they could not move forward without leaving a dangerous gap liable to attack or infiltration from the south, the new front must crystallize on their present positions north and south through Galatas.

Fortunately the troops under 5th Brigade command were able to hold until nightfall, and the withdrawal was carried out under cover of darkness, beginning even before sunset. Our men disengaged without difficulty, but owing to the lack of towing vehicles they had a good deal of trouble in getting their guns (mostly the Italian or French models, the latter taken over by the Italians and subsequently captured from them in the Western Desert) away to the rear.

Round Galatas little happened during the day. Small parties of Germans made a series of attacks towards the village from the prison area, but these were checked without much trouble. The guns and mortars we still had in action fired on any target that offered.

About noon the headquarters of the 4th New Zealand Brigade was heavily bombed from the air.

Canea old town was set on fire by German bombers and shipping was attacked in Suda Bay where an oil-tanker was hit.

The new front at least permitted the integration of the various New Zealand and Australian units fighting west of Canea. The 4th New Zealand Brigade, with Colonel Kippenberger's composite force, would hold in the north; the 19th Australian Brigade, which consisted of the 2/7th Battalion and half the 2/8th, in the south. It was a position imposed upon our Command by the exhaustion of the forward troops rather than one of its own choosing; the withdrawal signified the final abandonment of any attempt to dominate or overlook the Maleme aifield; and, if it led to the very needful reorganization of our position, it equally permitted the linking-up of Ringel's Group from the Maleme sector with Heidrich's forces who had been holding on in the prison area. The German menace to Canea was beginning to take shape.

Yet, despite this considerable withdrawal, the general feeling among the troops around Canea and Suda on that Friday was one of tempered optimism. It was believed (and in view of the tone of the official communiqués, this is scarcely surprising) that the German airborne landings at Retimo and Heraklion had been completely defeated and the enemy forces at those places annihilated. While it was known even among those who had not been themselves involved in the battle that we had withdrawn from Maleme under extremely heavy enemy pressure, it was supposed that the enemy's losses, inevitably exaggerated by popular report, had been on such a scale that they might well prove fatal to his enterprise if only the R.A.F.—in whose ability to encompass the impracticable the ground troops maintained a flatteringly naïve faith—could succeed in neutralizing his flow of reinforcements and supplies by a large scale bombing and interception programme.

It was, perhaps, fortunate for the peace of mind of these men, so sorely tried, that they were blissfully unaware of the handicaps and the responsibilities of our air forces in the Middle East.

For nothing now was interfering with the punctual arrival, departure and re-arrival of enemy aircraft at Maleme. A full seven miles separated our most advanced positions from that bitterly contested quadrilateral. All day the German aircraft landed uninterruptedly just as they chose. The early arrivals had paid the price on the two previous days. It had been high, but it had been sufficient. Maleme offered a safe landing now. It may well be that nearly two hundred troop-carriers alighted there in the course of the day.

It is true that the R.A.F., who were still doing what was possible to help in the defence of the island, managed to send Blenheims and Marylands to bomb the airfield in the evening. These aircraft were a heartening sight to those of our men who saw them come over, but the strike did little to impede the German operations. It was neither heavy enough nor sustained enough to do that.

General Freyberg, whose sense of realism was scarcely surpassed even by his outstanding courage, was the first to appreciate the significance of the loss of the airfield. In a signal to Middle East he stressed the fact that the enemy now possessed an operational aerodrome scarcely more than a dozen miles from Suda Bay, the only port which it was practicable for us to use for the maintenance of our principal force in Crete. Nor were landings being confined to the aerodrome, as we have seen. Nevertheless, Maleme was the supremely important point and Freyberg had intended yet another attack against it that night, even after the withdrawal to Platanias; but the threat to his flank from the Prison Valley area and the exhaustion of the troops under his command had rendered this impracticable. He therefore intended to consolidate his new position for defence. Two facts were inescapable; he could no longer take chances on the safety of his southern flank from attack and infiltration; and a large proportion of his men required a rest before they could engage in battle again.

But even to continue on the defensive was becoming a hazardous procedure. The enemy was now approaching equality of numbers, and in addition to the airborne landings Freyberg had received information that some ships had landed German troops on the Akrotiri peninsula behind Canea that day. Suda was now increasingly threatened, and Suda, let it be repeated, was the only port of supply available to his western force. The defensive fight could only be kept up so long as the maintenance of his troops in ammunition and supplies could be assured.

It was possible, he said in his report that help from the R.A.F., especially in fighters, might alter the outlook, but 'the next few days...are critical'.

It was certainly not an alarmist or defeatist statement; it merely drew attention to unpalatable facts.

On Saturday, May 24th, the German offensive from the air was intensified; and throughout the day supplies and reinforcements were poured into Maleme, troop-carriers arriving on the airfield at the rate of twelve in an hour.

Supported by bombing attacks upon our positions west of Canea the enemy's ground forces strove to press eastward and northward. During the morning the Germans reached the Aiya Marina ridge, and were engaged on the coastal road by our artillery. In the afternoon tanks and infantry assembled south of Theodhoroi Island and clashed with the 19th New Zealand Battalion which resisted stoutly. Fighting continued in the vicinity of the road till darkness fell, the little ground which was lost being recovered by counter-attack.

Near Galatas German attacks had been repulsed and we also held our own in the Prison Valley, but the fighting was not so severe. Further south beyond the road the 19th Australian Brigade was not attacked at all, being able to spend the day improving its defences.

So far so good. But it was perfectly clear that the German effort would be renewed on a larger scale next day, fresh and well-equipped troops being put in against the weary and depleted ranks of the defence.

Canea, which was still burning, suffered very heavily from the German bombers in the afternoon. It was much the heaviest attack that the Cretan capital had experienced. The enemy aircraft flew backwards and forwards over the town in perfect formation. Sometimes there were as many as sixty of them overhead at the same time; on no occasion while a raid was in progress were there less than a dozen. It was a perfect demonstration of pattern bombing. The Germans could afford it, for there was no fighter opposition against them. Lines of bombs were sown accurately across the town, for it was the German purpose to block its streets with rubble and cause the maximum difficulty to the troops and vehicles that had to be moved through it. Little was left of Canea except the water-front area.

On Sunday, May 25th, the Germans attacked in strength.

To appreciate the conditions under which our troops entered upon the last struggle for the defence of Canea and Suda, the extent to which they had been weakened and units had been broken up and 'cannibalized' must be taken into consideration.

The New Zealand Division which had done nearly all the fighting in this sector since the opening day was reduced to a total strength, including headquarters troops, of approximately 4,400. Of these, the 5th Brigade which had borne the brunt showed returns of about 1,380, the 4th Brigade of about 1,440, and the composite 10th Brigade about 800. In simple terms, the New Zealand Division was reduced to brigade strength, and each brigade was barely more numerous than a battalion should be.

Vasey's 19th Australian Brigade had as yet seen practically no fighting, since it had had to cover the unattacked Georgeopolis beach during the first day or two and had not been at all seriously involved since its shift to the Canea sector. But the original strength had only been that of a battalion and a half, and when Sunday's battle opened it could muster no more than 1,170.

Of the Greeks fighting in regular formations in the western sector of Crete there now remained about a thousand of No. 2 Greek Regiment in the neighbourhood of Mournies and Perivolia (S.S.W. of Canea); in unascertainable number still resisting around Alikianou on the further side of the Prison Valley; and about 700 men of No. 1 Greek Regiment near Kastelli in the far west.

For the previous two days the Germans had been landing troops quite unimpeded at Maleme. Even allowing for their losses they can scarcely have had less than 15,000 troops in the sector by the morning of May 25th. And they could now be reinforced continuously up to almost any extent.

Against them we could put into the line a total of something under 6,000 with another thousand or two who might be committed as a final reserve. Say 9,000 in all. Nine thousand men, all of them tired through the incessant strain and hazard of air attack, even when they had not been involved in the ground fighting; nine thousand men who had no reasonable hope of reinforcement or relief.

While the New Zealanders and the 19th Australiaa Brigade confronted the German advance from the west and south-west the troops in rear were being reorganized in four commands.

Lieut.-Colonel Healy, a gunner, was given command of the so-called 'Suda Brigade', a hybrid organization of about 2,000 rifles. It included a battalion of Royal Marines—previously manning searchlights—gunners of the R.H.A. and 2/2nd Australian Field Regiments, the 'Royal Perivolians' who had representatives of many untis in the ranks, and elements of two Greek battalions. This force was to take up a north-south support position along the line of a stream at Mournies two miles south of Canea. It was a position that might with luck hold for a very few hours, not longer.

Next, there was the Akrotiri Force under the command of Major Boileau, composed of the Northumberland Hussars, and the Rangers. These troops were to enjoy the inconvenient rôle of Mr. Facing-Both-Ways. They would have to be prepared to hold a potential 'stop-line' across the Akrotiri isthmus against attacks from the south while at the same time dealing with any sea or airborne troops who might be landed on the peninsula to the north.

Then there was the 'area reserve' which had not yet been committed to action except for a platoon or two which had rounded up some paratroopers—the 1st Welch Regiment (Lieut.-Colonel Duncan).

Finally, the defence of Suda itself was entrusted to the scratchiest of scratch forces under Major Farrier, composed largely of Greek gendarmerie, civilian volunteers and a few solitary details separated from their units by the eddies of battle—a Home Guard of the most rudimentary nature.

During the night of May 23rd/24th there had arrived for us at Suda a slight reinforcement of 200 which gave promise of better things to come. This was the vanguard of 'Layforce', commanded by Colonel R.E. Laycock and composed of parts of No . 7 Commando and Nos. 50 and 52 Middle East Commandos, numbering 800 officers and men and organized in two battalions.[1]

The spirit of the troops, everywhere, was still high, despite their grievous condition. Small arms ammunition was running so short that it had to be doled out a few boxes at a time as the limited quantity of transport vehicles permitted—and not by day when German aircraft were sure to be overhead. Also, the distribution of drinking water, in many instances strictly conserved, and of the dwindling supplies of food could only be undertaken at night. Medical stores were failing. Dressing stations and field ambulances were overcrowded with wounded men.

The enemy's assault on this fateful Sunday followed the pattern now becoming all too familiar through repetition. The morning was devoted to the preliminary 'softening up' from the air, during which

[1] It had been intended that these commandos should be employed in offensive and harassing operations, for which their training and equipment pre-eminently suited them. In the early part of the year plans were well advanced for an attack upon the Dodecanese to eliminate the danger of air and submarine attacks upon our communications from Africa to Greece. In this projected operation the commandos were to have played a prominent part. But the Dodecanese undertaking was abandoned, and presently, in view of the acute shortage of our manpower, it was found necessary to use these skilled assault troops as reinforcements for the defensive battle of Crete.

time our forward and rear areas were very thoroughly 'combed'. The R.A.F. from their bases in Africa, came again. Both in the morning and afternoon Marylands, Blenheims and Hurricanes attacked Maleme airfield, and at night four Wellington bombers did likewise. So far as could be ascertained these efforts had only a nuisance value.

In the early afternoon, after ample time had been allowed for the battering and riddling of their objectives, the German ground forces, nearly two brigades strong, went in to the attack.[1]

The first thrust was held, but following intensely concentrated mortar fire, the enemy at about 3 p.m. broke through along the coast on the extreme right of the 18th New Zealand Battalion and gained nearly half a mile. For some two hours the Germans persisted in their efforts to develop this success but the advance of the 20thBattalion— one hundred and forty strong—helped to keep them in check. Then the inevitable happened. Overborne by the heavy volume of mortar fire the defenders were pressed back to positions east of Galatas. The 18th New Zealand Battalion, which lost 99 killed and 150 wounded out of 450 of all ranks, was engaged by all three battalions of No. 100 Mountain Regiment on this day.

At Galatas the composite body known as Russell's Force which consisted chiefly of the divisional cavalry and petrol company with a party of the 19th New Zealand Battalion and some gunners—in all about 150 strong—continued to hold the village. Russell's men were machine-gunned from the air at tree-top level and, from now onward, were attacked repeatedly from the west and from the direction of the prison. Then, about 8.30 p.m., after the 18th Battalion had been forced back as related above, Colonel Kippenberger ordered Major Russell to withdraw his force behind the village to the east. This he succeeded in doing, the troops extricating themselves from a most difficult position, though not without considerable loss. The exultant Germans streamed into Galatas.

The trickle of stragglers moving back now thickened to a flood. A breach had been opened in our front, and the Germans in the village might be counted upon to assail our exposed flanks. The situation was critical. The safety of the whole line was in peril. Should it crumble the enemy might well be in Canea, even Suda, that night.

The day was saved by one of those spasmodic, improvised

[1] See Map 10.

counter-attacks which before now have stopped an army in full flood tide of success. First of all two of the light tanks of the Hussars clanked up the road into Galatas and out again shooting up the Germans in the streets. That gave a breathing-space, just time enough to compel the enemy to consider the desirability of adopting defensive precautions rather than of pushing on. But the tank crews had lost two men wounded in the course of the sally, a machine-gunner and a gunner-observer. They appealed for replacements. A machine-gunner and a truck driver from brigade headquarters volunteered, the latter being put through his paces in ten minutes.

A succession of reinforcements—small, well organized, well armed parties—were sent forward by Brigadier Inglis commanding the 4th New Zealand Brigade. These men were drawn from a dozen units and included even the members of the 'Kiwis', the New Zealand concert party which had been sent to Crete to enliven the presumed *longueurs* of the defenders. They were posted on ridges overlooking Galatas, and under cover of this makeshift line elements of the 5th New Zealand Brigade—two companies of the 23rd Battalion each eighty strong, a party from the 18th and two platoons of the 20th—were assembled for the counter-attack against the village. Four light tanks were now available; two of these were held back to cover the approaches to the next village, Karatsos, the other two were detailed to support the counter-attack against Galatas.

Then, as darkness thickened on that warm May night the motley force organized and led by Kippenberger in person[1] went forward to death and glory. It was Ethandune; it was the charge of the Worcestershire Regiment at Gheluvelt, the attack which saved the line at Ypres on that last day of October 1914.

The most English of our poets of this century writing of a battle that welded England a thousand years earlier has interpreted the essential spirit of that last broken charge:

> *When Alfred's word was ended*
> *Stood firm that feeble line*
> *Each in his place with club or spear*
> *And fury deeper than deep fear*
> *And smiles as sour as brine.*

---

[1] Colonel Kipppenberger who started off leading the counter-attack was unfortunate enough to sprain his ankle. He was passed by his men as they broke into a run, but followed them up to the village.

Wild stared the Danes at the double ways
Where they loitered all at large
As that dark line for the last time
Doubled the knee to charge—

And caught their weapons clumsily,
And marvelled how and why—
In such degree by rule and rod,
The people of the peace of God
Went roaring down to die.

It was with that spirit that they charged through the darkness on that Sunday in May, men of English blood from the land of the Southern Cross, casting their all into the battle of all mankind.

Back into Galatas they stormed, climbing over the low stone walls, swarming into the houses, firing when they could, clearing buildings with hand grenades when they possessed any, and then going in with the bayonet.

It lasted for twenty minutes, the quick flash of rifle fire, the rattle of automatics, the glowing red of the tracers...

Then the Germans broke. Those who were not killed in the streets and the houses, and most were killed, were swept away on the impetus of the attack. They vanished westward into the darkness, and the village was clear.

Again distinguished for his gallant and resourceful leadership was 2nd-Lieut. Upham of the 20th Battalion; although he had been wounded two days before, he had insisted on remaining with his men.

The action at Galatas was made memorable by that lost despairing heroism that has so often snatched victory from defeat: at Ethandune no less than at Ypres and over the skies of Britain as among those desert wastes where the bleak uninhabited of Ruweisat and Alam Halfa look down upon the curve of coast that bears the name of Alamein.

General Freyberg has described this action as 'one of the greatest efforts in the defence of Crete'.

After the conquest of the island, the Germans erected a memorial in the village to both Germans and New Zealanders who fell in the fighting at Galatas.[1]

And the supreme tragedy lies in the fact that the heroism was in vain. The counter-attack, in its reckless courage, deserved to have

[1] This memorial, erected in 1941, was removed by a later German commander in 1945.

turned the fortunes of the whole battle. How fit and appropriate if it had indeed done so; if in the obscure village of Galatas had been erected a single stone, like that which the visitor may see where the road from Ypres climbs the first shallow ridge near St. Julien, the stone which bears the sole inscription: *'Ici fut arreté l'envahisseur'*.

But it was not to be. The New Zealanders were weakened by the losses they had suffered; they no longer had enough men to hold the line. And troops of all units were now hopelessly mixed in the forward areas, complicating the task of reforming and regrouping them. The men were dog tired, wearied out by the strain of being under incessant air attack. But the Germans had broken into our forward positions in at least two places, and unless they could be driven out before dawn were likely to exploit their gains next day. So, even at this late hour—about midnight—consideration was given to the possibility of yet another counter-attack with a view to dislodging the enemy. But only the 28th (Maori) Battalion was sufficiently rested and organized to be committed, and its 400 men might have to face any number of Germans up to five battalions. There was no chance of success though Colonel Dittmer would have taken his men forward without demur.

There was thus nothing for it but a further disengagement and withdrawal to a new and shorter line which would be only about two miles in front of Canea; and this movement head to be carried out at once in order to take advantage of the hours of darkness. No avoidable delay could be risked in the issue of orders, for all telephone communications forward of divisional hadquarters had been destroyed by bombing, and messages must be conveyed to brigades and battalions by runner.

Late that night Brigadier Puttick signalled General Freyberg that he hoped to establish the new line but that his men were badly shaken by the severity of the air attacks and he feared that it might be impossible to get his guns away.

'I am exceedingly doubtful', he concluded, 'on present reports, whether I can hold the enemy tomorrow.'

An effort to reinforce Crete with the main body and headquarters of Layforce had failed by reason of the very rough weather. The troops left Alexandria in four destroyers on the 25th with the intention of coming ashore during the night; but the boats on which a quick landing depended, were washed away by heavy seas, and the flotilla, with fuel supplies running low, was obliged to return to Egypt.

Monday, May 26th, the seventh day of the battle, was described by General Wavell in his subsequent despatch as the critical day. In one sense, perhaps, the crisis had been determined—in favour of the Germans—on May 22nd when the counter-attack failed against Maleme airfield. In another sense, given the conditions which the defence had to face, the critical date was that when the German Command fixed the scale of attack. By May 26th was the day on which the break came, the day when evacuation was admitted to be a necessity.

The initiative now lay firmly in German hands, for the invaders numbered over 20,000, most of them concentrated between Maleme and Canea for the main threat against Suda.

General Ringel, commander of the 5th Mountain Division, who was in charge of the operation, had determined that on this day should be delivered the *coup de grâce*. The greater part of our forces had been drawn into the Canea sector, where intense German air attacks upon the rear areas were already producing a state of administrative confusion. For the frontal attack Ramcke's Group would move east along the coastal road against Canea; No. 100 Mountain Regiment would push through Karatsos; and Colonel Heidrich's No. 3 Paratroop Rifle Regiment, which had been fighting in the prison area since the opening day, would continue its pressure towards Canea from the south-west.

These converging columns, whose nominal strength amounted to at least seven battalions and whose actual numbers represented more than four, were preparing a knock-out blow for a force of three very weak battalions all of them wearied by the strain of constant vigilance, arduous battle and continual air attack. These defenders who occupied the angle formed by the coastal and the prison roads were to be pinned down and then shattered in front of Canea. Meanwhile their line of retreat was to be cut by a flank march through the hills to the south.

The roads from Canea to Alikianou (south-west) and from Canea to Stilos (south-east)[1] form, roughly, the sides of an isosceles triangle. If the Germans could move along the base line through the foothills from Alikianou to Stilos and thence on to the road to the south they stood a good chance of cutting off and capturing the whole of our troops based on Canea and Suda.

It was not at all a simple task which General Ringel set No. 85

[1] See Map 14.

Mountain Regiment. From its assembly point at Modhion (a little south of the coast road and about midway between Maleme and Platanias) it was faced with a march of nearly twenty miles as the arrow flies, much the greater part of it across trackless hills 'against the grain of the country'—up one ridge, down into the valley beyond, up to the next ridge, and so on. But if the Germans could reach Stilos and the through road at Neon Khorion that night their object could be achieved; if they could reach these villages by the following night they might still cut off the greater part of our forces, and the remainder could be pressed hard in pursuit. What von Stumme had conspicuously failed to do in Greece by his movement from the eastern coast into the Larissa plain or by his flank march from Yanina southward to the Gulf of Corinth, would be achieved in Crete by the fit young men of No. 85 Mountain Regiment. Or so it was hoped.

Over on our side of the line the disengagement of the forward troops had been going on during the night, following the glorious but vain counter-attack at Galatas. In effect, the 4th New Zealand Brigade, which had held the line during May 25th, now withdrew through the 5th Brigade, and the latter, so severely hammered in the first days of battle, found itself once more constrained to play the ungratifying part of Uriah the Hittite. The withdrawal was completed by 5.30 a.m. on Monday morning, and the line was now held, theoretically, by the 21st Battalion on the coast, the 19th in the centre, and the 28th (Maori) Battalion on the left with its flank on the Alikianou road. Beyond the road, southward, lay the 19th Australian Brigade. Behind the Australians was the Suda Brigade deployed along the line of the Mournies stream.

The New Zealanders, who had the remnants of their own 4th Brigade in support, were of course, battalions only in name. They had lost heavily in the fighting and had been reinforced by a number of small groups which had become separated from their own units.

The 3rd Hussars, now with five tanks of which only four were runners, lay in support south-west of Canea.

General Freyberg, from his new headquarters in a quarry not far from Suda docks sent an encouraging message to Brigadier Puttick but emphasized that the new line must be held at all costs. Yet Freyberg himself doubted if this could be done for long by the sorely tried New Zealanders. After signalling his apprehensions to Middle East Command he placed Brigadier Inglis, from the 4th New Zealand Brigade in command of a force which was to take over the line after dark. This new formation comprised the 1st Welch Regiment, the 1st Rangers, and the Northumberland Hussars.

Rumours were rife, and some men in the back areas believed that evacuation of the island had already begun. Actually, in anticipation of a general evacuation, base personnel who could be spared and dock workers from Suda had already been instructed to make their way as best as they could to the fishing village of Sphakia on the south coast of Crete. Unfortunately this instruction soon became generally known, and some stragglers from the combatant units made no further effort to rejoin but streamed off southward. In this fashion the Composite Battalion which had fought so finely around Galatas began to melt away.

As usual the Germans were content to allow the clear and cloudless morning to pass without initiating anything beyond extensive air attacks against our forward and rear positions. It is probable that they wished to hold us in front of Canea while the flank movement of No. 85 Mountain Regiment made headway. By one o'clock in the afternoon, however, the Germans were attacking vigorously along the Alikianou—Canea road at the junction of the New Zealanders and Australians, and were working round the southern flank of the Australians.

Brigadier Puttick, commanding the New Zealand Division, took so serious a view of the situation that he doubted if the front could hold beyond nightfall. In the mid-afternoon he started back to report in this sense to Freyberg at Force Headquarters and to recommend an earlier withdrawal. Since all telephone lines were down it was necessary for him to go in person; and since every vehicle moving by daylight was a certain target for the roaming Messerschmitts he set out to make the four-mile journey to Suda on foot. It was a measure of the extent to which essential communications had broken down that a divisional commander felt compelled to be his own messenger without the benefit of so much as a bicycle to carry him.

Puttick reached Headquarters only to be informed that there was no option and that his troops must continue to hold until the night relief could be carried out. He returned to divisional headquarters to find that the situation had changed for the worse; although a break-through along the coast road had been averted by a counter-attack supported by the remaining tanks, both Hargest who commanded the New Zealanders in the line and Vasey who commanded the Australians were agreed that the position could not be held.

Intelligence had arrived of German movement round the left flank, and pressure everywhere along the front was increasing.

At about twenty minutes to six, while Puttick was writing a report to Major-General Weston, the latter arrived at New Zealand Division headquarters. The local commanders—Brigadiers Puttick, Hargest and Inglis was present and Brigadier Vasey was available on the telephone—assured Weston that withdrawal should begin without delay if disaster were to be avoided, and suggested a shorter defensive line extending southward from the head of Suda Bay.

The brigadiers knew what their troops had endured and believed them to be almost at the end of their tether; but there is evidence to show that the units on the line felt themselves in no particular difficulties during the day. Certainly it seems that the enemy delivered no 'all out' assault. German accounts describe the capture of Galatas—abandoned by us at 2 a.m. that morning—and other attacks which were unnoticed by our men. But the threat to the left (southern) flank was very real.

Being unable to order withdrawal on his own authority, Weston set out for Force Headquarters. Since it took him an hour and twenty minutes to cover the distance it is to be presumed that he, too, travelled on foot.

Freyberg, however, remained adamant. The most he could promise was that Force Reserve should be moved up to take over from the New Zealand Division starting off within the hour, i.e. by 8.30 p.m.[1] At the southern end of the line the Australians would continue to hold, with the Suda Brigade.

Meanwhile Brigadier Puttick was anxiously awaiting the orders to withdraw that were expected to be the outcome of Weston's visit to Force Headquarters. The delays imposed by the breakdown of communications increased the tension of that day of maddening suspense and over-strained nerves. The Australians eventually received a personal authorization from Freyberg to fall back on the Suda Brigade's position along the Mournies stream, but when no communication had arrived for the New Zealanders at 10.30 p.m. Puttick took the responsibility of ordering the withdrawal of both Australians and New Zealanders to the line recommended by General Weston—southwards from the west tip of Suda Bay.

It was not until an hour and a quarter later that Freyberg's instruction came through. It ordered the troops to stand fast until

[1] Owing to delay in communicating the message and subsequent road blockages, Force Reserve did not, in fact, start moving until midnight.

Force Reserve arrived to take over.

By this time the retreat was already in progress and could not have been checked. The delays in the transmission of orders meant that when they arrived they were already inapplicable. Vasey's 19th Australian Brigade, for instance, had received specific instructions to hold along the line of the Mournies stream. By the time this message was received the Germans were known to be working past it without opposition on the south.

Each one of the three forward formations—New Zealand Division, 19th Australian Brigade and the Suda Brigade—received its order to stand firm until relieved *after* it had already begun its own withdrawal or after withdrawal on its flank had already compromised its own position.

Force Reserve, the final desperate hope, had started to move forward at midnight in ignorance of the fact that the troops whom it was to relieve had already begun to withdraw from their positions. An hour and a half later two despatch riders were sent off by Freyberg to countermand the advance, since everyone else was now moving backward. By the time that the message was received it was too late to check Force Reserve. The 1st Welch Regiment, the Northumberland Hussars, and the Rangers went on to offer the last resistance to the Germans west of Canea.

The remainder of our forces continued their retreat, the 19th Australian Brigade and 5th New Zealand Brigade dropping back to take up the position covering Suda, while the 4th New Zealand Brigade went on to Stilos, near the road to the south coast whither stragglers and base personnel in increasing numbers were now making their way.

While the forward units maintained military formation and marched in some kind of order, the rear echelons pressed on as best they could in the direction of Sphakia, moving sometimes without orders and usually without organization. For the first time there were some indications of a weakening in morale—but not among the fighting troops who had lately been in close contact with the enemy. These remained grimly determined to give blow for blow.

Freyberg knew that the end had come. In a despatch to Middle East Command drafted at 9.30 p.m. on May 26th (though probably held for some hours) he signalled the Commander-in-Chief in terms which left no room for ambiguity.

He reported with regret that in his opinion the troops in the Suda area had reached the limit of their endurance: no matter what decision might be taken by Middle East Command, the position at Suda from a military point of view was hopeless: his small, ill-equipped, immobile force could not stand up against the concentrated bombing which it had faced during the last seven days: it must be recognized that the difficulties of extricating the complete force in the Suda area were now insuperable, but provided that a quick decision was reached a certain proportion of the troops might be embarked: once the Suda sector was reduced the reduction of Retimo and Heraklion would only be a matter of time: the troops at Suda, with the exception of the Welch Regiment and the commandos were unfit for any offensive action. Freyberg concluded by saying that if a gain of time would help the general situation in the Middle East he would carry on, but would have to consider how this could be done: Suda Bay might be under fire within twenty-four hours: casualties continued to be heavy and most of the immobile guns had been lost.

It seems that even before this message reached Cairo Wavell had conferred with Admiral Cunningham, Air Chief-Marshal Tedder, General Sir Thomas Blamey, and the Hon. Peter Fraser (Prime Minister of New Zealand). The Australian General and the New Zealand Minister naturally expressed their anxiety as to the fate of their troops and the Admiral promised to prepare for the evacuation of Crete, a precaution that could hardly be delayed. Early on May 27th Wavell cabled home a description of the plight of Freyberg's forces; and, later in the day he received from London approval for the step which had now become inevitable if all who remained on the island were not to be sacrificed.

Surprising as it may seem reinforcements arrived in Crete during the night of May 26th. D. Battalion and the headquarters of Layforce had left Egypt again at 5.30 a.m., conveyed in H.M.S. *Abdiel* and the destroyers *Hero* and *Nizam*. After an uneventful passage they landed at Suda just before midnight. A litte later they were informed that our troops were in retreat and that they—the new arrivals— would form the rearguard.

4

Retimo

ON May 21st there was again no attack either by air or sea upon Georgeopolis. The 2/8th Battalion had already been moved westwards into the Canea sector and the 2/7th Battalion was to start that night in the same direction, leaving Brigadier Vasey with a staff but no fighting force. As we know, on the following day he was to be found commanding his own troops in a position south-west of Canea.

At Retimo,[1] the operations planned by Colonel Campbell the previous evening to clear his flanks were duly delivered at dawn, the 2/1st Battalion going for Hill A on the east, and the 2/11th Battalion attacking Hill B on the west.

At Hill A the Germans had been building up their strength during the night, and our attack was answered by a German counter-assault delivered with most effective support by the enemy's mortars. The Australians were checked and had to withdraw. Although the hill remained under fire from our guns, Australian battalion headquarters was equally at the mercy of the the the German mortar fire. Soon the Australians tried again and this time with success: by 10 a.m. the hill was in our hands, together with some guns which we had lost, and the Germans were retreating eastward towards the olive-oil factory at Stavromenos, pressed by the Greek battalion which was in support of the 2/1st.

Hill B was captured without much difficulty, but the 2/11th Battalion could make little further progress. The Germans were very strongly established in the coastal village of Platanes, and their machine-gun fire was more than our guns—Italian trophies with defective ammunition—could subdue. Then came a gratifying interlude when a flight of Dorniers swept over and bombed the enemy, and other German aircraft dropped supplies amongst the Australians. A Greek battalion which should have given support was stopped by fire at a ravine south-east of Perivolia; but by evening, after making a wide detour, our allies reached a position overlooking Perivolia from the south.

In the afternoon the Australians cleared the beaches between the two hills and among their prisoners was Colonel Stumm, commanding the regiment which had launched the assault at Retimo. Further inland, parties of the enemy had been at large, working through the hill villages of Maroulas and Adhele, where they captured an Australian advanced dressing station before being ambushed on the northern side of Piyi.

The situation at Retimo at the end of the day might be called

[1] See Map 12.

satisfactory, in as much as the main enemy forces had been driven in divergent directions, east and west; but our troops were running short of ammunition and other supplies, and in view of the isolated nature of their battle it was not easy to see how help could be sent. Ther Germans in Perivolia cut off communication with Suda and the west.

On May 22nd attacks were delivered against the enemy at Stavromenos, to the east, and at Perivolia on the western side of the airfield. The olive-oil factory at Stavromenos was treated to an artillery and mortar bombardment which would have been heavier had we possessed more ammunition. The attack, consisting of forty Australians and 200 Greeks, went in at about 6 p.m. but could not be pressed home against the stone walls of the factory. Eventually the Greeks were left in observation while the Australians, who had reached a position only forty yards from their objective, were withdrawn to defences near the airfield.

At Perivolia the Australians fared badly. They were checked by machine-gun fire east of the village and German fighter aircraft then attacked them, one company losing fifty men out of 120. Meanwhile the Greeks had lost heavily in an attack upon a church, south of the main road, which was occupied by a number of Germans. The only luck that came our way in this locality during the day was the surprising recovery of both 'I' tanks which had been lost on the opening day of battle. Fresh crews were selected to drive and fight them.

On the morning of May 23rd Colonel Campbell agreed to a three hours truce to enable both sides to bury their dead and collect their wounded. There was good reason for this arrangement for here, as elsewhere, the effect of hundreds of corpses exposed to the hot sun was well nigh insupportable. When the truce expired, however, Campbell was astonished to receive a demand from the commander of the German troops at Stavromenos that he should surrender with his entire force, on the grounds that the German attacks in other sectors had met with complete success and that no purpose could be served by prolonging the struggle here.

Campbell, being in complete control of his own sector, naturally received the demand with contempt and, as soon as the envoy had returned to the German lines, opened a fresh bombardment. He was the more encouraged in his defence by the fact that at the close of the period of truce about seventy German walking wounded had taken the opportunity pass over into his lines. Their arrival seemed to be an indication of declining morale and lack of adequate supplies among the dwindling German force.

It clearly needed only a little more pressure to destroy the German force around Stavromenos. But Campbell lacked the means to exert just that additional pressure. He had been short of ammunition almost from the first day, and he was fighting a lone isolated battle in what had to be recognized as the least important of the three[1] sectors. Even if he had enjoyed direct communication with either Suda or Heraklion, which he did not, it was doubtful whether any considerable reserves of guns or ammunition would have been available for him. For that reason he had to keep his force firmly in hand and only take such action as was necessary to ensure the defence of the airfield. He had now completely cleared up Hill A, where the enemy had given so much trouble at the start of the battle. His troops had buried 300 German corpses found on and around the hill; another 200 had been buried at Hill B, further to the west.

If, however, the air strip was securely protected and the enemy concentration at Stavromenos was being worn down, the powerful centre of resistance at Perivolia showed no sign of weakening. The Germans, variously estimated at 150 and 300, who had established themselves in the church a little to the south of the village presented an ideal target for a bomber. But we had no bombers. Instead, Force Headquarters, on the report of a liaison officer who had got through to Suda, detached a company of the Rangers and a 2-pdr. gun from the Canea-Suda area to dislodge the enemy. At 3 p.m. a message was sent to Retimo to inform Campbell that this detachment was on its way.

Towards evening enemy aircraft made a heavy attack upon Campbell's positions. No German reinforcements were flown in, but supplies were dropped in considerable profusion, some of them in the sea.

So in the Retimo area the enemy had made no headway, but he could afford to wait. Our men were feeling the strain and food supplies were becoming a real anxiety now that the rations that were left had to be shared with so many German wounded and other prisoners. 'The situation remained that of a beleaguered garrison whose fate depended mostly on events outside its own control.'

At dawn on May 24th the Rangers from Suda attacked the Germans in the church south of Perivolia. Seventy strong, the

[1] Three, because the Maleme sector had been eliminated by the withdrawal towards Canea.

275

Londoners were outnumbered probably by three to one, and such were the difficulties of communication that neither the 2/11th Australian Battalion nor the Greek troops knew that the attempt was to be made. It failed—as it was bound to do—and the Rangers withdrew by the way they had come, having established no contact with Campbell's forces, who were not seriously engaged during the day.

The Australians obtained some German supplies, here as elsewhere, by the pleasant expedient of signalling to enemy aircraft with their own devices. But, since the positions of the enemy pockets of resistance were now pretty well known to their higher Command, the opportunities for profiting by this unintentional bounty were diminishing. A small quantity of medical supplies was dropped by our own aircraft on Saturday night, but the ration situation was by this time getting acute. An attempt to supply the garrison by sea by means of light coastal craft had to be abandoned owing to choppy weather.

Much bravery of an individual and unorthodox nature was shown in this almost forgotten fighting around Retimo. The following story of one old priest of the neighbourhood, who bore his part in resisting the invader, is believed to be authentic.

A party of paratroops had seized a stone house in one of the villages and converted it into a strong-post. From their refuge they were machine-gunning anybody who appeared. Every attempt to shift them had failed, but some method of forcing them into the open had to be found. The priest ensconced himself in a house opposite, armed with a rifle. Then he sent a small boy with a hive of bees to creep up on the German's retreat from behind. The boy arrived at he house unobserved, climbed on to the roof and dropped the hive down the chimney. Very soon, pursued by the enraged bees, the Germans came racing into the street, and as they appeared the priest picked several of them off.

Force Headquarters found that increasing pressure in the Canea-Suda region prevented the despatch of a larger detachment to do what the Rangers had failed to do, but Campbell was certainly making the most of the resources at his command. At 4.30 a.m. on May 25th the 2/11th Australian Battalion, with one tank, was to have attacked the enemy south of Perivolia, but an accident to the vehicle caused the operation to be postponed for twenty-four hours. Later in the morning a captured German mortar was used to rout out and drive towards the coast a party of forty Germans from a spot south-east of Stavromenos.

Next day Colonel Campbell continued his operations in which the two 'I' tanks were to play a part. These vehicles had gone through a number of vicissitudes since the opening of the battle. Captured by the Germans on the first evening they had been retaken two days later; both had since become ditched and the new driver of one of them wounded.

At dawn on the 26th one tank went into action to help the 2/11th Australian Battalion in its attack upon the Germans at Perivolia, but the tank gun jammed and the effort failed. Shortly before noon, however, the same tank with its gun in order again, took part in a reconnaissance of the Stavromenos oil factory carried out by a company of the 2/1st Battalion. The small number of Germans defending the building made a poor show of resistance and the Australians seized it, taking forty wounded and forty unwounded prisoners.

The last remnant of Germans in this quarter, eighty strong, had withdrawn to a headland a mile or so further east, where they were kept under observation by a detachment of Cretan gendarmerie. Colonel Campbell was not concerned to lose lives in eliminating a force that constituted no further danger to him; nor did he desire the responsibility of supporting any larger number of prisoners. He already held 500, and, as already noticed, the feeding of them was causing him considerable embarrassment. He was worried by the shortage of rations and by the persistence of rumours that the evacuation of Crete by our forces was imminent. Since May 24th he had been out of touch with Force Headquarters, and with a view to obtaining information (and also supplies) he had sent the quartermaster of the 2/11th Australian Battalion to get what he could of both.

The quartermaster returned on the afternoon of May 26th with more sustenance for the spirit than for the flesh. He reported that at Headquarters there was no thought of evacuation and that reinforcements were to be expected; and he brought the first news of the Ranger's attack carried out on the 24th. The news of reinforcements was encouraging, and when the second tank was hauled out of its ditch and cajoled once more into running order Colonel Campbell decided to deal with the outstanding German stronghold at Perivolia on the following day.

Had the quartermaster left Suda even a few hours later, it is inconceivable that he could have failed to bring back a very different report of the shape of things to come.

5

Heraklion

THE first day's fighting at Heraklion[1] had left the Germans with a considerable footing over two miles east of the airfield, at a point on the coast where they were out of range. They were in possession, also, of the Greek barrack buidlings south of the airfield, and they controlled parts of Heraklion itself, as well as the beaches and approaches to the town on the western side.

[1] See Map 13.

German air attacks began before 5 a.m. on May 21st and were heavy and persistent enough to hamper our movements throughout the day. Supplies were dropped from the air for the Germans, and here, as in other places, our troops were able to secure a share by making use of captured ground-to-air signals. Reports said that the enemy had received supplies from small boats which had come into the beaches west of Heraklion but this may not have been so. The appearance of British warships off the coast at 7.30 a.m. was a heartening sight.

Colonel Brauer who commanded the Parachute Regiment had ordered a general attack upon the airfield just before midnight on Tuesday. Orders to his scattered forces appear to have been slow in getting through, for no attack developed until the morning of the 21st, and the whole operation consisted of independent efforts by separate detachments sometimes of only platoon strength.

Parties advanced from the east, making for East Ridge and the edge of the airfield. A group at 'Rattling Bridge' was dispersed by our artillery. Our 'I' tanks engaged with success light field guns along the coastal road and brought effective fire to bear upon Germans in East Wadi. In the afternoon Germans were rounded up at the village of Prassas, and as the Australians had surrounded the Greek barracks and cleared the 'Charlies' area, the airfield might be accounted fairly secure. At about 5 p.m., however, a number of German aircraft landed parachutists beyond East Beach where they were reported to be laying out a landing strip.

An attack upon our road block at Knossos had been repulsed with a loss to the Germans of thirty-five men.

Only in Heraklion town did the situation at any time look at all dangerous. The Germans had one battalion on the outskirts of the town and another some way away to the west covering the approaches from that side. Both were out of touch with their regimental commander, Colonel Brauer; but having intercepted during the morning a wireless message ordering a general attack on the airfield with all available forces on the eastern side, Major Schulz, who commanded the battalion in the outskirts of the town, determined to deliver a simultaneous attack.

Pressing in from the west and south, the Germans again reached the harbour and captured most of the town. The Greek troops, fighting from street to street, were running short of ammunition and on the point of surrender; but they were encouraged to rearm themselves with captured German weapons. Joined in the evening by a platoon of the Leicestershire and a platoon of the York and Lancaster they then succeeded in clearing the Germans from a great part of the town.

Here as at Retimo the enemy was still very far from securing his objective, and appeared to have little prospect of doing so without substantial reinforcements. These could, of course, arrive by air. On our side we had the advantage that Heraklion was not completely isolated and even now reinforcement was at hand.

It was true that no British transport could venture within fifty miles of Crete in daylight without risking attack from the air; but on the southern side of the island the 1st Argyll and Sutherland Highlanders had not arrived at Timbaki,[1] one of the few possible landing places along that bare and inhospitable coast. The battalion had been intended to protect the plain of the Messara, over which brood the considerable remains of the ancient Minoan hill fortress of Phaistos, and possibly establish a landing ground for our aircraft there. But since the arrival of another battalion—the 2nd Queen's—of the 16th Brigade was expected, it was decided that the Highlanders should move on across the island to join Brigadier Chappel at Heraklion.

[1] See Map 8.

On the morning of May 22nd the town of Heraklion seemed free from Germans, thanks to the efforts of York and Lancaster patrols and parties of Greek soldiery. Those of the enemy who remained in the barracks south of the airfield were eliminated. With the town fairly secure and direct threat to the airfield were eliminated. With the town fairly secure and direct threat to the airfield removed, the prospect seemed encouraging; but hostile snipers were active within our perimeter and the Germans were still in considerable strength to the eastward.

In this locality an attack, with tank support, was to have been delivered against the enemy's machine-gun posts. Unfortunately the traversing gear of one of the tanks was out of order and the engine of the other seized when its radiator was pierced. Black Watch patrols were busy near the airfield, but the Germans were too firmly ensconced at Rattling Bridge, East Wadi, and the ridge beyond the wadi to be shifted by any means at our command. As the enemy had penetrated into the hills south of our perimeter, a company of the Leicestershire was moved eastward to reinforce the Black Watch. Apex Hill was then cleared, and the remaining Germans in this area surrendered when artillery fire was opened on them.

All our movements were harassed by air attack, and in the morning a troop-carrier had actually attempted to land on the airfield under cover of a spray of machine-gun bullets for a fighter aircraft. Both carrier and fighter were driven off by the fire of our Bofors guns. The Germans dropped supplies to the east, south and west outside our perimeter and also within it. Perhaps on this day the *Luftwaffe* served us better than it did our opponents.

On at last one occasion Germans in the neighbourhood of Heraklion were seen to be driving Cretan women and children in front of them to shield their advance. The Greek commander thereupon sent the enemy a message that if this practice did not cease, all German prisoners in his hands would be executed. The message had the desired effect.

The systematic burial of the dead, an important task, could no longer be delayed. More than 950 Germans were thus disposed of by us, and another 300 bodies were accounted for by the Greeks. .

Thus passed another day on which we seem to have held our own. Yet, in the evening, two further bodies of parachutists were dropped, both coming down outside our perimeter. To the west of Heraklion about 300 men descended, while another 500 came down somewhere to the south-west of the airfield. This was sufficient indication that the enemy by no means intended to abandon offensive action at Heraklion.

And late that night German forces were reported to have established themselves astride the road that runs from Heraklion to the south coast where the Argyll and Sutherland Highlanders were located and preparing to move northwards.

Our efforts to reinforce and sustain Crete continued, but with little success. At 9.30 p.m. the 2nd Queen's, with 16th Brigade headquarters, left Alexandria for Timbaki. On this night, too, No. 24 Squadron South African Air Force was to have flown to Crete on a bombing mission, but bad weather kept the aircraft grounded at their desert aerodrome.

Friday, May 23rd, proved to be an eventful day at Heraklion. Aircraft dropped supplies to the Germans, and those in position east of the airfield received further reinforcements by air. Our impression that the enemy would hold fast on the west and south and make his chief effort from the east was confirmed during the day by the interrogation of prisoners as well as by observation. Two companies of the Leicestershire made a reconnaisance of these eastern positions where many machine-guns but few Germans were discovered.

Some anxiety arose as to the state of affairs on the Timbaki road. A ration truck sent to the road-block at Knossos had failed to get through, and two trucks sent down to make contact with the Argyll and Sutherland Highlanders were captured by the Germans. Then, about noon, two 'I' tanks arrived unexpectedly from Timbaki with the news that the Highlanders were on their way. These tanks being under orders for Suda, were sent on by sea together with the one tank still operating at Heraklion, and two field guns.

Earlier in the afternoon a single Hurricane from Egypt landed on the airfield. The return of Noah's dove can scarcely have brought more hope to the inmates of the Ark than did this first token of the return of R.A.F. fighter aircraft to active participation in the battle. Even the fact that it was speedily destroyed on the ground by half a dozen Messerschmitts could not dispel a wave of optimism among the defenders. To them it seemed an indication that the tide of victory was now definitely flowing in their direction, although it was actually ebbing, here as elsewhere.

About three hours later six more Hurricanes, following a dogfight over the town, came down to sanctuary upon the airfield. Four of them had received minor damage, and it was not widely realized at the time that they were all that remained of two squadrons which had been ordered to Crete. It had been intended that they should fly directly to Maleme to attack the German transport planes which were by that time arriving in untroubled succession on the airfield. They had been diverted to Heraklion—probably a mistake although they were too few in number to have affected the issue at Maleme.

The reappearance of the Hurricanes, which for the moment raised unrealized hopes among the defenders of Crete, had been made possible by the fitting of extra fuel tanks to enable them to cover the 350 miles each way from their bases in the Western Desert with a brief period of combat between arrival and departure.

It did not prove a success, and the following reasons, given by one of the pilots to the writer of one account of the Battle for Crete, explain why this was so:

> The additional tanks gave the Hurricane a range of 900 miles compared with the normal range of 600 miles. There were two additional tanks—one port, one starboard. The port tank emptied first, then the starboard tank. Air locks were liable to develop owing to bad refuelling or severe bumps in the air and throw the system out of commission. You never knew when the port tank emptied if the starboard tank was going to feed through. If your starboard tank refused to work over the sea that was the end.[1]

The Hurricanes had to shed their armour and reduce their ammunition load to carry the special tanks. The extra fuel load also meant a certain loss of power, and when they reached Crete they always ran into formations of Messerschmitts which outnumbered and could outpace, outclimb and outmanoeuvre them. In any case, the British fighters were so few that they could do little to blunt the edge of the *Luftwaffe's* vicious attacks.

Following a heavy raid upon the town, the German commander at 7 p.m. issued an ultimatum that Heraklion would be destroyed unless the Greeks ceased resistance. The ultimatum was rejected, but it was judged advisable to get the civilians away and this was done, except for the inmates of the hospital which contained many patients who could not be moved. The defence of Heraklion was now taken over by two companies of the 2nd York and Lancaster, a road-block being established west of the town.

It may here be recorded that next day German aircraft dropped leaflets which threatened death to all Greeks who continued to resist.

Heraklion appeared to be of increasing importance now that the *Luftwaffe* had demonstrated so unmistakably its command of the air. Whether our troops were to be sustained and reinforced in their defence of the island, or were to be brought away, the harbour at Suda, which no ship could even approach by day without running a frightful risk, could not be counted on. To use the tiny ports on the south coast also involved considerable hazard, but Timbaki was the

[1] Hetherington, *Airborne Invasion,* p. 116.

282

only one of these places which was connected to the north coast by a road fit for motor transport. And this road led only to Heraklion.

At sea, on their way to Timbaki, the 2nd Queen's and the headquarters of the 16th Brigade were ordered back to Alexandria early in the afternoon of this day, the danger of attack from the air being considered too great. This order was countermanded in the evening, and the ships steered north again, but at midnight they received fresh orders to return to Alexandria.

The Germans proceeded with an intermittent bombing of the town all day on May 24th, and continued to drop supplies to their troops both east and west of Heraklion. A considerable number—perhaps a battalion—of paratroops came down on the west; but patrols of the 2nd York and Lancaster discovered a hostile movement from west to east on the landward side of our perimeter. There seemed no doubt that the real build-up was to the east where the enemy on the ridges beyond East Beach was considered to be too powerfully established for our available troops to attack with any prospect of success. Five of our Hurricanes, however, made a number of sorties against these positions. German aircraft were now making unopposed landings on the relatively smooth surface of Mallia beach fifteen miles along the coast to the east—yet another instance of the extent to which the enemy was dispensing with the airfields which at one time had appeared to be essential to his success in Crete. It was becoming clear that while Brigadier Chappel was master in his own house, his writ did not extend any great distance beyond it and that the new build-up by the enemy far away to the east was probably in preparation for an Italian landing from the Dodecanese.

The extent to which our force at Heraklion, though successful in the defence of the airfield and town, was gradually passing from the role of besieger to that of besieged is shown by the difficulty which the Argyll and Sutherland experienced in fighting their way through to the perimeter.

Leaving one company to cover Timbaki and the potential landing-ground at Ay Dheka near the south coast, the battalion by a forced march north during Friday night had reached the approaches to the perimeter west of Heraklion, only to find that, as had happened to the Athenians of Nikias at Syracuse or the Gauls of Vercingetorix at Alesia, an outer perimeter was growing up and that this must first be forced. The new German arrivals by parachute dropped slap into the battle that was in progress on this side, and their intervention contributed to the repulse of the first attempt of the Highlanders to break through.

On May 25th the enemy made an assault upon Heraklion from the west. He encountered two companies of the York and Lancaster and one of the Leicestershire who counter-attacked with the support of artillery and two light tanks. The Germans were driven from the outskirts of the town, but fell back upon a strongly organized, machine-gun defence which effectually checked the progress of our men.

The Greeks who had been relieved of the responsibility for Heraklion were now reorganized as two battalions and located at Arkhaia Knossos: they guarded the hospital and were charged with preventing the enemy from blocking the Knossos road.

The first party of the Argyll and Sutherland Highlanders had begun to enter the perimeter on this Sunday morning. The main body of the battalion—really half the battalion—did not succeed in getting through until a little before midnight. Only the carriers and a few trucks came in by road, the others making their way across the hills. The Highlanders were certainly a welcome reinforcement and their arrival established the fact that the Heraklion garrison was still in touch with the outside world.

During the night of May 25th/26th bodies of German troops, using local mules for pack transport were moving in a wide arc from the west to the east side of our perimeter. Perhaps the seaborne Italian expedition from the Dodecanese was even now at hand. Meanwhile, the Australians who were holding Apex Hill, two and a half miles south of the airfield, found themselves cut off, and were obliged to fight their way back to the Black Watch lines. They arrived about 8.30 a.m. on the 26th having killed many Germans.

At 6.30 a.m. part of the Argyll and Sutherland Highlanders had been caught by the Germans on an open hillside east of Heraklion, and suffered considerably from ground and air attacks. A counterattack by two companies of the Leicestershire miscarried, partly owing to the activity of the German aircraft, so this quarter continued to give cause for anxiety all day.

The enemy certainly showed an increasing tendency to assume the initiative, though he was still content to avoid a general engagement and to strengthen his concentration about four miles to the southeast of the airfield. He was by this time estimated to have not more than 250 men still in position to the west of Heraklion (left there, presumably, to mask the departure of the remainder and to prevent us denuding the garrison of the town for operations elsewhere); about 700 established across the road to the south near Knossos, where the Greeks were engaged in desultory encounters; and a force of unknown size, but certainly considerably larger than either of these two, away to the east. Here, where the Germans had been daily reinforced by airborne troops since the original assault, seemed to be the chief menace. An attack might be launched in considerable force even before any Italians appeared.

And what of our reinforcements? At 7.30 p.m. on the previous evening the 2nd Queen's and 16th Brigade headquarters had again embarked for Timbaki; but this, their last attempt to reach Crete, ended in another failure. From 10.45 a.m. on the 26th the ships were attacked again and again by dive bombers; frequent changes of course brought no relief, and, after considerable damage had been done to the landing craft, the order was given to return to Alexandria.

CHAPTER V

Evacuation

1

The Road to Sphakia

AS already related, it was on May 27th that the authorities at Home sent their approval for the evacuation of Crete. A provisional plan had already been worked out for the withdrawal of the troops engaged in the Maleme-Canea— Suda area: they were all to make for Sphakia, the fishing village on the southern coast, by the rough mountain road which provided their only line of retreat.[1] It was just a week since the first glider had drifted down towards the Tavronitis river bed and the first paratroops had dropped from the skies above Maleme and Canea.

General Weston, who commanded the rearguard, planned a series of delaying actions while the main body made its way, largely on foot, across the island to Sphakia. At least one advantage helped to compensate for the many trials and tribulations of the retreat: there was only a single road to follow through the mountains, so, unless the enemy employed more parachutists, it would be difficult for him to cut off the main body. It would be necessary for him to deploy in order to force each rearguard position, for the nature of the country rendered flank movements scarcely practicable.

A detachment of Layforce 200 strong took up a position during the night of May 26th/27th in the town and docks of Suda, with orders to fight a delaying action. The main body of Layforce, which had just landed, was marched immediately to the Stilos area where,

---

[1] The Germans, it appears from their official accounts, expected our force to fall back eastward from Suda and link up with Colonel Campbell's force at Retimo.

with two 'I' tanks and three carriers it occupied the next rearguard position. These commando troops, who had been trained for a very different purpose, were at some disadvantage, for they possessed no artillery or mortars and only sixteen Bren guns. But they were coming fresh into action.

Except for the gallant 200, and for various stragglers, Canea and Suda were vacated by our forces during the night, but not without some confusion, as more and more men took the route which led to the south. Transport moved in haphazard fashion, and many of the vehicles broke down upon the mountain road leaving stranded staff officers who sought to control and organize the column. The road was so packed with refugees and stragglers that despatch riders found it difficult, if not impossible, to force a passage: hence it was that General Weston was unable to exercise command over the whole rearguard operations which were efficiently conducted, nevertheless by the New Zealand and Australian commanders and Colonel Laycock who worked well together.

The coastal defence and anti-aircraft guns had been destroyed and the detachments ordered to Sphakia, their presence naturally increasing the congestion on the road. From the Akrotiri peninsula the men of the 151st Heavy A.A. Battery crossed Suda Bay in small boats, since Suda was already in enemy occupation by the time they had destroyed their guns. Gunners of the 20th Heavy A.A. Battery, who had been given defence duties in Suda docks, found it hard to believe that evacuation had been ordered and remained at the docks with Laycock's men.

Now our thoughts must turn to Force Reserve, made up, as will be remembered, of the 1st Welch Regiment, The Rangers, and the Northumberland Hussars. This improvised 'brigade' was commanded by Lieut.-Colonel Duncan of the Welch, for Brigadier Inglis had never been able to join it.

The advance continued through the night with the expectation of coming upon and relieving the New Zealanders and Australians who had already been withdrawn. Had the newcomers but known it, there were no troops between them and the Germans who were about to advance in vastly superior force.

About dawn of the 27th the Welch halted and took up a position about a mile west of the outskirts of Canea, with the right of the battalion resting on the coast. The Rangers were kept in close support and the Northumberland Hussars, on the left, held the line of the Mournies stream. The pressing need was to obtain contact with our own troops, but none of the patrols sent out for this purpose were seen again. Already the Germans of No. 141 Mountain Regiment were moving round the southern flank of Force Reserve.

About 8 a.m. the enemy developed his frontal attack, putting in Group Ramcke, No. 100 Mountain Regiment and No. 3 Parachute Regiment—the greater part of a division of good German troops, rested, well equipped and eager for action. Our men offered a stout resistance. All through the morning the struggle continued, but at two o'clock in the afternoon the Germans broke through the sorely harassed line of posts at three points and entered Canea. At 6 p.m. the mayor made a formal surrender of the town.

Even now an effort was made to withdraw our troops and reform in front of Suda, but we had suffered too heavily and only a few groups were able to break away. A party of the Welch, near the coast, is known to have maintained the fight as late as the morning of May 28th; but only about 150 men out of the 1,200 of Force Reserve who had been engaged made their escape. The German advance had been slowed and valuable time gained thereby, but the price we paid was a grievous one.

Meanwhile No. 141 Mountain Regiment was pushing on south of Canea in the direction of Suda. Here the 5th New Zealand and 19th Australian Brigades had taken up a defensive position along a slightly sunken road known as 42nd Street[1] which ran between olive groves about a mile west of Suda. On came the German vanguard, a battalion strong, hastening forward somewhat incautiously in its desire to maintain close contact with its retreating enemy and perhaps paying insufficient attention to the possibility of an ambush or counter-attack. It may well be that the Germans did not expect to encounter any serious resistance at this stage. Between ten and eleven o'clock that morning they came up against the positions held by the New Zealanders and Australians.

[1] See Map 11.

Without waiting for the attack to develop in force the Maori battalion and 2/7th Australian Battalion went in to counter-attack with the bayonet.

No one knew how it started. Some thought the New Zealand battalion was the first to go forward, some thought the Australian. In any case it seems that there was a degree of spontaneity about it. Captain Rangi Royal of the Maori battalion was seen to leap up on the side of the sunken road, brandishing his revolver and waving his men on. In a few minutes the whole line was scrambling forward.

It was one of those surprises which are liable to upset the balance of any advancing force. Without help from the air, without any preliminary bombardment, without much supporting fire, the Australians and New Zealanders flung back the German vanguard for as much as a mile and a half, inflicted upwards of 150 casualties and captured a quantity of material.

The official German account of this action is somewhat sketchy, but admits that the fighting was fierce and costly—'every tree had to be fought for'—and that heavy casualties were suffered by the battalion. By the afternoon the enemy was established on the high ground south-east of Canea, but all thought of rushing Suda that day was abandoned by him. He contented himself with keeping our positions under heavy fire from machine-guns and mortars.

But the frontal attack from the direction of Canea was not the only threat which the New Zealand and Australian rearguard had to face that day, for the turning movement by No. 85 Mountain Regiment (Colonel Krakau), now constituted a grave menace to the southern flank and rear of the two brigades.

It will be remembered that this force had been despatched by General Ringel with the object of getting to Stilos as speedily as possible and from that point establishing a position astride the line of our retreat a mile or two to the east in the direction of Neon Khorion. As in the case of the German airborne landing at Corinth, which strove to cut off the retreat of our forces from Greece, this attempt came just about twenty-four hours too late to achieve any important success. For this the chief credit must go to the magnificent defence put up by No. 8 Greek Regiment at Alikianou. For three days (May 23rd-25th) they had stubbornly resisted first the paratroops, then No. 100 Mountain Regiment and finaly No. 85 Mountain Regiment.

Since no progress could be made until Alikianou had been taken the German command laid on a set-piece attack for the morning of May 26th. For half an hour the village was heavily dive-bombed; then the German mountain infantry moved forward. They found Alikianou deserted. The Greeks had quietly slipped away into the hills during the night. It had been a model resistance, holding up strong German forces for several valuable days and eventually leaving them to spend their full-scale attack upon a deserted position.

It is a flattering reflection that contemporary German accounts

assumed that Alikianou had been held by a British detachment throughout these days.

After occupying the abandoned village, Colonel Krakau's force, accompanied by a mule train, began to push eastwards across the foothills. The resistance at Alikianou had suitably impressed the enemy, and the commander of the leading battalion was surprised not to encounter any British troops on the heights above the village. The Germans pushed on, but moving, as has been indicated, against the grain of the mountain ridges, and constantly harassed by guerrillas, they only succeeded in covering five miles of up-and-down going in the course of the day. At nightfall they were not yet round the southern flank of our position.

Even so, the Germans had made enough progress to compel the withdrawal of the Australian and New Zealand brigades. General Weston brought them back during the night to the neighbourhood of Stilos.

In the Suda docks area Laycock's detachment had been engaged with parties of Germans, but managed to break contact at nightfall and then to retire upon the defile at Beritiana where it joined another detachment of Layforce, something over a company strong, and also two companies of the 28th (Maori) Battalion under Captain Rangi Royal, one of the heroes of the 42nd Street action. The Maoris had been retained to strengthen this position when their own 5th New Zealand Brigade was withdrawn to Stilos.

The main body of Layforce was now located at the village of Babali Khani, three miles further back on the road to Sphakia. The 4th New Zealand Brigade was making for Askifou where a high valley, called 'the Saucer' because of its shape, lay deep among the mountains—a tempting landing-ground for German parachutists intent upon the interception of our retreat. North of the Saucer General Weston had his headquarters for a time. Force Headquarters was making for Sphakia so that General Freyberg could control the arrival and disposal of his troops and their embarkation.

Wireless contact with Middle East Command had broken down in the course of the day, though not before a signal had been received from Wavell confirming approval of the evacuation and Freyberg had given an outline of his plans. He reckoned to have ready to embark on the night of May 28th/29th about 1,000 men, and on the three succeeding nights, 6,000, 5,000, and 3,000. At this time it was hoped that a large contingent of the force at Retimo might reach

Sphakia. Freyberg was giving priority to the wounded, then to the fighting troops, units which had been longest in action receiving special consideration.

Since Sphakia was to be the final location of Force Headquarters the Naval Officer in Charge at Suda had sent a wireless set by motor launch to ensure communication. The launch never reached Sphakia. It was seen by the Germans and sunk by air attack.

On the morning of Wednesday, May 28th Freyberg reported to Middle East Command from his rudimentary Headquarters at Sphakia,[1] using an R.A.F. wireless set, the only one available.

He asked if embarkation could be expedited: it had proved impossible to break contact with the enemy, and it was most unlikely that resistance could be prolonged until the night of May 31st/June 1st: only the New Zealanders and Australians were able to find detachments fit to fight: at a generous estimate the combatant troops now numbered less than 2,000 with three guns, a total of 140 rounds of gun ammunition, and three light tanks[1]: tomorrow night (29th/30th) would be the last chance to get the troops away: there were many unarmed stragglers: every effort would be made to embark the fighting troops tomorrow, and any left over would be directed to Port Loutro for evacuation on the following night.

But the main effort of the Mediterranean Fleet was directed that night to Heraklion, where were concentrated five battalions whom it might prove impossible to rescue if their evacuation were to be postponed for even another twenty-four hours. Somehow General Weston would have to hold off the enemy pursuit to Sphakia throughout the whole of Wednesday and Thursday.

The most immediate threat that morning came from the German mountain troops who for the past two days had been moving across our southern flank in the direction of our line of retreat to Sphakia. They had just failed to reach Stilos on the previous evening, but at about 5.30 on Wednesday morning they moved forward against the remnants of Hargest's 5th New Zealand Brigade and the 2/7th Australain Battalion which had reached the village during the night.

The Anzacs were ready to receive the complete mountain battalion which seems to have been committed to the attack, and repulsed it without much trouble. The Germans remained in contact

---

[1] Some of his staff officers and part of his headquarters personnel were still on their way across the mountains.

[1] This proved something of an underestimate.

and it was clear that the position could not be held for long without supporting artillery. A message was sent back to the 4th New Zealand Brigade, now at Askifou over sixteen miles south along the road, asking that three of the four guns there should be sent forward. When this proved impossible, Hargest and Vasey, using the discretion which was allowed them in view of the conditions of the retreat, decided to break off the action and continue the retirement by day. This involved considerable risk, but the troops were considered to be in no condition to fight all day and march by night. And for once we were lucky. The *Luftwaffe* failed to put in appearance in strength, although the weather was clear and bright. German air activity was on a notably diminished scale throughout the day in this area, being primarily concentrated against the defenders of Retimo and Heraklion.

The withdrawal of the Anzacs, which began at about 10 a.m. left the detachment at Beritiana, two or three miles further north, in a precarious position. No message seems to have been despatched, or at any rate received, at Beritiana, informing the troops there of the enemy concentration against Stilos and our imminent withdrawal from the village.

The force at Beritiana had troubles of its own to face, quite apart from the uncovering of its rear at Stilos. As early as 6 a.m. a specially formed pursuit detachment had begun to advance from the north. This detachment had been given the task of following up the retreat by the coast road and clearing a way through to Retimo and Heraklion. It was composed of fresh troops who had not yet been in action—one motor-cycle battalion, one mountain battalion, some mountain batteries and a section of engineers for dealing with demolitions. On any ground where it could find room to deploy it would obviously be able to overwhelm the weak rearguard detachments opposed to it.

A powerful attack was delivered with mortar and artillery support. All through the morning the defenders held their own, but by noon the enemy succeeded in dislodging them. The two Maori companies fought their way back, covering a distance of twenty-four miles before they rejoined the main body. In the process they only lost two men killed and they managed to bring back their eight wounded. The Layforce detachment was much less fortunate. It was completely cut off by the German mountain troops, who had now established themselves in a dominating position at Stilos. Laycock himself and his brigade-major managed to get away by driving slap through and over the Germans in one of the two tanks that had remained with the rearguard. Later they rejoined the main body further back, driving in with their tank still swathed in its camouflage netting. For the fate of the remainder who survived we have only the German official account, but it appears that they were all rounded up and captured.

The enemy advancing by the road, now made contact with No. 85 Mountain Regiment, which had made the long cross-march over the ridges. An advanced party was pushed on ahead to clear the next rearguard position. Now that the Beritiana detachment had been annihilated or dispersed and the two nominal brigades which had been in position at Stilos were withdrawing southward towards the Askifou valley, the main body of Layforce just north of Babali Khani formed the rearguard. It had the 2/8th Australian Battalion in support, and also enjoyed the assistance of one of the very few remaining 'I' tanks. So long as this force remained in position it blocked the main routes to both Retimo and Sphakia, for the road fork was four miles further on.

The Germans delivered their assault early in the afternoon. A motor-cycle company led the way, followed by engineers, artillery, anti-tank guns and infantry. Attempts to rush the position failed in the face of steady rifle fire, and the motor-cyclists, who, as was not unusual, took the first knock, seem to have suffered heavily. The solitary tank did good service in holding off the German infantry; then German reinforcements arrived in the shape of a battalion of No. 85 Mountain Regiment. This battalion endeavoured to work round the western flank of the defence, while our men were pinned down by mortar fire from in front, but the Australian battalion, which was fed into the line company by company, countered this threat. So, although very hard pressed at times, Colonel Laycock's force was able to hold on until nightfall. As on previous occasions, our troops endeavoured to make up for their lack of fire power by local counter-attacks, usually in platoon strength but sometimes with parties of seven or eight men, wherever the enemy had worked in to close quarters. Our position had been well chosen, and the German commander, in his report of the battle, complained that his artillery support was ineffective owing to the difficulty of obtaining observation. And again it may be noted that the German infantry showed to no particular advantage in battle when lacking the close support of the *Luftwaffe;* and the small-scale counter-attacks undertaken by Layforce at dusk effectively discouraged the enemy from engaging in night operations.

Layforce had held the position for as long as had been planned. Shortly after 9 p.m. the troops began to pull back, and, leaving roadblocks to delay the enemy' pursuit, moved off towards the concentration point at the Askifou 'Saucer'. The Germans made no attempt to follow up.

While Layforce was engaged in this successful rearguard action on Wednesday afternoon the bulk of our forces continued the retreat along the *via dolorosa* that led southwards to Sphakia and—perhaps—to safety. For most of the men taking part it was now a test of sheer endurance. For only a small proportion was there any longer a question of fighting. The remainder had just to keep footslogging along the stony mountain road, with stiff and aching limbs, with broken boots and with a torturing over-powering thirst; for there were no streams and only occasional wells along this mountain route. Often when a body of men reached one of these wells and clustered round to fill their water-bottles if they had them—empty bully-beef tins if they had not—the cry would go up 'Jerries overhead!' and all would fall flat on their faces, hoping the enemy pilots had seen nothing. To run for cover was the greatest mistake; it merely drew the attention of the hostile aircraft.

This is how it appeared on that Wednesday, May 28th, to Dr. Theodore Stephanides who took part in the withdrawal to Sphakia:

> On our way I noticed that though the men around us were straggling along anyhow, they did not seem too depressed on the whole; many of them would crack an occasional joke or sit down at the side of the road fur a quiet cigarette. As a matter of fact, it had not occurred to me that this was the first lap of a wholesale evacuation. I thought that we were 'only retiring to another defensive position prepared in advance' owing to a temporary reverse, and that long-range fighters would reach us somehow to enable us to clear the Germans out of the island. It certainly never entered my head that it was *we* who were being turned out....

> ...we saw units withdrawing in perfect order with their rifles and all their equipment. They were marching in sections, generally in single file owing to the terrain, under their officers and N.C.O.s, who ordered them when to scatter and take cover and when to reform. It was very heartening to watch the calm and competent way they went about it....

> Enemy air activity became more marked about this time, and suddenly we heard a loud droning from over the hills to the

northeast. Then thirty or forty planes swept unexpectedly out of the skies, and after bombing the village we had just left, swooped roaring in our direction...fortunately we saw an old disused limekiln a few yards away and tumbled into it just in the nick of time. The upper part of this kiln had collapsed, but the bottom was some four feet below the surface of the ground and filled with a dense tangle of weeds and brambles, into which we burrowed and lay hidden. We were a hundred yards or so from the main road, and a small group of houses which the Germans, for some reason or other, began bombing and machine-gunning with great persistance although, as far as I could see, there was nothing to warrant such an expenditure of munitions.

For minute after minute, each one of which seemed an hour, that heart-stopping racket went on. Our refuge heaved and rocked and I was afraid that it would cave in on us; every now and then chunks of earth and stones spouting up from the explosions rattled on our steel helmets, and although we were below ground level the blast was so strong that it felt like a thump in the solar plexus....

Time seemed to have been petrified... but at last, what seemed an age, the planes departed and we crept dazedly into the open and resumed our march. Two or three houses which had just been strafed were on fire and sending up thick columns of smoke, there was a number of huge craters on and around the road and one smashed truck with its driver lying dead beneath it. That, as far as I could see, was the total result of all that late sound and fury.

Soon heads began to appear from all sorts of unexpected hiding-places, followed cautiously by their owners, and the southward retreat continued as before!

And here is the impression of Captain Peter McIntyre, New Zealand Official War Artist, of the same agonizing period:

As far as one could see, a long straggly line of men trudged up the mountain, and all along the roadside men lay exhausted. The planes were circling now, so we left the road and clambered up from the floor of the ravine below, where the rocks and trees gave some sort of cover. Single file, the endless line climbed up and up. Men lay asleep or done up across the track, but the others just stepped over them and on. The track was strewn with gear— empty water-bottles, pieces of webbing, greatcoats.

Sometimes down the face from the rock the wreckage of army trucks would be strewn where they had plunged headlong off the road when attacked by bombers. You would notice dimly the

¹ Stephanides, *Climax in Crete*

personal gear strewn around these trucks—a mess tin, a pocket tin, a pocket book, a photograph, or an Australian hat.

A song kept humming through my head. Gradually I became more conscious of it. I could swear I had heard snatches of it whistled from the columns in the valley. The song of the retreat, 'Waltzing Matilda'—ridiculous in a way and quite inappropriate but somehow expressive of the hopes of these men, hopes of seeing Australian homes or New Zealand homes again. The broad Aussie hat lying by the broken truck sent it through my mind again. 'You'll come a waltzing Matilda with me?' Still, the ravine wound up and up. Legs were like lead now, and you trudged in a foggy coma, conscious only of aching feet and the raw patch on your hip where the rifle chafed. The sweat ran down your face and stung your cracked lips. Sometimes a creaking wisecrack would come from somewhere down the column.

Once, out of a fog of tiredness I became conscious of a bewildering sight. There in the midst of a retreating army was a young girl, a pretty blonde, no more than seventeen, with her hair down and carrying a rifle. The men stared in curiosity as they passed, but in their weariness they made scarcely a comment. Only one, a New Zealander with an inch of stubble on his grimy face, raised his hand in salutation. Who she was, or whether she ever got through to the coast, we never knew.

At last, at weary last, there was the top of the pass. Below us and ahead lay a beautiful plain like a cup in the mountains. There were green fields in a vari-coloured pattern and little white villages clustered under the edge of the hills. Across the plain, the khaki columns crept like ants making thin wavering lines into the distance. We came on a line of huge forests. Other armies must have passed through here in some forgotten age. In the intervening years this 'happy valley' could have seen but little of passing life, lying as it did high and remote in the mountains. Now it was witness of the British Empire fighting its rearguard action for life. It saw dive-bombers and the hurtling trucks and heard the rattle of machine-guns. Civilization had caught up with it.

There were wells here and cold water, giving wonderful relief to raging thirsts. You gurgled it down, letting it spill over and run down your chest. Then...sling your rifle again and march, march. The plain narrowed at the far end into another pass, and the bombers were pasting it. The line of men would move on and up, and then the planes would come and the line of khaki would melt into the rocks. The crash of bombs echoed through the mountains. Huge clouds of smoke and dust belched upwards from the passes.

Somewhere here, two of us, a red-headed Irishman called Barry Michael and myself became separated from the rest of our squad. Too tired to care we went on. All through the hot afternoon we dragged. Once we had to crouch under some boulders while the planes bombed all around us. I remember looking up once to see three great bombers sweeping over the hilltop straight for us. We saw the bomb leave its rack. 'Jesus!' said Mick, and we tried to melt under the stones.

The crash came almost as a relief, for it was yards away on the hillside.

'And to think right now I might be sitting in a Dannevirke pub', says the Irishman.

By dark we were marching down through a great chasm in the mountains. Below the road, the cliff fell away sheer to the depths of the ravine. Down there we could see another line of men stragling down to the sea. With the darkness came the longing for sleep. Your feet seemed to move mechanically. Your whole body ached. The rifle had become an impossible leaden weight and the webbing chafed until on your hips and shoulders there were raw patches. We had had little sleep in over a week. Nerves were ragged, and we had seen little enough food even in the first days and scarcely any at all in the last three days. We had marched at a hard pace all through the night, through the next day, and into the night without more than a few ten-minute rests.

Thoughts were muddled and senseless now, drifting in irrelevant fashion to things years back. Tempers flared up out of tiredness. I remember threatening to swipe Mick when he brushed against me. The things around me, the dark pine trees against the sky, began to fade. I remember crashing in the ditch beside the road. I could hear the feet tramping just beside my head, but could feel nothing. I felt myself sinking into deep luxury.

The will to live, the instinct for survival, seems to rise in aid of a man when most needed and becomes the dominating thought and driving force. I could not have slept more than an hour until I was awake again to find the faithful Mick in the ditch beside me. The heavy tramp of feet and the silent mass of men that streamed past brought back that clear thought, 'Get to the coast!' and we dragged ourselves, numb and heavy, into the column.

Of the next hours I have no recollection whatever, except of an all-enveloping thirst, until next morning when we climbed into a hole in the cliff-face.

2

Passage from Heraklion

BRIGADIER Chappel's position was by no means an easy one. During the night of May 26th/27th he explained his problem in a message to Middle East Command whence it could be transmitted to Creforce, for Chappel had no direct communication with Freyberg.

Briefly we could defend the existing perimeter, which was exposed to the enemy's fire, but were powerless to prevent his reinforcement by air so that our position might eventually become untenable; we could attempt to clear the roads to the west and the south-east but there was little object in trying to do so unless reinforcements or supply columns could be sent in by these routes; or we could launch an attack upon the principal German concentration, to the southeast near the village of Elia, which would be a hazardous operation with the forces available.[1]

During May 27th, Middle East Command provided the answer to the problem, and the answer was contained in one word—evacuation. This news was not at once made known to the troops who were ordered to act aggressively as opportunity offered.

German air attacks occurred at intervals during the day, and a convoy of trucks which it was hoped could be rushed through to the south was held up by the enemy at Knossos. From 8.30 a.m. onwards German supplies and reinforcements were dropped to the west and the east—but mostly to the east—of our positions, and East Hill and 'Charlies' were shelled. The 2/4th Australian Battalion and the Argyll and Sutherland Highlanders sent out fighting patrols to investigate German activity at Apex Hill which was shelled by our artillery.

During the afternoon two Hurricanes landed on the airfield, but one sustained damage when it attempted to take off again.

On May 28th, Admiral Cunningham decided that the Heraklion garrison—five battalions and twenty-four guns—must be evacuated that night and Brigadier Chappel was so informed by Middle East Command. Orders were then issued and preparations began.

An exceptionally heavy air attack was delivered during the afternoon, and evidence seemed to be accumulating that the very next day might see a ground offensive launched in force from the

[1] See Map 13.

east. On the morrow, indeed, the first Italian troops were to land in the eastern part of Crete. The Italian commander in the Dodecanese had offered to participate with his forces as early as May 22nd; this offer, which was referred upward until it reached Field-Marshal Goering, was accepted, and the Italians had been asked to undertake the occupation of the eastern part of the island. Meanwhile Colonel Brauer was hastening his preparations for the assault upon the Heraklion airfield, but was compelled to report that he would not be ready before the afternoon of the 29th.

The Germans flew in substantial reinforcements during May 28th. Our estimate was that two battalions were dropped to the east of the perimeter, about seventy troop-carriers being employed. One carrier came down near Apex Hill. The hospital at Knossos, hitherto respected by the enemy, was heavily mortared and machine-gunned; and when a protest was made the excuse was given that the place was being used as an artillery observation post. This, of course, was not the case; it seems that the Germans were stung to this act of savagery by the good shooting of our gunners.

The hospital at Knossos was isolated and practically surrounded so there could be no thought of bringing the wounded away when the garrison embarked. Likewise, a platoon of the Black Watch, holding a road-block in the vicinity, had to be left to shift for themselves; and the Greek troops had taken to the hills and were out of touch with our command. With these exceptions, the garrison concentrated in an inner perimeter which the York and Lancaster would hold as a covering position, being the last troops to leave. By employing delayed-action fuses, it was arranged to explode an ordnance dump and a petrol dump—not before 6 a.m. on May 29th.

The cruisers *Orion, Ajax* and *Dido,* and the destroyers *Hotspur, Decoy, Kimberley, Hereward, Jackal* and *Imperial* had sailed from Alexandria at 6 a.m. on the 28th. In negotiating the 25-mile wide Caso Strait the ships had to run the gauntlet of air attacks as was expected; and about 9 a.m. *Ajax* was so narrowly missed by a bomb that a fire was started and she was ordered back to Alexandria without completing the passage to Heraklion. It was not until 11.30 p.m. that the remainder of the fleet arrived off the port. Only three and a half hours remained to carry out the embarkation before the approach of daylight would compel the ships to leave. The Navy lost no time. While the cruisers lay outside the harbour the destroyers went in to the main jetty and acted as lighters, ferrying the troops to the cruisers before taking in their own complements. In this fashion

Brigadier Chappel's entire force, over 4,000 strong, was embarked, and the ships sailed at 3 a.m. on the morning of May 29th.

So far all had gone well. The enemy had made no sign. The first mishap was that to the destroyer *Imperial,* whose steering gear broke down as the result of the bombing attacks during the outward passage. She was abandoned and sunk, the ships's company and the troops being transferred to the destroyer *Hotspur.* Then, soon after sunrise, when the ships had entered Caso Strait, the *Luftwaffe* struck and struck again. *Hereward* was hit and forced to steer for the Cretan coast where she ran aground, most of those on board eventually becoming prisoners of war. Damage to the *Decoy* caused speed to be reduced to 25 knots, and the cruiser *Dido* was also hit. During repeated attacks the *Orion,* which carried 1,100 troops, was hit three times, losing her captain and 90 others killed and 275 wounded: one bomb passed through the bridge of this cruiser and exploded in the stoker's mess deck. Yet, so damaged as to be almost out of control, she staggered on towards Alexandria.

The ships were picked up by Fulmars of the Fleet Air Arm shortly before noon, and the German attacks, in which it was reckoned that over 100 aircraft were employed, gradually died away. We had suffered a grievous loss in troops and seamen—over one hundred killed and more than three hundred wounded—while the damage done to the ships caused difficulties in completing the evacuation which, with the departure from Heraklion, had only begun.

It was particularly galling to have to pay such a heavy price for the extrication of our troops from Heraklion, after the smoothness with which the assembly at the harbour and the actual embarkation had taken place. However, taken as a whole, Heraklion may be regarded as the most satisfactory of the three engagements which make up the Battle for Crete. The garrison had most effectively defeated the German airborne attack on the opening day and then, for the remaining eight days, had maintained itself and defended the airfield by vigorous action against ever increasing numbers of the enemy.

3

The End at Retimo

AS we know, at Retimo,[1] Colonel Campbell's main preoccupation was to re-establish contact with the outside world. Attempts to drop him supplies from the air during the night of the 26th/27th failed because there were no ground flares, and without these to guide them the pilots could not locate our positions.

The fresh attack upon the German stronghold at Perivolia, which cut our communications to the west, was duly delivered at dawn of the 27th, but met with no success. One of our tanks had its track smashed by a mortar bomb, and the other was penetrated by an armour-piercing shell and set on fire; even so, two companies of the 2/11th Australian Battalion almost got to grips with the Germans before they were pinned down by such a volume of machine-gun fire that they could not stir before dark. Also, they were attacked from the air.

At 3 a.m. on May 28th, however, two companies of Australians forced their way into Perivolia and killed about eighty Germans before they withdrew.

During the night a landing craft had arrived from Suda with a cargo of two days' urgently required rations. But it brought no message regarding evacuation, although orders to that effect had been issued by Force Headquarters on the morning of the 27th, and a column of men was already streaming southward. Actually the landing craft had made too hurried a departure from Suda on the previous evening. General Freyberg did send an officer down to the harbour after the decision to evacuate was made known; but the vessel had already departed for Retimo. It seems that Colonel Campbell's detachment was dogged by sheer bad luck. Force Headquarters, arriving at Sphakia on May 28th learned with concern that no instructions regarding evacuation had been sent to

Retimo; and from Sphakia to Retimo there was no means of communication. All that could be done to remedy this disastrous omission was to signal Middle East Command a request that an aircraft be sent to fly over Retimo and drop a message instructing Campbell to prepare for evacuation as soon as possible: to begin a withdrawal that night on Plaka,[1] fifteen to twenty miles to the south across the mountains, where his troops would be embarked; to occupy concealed positions at Plaka by first light on May 31st; and to hand over all German prisoners to the Greeks.

[1] See Map 12.

[1] See Map 8.

It was also suggested that a sum of £1,000 in drachmas should be dropped as a practical means of assisting stragglers, who might be unable to rejoin the main body, to escape subsequently by caique. This constitutes probably the first instalment of the many subsidies that were introduced into Greece by 'irregular' means in the course of the next few years. Not all of them served so useful a purpose.

On this day Colonel Campbell was interested to learn from a B.B.C. broadcast that 'the situation in Crete is extremely precarious'.

Next day, Thursday, May 29th, an aircraft from Egypt flew over the Retimo position and dropped a message bidding the garrison evacuate, couched in slang phraseology that would not be comprehensible to the Germans if they should pick it up. There is no evidence that this message was ever found. In the evening a Hurricane was sent with a further message. But with so many Messerschmitts roaming the air above Crete it is not surprising that the solitary Hurricane did not return.

That day the Germans began to close in from the west. A body of their motor-cyclists entered Retimo during the afternoon, and made contact with the Germans at Perivolia. Even the little force on the headland far away to the east moved forward to take up fresh positions before dark. During the night the four Greek battalions which had been stationed in the centre between the two Australian battalions slipped away into the hills. The end was at hand.

Colonel Campbell's force was indeed in an impossible position. Of his original numbers, about 1,000, with which he had started to give battle he had lost a comparatively small proportion, but he had rations for only one more day and he had no clue at all to the situation in other parts of the island, and did not know whether his force would be able to march or fight its way to the south coast. And so signals were sent out to sea during the night in the hope that they might attract the attention of some stray British craft.

But by this time there were no British ships anywhere in the waters to the north of Crete.

The end came on the morning of Friday, May 30th. After dawn German army trucks could be seen pouring out along the road from Retimo to Perivolia. They could only have come from the Canea sector, and this was the first definite indication to Colonel Campbell that our resistance in that quarter had entirely ceased.

Lacking any orders, Campbell still maintained his purpose to continue the defence of the airfield. With the exception of one

Company of the 2/11th Battalion, which was left to fight a holding action at Perivolia and was overrun by sheer weight of numbers and metal, he withdrew all his remaining force to a smaller perimeter in the immediate vicinity of the landing-ground. But the Germans came on. There were two tanks and several field guns with the advanced force; and as Campbell grimly noted that they were moving to the south, taking up the positions formerly held by the Greeks, he knew that his situation was hopeless.

Resistance could not, in the opinion of the garrison commander, have been prolonged for more than another hour, in view of the commanding position which the German tanks and guns would be able to take up and his own shortage of ammunition. The chances of getting through to Sphakia (for Campbell had heard nothing of the plan to evacuate his force from Plaka Bay), were extremely slight. It was a three-day march, even if the way were clear, and his men had no rations beyond that day. Nor was it possible, owing to the lack of communications, to pass any quick messages through to the forward companies telling them to attempt to fight their way through.

Campbell had no alternative.

He was himself in personal command of the 2/1st Battalion and he sent a message through to the commander of the 2/11th.

'I am going to capitulate' it read. 'I advise you to do the same. Destroy all weapons you possibly can.'

Then he drank the bitterest cup of war. Accompanied by two of his officers, he walked forward under a white flag and gave in his surrender.

The commander of the 2/11th Battalion, called a conference of his senior officers. They discussed the alternatives of fighting it out, surrendering or taking to the hills. The first was ruled out as useless, considering the positions which the Germans had already established. Even while the officers conferred, mortar shells were bursting all round battalion headquarters. The troops were recommended to surrender or to attempt to make their escape in small parties.

A fair proportion chose the latter and, helped and fed by the Cretans, managed to get through eventually to the south coast.

Of the 1,000 who formed the Retimo garrison on May 20th about 160 had been killed in action; 140 made good their escape, the remaining 700 were taken prisoner.

One can feel only deep sympathy for Colonel Campbell and his gallant troops. The Retimo garrison had done all, and in fact more than could be expected of it. Though lacking anti-aircraft guns it had successfully frustrated the airborne assault upon the landing-ground and, though seriously short of ammunition and supplies of every kind, it had driven the invaders beyond mortar-range of the ground and had contained them there. It had killed about 700 Germans, a high proportion of the total of enemy dead in the whole of Crete. The ten days fighting at Retimo ended in surrender only because the battle had been lost elsewhere.

Part of the German column from Suda continued eastward from Retimo and reached Heraklion on the afternoon of May 30th, 36 hours after our garrison had left. A motor-cycle detachment pushed on eastward again, and on the same night met Italian troops on the Gulf of Mirabella. The whole of the north coast of Crete was in enemy hands.

4

Last Scenes at Sphakia

The road to Sphakia stopped two miles short of the coast. Beyond that the last stage of the journey involved a climb down a 500-foot cliff by a precipitous goat-track to the water side, where a shallow beach of shingle, less than 20 yards wide and 150 yards long, provided the only assembly point for the men about to embark. In the course of Wednesday, May 28th, the headquarters troops of Force and of the R.A.F. had gradually arrived, and the latter operated their wireless transmission set in a cave a mile along the coast to the east.

After dark the destroyers *Napier, Nizam, Kelvin* and *Kandahar* arrived off the coast. They had brought rations, which were understood to be in urgent need, and they had come to take off the first instalment of troops from the beaches.

Unfortunately the rations consisted chiefly of flour and matches—flour and matches when bully beef and biscuit were in urgent demand.

The destroyers lay off shore for about five hours that night, and during this time they were able to take on board 200 walking wounded and 800 unwounded troops, the latter figure including almost all the remaining R.A.F. personnel on the island. It was not an excessively large number, having regard to the time and the ships available. That it was no greater was due to the difficulty found in dispersing and concealing troops before darkness and yet having them in readiness upon the beach so as to save time when the ships' boats touched down. Time was lost, also, through 'gate-crashers' having to be turned back. It was clear that more carefully organized methods and a general speeding up would be necessary if the whole force were to be got away.

The original schedule had laid down a period of four nights for the evacuation of Sphakia, of which this was the first night. But the likelihood that it would be possible to spread either the resistance or the embarkation over so long a period had now greatly diminished. · On the one hand, the Germans were advancing along the road from the north. They might at any time over-run the numerically weak, ill-equipped and physically exhausted improvised units that were successively doing duty as rearguard. They might drop a formidable force of parachutists either in the Askifou plain or at Sphakia itself to render the embarkation still more hazardous and perhaps impracticable.

Nor could the Royal Navy guarantee shipping for the evacuation for a further three nights. The losses taken had been severe, and Admiral Cunningham had to consider his other commitments in the Mediterranean. The Army and Air chiefs in the Middle East, Wavell, Blamey and Tedder, were equally reluctant to request him to hazard valuable ships and lives night after night. It became a matter of grim accountancy. What losses in ships and crews would Cunningham be justified in risking in order to bring off the thousands that still remained in Crete? The decision was rendered the more difficult because no certain figure could be given for the troops on the island. Not enough was known about the losses we had suffered in battle or about the location of the various bodies of men in western Crete: another of the consequences of the breakdown of communications due to the enemy's air domination.

Wavell felt that he could not ask that anything larger than destroyers should be risked in further evacuations, and the Admiral came to the conclusion that the last attempt at evacuation would have to be made on May 30th/31st, one night earlier than had been planned.

In the event, it was a little better than that. The Navy did send cruisers to take part in the evacuation on the night of May 29th/30th, and the evacuation was subsequently extended up to the scheduled date of May 31st/June 1st.

The Anzacs of the 5th New Zealand and 19th Australian brigades had been plodding south throughout most of the previous day and far into the night. Not intil about 3 a.m. on the morning of May 29th did they reach the green valley of Askifou where a large part of the remainder of the force was now concentrated, in preparation for covering the final ten-mile stretch to the sea. The resistance put up by Layforce at Babali Khani on the previous day had proved effective in staving off close pursuit. And when the enemy started moving forward at dawn on the 29th the landing column took the road to Retimo to complete the reduction of Colonel Campbell's force. It was some time before No. 85 Mountain Regiment, who were charged with the pursuit to Sphakia, began to approach the Saucer in sufficient strength to deliver an attack. The 23rd New Zealand Battalion, now only 160 strong, was posted with a detachment of the 2/8th Australian Battalion at a pass about three miles north of the northern rim of the Saucer, but no attack developed during the morning.

General Weston, in conference with his three brigadiers, Hargest, Inglis and Vasey, at one o'clock that afternoon, decided that the Saucer could be held until nightfall by the 4th New Zealand Brigade which would then retire to the coast. The Australians with the Royal Marine Battalion would take up a final defensive position at Vitsilokoumos, a particularly strong point where the road winds and narrows rather more than two miles north-east of Sphakia: they would have the three remaining tanks and three Bren carriers under command. Layforce and the 5th New Zealand Brigade would move south to the dispersal area and the beach.

Still the Germans refrained from pressing the pursuit. The forward New Zealand company covering the northern approach to Askifou was engaged by the enemy advanced guard in the afternoon but managed to hold the attack without difficulty. For the second day in succession there was comparatively little air activity except when sixty aircraft delivered attack upon Sphakia and the adjacent beaches between 6 and 7 p.m.

After resting for a good portion of the day the troops, other than the 4th New Zealand Brigade, began to move south again along the road during the afternoon. The withdrawal of the 5th New Zealand Brigade was carried out in particularly good order, the troops moving in single file and at well-spaced intervals. After dark the 4th New Zealand Brigade in their turn began to withdraw towards the dispersal area near the coast.

As the evening haze began to gather, a powerful convoy of ships approached the coast of Crete. It arrived off Sphakia about 10 p.m. Here was the troopship *Glengyle,* the cruisers *Phoebe* and *Perth,* the A.A. cruisers *Calcutta* and *Coventry,* and the destroyers *Jarvis, Janus* and *Hasty.* Pickets had been posted at the various approaches to the beaches to prevent a repetition of the gate-crashing incidents of the previous night, and if the system of embarkation proved somewhat inelastic and produced occasional vexatious delays before the units due to be taken off could be assembled, it at least avoided the dangers of uncontrolled embarkation. Naval officers were sent on shore to explain the procedure, and the vital necessity for absolute stillness in the event of enemy planes coming over to drop flares. The quiet and business-like way in which the naval men spoke seemed to brace everybody's nerves and to give them renewed confidence.

For more than three hours on that still night the large, flat-bottomed, shallow-draught boats plied backwards and forwards across the glass-smooth waters under the tranquil summer sky. In almost total silence the weary, stumbling, khaki-clad figures limped aboard the ships, some still carrying their rifles, some without them. The walking wounded needed a little extra care and time to get them safely from shore to ship. When the time for putting to sea arrived shortly after 3 a.m. 6,500 of the men who fought at Maleme and Canea had been taken on board. Whatever might happen subsequently it had already been possible for the Royal Navy to lift a larger number of men from the island than had been contemplated by Freyberg three days earlier.

German aircraft were soon overhead next morning and hunted the convoy for several hours, but except that H.M.A.S. *Perth* received a hit in a boiler room and suffered some casualties the attackers met with no success. In the later stages of the passage a few long-range R.A.F. fighters flew to see the convoy home.

On the morning of May 30th over 10,000 men still remained concentrated around Sphakia and on the ten-mile stretch of road to the north.[1] It had been planned that four destroyers should be despatched that night to complete the evacuation but as these could only convey 2,000 men between them Admiral Cunningham now agreed to extend the evacuation by another night, seeing that some R.A.F. fighter cover was available for part of the return passage.

---

[1] The official estimate of 'Creforce' that morning was 7,000, but this figure underestimated the number of stragglers who were making their way back to the coast independently.

Vasey who was in command of the rearguard on the road to Sphakia determined to hold the attackers off his main position at Vitsilokoumos by making full use of his tanks and carriers in a delaying action. It would be their task to cover the successive demolitions in turn, deal with the motor-cyclists who normally formed the reconnaissance element of the German advance, and subsequently to fall back when the enemy pushed forward in some strength. There did indeed appear to be a good opportunity of the armoured fighting vehicles to engage an enemy vanguard that was unlikely at first to enjoy much assistance from support weapons; and in its way the day's fighting proved to be a rather neat and satisfactory business.

Before 7 a.m. the two leading companies of No. 100 Mountain Regiment, having pushed on past the Askifou plain, began their attack. Contrary to expectations they were supported by three light tanks, and one of the British tanks was speedily knocked out. The other two then withdrew behind the first of the demolitions which had been prepared by the 42nd Field Company R.E.

The new position which they took up after the demolition had been blown was about a mile south of Imvros at a point where a bend in the road concealed our tanks from view while providing them with good observation of the southern exit from the village. About 11 a.m. the Germans succeeded in dislodging our troops from this position, too. The road here runs along a ridge, with the ground dropping away sharply on either hand; so when the Germans found their frontal assault held up their infantry advanced over the ground immediately below the road where they were unopposed, since it proved impossible for our tanks to depress their guns sufficiently to bring fire to bear.

And so it went on all through the morning and afternoon, the two tanks and the three carriers making a fighting retreat from one road bend to another and pulling back only when the hostile infantry threatened to gain the road in their rear, or when anti-tank weapons began to come into action against them. Once the Germans were caught napping when, their infantry having just taken up a new forward position, one of our tanks and two Bren carriers slipped back up the road to surprise with a burst of fire a party of about forty Germans. Few of these survived.

By 5 p.m. the two tanks were back on the main Australian position. But both were finished. They had steering, brake, engine and clutch troubles, and so they were wrecked in positions where their ruined hulls would help to strengthen the existing road-blocks. The Germans made contact before dark, but the commander of No. 100 Mountain Regiment was sufficiently impressed with the natural strength of the position to refrain from attacking it. He gave orders for a company to move out on either flank during the night so as to effect an envelopment at dawn next morning.

During the day two Sunderland flying-boats had arrived at Sphakia and, in accordance with orders from Middle East Command, General Freyberg and his staff were taken off, General Weston being left in charge of the final stage of the evacuation.

It was perhaps the moment of deepest tragedy in Freyberg's life. Through no fault of his own the battle had been lost which above all others he would have wished to have won. He had been in supreme command and his New Zealanders had endured the longest and severest part of the fighting; but without any means of countering the deadly and persistent air assaults of the enemy they had been powerless to turn the fortunes of the day.

The problem of rations and water had become acute. The Australians posted on the crest of the ridge, a good two-hour climb from Sphakia, were already suffering acutely from the shortage, and the supply of rations on the beach of Sphakia was not large. No trucks could have been got down the hill path to fetch supplies (in any case, there were now very few trucks left) and the force possessed no mules. So volunteers were called for to climb and bring food up to the Australians. In order to have their hands free these men, many of them Australians too, took off their shirts and turned them into improvised haversacks. Thus they climbed the cliff and fed their fellows of the rearguard which was enabled to hold on throughout the ensuing day.

The night's evacuation brought a sharp disappointment. Four destroyers had started from Alexandria; only two arrived off Sphakia. One of the four had been stopped and then turned back by enemy attack, the other, suffering engine trouble, had been compelled to return to port. The two which did arrive, *Napier* and *Nizam,* undertook to carry double their quota of 500 each, but the revision of the embarkation plans could not be effected with sufficient speed. To avoid over-crowding, with its concomitant danger of enemy air observation and bombing, only those who were actually to be embarked had been allowed to move from their dispersal areas on to the beach. The discipline of the evacuation, perhaps open to criticism at first, was now perhaps too rigid and the beach-masters were constrained to 'go out into the highways and byways and compel them to come in'. And this took time, with the result that when the hour of 3 a.m. arrived only an additional 400 men had been embarked over and above the first thousand. The ships were dive-bombed during the return passage, but both arrived at Alexandria unscathed.

When Saturday, May 31st, dawned there were still something like 9,000 troops left on the island, concentrated now in a very small area covering Sphakia. Of this number, less than half were fighting troops. This category comprised approximately 1,100 New Zealanders (about 950 of these belonged to the battle-worn 5th Brigade, for most of the 4th Brigade had been taken off on the previous night), 1,250 Australians, 550 Marines, 500 of Layforce. The remainder was composed of varied base personnel and whatever was left of the static defence troops from Suda.

The Australian rearguard at Vitsilokoumos held positions on either side of the road in considerable strength. On their right Layforce (until relieved by the Royal Marines and the Maori battalion) formed a defensive flank; on their left, elements of the New Zealand brigades were in position. The commander of No. 100 Mountain Regiment, according to his own account, finding that our front was more extended than he had supposed and that neither of his two flanking companies actually overlapped the defence, decided upon a wider enveloping movement. Two more companies were therefore detailed to move off into the mountains, one upon either flank, with a view to descending upon Sphakia from the east and from the north-west respectively. He hoped that it would be possible to effect this final envelopment at dawn on June 1st, but having regard to the natural strength of the position (and with a curious absence of any sense of urgency), though he now had good observation of our position from a hill on the eastern flank, he decided to postpone his attack until he could obtain air support.

Up on the steep escarpment with his back to the southern sea, Vasey surveyed his position and felt confident that his men could hold at any rate throughout the day—provided that there were no infiltrations through to the beach. On the previous day two German patrols had worked their way down close to the cave where Creforce Headquarters was now established. These patrols had been destroyed, one by the platoon which 2nd-Lieut. Upham led with his usual skill and daring. To this gallant officer who, despite wounds and sickness, had achieved so much was to come the fitting award of the Victoria Cross.

Nothing seemed more surprising at the time than the failure of the enemy to take advantage of the situation by dropping parachutists at Sphakia and thereby deranging and perhaps preventing our evacuation. The Germans knew perfectly well, from the evidence of their aircraft, that the whole of our force from Maleme-Canea-Suda was making for that tiny fishing village. A comparatively small number of airborne troops could have seized and held the place and stood a good chance of destroying our troops piecemeal as they came from struggling across the Cretan mountains. Yet this was not done. Perhaps the explanation lay in the fact they had no more parachutists immediately available for such an operation. If so, this was the result of the heavy losses we had inflicted on them during the struggle.

That, as it happened, was not the worst of Weston's anxieties during the day. Wireless communication with Middle East Command was now only intermittent, and Creforce was under the impression that evacuation was not to be extended to cover the night of June 1st/2nd. But during the afternoon a signal came through to say that the last evacuation would take place on the coming night. It was hoped to send enough shipping to embark 3,600, and a couple of Sunderlands would also be sent, in one of which Weston himself was instructed to leave.

It needed no very elaborate calculations to discern that something like 5,500 men would still be left behind when the ships drew away from Sphakia for the last time. The problem of feeding those troops who still remained was already causing the utmost anxiety, for the remaining rations were not sufficient to provide for the force beyond that day. Already the men were on short commons and many were desperately hungry. Continued resistance at this stage depended even more upon more food than upon more ammunition. Weston signalled Middle East Command to this effect in the early evening and asked for a directive. But the batteries of the remaining wireless set in the cave at Sphakia were now failing and no reply was ever received.

The decision to abandon some 20 per cent of the defenders of Crete had not been lightly taken. While humanity prompted that every possible effort should be made to rescue these long-suffering troops, the dangers of sending shipping yet again into these waters had to be taken into account. It would be no act of humanity and a poor economy of force if more men were to be lost in attempting the rescue than could be saved by extending the evacuation over a further night. But transcending this was the wider consideration of Mediterranean strategy. It was not only the lives of the men in Crete that were at stake. It was the lives of the men in Malta, the men in Tobruk, conceivably also the men in Cyprus. Let the Royal Navy once be weakened beyond a certain point and the consequences were beyond all computation. It was said of Jellicoe in the previous world war that he was the only man who could have lost the war in a single afternoon. Admiral Cunningham in the present conflict shouldered a responsibility scarcely less awful.

The decision had to be taken. Everything available was to be scraped together for that night's evacuation. After that the ships would not return.

At eleven o'clock that night they arrived—the cruiser *Phoebe*, the minelayer *Abdiel*, the destroyers *Jackal*, *Kimberley* and *Hotspur*. Three landing-craft had been left behind after the previous night's evacuation: dragged ashore they remained concealed in caves all day. Now they were loaded up with the first wave of troops to leave.

The order of embarkation allowed for the passage of the remainder of the 4th New Zealand Brigade (about 200), the 5th New Zealand Brigade (950), the 19th Australian Brigade (1,000-1,250), Layforce (500) and the Royal Marine Battalion (550) in that priority. Strong guards had been posted at the beach approaches in order to ensure this priority for the organized formations and to prevent the boats being swamped by any undisciplined rush of stragglers and others. It had to be done.

At first all went smoothly, the New Zealanders were embarked in an orderly manner, and the time-table seemed to be well ahead of schedule. But the news had got round that this was the last night of evacuation, and more men, seeing the certainty of capture if they were left behind, surged towards the beaches. The guards at the approaches were either withdrawn too early or were overwhelmed by the human tide—it is not quite clear which—and confusion reigned. It was rendered the worse by the fact that the Navy on each of the previous nights had been able to lift numbers in excess of its estimate. This led to extra troops being allowed to station themselves at the approach to the beach so as to be within summons. As a result the men of Layforce found themselves unable to break their way through the rabble of refugees and very few actually reached the boats. The Australians who had held the final position on the escarpment found themselves impeded in the same way; and, owing to a faulty transmission of orders, the 2/7th Australian

Battalion was not included in the lists supplied to the officers controlling the movement to the beaches. Of nearly 500 officers and men still left in the battalion only 16 succeeded in getting through to the boats. When the ships sailed at 3 a.m. they carried 4,050 men, a figure that exceeded the estimate by over 400. But it might have been larger still.

Before leaving by air, in accordance with his instructions from Middle East Command, General Weston had issued the following instructions to Lieut.-Colonel Colvin of Layforce, the senior officer remaining on the island:

'In view of the following facts:

(a) My orders direct me to give preference to fighting troops. This has reduced the active garrison below what is required for resistance.

(b) No rations are left this Saturday night. Most of the troops are too weak owing to shortage of food and heavy strain to organize further resistance.

(c) The wireless will give out in a few hours and the risk of waiting for instructions from Middle East cannot be accepted, as this will leave the officer in charge without any guidance as to his course of action.

(d) There is no possibility of further evacuation.

'I, therefore, direct you to collect such senior officers as are available in the early hours of tomorrow morning and transmit these orders to the senior of them.

'These orders direct this officer to contact with the enemy and to capitulate.'

The sum of £1,000 was handed over to Colvin so that individual groups of men might be able to purchase means of escape.

The decision to surrender came as a thunderclap to the majority of the troops when Colonel Colvin and his officers informed them that no alternative remained. Attempts were made to tear down the white flag that was hoisted above Sphakia as an indication to German troops and aircraft that the end had come. The hope that springs eternal, and never more certainly than among men in extremest danger, had led some to believe that there would yet be one further night of evacuation—nor was it an altogether unreasonable hope, in view of the repeated changes which the time-table had undergone. But when it was realized that the rations were exhausted, and that small-arms ammunition also was running out, the situation had to be accepted. No serious defence would have been possible against the assault which a conscientious but unimaginative German commander, fighting, like Tybalt, 'by the book of arithmetic', was planning against men too weary and weak with hunger even to crawl forward and surrender. Foreseeing this, and foreseeing also that the German advanced forces would have carried no superfluous stocks of food with them, Weston immediately upon his arrival at Alexandria had signalled Middle East Command requesting that sufficient food be dropped by air at least to enable the men to march as far as some locality where the Germans might be expected to feed them. This was done without delay.

Before the final evacuation General Wavell had sent the following signal to Major-General Weston, R.M., the commander of the rearguard.

> You know the heroic effort the Navy has made to rescue you. I hope you will be able to get away most of those who remain, but this is the last night the Navy can come. Please tell those that have to be left that the fight put up against such odds has won the admiration of us all and every effort to bring them back is being made. General Freyberg has told me how magnificently your Marines have fought and of your own grand work. I have heard also of the heroic fighting of young Greek soldiers. I send you my grateful thanks.

Though there was now no alternative to surrender, it seems that groups here and there ignored the recommendations or orders from above and continued to resist with such ammunition as they still possessed. At any rate the German accounts gravely record a dive-bombing attack upon our positions which began at 8.30 a.m. and was followed by an artillery bombardment which 'forced the enemy to leave his positions and seek safety by dispersion in the fields'. Thereupon the elaborate enveloping movement by the two flanking companies was set in action, but it was four or five hours before the Germans reached Sphakia, and not until eight o'clock on the evening of June 1st were they able to report the coast for a distance of three or four miles on either side of the village firmly in their hands.

Not all of the 5,000 men still left in the southern part of Crete became prisoners of war. Major Garrett of the Royal Marines finding a landing craft which had been beached after the night's evacuation (and which contained some much needed rations) soon got it afloat and, accompanied by four officers and 134 other ranks, departed in the direction of the tiny uninhabited island of Gaudhopoula a dozen miles to the south, just as German aircraft came over to dive-bomb Sphakia and the Australian position on the escarpment.

The party reached the island and lay up during the day. At nightfall they made a fresh start and, with the assistance of a small-scale map of North Africa and the eastern Mediterranean, set a course for Tobruk, the nearest point in British hands on the African coast. And that was a mere trifle of 200 miles away. There was no chance of the available petrol carrying the craft anything like the required distance; in fact, it gave out on the following evening. After that they drifted at sea for a week. Finally, on June 9th, when the party was enduring the last extremities of hunger and thirst, land was sighted and the boat ran aground some miles east of Sidi Barrani and comfortably behind our forward positions in the Western Desert. There had been two deaths from thirst and exposure; the remainder of the castaways were in farily good shape.

Three other landing-craft, each as an independent venture, made the passage from Crete to Africa, their occupants totalling 136 of all ranks. Over 400 others, mostly in small parties, arrived, some making the African coast as late as September. Two groups, in all 13 officers and 68 other ranks mostly of the 2/11th Australian Battalion, were rescued by submarine.

Others of our men, as well as those from Sphakia, succeeded in escaping from the south coast of Crete. It will be recalled that when our troops left Heraklion an outlying platoon of the Black Watch in the neighbourhood of Knossos could not be informed of the evacuation and so were left behind. This party successfully extricated itself and, moving south across the island, joined forces with the headquarters company of the Argyll and Sutherland Highlanders, which had been left at Ay Dheka, a few miles from the south coast, to protect prospective landings in that area and the landing-strip which it had been intended to construct in the broad Messara plain. The united forces moved back to the shore in the neighbourhood of Timbaki on May 30th. The following day they were joined by about one hundred Australians from the 2/11th Battalion who had made their way across the mountains from Retimo after the surrender. No Germans were anywhere in the neighbourhood, and on June 1st a Blenheim dropped rations to the party. But the coast was almost uninhabited and no boats could be found, apart from three damaged vessels which had been abandoned after the troops had been put ashore during the preceding week. One of these, a landing-craft, was got afloat with great difficulty on the evening of June 2nd, packed with 11 officers and 66 other ranks, and sailed for the Egyptian coast. Early on the following morning the craft was sighted and stopped by an Italian submarine which took off all the officers except two and then allowed it to proceed on its course. No further misfortune befell this bold enterprise, and the troops reached Mersa Matruh on June 5th.

As soon as the Germans obtained control of the southern beaches they removed boats of any size and aircraft were detailed to patrol close in shore, rendering escape doubly difficult. Many of our men took to the mountains and were sheltered by Cretans. The Germans who, on the whole, had treated the captives taken at Sphakia with reasonable humanity as men who had suffered honourable defeat, presently grew impatient in the knowledge that armed British troops were still at large in the mountains assisting the Cretan guerrillas. The following appeal is a mark of the irritation which their presence caused to the enemy command:

SOLDIERS

of the

ROYAL BRITISH ARMY, NAVY, AIR FORCE!

There are MANY OF YOU STILL HIDING in the mountains, valleys and
villages.

You have to PRESENT yourself AT ONCE TO THE GERMAN TROOPS.

Every OPPOSITION will be completely USELESS.

Every ATTEMPT TO FLEE will be in VAIN.

The COMING WINTER will force you to leave the mountains.

Only soldiers who PRESENT themselves AT ONCE will be

sure of a HONOURABLE AND SOLDIERLIKE

CAPTIVITY OF WAR. On the contrary who

is met in civ clothes will be treated as a spy.

THE COMMANDER OF KRETA

Notwithstanding this threat, there were still about 500 British soldiers at large in the island as late as the close of 1941.

CHAPTER VI

Conclusions

I

The Loss

THE strength of the British garrison in Crete on May 20th, when the attack started, amounted to 28,614. Of these 14,967, or rather more than 52 per cent of the total, were eventually evacuated to Egypt. This compares unfavourably with the evacuation from Greece, when approximately 75 per cent of the expeditionary force was successfully withdrawn. Moreover the proportion is really lower still, as over 3,000 more troops, consisting of the 1st Argyll and Sutherland Highlanders, two Middle East commandos and a battalion of Royal Marines, were landed after the battle had begun.

The final figures issued by Middle East Command in November 1941 are as follow:

	Original Creforce	Arrived from Greece and remained	Reinforcements from Egypt	In Crete May 20th
British . . .	5,200	6,399	3,464	15,063
Australians . .		6,451		6,451
New Zealanders .		7,100		7,100
Total . .	5,200	19,950	3,464	28,614

	Losses		
	Evacuated to Egypt	Total	Percentage of Grand Total
British . . .	7,289	7,774	57
Australians . . .	3,119	3,332	24.4
New Zealanders. .	4,559	2,541	18.6

As we know, the New Zealanders bore the brunt of the fighting at Maleme, and about 800 of those who took part in the retreat to

Sphakia had to be left behind. The Australian losses are largely accounted for by the fact that the Retimo Force which could not be brought away was, apart from Greek troops, exclusively Australian; also, the 2/7th Battalion of the 19th Australian Brigade, which fought the final rearguard action on the plateau above Sphakia, was left behind owing to the breakdown of the evacuation arrangements at the beach on the final night.

Of the British losses, about one thousand were suffered on May 27th when Force Reserve—the 1st Welch Regiment and the remnants of the Rangers and Northumberland Hussars—went forward, after the general withdrawal had begun, to stand the shock, unsupported and vastly outnumbered, of the German advance on Canea and Suda. The commando troops who composed Layforce also lost heavily, and few succeeded in getting away.

As ever, the Army in its need had been able to count upon the utmost devotion and self-sacrifice of the Royal Navy. On June 2nd, Admiral Cunningham, commanding the Eastern Mediterranean Fleet received from General Wavell the following message:

'I send to you and to all under your command the deepest admiration and gratitude of the Army of the Middle East for the magnificent work of the Royal Navy in bringing back the troops from Crete. The skill and self-sacrifice with which the difficult and dangerous operation was carried out will form another strong link between our two services. Our thanks to you all and our sympathy for your losses.'

The losses of the Fleet were grave indeed. Over 2,000 officers and seamen were dead. Three cruisers and six destroyers had been sunk. Two battleships, one aircraft-carrier, two cruisers and a destroyer had suffered such damage as would take some months to repair. Cruisers and destroyers to the number of nine were less badly hit.'

The official German figures show the combined losses of the Army and *Luftwaffe* as:

	Killed	Wounded	Missing	Totals
Officers . . .	169	143	56	368
Other Ranks . .	1,802	2,451	1,832	6,085
Totals . . .	1,971	2,594	1,888	6,453

This figure was confirmed by General Student, commander of the XI Air Corps, in his subsequent interrogation after the war. Though it falls far below our own contemporary estimates,[1] it is higher than the losses to which the Germans admitted for the whole of the fighting in Yugoslavia and Greece during the previous month. Nevertheless the totals cannot be accepted as accurate.

The Australian War Graves Commission which visited Crete in June 1945 counted 4,000 German graves in the Maleme-Canea-Suda area alone. About 1,700 of these were around Galatas. For Retimo and Heraklion the estimates vary. The lowest figure for German dead at Retimo is 300, and it is more likely to have been in the neighbourhood of 700. For Heraklion the lowest estimate is 600 and it may well have been over twice that number.

This would give a minimum of 4,900 killed (which may include many of those drowned in the seaborne expedition). A New Zealand estimate adds 200 for those drowned when aircraft crashed into the sea, and 500 more who are likely to have died of wounds in hospitals in Greece. Its calculation of two wounded for every one killed, would add a further 11,200, bringing the total up to the very high figure of 16,800. There is no means, however, of confirming these estimates.

Assuming (which is very likely) that the Germans officially listed as missing were in fact killed, there is no excessive discrepancy between the German figure, which would amount to 3,859, and our minimum figure of 4,900. It would seem, therefore, that the German losses can scarcely have been less than 8,000 and may have been considerably higher.

But though these are small numbers compared to the gigantic losses which Hitler was very shortly to incur on the Russian front, they do represent a high loss in proportion to the total of troops engaged. And these losses were suffered by specialist troops.

Our own contemporary estimates of enemy aircraft destroyed were likewise greatly in excess of the actual losses. Unofficial estimates verged on the astronomical, and the calculated figures issued by authoritative sources placed the German losses in aircraft at about 180 bombers and fighters and 250 transport planes destroyed. The actual losses from May 13th, when the air attack upon Crete began, until the end of the battle amounted to 4 long-range reconnaissance aircraft, 19 bombers, 9 dive-bombers, 35 fighters, and 80 transport aircraft, a total of 147. In addition, 4

[1] General Freyberg placed the enemy losses at 17,000 (including 6,000 drowned). General Wavell's figure was 12,000 to 15,000 and Mr. Churchill's estimate in the House of Commons was much the same.

bombers, 2 dive-bombers, 13 fighters and 45 transport planes were more or less seriously damaged. To these may be added a further 73 (7 bombers, 9 dive-bombers, 17 fighters, 39 transport planes and one coastal patrol machine) destroyed on operations in this theatre of war (chiefly as the result of crash landings) not directly due to British or Greek action. Eighty-four more machines were damaged in this manner.

Directly and indirectly, the battle for Crete therefore compelled the Germans to write off nearly 370 first-line aircraft for the time being, of which 220 were a dead loss.

2

Policy and Performance

THE loss of the battle for Crete proved a bitter disappointment to the public at home. To many it seemed the crowning disaster in the long series of humiliations and defeats that seemed inseparable from British diplomacy and British arms. To understand the particular quality of disappointment it must be remembered that the tale of misfortune and mismanagement that starts far back in the period of the Manchurian incident nearly ten years earlier had seemed to reach a climax in the tragic events of May and June 1940, when the German armies swept irresistibly across the Low Countries and France, and Britain was left alone to face the tempest.

Then the cloud had lifted. To the miracle of Dunkirk had succeeded the miracle of the victory of the Royal Air Force over the skies of Britain, a battle rightly recognized at the time as decisive in the war, perhaps decisive in the history of the world. The winter had seen the no less astonishing victories of the Greeks in the Pindus and Albania and Wavell's sweep across Cyrenaica, gathering in prisoners by the twenty thousand at every stride. Ignoring the fact that the German ground forces had not been confronted since they swept our troops from the Continent of Europe, there was a tendency to believe that the tide was indeed on the turn and that our armies were adequate in equipment and battle practice to engage the Germans with reasonable hope of success in country where the enemy superiority of numbers could not be effectively employed.

The rapidity with which the Germans blasted their way through to victory in the three weeks' campaign in Greece administered a sharp rebuff to these hopes. But excuse could be found. The collapse of Yugoslavia, with the consequent uncovering of the flank of our prepared position; the inability of the Greeks to co-operate in our subsequent retreat to new positions; they heavy losses of our air forces at a comparatively early stage; the paralysing influence of defeatism in certain Government quarters in Athens—all these could be urged in partial explanation of our rapid expulsion from the mainland.

But Crete seemed to provide a real prospect of breaking the Nazi wave. British forces had been established in the island for six months—and therefore it might be assumed that all was in readiness to meet an assault. The enemy had no considerable volume of shipping easily available for a seaborne invasion, and in the improbable event of the Italian fleet putting to sea in strength—well, our Mediterranean Fleet with memories of Cape Matapan was waiting in anticipation. If he sought, as seemed most probable, to storm the island mainly or wholly by airborne assault, he was attempting a task never yet achieved in war and one upon which he had been unable to embark in the previous summer and autumn despite the fact that Britain had lost the entire armament of its Expeditionary Force in her Continental campaign.

So ran the line of argument, sound enough so far as it went. It seemed reinforced when early in May, Mr. Churchill, in his most defiant mood, announced roundly that 'we intend to defend to the death, without thought of retirement, both Crete and Tobruk...Let there be no thought of cutting our losses.' Tobruk had already successfully withstood one head-on assault and its defenders showed no signs of flagging; it seemed reasonable to hope that the defence of Crete would prove no less successful.

Yet Crete was attacked and taken by the Germans after twelve days' fighting and almost half of the force of British, Australian and New Zealand troops was left behind, either killed or captured on the island. It was taken solely by airborne assault, for no troops were landed from the sea until the decision to evacuate had already been made and the first embarkation of our troops was on the point of proceeding. It was taken, despite the fact that the attack conformed closely to the pattern that had been anticipated, and that as regards both time and place, as well as method, our information and estimates had been shown to be remarkably accurate.

Crete was attacked and taken; yet it had been defended more on military, than on political grounds, and because the War Cabinet, with the concurrence of their military advisers, had decided that it could be defended with a reasonable hope of success.

The battle for Crete will, perhaps, be matter for discussion as long as the ways and means of making war exercise their strange and terrible fascination upon mankind. Regarding the broad, major reason for our defeat need be no doubt or dispute at all. The explanation for the German conquest of Crete may be found in two words—Air Power.

We lost Crete because we were unable to provide air fighter cover for our troops and only negligible bomber support. The Germans, on the other hand, committed their available air forces, consisting of over 1,200 planes of various types up to the hilt at every stage of the battle. In the preliminary bombing and machine-gunning of our defence positions, in the transport of troops to the landing-places and finally in the close support given by low-flying fighter aircraft to their ground forces both in attack and defence, the *Luftwaffe* played a decisive rôle. It was omnipresent; our own air support, for reasons that we have seen, was practically non-existent.

Such a disparity in a vital arm of warfare was almost bound to be decisive. One must repeatedly emphasize how much an air attack against which there is no fighter defence tends to immobilize the functioning of the defence from the chief command downwards. Under such circumstances, direction and execution are so hampered and restricted that the initiative must be surrendered to the enemy. Plans, communications, maintenance, attack and counter-attack—all the normal operations of an army in action become difficult almost to the point of impossibility. They are, indeed, subject to a form of effective strangulation.

We may now consider whether it was necessary that the battle should have been fought at all.

The Royal Navy had been insistent from the first upon the importance of securing Crete in the event of Axis aggression spreading to the eastern Mediterranean. Crete was a valuable cover for our naval base at Alexandria. The threat of air attack to our forces in the eastern Mediterranean came principally from the Italian bases in the Dodecanese and these could themselves be largely neutralized and always threatened so long as we were in actual control of Crete. So Crete was an outlying defensive post of our Middle East position. Once let if fall, and enemy aircraft would be established dangerously nearer to Alexandria and our Middle East bases; and the prospect of eliminating the Axis hold on the

Dodecanese disappeared. Moreover, the German conquest of Crete would bring into being a new 'narrows' in the Mediterranean. Convoys to Malta from the west already had to run the gauntlet of the eighty-mile wide channel between Sicily and Cape Bon in Tunisia; convoys from the east would be faced with a second 'narrows', the two hundred-mile wide channel between Crete and the hump of Cyrenaica. The ebb and flow of battle carried our armies backwards and forwards over the Libyan desert, but during the greater part of the eighteen months between the loss of Crete and the Allied landings in French North Africa the Cyrenaican bastion was in enemy hands, and German aircraft, operating from Africa or from Crete, consequently took grievous toll of our shipping.

Yet the case for holding on to Crete is by no means so solidly established as might appear. While it was desirable to retain any and every position which might widen and strengthen the *glacis* of our main keep in the Middle East or which might provide us with a foothold for a subsequent jump back into Europe, the maintenance of our forces in any such outlying positions needed to be justified both on strategic and on administrative grounds.

Any scheme for the defence of Crete had to take into account the weakness of our air power in the Middle East and our inability to provide adequate fighter cover for our troops. We refrained from extending the number of airfields beyond Heraklion, Maleme and Retimo for the sufficient reason that we possessed neither the aircraft to station there nor—and this is of cardinal importance—the anti-aircraft guns to defend them. The example of Norway and the much more recent example of Greece were sufficient to show that a few aircraft operating from a few air bases are almost helpless and must speedily be annihilated by a force working from numerous bomber and fighter bases near at hand. Therefore, any defence of Crete must be a defence by the army and the fleet with only such assistance as could be given by night attacks upon the enemy's bases by our bombers from Egypt. From the first, then, we were certain to be fighting under one of the gravest handicaps possible in modern war.

Yet even supposing that we had never been attacked in Crete, or that, having been attacked, we had successfully repelled the invasion, the continued presence of a British garrison on the island would have constituted a most serious drain upon our man-power, never excessive, in the Middle East. It would have represented a dispersal of force quite contrary to all the principles of war. It is true that we left one force detached in Tobruk throughout almost the whole of this year; and we maintained another garrison in Malta for a full two years under the perpetual shadow of hostile attack. But we needed Tobruk as a means of hampering the enemy and rendering difficult the supply of his forward troops in the desert, and Malta, a valuable link in our Mediterranean communications, was subsequently to cover the invasion of Europe by way of Sicily. We did not need Crete for an offensive purpose, because the best way of return into Europe could never be through Greece; and when it was eventually possible to go back into Greece in the autumn of 1944, we were able from our advanced bases in southern Italy to bypass Crete with the greatest of ease. Crete was not necessary to us, therefore, as an *offensive* position.

Moreover, the problem of its maintenance would have been extremely formidable. The feeding and supply of the garrison, to say nothing of the 400,000 inhabitants cut off from all traffic with the mainland of Europe, would have been a constant drain upon our resources and our shipping. The absence of any ports on the south coast and any adequate means of transport to the main towns on the north must have meant that our convoys would have to continue to run the gauntlet of the narrow strait of Kithira or the still narrower strait of Caso under the eyes of the *Luftwaffe* and the *Regia Aeronautica.* Again and again our shipping was strained to the utmost; might not the necessity of keeping Crete supplied have produced disaster at some more vital point?

Therefore it is clear that the continued maintenance of British or allied forces in Crete must have involved an extremely serious drain upon our shipping and a dangerous dispersal both of troops and aircraft, while the compensating advantages are less easy to see. Of these advantages not the least important—taking a very long view—would have been the preservation of a part of the kingdom of Greece from Axis domination. Had it been possible for a Greek Government to continue to function on Greek soil it is arguable that the tragic developments which later troubled the internal life of that heroic but ill-starred nation might never have occurred. The rift which widened between the Government in exile and what came to be a *de facto* Government in the mountains, one of the causes of the tragedy of December 1944, would at least have been diminished.

It may well be that, having beaten off an assault, we might subsequently and in our time have found it necessary to evacuate

Crete, just as we had found it necessary to evacuate scarcely less defensible Channel Islands a year earlier. That is by no means improbable, in view of the facts stated above. But it scarcely establishes a case for giving up the island without a fight. Let the enemy first attack, let him be allowed to break his teeth upon the island; *then,* in our own good time, if circumstances should so demand, let us withdraw at leisure and without loss.

The case for contesting an invasion of Crete was most eloquently and cogently stated by the Prime Minister in the House of Commons in the debate on June 10th, 1941. The fighting defence of Crete formed part of the strategy of rearguard actions, the only reasonable alternative to capitulation which we could adopt after the disaster in France and the simultaneous extension of the war to the Mediterranean. It was necessary that, despite our inadequate resources, our strategy should reverse the disastrous methods of our diplomacy during the previous decade, that it should avoid above all a policy of military appeasement which would surrender position after position to the enemy on the grounds that we were not yet strong enough to defend them with the certainty of success.

The word on this subject is with Mr. Churchill.

> The choice was whether Crete should be defended without effective air support or should the Germans be permitted to occupy it without opposition. There are some, I see, who say we should never fight without superior or at least ample air support, and ask when this lesson will be learned. But suppose you cannot have it. The questions which have to be settled are not always questions between what is good and bad; very often it is a choice between two very terrible alternatives. Must you, if you cannot have this essential and desirable air support, yield important key points one after another?

> The further question arises as to what would happen if you allowed the enemy to advance or overrun without cost to himself the most precious and valuable strategic points? Suppose we had never gone to Greece and never attempted to defend Crete! Where would the Germans be now? Suppose we had simply resigned territory and strategic islands to them without a fight! Might they not at this early stage of the campaign in 1941 already be masters of Syria and Iraq and preparing themselves for an advance into Persia?

> The Germans in this war have gained many victories. They have easily overrun great countries and beaten down strong powers with little resistance offered to them. It is not only a question of

the time that is gained by fighting strongly even at a disadvantage for important points, but also there is this vitally important point of stubborn resistance to the will of the enemy. I merely throw out these considerations to the House in order that they may see that there are some arguments which deserve to be considered before you can adopt the rule that you have to have a certainty of winning at any point, and if you have not got it beforehand clear out.

The whole history of war shows the fatal absurdity of such a doctrine. Again and again it has been proved that fierce and stubborn resistance even against heavy odds and under exceptional victory. At any rate the decision to fight for Crete was taken with the full knowledge that air support would be at a mimimum, as anyone can see, apart from the question of whether you have adequate supplies or not.

Our defence plan, therefore, had to aim at inflicting a sufficiently sharp rebuff upon the enemy to compel him to withdraw, at any rate temporarily, from the assault; after which we should be in a position to maintain ourselves in Crete or to withdraw quietly from it if the maintennce problem proved beyond our capacity. Our ground troops and our fleet would have to meet the onslaught of a powerful airborne force, followed up in all probability by a seaborne assault, and covered at all times by fighter and bomber aircraft to which we could provide no adequate reply in kind. What strategy could we adopt which could offer any prospect of success?

Again let us quote Mr. Churchill, in his speech to the House of Commons, since none can summarize a plan more succinctly than he.

Our Army was to destroy the airborne attacks, while the Navy held off or destroyed the seaborne attacks. But there was a time limit. The action of the Navy in mounting the northern seaguard without adequate air defence was bound to be very costly. We could only stand a certain proportion of naval losses before the northern seaguard of the fleet would have to be withdrawn. If meanwhile the Army could succeed in biting off the head of the whole terrific apparatus of the airborne invasion before the naval time limit, or loss limit, was reached, then the enemy would have to begin all over again, and having regard to the enormous unprecedented scale of the operation and the losses he would have to incur, he might well for the time being at least have broken it off. At any rate there would have been a long delay before it could be mounted again. That was the basis on which the decision was come to.

And now one may consider to what extent we might have made better preparation for the defence of the island against the time of trial; and if, during the twelve days battle, the Germans might have been forced to pay a heavier price for their success.

It is true that we had been in almost undisturbed occupation of Crete for six months, and at first sight one might conclude that there was ample time and opportunity to take whatever defnsive measures were necessary. But Crete must be viewed against the background of the whole Middle East Command, laden with tasks and responsibilities which its resources were inadequate to discharge with success. General Wavell's straitened means of making war compelled him to adopt a series of shifts and expedients, and minor changes of policy, to meet contingencies as they arose. Risks had to be run. Changes in the dispositions of our forces and the allocation and re-allocation of munitions, supplies, material and shipping had to be made as the march of events appeared to dictate. And officers had often to be found suddenly for new commands which might diminish or grow in importance, varying with the fluctuations of the Mediterranean struggle. Under such circumstances some mistakes and miscalculations were sure to arise. And Fortune was not always on our side.

When a refuelling base for the Royal Navy was established at Suda Bay some protective armament—primarily a Fleet responsibility—was required and provided at Suda. But the defence of the whole of Crete against any form of attack was a much bigger proposition and one which we had not the resources to undertake except by slow degrees. As already related, Middle East Command planned to provide a garrison of one division, and preparations to house supplies, equipment and munitions for such a formation were taken in hand. The work, perforce, proceeded slowly. And when we decided to intervene in Greece troops and stores and shipping, as many and as much as could be spared, were required for the venture on the mainland. We were always short of the transport, material, tools and labour needed for even the preliminary work in Crete where the construction of dumps and installations went on concurrently with the digging and camouflaging of gun-positions, posts and entrenchments in the Suda area and around the airfields.

Then Crete was called upon to fulfil an additional purpose which influenced to a very great extent the conditions under which, ultimately, it was to resist the German attack. When the evacuation of our forces from Greece began the island was used as a transit camp to permit of rapid shipment from the mainland by ensuring a quick turn-round for vessels which would otherwise have had to make the much longer passage to Egypt. This is not to say that the troops who had fought in Greece were expected to defend Crete. They were not. Only lack of time, and shipping difficulties, prevented the relief of the men from Greece by the fresh formations to be provided by Middle East Command. It was the fortune of war, and very much to be regretted, that two brigades of the New Zealand Division, a goodly proportion of the Australians, and such British units as the Rangers and the Northumberland Hussars should have been obliged to undergo so soon this second ordeal.

The ground defence of the airfields, in the absence of support from the air, called for special measures: special equipment and armament and special training of the troops. We had had no experience of the form of attack which was expected—sustained air bombardment followed by airborne assault of infantry. None of the three airfields—Maleme, Retimo and Heraklion—had been laid out with any regard to facilities for ground defence, and the siting of anti-aircraft batteries presented some problems difficult to solve. Guns might be called upon to engage at different times, and at different ranges and heights, bombers and fighters, gliders and troop-carriers. Without becoming too technical it may be observed that a wide arc of fire entailed difficulty in providing protection and camouflage for the gun. We had not the means to construct the alternative positions and the dummy positions which were needed to complete a sound scheme of defence.

Infantry dispositions to meet an assault from the skies had, of course, to cover the vicinity of each airfield; but there was no telling where parachutists might drop or troop-carriers land, so that most units were committed to the defence of a wide area. Those located on the coast had also to keep in mind the possibility of a landing from the sea. Few of the troops had much opportunity for training or to practice themselves in their appointed rôles, and those who had fought in Greece needed a period for rest and recuperation before being committed to battle again.

Aerial reconnaissance, as carried out by the few aircraft we maintained upon the island up till May 19th, was doubtless of value, but it might have been wiser to have withdrawn them from Maleme much earlier and to have destroyed the airfield. As it happened, our aircraft departed on one day and the German assault was delivered on the next.

329

Yet it is wrong to attach an over-riding importance to the airfields as though the invasion could have been defeated simply by our retaining possession of all three of them. Their value to the Germans was undeniable, but the loss of Maleme airfield must be regarded as a serious set-back rather than a decisive blow. If it had been recaptured the enemy might have experienced great difficulty in using the bed of the Tavronitis as a landing ground. Even so, there were other places where the troop-carrying aircraft might have been crash landed, and in such numbers as to decide the issue in favour of the invaders. The whole conception of Maleme as the single point where the enemy could reinforce by troop-carrier implies too rigid a conception of his potentialities, and makes no allowance for the flexibility of his methods and his undoubted gift for improvisation in the field. German parachutists were already at work by the end of the first day preparing alternative landing grounds, notably one in the prison area where there is a considerable expanse of open meadowland.

At Heraklion, where we retained firm control of the airfield throughout the operations, the enemy managed to land a stream of troop-carriers several miles to the east in a locality out of range of our field-guns. When we evacuated Heraklion this concentration was being built up into a force which, in a day or two, would probably have been strong enough to take the initiative and attack with every prospect of success.

To our commanders and troops at Maleme the comparative importance of the airfield as such, mattered little: it was their business to defend it, and to destroy the invader wherever encountered. And because the airfield was lost, the reasons for our failure to retain it have been the subject of some discussion.

In the first place, the timing of the enemy's operations at Maleme was excellent. The troop-carriers arrived swiftly on the heels of the bombers and the machine-gunning fighters; as they were intended to arrive, but did not, at Retimo and Heraklion. Under the weight of the air bombardment it is easy to understand that the anti-aircraft defence was not so effective as it might have been. Our batteries lacked the training to counter with success the systematic attack by the low-flying aircraft which supported the airborne assault.

It was the opinion of the Inter-Services Committee who reported on the action of the Battle of Crete that 'The main feature of air operations in Crete was the employment of low-flying aircraft to support the airborne and parachute troops'. The entire conduct of the operations was dependent upon this support, and it was the view of the Committee that once the troops had landed the destruction of these supporting aircraft was of equal if not of greater importance than the destruction of the reinforcing airborne troops.

And it was the heavy, systematic and persistent attacks by the enemy aircraft, bombers and fighters alike, which took heavy toll of movement by daylight and almost destroyed our means of communication, grievously hindering, if not altogether preventing, the transmission of orders and information. So counter-attacks were delayed and, when delivered, were often made in insufficient force because the novel methods and widespread nature of the German assault made the focal point of the battle difficult to determine. Commanders were conducting an all-round defence and rightly hesitated to leave any localities empty of troops; they had been warned, also, against attempted landings from the sea. Add the difficulties already mentioned, also the lack of tools, transport and support weapons, and the failure at Maleme becomes easy to understand.

Certain it is that here and elsewhere the odds against us were very great. We did what we could; and the last word on the matter may well be provided by the Inter-Services Committee:

> The major lesson of the campaign was that to defend with a relatively small force an island as large as Crete, lying under the permanent domination of enemy aircraft and out of range of our own, was impossible.

Whatever criticism is made of our preparations for defence and of our conduct of the battle, it remains true that we inflicted a decided repulse on the enemy during the initial days of the battle and that we threw his general plan of campaign badly out of gear. It is one of the strange ironies of the war that the Battle for Crete which caused such grave searchings of heart at home and which was so intensely studied by Allied staffs as a model of airborne tactics was considered by the Germans themselves to be their first serious setback.

Of the grave miscalculations of their Military Intelligence we have already spoken. For the first time in the war the German losses in picked troops proved to have been far higher than had been estimated. This had important consequences for the future.

> The Führer was most displeased with the whole affair, admitted Student. Our losses in Crete were very high for that time. We had been lucky so far, as the whole French campaign had not cost us as many lives as a single battle in 1870. It was the

> same with the Balkan campaign, excluding Crete. Crete alone
> cost us 4,000 killed and missing out of 20,000 men thrown in.[1]

There was one direct consequence of the German heavy losses and delayed victory in Crete. Hitler became affected with a distrust of airborne operations in general and in particular of the development of the German offensive in the Mediterranean by these means. To British observers it seemed logical that the Germans should exploit their victory by a further operation in the direction of Cyprus and thereafter into Syria and Iraq. The conquest of Cyprus would have presented greater problems in view of the fact that, unlike Crete, it lay outside the range of effective German fighter support. But who shall say that, if Crete had been abandoned or but lightly held, such an operation might not have been most strongly urged by a Command flushed with easy success and, under such circumstances, sanctioned by the Führer. And beyond Cyprus lay Syria and Iraq, both ripe for German penetration in that critical month of May, 1941.

Student was perfectly prepared to continue what he had begun.

> After Crete I proposed that we should make an attack upon
> Cyprus in order to make a jumping-off ground for an air attack
> and paratroop attack on the Suez Canal. But Hitler rejected it
> because of the losses we had received in Crete.

None can deny that the tide was flowing strongly in favour of a powerful exploitation of the German position in the eastern Mediteranean during the early summer of 1941. In the space of two months Yugoslavia had been conquered, Greece had been conquered, Crete had been conquered; Wavell's weakened forces had been swept out of Libya; Iraq had succumbed to the influence of the Axis powers and was looking westward for German assistance during the crucial weeks of May; in Syria Marsahl Pétain's subordinates were proving a great deal more than complacent to the German requirements in the way of airfields. Granted that Hitler's eyes were now set upon Russia, yet with the immense and practically unimpaired resources in man-power which he commanded, with his vast stocks of war equipment available, it might have proved possible to detach sufficient force to secure the immense strategic and economic prizes which the Middle East had to offer. Crete was a poor reward for so much planning, such loss of skilled fighting men and such expenditure of aircraft unless it were a stepping-stone to

---

[1] Interrogation of Colonel-General Student, War Office Intelligence Review, November 1945. Quoted by Milton Shulman, *Defeat in the West*, p. 59.

greater things. The revolt in Iraq and the sinister developments in Syria during that very month pointed the way. But Hitler, never sufficiently alive to the importance of the Mediterranean to the grand strategy of the war, was blind to the omens. And in part at least this obliquity of vision was the outcome of the losses suffered by his picked troops in Crete during ten days fighting in May.

General Index

335

Index to Formations and Units